A century of **PARIS**  *Roubaix*

Pascal Sergent

Preface

Perhaps the reference is a little abrupt but I take hold of it as it comes to mind; Napoleon contended that "a head without a memory is like a fortress without a garrison", as an expert it was a pragmatic way of emphasising the importance of the lessons of history.

And this is what we are offered; history, to celebrate the Centenary of the oldest of the greatest cycle races, Paris-Roubaix. Yet perhaps, it is more its eccentricity than its antiquity that has made it so popular, a race that insists in these times of rapid progress on launching its riders onto the most anachronistic and accursed roads that it can find. "The last touch of craziness in cycling" as Jacques Goddet put it a few years ago.

From 1896 with the victory of the German Josef Fischer to our modern heroes a century later, the history of Paris-Roubaix is rich in exploits and sporting dramas; and the dust or the mud of the cobblestones of the North have been here and there spattered with the sweat and sometimes even the blood and the tears of those brave champions who attacked them, intrepid and joyful at the start of every April except those of the war years.

The following pages will relate all this in detail. These pages constitute the official book of the centenary of Paris-Roubaix; they trace ninety three years of this magical competition, of this pagan spectacle, which regularly inflames thousands of spectators and millions of television viewers. Proof that man's emotional capacities are timeless and that - Napoleon was right - an outmoded race, on archaic roads with machines that were conceived many years ago preserves intact its usefulness and seduction.

This is the image we wanted to transmit, a treasury of memories for those already affected by Paris-Roubaix and a legacy for those who will be. For this project to succeed it has been necessary to call on the goodwill of a whole number of individuals but above all on that of the author, Pascal Sergent. To Paris-Roubaix he is both a curator and a historian. Already the author in two volumes of the history of this Northern Classic, he tracks down and collects posters, newspapers, photos, documents and objects which he conserves with meticulousness and a rare passion.

For this centenary book he has re-opened his collection and taken up his pen again. His work bears the stamp of exactitude and precision and if I add that he is also involved in the official film, Paris-Roubaix 1896-1996 ' le centenaire ' an exhibition, and a symposium you will acknowledge that with this inquisitive and resourceful Roubaisan, Paris-Roubaix has found its keeper.

I must add in passing that as far as passion or even accuracy is concerned Pascal Sergent is not the only one with such noble feelings for Paris-Roubaix. There are many others, people as important as the mayor of Roubaix, René Vandierendonck who based his new year's speech on the theme of the centenary of Paris-Roubaix and who organised a superb celebration in honour of Gilbert Duclos-Lassalle, twice winner of the event, at the time of his retirement from competition. The Velo Club of Roubaix with Jean-Claude Vallaeys its general secretary, the mail order firm La Redoute with François Sénéchal its Sponsorship Director. They are all fans of the race and are all convinced that for the image and the morale of the town the fame of Paris-Roubaix is a blessing.

For those elected to administer the region and to preserve its heritage, in particular Jacques Donnay the President of the Conseil General of the North and his Vice-President Claude Larcanché, who are responsible for the roads, both are aware that they have a part to play in the annual passage of the riders over their cobbled roads. Are they too severe? Will they will be restored ? Will they draw back from tarmac ? Fortunately they will be protected. The North has to keep its character and its soul and Paris-Roubaix will play its part. The region is slowly escaping thankfully, from the reputation which was epitomised by the expression "The Hell of the North".

As the scales tip the other way the region wants to take advantage of its sense of identity and its cobblestones which are the remnants of another age. We the directors of the Tour de France, the heirs of Henri Desgrange and Jacques Goddet, guardians of the title and of the character of Paris-Roubaix, responsible for its organisation, its route, are conscious of the opinion of the whole of the cycling world. Naturally we are thrilled and delighted at the positive and consensual attitude shown towards the "Queen of the Classics".

It has always been subjected to intensive preparation. For many years it was Albert Bouvet, now it is the turn of Jean-François Pescheux and his team who are the keepers of its orthodoxy, of the indispensable balance between excess and overcautioun in the search for difficulties to be surmounted between Compiègne and Roubaix. Born of the peloton they know how far they can go.

Motivated by enthusiasm and guided by experience we hope that the collective emotion and the festive atmosphere will be present on the roads of the North when this beautiful and cruel adventure unrolls before the television cameras, the god of the valiant centenary, our Paris-Roubaix.

Jean-Marie LEBLANC

To the memory of Paul Depoortère,
my grandfather, without who,
among others, the names of Lapébie or Coppi
would have no doubt remained unknown.

Pascal Sergent

Roger De Vlaeminck, "Monsieur Paris-Roubaix" accompanied by the author Pascal Sergent and the original publisher Michel De Sutter in front of "de Eecloonaar" at Eeklo.

My parents were gluttons for work, they bled themselves white and never counted the hours. They even worked on Sundays. Except some time in April during the 1970's when my father went so far as to switch on the television to follow a cycle race : the Paris-Roubaix.

Fred De Bruyne was the commentator and the pictures were in black and white. To start with he spoke calmly, but as time went on and the finishing line approached he was almost yelling.

His enthusiasm was contagious and I was carried to fever pitch.

I was sitting on the edge of my chair.

And each time it was Roger who won.

"The Gypsy" the unbeatable Roger De Vlaeminck.

I can only remember the times when Roger carried it off.

Either it was my father who knew when he had to switch on the television set, or it was me who believed that only De Vlaeminck's victories were worth remembering.

The publishing of this book will rectify this error of judgement.

I dedicate my involvement in the production of it, to all the actors and all the extras in this spectacle which is renewed every year.

Michel De Sutter,
Original Publisher

Théodore Vienne

Industrialist at Roubaix

and his friend **Maurice Perez** were promoters
of track racing at the "Velodrome Roubaisan".

The following year, Vienne created one of the key events of cycling

PARIS-ROUBAIX

Quarante-et-unième année. — N° 112

EN VENTE A PARIS

Mardi 21 Avril 1896

ÉDITION

Journal de Roubaix

ÉDITION

5 C^{MES.}

5 C^{MES.}

TARIF D'ABONNEMENTS	Bureaux & Rédaction :	ABONNEMENTS & ANNONCES
ROUBAIX-TOURCOING, LE NORD et les DÉPARTEMENTS LIMITROPHES	ROUBAIX, rue Neuve, 17 — TOURCOING, rue des Poutrains, 42	Les Abonnements et Annonces sont reçus :

AGENCE PARTICULIÈRE A PARIS : 26, rue Feydeau

DIRECTEUR-PROPRIÉTAIRE : ALFRED REBOUX

LA COURSE VÉLOCIPÉDIQUE PARIS-ROUBAIX

MINISTRES & FRANCS-MAÇONS

Nos ministres ne se lassent pas de parler à la franc-maçonnerie. Dernièrement, c'était M. Combes qui haranguait ses frères; hier, c'était M. Guieysse qui, présidant le banquet de la Loge les « Vrais Amis », prononçait un discours.

M. le ministre des colonies a constaté que « les franc-maçons actifs sont en majorité dans le ministère ». On le savait. Dans une réunion maçonnique, tenue quelque temps après l'avènement du ministère Bourgeois, quelqu'un avait déjà fait remarquer que le Grand Conseil de la franc-maçonnerie pourrait très bien être remplacé par le Conseil des ministres. C'est assurément un très juste sujet de satisfaction et d'orgueil pour la franc-maçonnerie.

Mais pour l'immense majorité des Français, qui sont des profanes, cette identification du gouvernement de la France avec une secte, qui ne compte après tout que quelques milliers d'adhérents, est plutôt un sujet d'étonnement, sinon de scandale.

On ne sait pas au juste, dans la franc-maçonnerie entourée de mystère, de quels engagements particuliers un ministre franc-maçon est tenu envers ses co-initiés, à l'exclusion et au préjudice des autres Français.

D'ordinaire, les hommes politiques qui ont l'honneur d'être placés à la tête du gouvernement de leur pays ont la prétention d'être le gouvernement de la majorité et, à beaucoup d'égards, le gouvernement de tous. Ils se défendent de relever d'aucune coterie, d'appartenir à aucune petite Église. Ils considèrent qu'ils sont au pouvoir pour y être les serviteurs de l'intérêt général et de l'intérêt public. Il y a sûrement de bonne raison aussi dans leur parti.

Mais un parti n'est pas une franc-maçonnerie. Il y a des mots qui ne peuvent être réunis sans discordance. On ne comprend pas une justice maçonnique, une administration maçonnique, un gouvernement maçonnique.

Un magistrat, un administrateur, un ministre, un chef de gouvernement, s'il a jugé à propos avant d'être revêtu de ses fonctions de s'affilier à quelque secte, devrait les oublier aussitôt qu'il entre en charge et s'en cacher. Il devrait dire à ses compagnons : « Je ne vous appartiens plus. J'appartiens à la justice, à l'administration, à la France. Ce n'est pas pour vous que je juge, que j'administre, pour vous que je gouverne. Laissez-donc de me regarder comme l'un des vôtres, et de me souffler à l'oreille vos mots de passe et de reconnaissance. Je ne les comprends plus. »

Nos ministres actuels n'ont pas de ces scrupules. Ils laissent dire et ils prouvent, par leur conduite, qu'ils sont le ministère de la franc-maçonnerie, le gouvernement d'une secte. Depuis qu'ils ont entre leurs mains les affaires de la France, ils se déclarent francs-maçons plus que jamais, si l'on en croit les actes qu'ils ont établi le siège du gouvernement.

M. Guieysse le disait assez ingénieusement — « Quant à moi, je n'ai jamais été aussi

rester, en nous périssons! » On a même cru entendre autre chose.

Mais à force d'écouter ce qui se murmure dans les Loges, le ministère de la franc-maçonnerie ne perçoit plus rien de ce qui se dit tout haut, partout ailleurs.

INFORMATIONS

L'impôt sur le revenu et les menus générale

...

Les perceptions supprimées

...

Les grèves pendant le mois de mars

Le Bulletin de l'Office du Travail publie les renseignements suivants :

...

Le départ, à la Porte-Maillot, à Paris

...

Un service de navigation directe entre le Canada et la France

Le Parlement canadien a voté une subvention pour un service de vapeurs là-course entre le Canada et la France. La ligne reliée du Canada en Angleterre s'ouvre à bien des points de vue fort intéressant.

Expérience curieuse, vivra probable

...

L'expédition de Dongola

Londres, 19 avril. — ...

La révolte des Matabélés

Londres, 19 avril. — ...

Un accident de chemin de fer

...

Une interview du président Krüger

Le Temps publie le compte-rendu d'une visite faite par son correspondant au Transvaal au président Krüger. De ce compte-rendu, nous détachons le passage suivant relatif au voyage du président Krüger en Europe :

...

Le nouveau bourgmestre antisémite de Vienne

Vienne, 19 avril. — ...

PARIS-ROUBAIX

La Grande Course Vélocipédique

DE DIMANCHE

Le départ, Porte-Maillot, à Paris

(D'un correspondant particulier)

Paris, 19 avril. — « Paris-Roubaix ! Rendez-vous de Paris-Roubaix ! » telles étaient les exclamations que l'on entendait, à peu près universellement, depuis quelque temps, dans ce milieu spécial qu'est le monde des professionnels de la vélocipédie. Peu cependant la date de l'épreuve approchait, plus l'animation devenait grande, les pronostics allaient bon train.

...

19th april 1896
The legend begins

Cl. Panajou Freres (Bordeaux)
III
FISCHER (Allemand)

Josef FISCHER
(Germany, 1865-1959)

The first great German champion, he remains the only German winner of Paris-Roubaix.

1893 : Moscow-St Petersburg
1895 : Trieste-Graz-Vienna
1896 : Paris-Roubaix,
        German Champion (Motor-paced)
1899 : Hamburg Four Day
1900 : Bordeaux-Paris, 2nd Paris-Roubaix

"Without any doubt, the most interesting attempt at sporting decentralisation which has been attempted since cycling became the most popular French sport, is that of the Roubaix Velodrome. Established in 1895 at a time when all attention focused on Paris, the sole home of a cycle race, it can be said without exaggeration that the Roubaisan track quickly became famous throughout the whole world. Its history is intimately linked to French sport".

These lines were written in 1898 by Victor Breyer one of the most famous chroniclers of la Belle Epoque. Breyer summed up the birth of the Roubaix Velodrome, which attracted thousands of spectators each Sunday, the place that became the setting for the first Paris-Roubaix finishes. Opened on the 9th June 1895, this velodrome hosted the track stars of the day; Banker, Jacquelin, Ellegaard, and the famous black American sprinter Major Taylor who in 1901 made his French debut at Roubaix.

Towards the end of the last century the town of Roubaix was booming thanks to its flourishing textile industry. Sunday was the worker's only day of rest and, for many, the highlight of the week was a trip to the Roubaix track to see the racing.

At the beginning of 1896 two mill owners, Theo Vienne and Maurice Perez, had a brilliant idea. Why not organise a road race which would start in Paris and finish at their velodrome? They wrote to Paul Rousseau director of the daily newspaper, "Le Velo":

"Dear Mr Rousseau,

Bordeaux-Paris is approaching, and this great annual event which has done so much to promote cycling, has given us an idea. What would you think of a training race which preceded Bordeaux-Paris by four weeks?

The distance between Paris and Roubaix is roughly 280 kilometres, so it would be child's play for the future participants of Bordeaux-Paris. The finish would take place at the Roubaix Velodrome after several laps of the track. Everyone would be assured of an enthusiastic welcome as most of our citizens have never had the privilege of seeing the spectacle of a major road race and we count on enough friends to believe that Roubaix is truly a hospitable town. As prizes we have already subscribed a first prize of 1,000 francs in the name of the Roubaix velodrome and we will be busy establishing a generous prize list which will be to the satisfaction of all. But for the moment can we count on the patronage of "Le Velo" and on your support for organising the start?"

Paul Rousseau seemed to be immediately captivated by the plan. Victor Breyer the newspaper's cycling editor was given the task of inspecting the route...by bicycle! However, one of his colleagues, Paul Meyan, had acquired a superb six horse-power Panhard and offered to take him as far as Amiens, the young Breyer's first experience of a motor car.

The next day Breyer took to his bicycle. The journey from Paris to Amiens has been pleasant, but the second stage to Roubaix was a real nightmare. The weather grew worse and the rain heavier, making the uneven cobblestones even more hazardous. He did

1896

not reach his goal until the evening and arrived exhausted, muddy and frozen and decided to send a missive to Paris demanding that this "diabolical plan" be cancelled. He said that it would be dangerous to launch the riders on such a terrible route. Eventually, a refreshing night and the enthusiasm of the sportsmen of Roubaix dissuaded him from doing so. Paris-Roubaix would be disputed on the 19th April, Easter Sunday. When this was announced Vienne and Perez were confronted with several protests. The clergy were worried; would some of their flock miss the mass merely to get to the finish of the event? Even more sacrilegious, would the riders be starting so early in the morning that they would be unable to attend the traditional Easter service? Tracts were printed denouncing the casual way in which the religious feelings of the population of Roubaix were being ignored. To appease his critics, Théodore Vienne announced that a special mass would be celebrated in the Chapel of the Family of Orleans, barely two hundred metres from the start at the Porte Maillot. The plan proved to be impossible due to the very early hour but Vienne certainly did not publicise the fact.

In Paris on the day before the event, the contestants arrived at the "Brasserie de l'Esperance" (Bar of Good Hope) which had remained open all night. Among them Maurice Garin - who five years later was destined to win the Tour de France. He was defending the colours of the Roubaix cycling club and had been preparing specifically for the race by training over the route. With him was the Dane from Dieppe, Charles Meyer, the winner of Bordeaux-Paris, a few chairs away from him was the "crack" Welshman Arthur Linton, feared by all of them as he was never a man to race for second place. One hundred riders had

enrolled but in spite of the tempting first prize, half of them failed to turn up at the start. Among the defections were several potential favourites such as Franz Gerger, Gaston Rivierre and ...Henri Desgrange.

At the edge of the Bois de Boulogne, in the Cafe Gillet, forty five professionals and six amateurs from Lille came to sign the start sheet.

At 5.20 am Victor Breyer started to call the riders with one eye on the list of starters and the other on the sky. The tension mounted. The starter waited until 5.30 am, then Paul Rosseau stepped forward and gave the signal.

PIONEERS WHO SAW THE BIRTH OF THE LEGEND

In the front rank the favourites, Charles Meyer, Josef Fischer, Maurice Garin, Paul Guignard and Arthur Linton started flat out behind their pacers on their bicycles.

At the first control, at St Germain, after thirty two minutes of racing, Linton, Fischer, Meyer, Guignard, Stein, Garin and Sardin went thorough a minute in front of the rest of the group. The passage through the great forest of St Germain inspired Linton to attack. At Beauvais he was the first to arrive at the control. Joseph Fischer decided to make his move and at the end of a tremendous pursuit over many kilometres he caught the race leader. At Amiens the gaps were considerable. Garin went through five minutes down, Meyer was at twenty three minutes and Lucien was at almost an hour. Shortly after the exit from the town a dog ran across the road. Linton crashed. His hopes of victory rapidly evaporated as Fischer continued at his infernal pace. The hill at Doullens was quickly

1896

Josef Fischer in action...

scaled up by the German who preceded Garin by 11 minutes, Linton by 18 minutes and Meyer by 25 minutes. Behind, it was a rout. Fischer looked to have the race in the bag, but then he suffered two setbacks. At Hénin-Liétard a horse took fright as the bizarre cavalcade passed by, and bolted. Fischer only narrowly avoided it. A little later a herd of cows suddenly spilled onto the road from a field and blocked the way. But the German took it all in his stride, and the final kilometres became a triumphal procession. Seclin, Lesquin and Hem were filled with thousands of spectators. Bicycles, tandems and even triplets were very much in evidence. Paris-Roubaix had become a great event, everyone wanted to see the champions pass through.

In this crowded chaos, Maurice was robbed of his second place. He was delayed by a crash between Ascq and Forest when a tandem collided with a triplet that was pacing him, ridden by the two Acou brothers and ...Mrs Acou. With blood coming from his shoulder and the back of his neck he passed out by the side of the road as Meyer overtook him without a second glance. The crowd which had been waiting at the stadium was kept informed of the progress of the race thanks to a series of telegrams sent from the various controls along the route. At about 2.40 the Union of the Trumpets of Roubaix, given the task of signalling the arrival of the riders, blew their first fanfare. Officials and gendarmes redoubled their vigilance to ensure that no last minute incident would spoil the climax of the race. The thousands of privileged

spectators rose to their feet. 'Bravos' rang out. The Musical Society of the Velodrome played the national anthem. Fischer appeared. The cheers redoubled. Fischer completed the required six laps before signing the arrival register with a glass of champagne in his left hand. Soaked by sweat and and caked with dust, he disappeared behind the bouquets given by the manager of the velodrome, the Roubaix Cycling Club and the Corporation of Roubaix.

Thirteen minutes later the trumpets heralded the arrival of the next two contestants who were given as warm a reception as the winner had received. Meyer appeared on the track, followed by Garin. The latter finished exhausted and Doctor Butrille was obliged to attend to the man who had been run over by two machines! As rain began to fall the other finishers started to arrive. Poor Arthur Linton was fourth, victim of several punctures as well as his crash. Then there was Stein, Boinet, Eo, Ariès Pachot and a certain Mercier, 2 hours and 16 minutes after Fischer. He received a basket containing a dozen bottles of champagne which were consumed the same evening during a celebratory dinner at a Roubaix hotel. As soon as Vendredi, the coloured rider from Paris arrived 17th, the finishing control was transferred to the Café Richelieu on the Boulevard de Paris. The establishment remained open until 6.00 pm during which time another 28 contestants appeared to sign the finish sheet.

The winner's time of 9 hours and 17 minutes exceeded even the most optimistic expectations. In fact, for the first time ever for an event over such a long distance, the winning average exceeded 31 kph. At the end of this inaugural day the local elected representatives, in the presence of Paul Rosseau, warmly congratulated Théodore Vienne and Maurice Perez. As for Linton, after his unhappy race over the Northern cobblestones, he went on to win that year's Bordeaux-Paris, in spite of suffering terribly. Two months later his life came to an end in his home town of Aberdare in South Wales. The cause of death was given as typhoid fever but his friends said that his heart was just worn out.

After his victory in Paris-Roubaix, Josef Fischer became a legend in his own right. Winner of the Bordeaux-Paris four years later, he rode the first Tour de France in 1903, before moving to Paris. He embarked on a career as a taxi driver but was obliged to return to his home country when the First World War broke out.

1896

1. Josef FISCHER (Germany)
2. Charles MEYER (Denmark)
3. Maurice GARIN (France)
4. Arthur LINTON (Great Britain)
5. Lucien STEIN (France)
6. BOINET (France)
7. EO (France)
8. ARIES (France)
9. Gaston PACHOT (France)
10. MERCIER (France)

Fischer
PREMIER ARRIVÉ

Meyer
DEUXIÈME ARRIVÉ

Garin
TROISIÈME ARRIVÉ

Maurice Garin
on home ground

At the beginning of 1897 the people of Roubaix were preparing for some important forthcoming events; the Cycle Show, the municipal elections and ... Paris-Roubaix. The city's sports fans were all hoping for a victory by Maurice Garin who had a cycle shop in the centre of the town and who wore the colours of the local club. Vienne and Perez were hoping that the second edition of the race would be at least as popular as the first when thousands of spectators lined the route and invaded the stadium. However the riders were slow to enrol for the event. A large number of amateurs were attracted, spurred on perhaps by the commemorative medal given to every rider who finished the course in less than 24 hours, but only 45 professionals, of whom a mere 32 actually started, seemed interested. This defection was to remain one of the principle worries of the organisers for many years to come.

But in spite of the lack of quantity there was plenty of quality. In the absence of an injured Josef Fischer a number of riders were contesting the honour of being his successor. Among them were the Dutchman Mathieu Cordang, Charles Meyer who had already proved his worth over the route and the Swiss Michel Frédérick. Opposing them were several motivated Frenchmen such as Gaston Rivierre, considered to the best rider on current form, Maurice Garin naturally, Aries, Ducom and Bagré. The day before the event was cloudy and the atmosphere heavy. Rain was forecast would not help the condition of the roads, especially when the route passed through the coal mining section where coal dust was everywhere which.

The aptly named 'Bar of Good Hope' was full of pacers who had come to pick up some last minute tips. Some of the riders as well spent the whole night chatting to the locals.

Mathieu Cordang was the pre-race favourite at 5-2 in front of Frédérick and Rivierre both at 3-1 and then came Garin at 5-1 and Bertin at 10-1. Cordang, a former World Champion over 100 kilometres seemed to be the man to beat. He spoke no French but after his arrival in the French capital he made the organisers aware of the fact that he was suffering from stomach pains. Frédérick said that he was disappointed with his performance the previous season and was counting on Paris-Roubaix to make up for it. Rivierre seemed quite calm but thought that the distance was a little short - after all he was known as the "marathon man". And what about Maurice Garin ? According to numerous observers 'the little chimney sweep' had the edge. He compensated for his small stature by his class and his legendary will to win.

Sunday 18th April 1897, 6.00am and the amateurs had just started. The rain-soaked boulevard was now free for the professionals. The weather conditions increased the worries of the competitors, who were already well aware of the difficulties of the route. When a nervous Victor Breyer called the competitors to the line, the sun broke through the clouds.

At 6.30 am and the starter released the 32 men. Immediately Rivierre attacked followed by Frédérick, Garin and Cordang. In the conditions it was important for the favourites to be at

1897

Maurice GARIN
(France, 1871-1957)

One of the greatest champions of the heroic era. The 'little chimney sweep' won the main races and was in at the birth of modern cycle racing, winning the inaugural Tour de France.

1893 : Paris 800 Kilometres
1894 : Liège 24 Hours
1896 : 3rd Paris-Roubaix
1897 : Paris-Roubaix, Paris-Royan,
        Tourcoing-Bethune-Tourcoing
1898 : Paris-Roubaix, Tourcoing-Bethune
        Tourcoing, 2nd Bordeaux-Paris
1900 : 2nd Bordeaux-Paris, 2nd Bol d'Or
        3rd Paris-Brest-Paris
1901 : Paris-Brest-Paris
1903 : Tour de France

Atmosphere at the 1897 finish.

Le Petit Journal

Le Petit Journal
CHAQUE JOUR 5 CENTIMES

Le Supplément illustré
CHAQUE SEMAINE 5 CENTIMES

SUPPLÉMENT ILLUSTRÉ
Huit pages : CINQ centimes

ABONNEMENTS
—
	SIX MOIS	UN AN
SEINE ET SEINE-ET-OISE	2 fr.	3 fr. 50
DÉPARTEMENTS	2 fr.	4 fr.
ÉTRANGER	2.50	5 fr.

Douzième année   DIMANCHE 1ᵉʳ SEPTEMBRE 1901   Numéro 563

MAURICE GARIN
Vainqueur de la course Paris-Brest

the front. This rapid start was but a foretaste of things to come; an incessant battle right up to the winning post.

When Cordang went on the attack, he did so with a double purpose, to test, but above all to intimidate his adversaries. He passed St.Germain and then went through Beauvais with a lead of seven minutes over Frédérick and eleven minutes on Garin. As Cordang continued to be riding effortlessly it seemed that the victory would again go to a foreigner. However, a battle was raging behind. Garin was sticking to his plan of waiting for the cobbles before really entering into the action. Then, on the hill at Amiens, Frédérick closed the gap to less than three minutes on the leader. Garin, riding like a metronome, had stabilised his deficit at 11 minutes. Just before Doullens Frédérick caught Cordang.

But Northern hopes seemed to be dashed when Garin went through, trailing by twenty five minutes. The little chimney sweep realised now was the time to increase the pace. On the road to Arras Cordang showed the first signs of weakness and allowed Frédérick to pass him, but not for long. But then Garin caught Frédérick at the entrance to Seclin. Cordang had passed through a mere two minutes previously. After an intense effort lasting a few kilometres Garin was on Cordang's wheel. At the velodrome thanks to the dispatches announcing the position of the leaders, the crowd was in a euphoria of excitement.

Ten thousand spectators eagerly awaited the victory of the local man. At 4.45pm the trumpets sounded to announce the arrival of the first man at Hempempont. Seven minutes later a suffering Frédérick passed through. He had just hit a cyclist coming in the opposite direction. His machine was damaged. The bets were still being taken when the trumpets played a second fanfare; this time to mark the arrival of the leaders.

As the two champions appeared they were greeted by a frenzy of excitement and everyone was on their feet to acclaim the two heroes. It was difficult to recognise them. Garin was first, followed by the mud-caked figure of Cordang. Suddenly, to the stupefaction of everyone, Cordang slipped and fell on the velodrome's cement surface. Garin could not believe his luck. By the time Cordang was back on his bike he had lost 100 metres. There remained six laps to cover. Two miserable kilometres in which to catch Garin. The crowd held its breath as they watched the incredible pursuit match. The bell rang out. One lap, there remained one lap. 333 metres for Garin who had a lead of thirty metres on the 'Batave'.

A classic victory was within his grasp but he could almost feel his adversary's breath on his neck.

Somehow Garin held on to his lead of two metres, two little metres for a legendary victory. The stands exploded and the ovation united the two men. Garin exulted under the cheers of the crowd. Cordang cried bitter tears of disappointment. As he got off his machine the winner did not forget him; " I won but I have to admit that Cordang was the strongest. The next time I will win by a much bigger margin..." Frédérick finished third at fourteen minutes and Rivierre was fourth. Fischer's record was far from being beaten but the adverse weather conditions were not conducive to a fast race.

Paris-Roubaix brought tremendous prestige to the winner and little by little the race established its own identity, even if Bordeaux-Paris remained the key event on the calendar. Rivierre found this event more to his liking and was to win it several weeks later ahead of Cordang who seemed doomed to second places.

1897

1. Maurice GARIN (France)
2. Mathieu CORDANG (Holland)
3. Michel FREDERICK (Switzerland)
4. Gaston RIVIERRE (France)
5. Léopold TROUSSELIER (France)
6. BOINET (France)
7. AIRES (France)
8. GUILLOCHIN (France)
9. LEOPOLD (France)
10. Marcel KERFF (Belgium)

JREAUX & RÉDACTION

, Grande-Rue, 71. - Tourcoing, rue Nationale, 78

cteur-Propriétaire : ALFRED REBOUX

ABONNEMENTS & ANNON

Les Abonnements et Annonces sont reçus : à ROUBAIX, Grande-Rue, 71. — A L
à PARIS chez MM. HAVAS, LAFFITE et Cⁱᵉ, place de la Bourse, 8,
A BRUXELLES, à l'OFFICE DE PUBLICITE.

PARIS-ROUBAIX

La grande course de bicyclettes et d'automobiles de dimanche. — Le départ de Paris
En route. — Les contrôles. — L'arrivée au Vélodrome roubaisien

GARIN VAINQUEUR

Le record de Fischer battu

UN TERRIBLE ACCIDENT

La toiture d'une baraque qui s'effondre. — Neuf blessés

L'ARRIVÉE DES AUTOMOBILES. — LES COURSES DE VITESSE

La course Paris-Roubaix a eu lieu dimanche pour la | mètres de Paris, pour éviter la traversée du Bois de Bou-
troisième fois. Malgré les circonstances les plus défavo- |

(left column fragments)
cats faisant partie de
rgane socialiste révo-
bsorbé 12,000 francs
cidé de mettre à la
élections cantonales
a bonne foi de leurs
a condamné les pré
puy, Arnaud, Vie
5 francs d'amende et
enseurs de la disso-
t en l'ordonnant si
yndicats des mineurs
es usines du Saut-du-

BLIQUE A NICE
dentiel est arrivé ce
s 32. Sur le quai, M.
nicipales ont reçu le

(right column fragments)
Voici les
journée de
St-Germa
9 h. 50 ma
Chevalier,
ordre à 7 h
nier, Girar
mont passe
Meauline,
reparti.
Beauvais
9 heures 50
et Chevalie
et Berlin à
chon à 10 h
Liégeois et
conseil 10
Premier
10 h. 31;
bert et Dec
10 h. 34,30
Leglndic, 1
Osmont pas
truyst, 11 h
passe à 11
Breteuil
Garin, 10 h
10 h. 46: 4

The little chimney sweep's double

As promised Garin returned in 1898. Motivated by his characteristic will to win the little chimney sweep wanted to confirm his previous success which he considered to somewhat 'tainted'. However, his preparation was interrupted by a crash and he appeared at the start covered in bandages like a mummy ! To compensate for the declining number of starters, the organisers decided that the pacers could use motorcycles and even cars as well as bicycles. To add to the confusion, there was a second Paris-Roubaix to be held on the same day - for motorcyclists ! The Chief of Police in Paris was of the opinion that the capital already suffered from too many traffic jams and demanded that the start be transferred to Chatou in the Northern suburbs. On the 10th April 1898, only thirty-four riders were present at the starting control. Among them were the 'old guard' led by Auguste Stéphane, thirty-five years old, who had his moment of glory in 1892 when he triumphed in Bordeaux-Paris, the inevitable Charles Meyer, and the former holder of the hour record Jules Dubois who had been French champion back in 1895. Opposing them were Gaston Rivierre, the little climber Edouard Wattelier who was making his debut in the classic, then an astonishing young Belgian, Arthur Vanderstuyft who was a miner by profession and who had passed the previous winter down the pits, and finally a 15-year-old, Milcent, who was to cause a crash at the start of the event.

At 7.00am Paul Rousseau called the riders to order and released the thin bunch of contestants. On the hill at Croix-de-Noailles a few hundred spectators were waiting stoically in the rain to see the men pass. Wattelier displayed his climber's talent and was first over the hill ahead of a watchful and determined Maurice Garin. The early part of the race was animated by Auguste Stéphane. At Achères a closed level crossing helped him to go clear, firstly in company with Jules Dubois and then alone. On the road to Breteuil, Garin took the initiative, caught

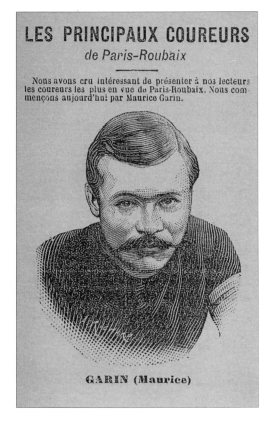

and passed the leader who was almost double his age and had certainly ridden twice as many miles!

There were still hours to go to the finish line, but the outcome of the race was being decided aready. Garin was putting the issue beyond doubt. At Breteuil his advantage was one minute over his nearest rivals, four at Amiens, ten at Doullens and twenty at Arras before crossing the worst sections of the cobblestones. The North was celebrating its hero. Nothing could stop him. This time the champion, without any possible argument, was proving himself to be the best and in the process also proving that his previous year's victory was a worthy one. In spite of the rain, aware of the progress of the race, the stadium was under siege by the local fans.

When Garin entered the arena it was perhaps the noisiest reception of all time. It caused him to forget all the mud, the rain, the tiredness; everything. The man who was one of the greatest champions of the 'heroic' era was to carry off many other marathon victories such as Paris-Brest-Paris in 1901, Bordeaux-Paris in 1902 and of course the very first Tour de France. However, as he was to confirm at the end of his long life, that April day in Roubaix was the finest of his career. Behind him, twenty minutes down, Stéphane arrived covered in blood. In the last few kilometres he had been the victim of several accidents. The others finished at intervals of several minutes in the order of Edouard Wattelier, Bertin, Charles Meyer and finally eighteenth and last Vanderstuyft who had been in the saddle a full seven hours longer than the hero from Roubaix, who had covered the 258 kilometres in 8 hours, 13 minutes and 16 seconds. To put this performance in some kind of context the winner of the motorcycle race finished the course in 7 hours and 29 minutes, a mere forty-five minutes faster than the 'little chimney sweep'.

1898

1. Maurice GARIN (France)
2. Auguste STEPHANE (France)
3. Edouard WATTELIER (France)
4. Jean BERTIN (France)
5. Charles MEYER (Denmark)
6. Rodolfo MULLER (Italy)
7. Gaston HERRINCK (Belgium)
8. Jules CORDIER (France)
9. LIEGEOIS (France)
10. MONACHON (France)

PARIS

PARIS-

10 A

Le départ des motocycles. — GARIN, le vainqueur, au

STÉPHANE et MEYER. —

(PHOTOGRAPH

ROUBAIX
1898

...t de Chatou. — Trois vieux de la vieille : Jules DUBOIS,
...e départ des bicyclettes.

(...DE J. BEAU.)

Quarante-quatrième année. — N° 94   (EDITION DU MATIN)   MARDI 4 AVRIL 1899

Journal de Roubaix

TARIF D'ABONNEMENTS ... | Bureaux et Rédaction : Roubaix : 71, Grande-Rue. — Tourcoing, rue Nationale, 78 | ABONNEMENTS ÉTRANGERS ...
Directeur-Propriétaire : Alfred REBOUX

Paris-Roubaix 1899

VOIX CONCORDANTES

L'APPLICATION DE LA LOI
sur la responsabilité des accidents du travail

L'AFFAIRE DREYFUS
LES DOCUMENTS
Les dépositions de MM. Charles Dupuy et Cavaignac

La déposition de M. Dupuy

La déposition de M. Cavaignac

INFORMATIONS
Le Président de la République aux contres d'Artenil

La mission Marchand. — Nouvelles officielles. — L'arrivée de la mission à El-Cocto. — En route pour Djibouti.

Mort du marquis de Chasseloup

Une nouvelle victime de la catastrophe de Toulon

Les Sacres occasionnelles à Paris

A la recherche de l'explorateur Andrée

Excuses de M. Mac Kinley à propos des incidents de Samoa

LE CRIME DE CHOISY-LE-ROI

Les projets de Mme Marie du Sacré-Cœur

LA TÉLÉGRAPHIE SANS FIL
Expériences françaises. — Au-dessus de Paris. Sept kilomètres.

LE NAUFRAGE DU "STELLA"
Les victimes

LA COURSE PARIS-ROUBAIX
4e ANNÉE

Le départ. — Sur la route. — Au Vélodrome. — Les dépêches. — L'arrivée du premier motocycle — L'arrivée de Champion. — Les 2e et 3e coureurs. — Une lutte sur la piste. — Les accidents. — Garin, Fischer et Bouhours abandonnent la course. — Les courses régionales

CHAMPION

LE DÉPART

LES PARTANTS

SUR LA ROUTE

MOTOCYCLES

LE PREMIER

AU VÉLODROME

Success for a 'stayer'

In 1899 and 1900 the organisers persisted in keeping the motorcycle pacers. It meant that track racing's motor-paced specialists were attracted in great numbers to this race over the cobbled roads. The favourable weather conditions were to help two 'stayers', well used to sheltering behind their motorbikes, to fly to victory. Without taking anything away from their victories, the winners of 1899 and 1900 were not great roadmen, but accumulated their successes on the track. On the 2nd April 1899, just for once the weather was superb, without a breath of wind, but to everyone's regret the number of starters did not increase. This time there were only thirty-two who replied when the starter called their names a few moments before the start. Among them, of course, Maurice Garin who had topped a poll of possible winners, organised by the 'Journal of Roubaix'. Josef Fischer, the very first winner, also returned to the race which had him famous, then several young ones such as the Frenchman Jean Fischer who was no relation to the German, Ambroise Garin, the brother of Maurice, several 'stayers' such as Emile Bouhours, Paul Bor and Albert Champion. Everyone was fascinated by these track riders and wondered how they would perform on these difficult roads. The surprises were not too long in coming. The first retirement was announced - it was none other then the 'little chimney sweep'.

He put his foot to the ground at Vallangoujard . His pacing car had broken down and twelve long minutes crawled by as the mechanics carried out the necessary repairs. According to the champion it was too long, much too long! He swore he would not restart and in spite of the pleas of his pacers he was content to stay seated by the side of the road waving ironically to the other competitors that he had not long been dropped. In the meantime, the young Albert Champion riding close to his pacer Broc, thought only of maintaining an infernal pace and escaped clear of the field. The general opinion was that the adventure would not last for long, for this outsider with a minimum of experience of this type of event was only twenty one years old.

His rivals were prepared to give him certain amount of rope

Albert CHAMPION
(France, 1878-1929)

He first found fame as a world record holder over just one kilometre but made few excursions into long-distance road racing.

1898 : World Tandem Record
1899 : Paris-Roubaix
1904 : French Champion (Motor-paced)

1899

Albert Champion signs the start sheet

and only occasionally increased their pace. After Beauvais, Ambroise Garin, Pierre Chevallier and Jean Fischer decided to it was time put a stop to this amusement and joined forces to bring back Champion . But their hopes were in vain as it became evident that they could make no impression on this champion of the track . Only Emile Bouhours proved capable of reducing the gap. At the control in Amiens, the half-way point, he was only two minutes behind the lone fugitive. Bouhours' superb pace caused everyone to believe that it would not be long before the junction was made. But, sadly for the sporting interest in the event, Bouhours advance was halted as he exited the town.

An imprudent spectator was crossing the road at the very moment when Bouhours' pace car arrived on the scene like a whirlwind. While the driver pulled on the steering wheel in a desperate attempt to avoid a catastrophe, the wing of the vehicle caught the spectator. Bouhours, in his wake was unbalanced and crashed heavily onto the road. So Champion's only potential rival was eliminated. The man at the head of the race was never caught, but he did have to endure a very bad patch on the road to Arras. On the first cobblestones, which were completely new to him, he was riding

at walking pace, to the surprise of the spectators. The thirty seven kilometres which separated Arras from Seclin caused him two hours of suffering. Fortunately Champion's lead was considerable. Moreover, behind, his adversaries were scarcely any fresher. At the velodrome, the welcome was as warm as usual as Albert Champion arrived a clear winner. Worn out but more than twenty three minutes in front of a chasing pair which comprised the unexpected Paul Bor who finished second and the young Ambroise Garin to complete the podium at Roubaix. The 258 kilometres were covered in 8 hours 22 minutes and 53 seconds, which was more than ten minutes longer than Garin's record, established in atrocious weather conditions.

As for Champion, his cycling career did not continue very long. He crossed the Atlantic to ride motor-paced events on the American tracks at a time when such hazardous races were little known in that country. Then he returned to France to pick up the 'stayers' title in 1904. He had caught the motoring bug. When he returned to America he created a spark plug for combustion engines which still carries his name. He thus became a prosperous industrialist. In Paul Bor's case it should be remembered that he was known by very few before this second place, and even the most well informed cycling followers were surprised. His success three years previously in a Paris-Rouen race for amateurs, was hardly a pointer to such an astonishing performance. Before returning to anonymity, he broke, on the 8th September, the World one-hour track record behind pacers mounted on motorised tricycles at the Parc des Princes. In actual fact, of this totally unexpected top three, only the young Ambroise Garin was able to surpass his third place on these Northern roads.

1899

1. Albert CHAMPION (France)
2. Paul BOR (France)
3. Ambroise GARIN (France)
4. Pierre CHEVALIER (France)
5. Eugène JAY (France)
6. Marcel KERFF (Belgium)
7. Lucien ITSWEIRE (France)
8. DUBUS (France)
9. L.DELATTRE (France)

Champion at the velodrome

Emile BOUHOURS
(France, 1870-1953)

Like Albert Champion, Bouhours made his name as a track rider - setting no fewer than 24 world records.

1897 : French Champion (Motor-paced)
1898 : French Champion (Motot-paced)
1900 : Paris-Roubaix,
French Champion (Motor-paced)
1902 : French Champion (Motor-paced)
2nd World Championships
(Motor-paced)
1903 : 3rd World Championships
(Motor-paced)

Bouhours demonstration

The second success of a 'stayer' took place in 1900. It was the time of the 'Belle Époque'. Paris was bubbling over with vitality. The town was playing host to two prestigious events; the International Exhibition, the most successful of all time according to the experts, and the Olympic Games, the second Olympics of the modern era.

On the other hand Paris-Roubaix found itself on the edge of the abyss. In spite of all their efforts, the organisers were only able to attract twenty three entrants. Certainly some stars were present, such as Maurice Garin who had been preparing behind his brother's motor tricycle for nearly two months at the Roubaix Velodrome. It would seem that this year he was determined that his race would not finish at Vallangoujard! Emile Bouhours also returned, anxious to avoid the fate which had eliminated him twelve months before. Then there was the eternal Josef Fischer and two local men Lucien Itsweire and Oscar Lepoutre. The debut was announced of the promising young Parisian by the name of Hippolyte Aucouturier . Early on this Sunday morning in April at Chatou the atmosphere was a little sad when the bunch of only eighteen riders started out in the direction of Roubaix. Vienne and Perez asked themselves if in the circumstances they should persevere or once again modify the formula of the event. But the race rapidly reasserted itself and Bouhours recovered his confidence by making an excellent start. The struggle was relentless as Maurice Garin quickly took over the lead, soon to be taken over himself by Fischer. The German was returning to the front rank. That he was enjoying excellent form was to be confirmed a few weeks later when he was victorious in Bordeaux-Paris. But he suffered numerous punctures, and an accident on the road to Arras put paid to his chances as it robbed him of his pacers for approximately twenty kilometres. Bouhours took advantage of the situation to catch Fischer and then pass him when he was in the process of repairing a sixth puncture !

The motorised pacers after the finish

Josef Fischer enters the velodrome.

Maurice Garin was hardly more fortunate, in additon to the usual hazards on the road, this time he also had to content with two closed level crossings where he lost precious minutes. The way was clear for Bouhours who impressed everyone with his resistance over the cobbles. The man from Normandy arrived at the velodrome, riding with an impressive speed behind his pacers, covering the 269 kilometres in 7 hours 10 minutes and 30 seconds at the astonishing average speed of 37.35 kph. The old record had been beaten by more than an hour Fischer held on to his second place, ten minutes down on the winner. Then Garin arrived another 28 minutes later. The local man received his usual enthusiastic reception but on his arrival at the track to the stupefaction of the crowd he rode onto the grass and refused to do the obligatory six laps of the track.

As the crowds gathered around him it was obvious that he was sullen and morose. He waved his arms in anger and accused his adversaries of being responsible for the two closed level crossings. " I don't care at all about the six laps of the track. I have arrived at Roubaix and for me that is the important thing. I refuse to go any further," he declared at the top of his voice.

The commissaires were embarrassed. It was essential to settle the affair before the next man arrived in fourth place. They decided to bring the finishing sheet to him to sign. Garin signed with a total indifference. In spite of the rules, but above all to avoid a scandal, he was officially classed as third by the judges. After his two successes in 1897 and 1898 and his third place in 1896 this was his fourth and last podium of the event. For the moment this was a record. Only seven other riders finished at Roubaix. Itsweire, Lepoutre, Simon, Dubreucq, Aucouturier, Pagie and Pothier, tenth and last and a full 4 hours and 40 minutes behind Bouhours. Several supplementary accidents affected the race, the most spectacular of which was at la Croix-de-Noailles. Caused by a collision between two motorcycles, a dozen people were injured, the most notable of which was the wife of a Member of Parliament. These incidents convinced Vienne and Perez that they should do away with motorised pacers. After the old formula was abandoned Emile Bouhours would never return to the race. He stayed faithful to track racing and was to carry off four national titles and twice stood on the podium at the World Championships, at a time when competition was fierce.

1900

1. Emile BOUHOURS (France)
2. Josef FISCHER (Germany)
3. Maurice GARIN (France)
4. Lucien ITSWEIRE (France)
5. Oscar LEPOUTRE (France)
6. Edouard SIMON (France)
7. Edmond DUBREUCQ (Belgium)
8. Hippolyte AUCOUTURIER (France)
9. Emile PAGIE (France)

Lesna : Paris-Roubaix before Bordeaux-Paris

At the beginning of 1901, the organisers took several important decisions for the evolution of their event. The abandonment of motor pacing was confirmed. Next the patronage of the sixth Paris-Roubaix was assured by the new sporting daily, 'L'Auto-Vélo'. By the way of retaliation 'Le Velo' announced its own version of Paris-Roubaix to be held on the same day, with the finish to be held in the Barbieux Park. The affair became so serious that the government decided to forbid any other event entitled Paris-Roubaix which finished anywhere near the velodrome. In the face of such difficulties and pressures, the management of 'Le Velo' decided at the end of March to cancel its plans.

As in the heroic times, the start from the Porte Maillot, was easily accessible to the Parisians. The course reverted to its original length of 280 kilometres. From the Porte Maillot the riders left in the direction of Brezons, then Houilles, Conflans, Pontoise, Ennery, Hérouville, Vallagoujard, Aublainville, Méru, Corbeil, Bois-de-Molle, Voisinlieu, Beauvais, Flers, Dury, Amiens (145kms) Villers-Bocage, Doullens, Mondricourt, Beaumetz, Arras (214.5 kms), Hénin-Liétard, Carvin, Seclin (251.5kms) Wattignies, Faches, Lesquin, Ascq, Forest, Hem and finally the velodrome to conclude the festivities. A few days before the event, Alphonse Steines inspected the roads and affirmed that although while they were not impractical, they were not very good, especially after Hénin-Lietard. At Roubaix, on the day before the race, the public were looking forward to the event. The velodrome had been renovated and was as new. At the 'Brasserie Moderne' as the rumours multiplied, firm bets were being taken. Lepoutre, Fischer and Ambroise Garin were at 2 to 1, Lesna at 5 to 1, Wattelier and Lorgeou at 10 to 1. However, one name was everyone's lips; that of Jean Gougoltz.

This man, the champion of the six-day track races, had recently converted to the road and was said to be on form. On 7th April 1901 at 4.40am, the morning was damp. The first to sign the start sheet, a certain Barbrel, appeared to be confident. He wanted to arrive at Roubaix and immediately return over the route in the opposite direction as training for the second Paris-Brest-Paris! Meanwhile, the favourite, Gougoltz, was taking breakfast. Unlike Gougoltz, who was a little tense, Lensa appeared unperturbed: "The mud? It doesn't frighten me. I've seen a' lot of it," he shrugged. The control closed at six o'clock. Under the rain, the muffled-up competitors converged towards the 'Restaurant Gillet' on the Boulevard Maillot, where as in the good old days the start was going to be given. Henri Desgrange, the new man in charge, called the riders to the line.

At precisely seven minutes past six, Mercier lowered the flag. Thirty nine professionals and twenty one amateurs launched themselves in the direction of Bezons.

1901

LESNA

Lucien LESNA
(France, 1863-1932)

A champion with exceptional endurance, Lesna was 26 years old before he rode his first race.

1894 : Bordeaux-Paris
1895 : French Champion (Motor-paced)
1896 : Champion of Europe (Motor-paced)
1898 : Champion of Europe (Motor-paced)
1901 : Paris-Roubaix, Bordeaux-Paris
1902 : Paris-Roubaix, Marseilles-Paris

Claude Chapperon at the finish.

The first serious attack came from Lorgeou and a little before Beauvais the battle was unleashed. Gougoltz and Lesna were alone in the lead. In less than thirty kilometres the 'tandem' had already relegated the pursuers to nine minutes. While Gougoltz was confirming the good things that had been thought of him, his pace suddenly became somewhat irregular. Lesnam, an experienced roadman, realised that his adversary was the victim of a monumental 'fringale', a hunger knock, His pacers, not used to this sort of event had no food to give him. Timidly Gougoltz asked Lensa for a piece of bread but apparently Lensa had never been so deaf! No doubt his ear ducts had been blocked by the efforts he had been making . Gougoltz weakly mumbled to his adversary and pacers; "Bandits, you're all bandits, I'll kill you all..." before saying good-bye to them. He finally arrived at the velodrome in eighteenth place 3 hours and ten minutes behind the winner. Amiens, Doullens, Arras, Seclin, the towns slipped by as the gap continued to grow. Ambroise Garin and Lucien Itsweire were the best, but a long way behind the leader. The sun shone down on Roubaix and ten thousand spectators filled the velodrome. At 5.06 pm the trumpets announced Lensa's arrival. He was not in the least tired and covered the last kilometre in 1min 37sec to well deserved applause. Twenty six minutes later Ambroise Garin, disappointed at having been unable to close the gap on Lensa, crossed the finishing line.

The only setback of the day was caused by a confused leader of the band. He believed that the winner was German (Lensa had been transferred to Berlin from where he had sent his entry). Then he thought he was Swiss, but eventually the conductor consented to play the Marseillaise as Lensa really was a Frenchman ! The next day at the 'Bar of Good Hope' discussions, excuses, complaints and grievances were all on the programme. Gougoltz was sure that with some food he would have won. Frédérick, the 'other' Swiss complained about the nails in the road. But Lensa had added his name to the list of winners after a lone break of one hundred and forty kilometres. Excellent training for Bordeaux-Paris which he also mastered a little later.

1901

left :
Lucien Itsweire (F) poses
for the photographer.

1. Lucien LESNA (France)
2. Ambroise GARIN (France)
3. Lucien ITSWEIRE (France)
4. Alphonse SEYS (Belgium)
5. Louis SCHULLER (France)
6. FOUREAUX (France)
7. Jean FISCHER (France)
8. Edouard WATTELIER (France)
9. Pierre CHEVALIER (France)
10. Georges PASQUIER (France)

Lucien Lensa on his 'cleveland'...

J. FISCHER, vainqueur en 1896

LA CAUSE DU SUCCÈS

Paris, 28 mars.

Roubaix qui est incontestablement la ville la plus sportive de France, vit dans la fièvre annuelle de la course cycliste Paris-Roubaix.

Pourquoi cette fièvre, pourquoi cet enthousiasme pour une épreuve moins longue que Bordeaux-Paris ou Marseille-Paris, sur un parcours moins accidenté que celui de Paris à Brest ? On pourrait trouver de multiples raisons. Celle d'abord que les grandes courses sur route aboutissent toujours à Paris, cet éternel accapareur, tandis que celle-ci a son point d'arrivée à Roubaix. Celle ensuite que les épreuves annuelles qui ont sept années d'existence se comptent en France et qu'il n'en est qu'une qui soit plus ancienne. Celle enfin que je crois très sérieuse et qui consiste en la suppression des voitures automobiles comme mode d'entraînement.

Ceux qui ont suivi depuis le début les courses cyclistes savent que le seul mode d'entraînement usité jusqu'en 1894 fut la bicyclette, puis intervinrent successivement et d'une année les tandems, les triplettes et les quadruplettes. Mais comme le cycliste veut toujours aller plus vite on mit à sa disposition ensuite les motocycles, les voiturettes et les grosses voitures.

...vint alors la suppression des courses d'automobiles qui provoqua l'interdiction de l'entraînement mécanique dans les courses cyclistes. C'en était fait de la vitesse qui parmit à Huret de venir de Bordeaux à Paris en 16 heures, mais c'était avant rendre à l'homme l'intérêt puissant du temps jadis : l'homme luttant à armes égales avec ses adversaires.

Un vestige du temps passé subsista encore l'année dernière, car les voitures automobiles, si elles ne pouvaient précéder les coureurs pouvaient encore les suivre, avec dans leurs flancs, des entraîneurs, des machines de rechange et des victuailles !

Cette année rien de tout cela : l'homme est seul sur la route avec comme seulement ses entraîneurs à bicyclette !

Eh, en somme, c'est bien là la grande lutte sauvage de la route, avec toutes ses péripéties angoissantes, les dépêches apportant au Vélodrome les détails du combat et le déboulé final, sur le ciment, du vainqueur acclamé par des milliers de poitrines !!

C'est de là vraiment que vient l'enthousiasme considérable qui accueille cette année les septième Paris-Roubaix.

Ne cherchons pas ailleurs !

H. DESGRANGE.

✠ La Course

Quand, en 1896, fut décidée la première course Paris-Roubaix, les hardis créateurs ne s'attendaient pas à voir leurs efforts couronnés de succès et, surtout, ne prévoyaient pas que cette épreuve cycliste, devenue traditionnelle, prendrait une telle place dans les mœurs de notre région. On ne peut bien affirmer que Paris-Roubaix est maintenant inhérente aux habitudes, aux mœurs du Nord de la France.

L'imposante manifestation a eu le don de passionner les sportsmen et d'intéresser les profanes !

Nous allons essayer de dépeindre le côté « psychologique » de la course si nos lecteurs veulent bien suivre avec nous les coureurs.

Chatou : cinq heures du matin ! Les lueurs de l'aube à peine apparues...

L'ARRIVÉE DE FISCHER EN 1896

pourtant il y a au départ une foule nombreuse, sportsmen acharnés, curieux indifférents, gavroches goguailleurs ! Il y a aussi les amis, les parents qui viennent donner les dernières recommandations, déposer les derniers baisers sur les fronts qui vont se couvrir... de boue sûrement, de gloire peut-être !... Car on peut bien affirmer que Paris-Roubaix...

---

maintenant inhérente aux habitudes, aux mœurs du Nord de la France.

L'imposante manifestation a eu le don de passionner les sportsmen et d'intéresser les profanes !

Nous allons essayer de dépeindre le côté « psychologique » de la course si nos lecteurs veulent bien suivre avec nous les coureurs.

Chatou : cinq heures du matin ! Les lueurs de l'aube sont à peine apparues et pourtant il y a au départ une foule nombreuse, sportsmen acharnés, curieux indifférents, gavroches goguailleurs ! Il y a aussi les amis, les parents qui viennent donner les derniers soins, faire les dernières recommandations, déposer les derniers baisers sur les fronts qui vont se couvrir... de boue sûrement, de gloire peut-être !...

La concurrents ont quitté restés et parcouru, se rangent à l'appel de leurs numéros, jettent un coup d'œil scrutateur sur la frêle machine qui va, de si on qu'ils vont tenter de conduire à la victoire, ce se mettent en selle ! Les uns sont gais, les autres sont graves, les uns énervés, les autres impassibles, mais tous attendent impatiemment le signal du starter.

Celui-ci prononce bientôt l'habituelle formule !

---

gloire ! Chacun voudrait lui serrer les mains, le féliciter, tant est grande et unanime l'admiration que provoque son inépuisable vaillance !

Combien la vue de cette foule délirante, l'ardeur de ces frénétiques bravos, doivent réconforter l'énergie et lui faire oublier les misères du parcours. Certes la route fut dure, mais la joie est grande, et on devine que sous la couche de boue amassée le long du chemin son visage reflète une ineffaçable impression de bonheur et de gloire !...

Si ces moments de triomphe laissent un inoubliable souvenir à l'homme qui en est l'objet, je pourrais aussi, à ceux qui y assistent, de véritables émotions. Et voilà pourquoi ceux, sportsmen ou réfractaires, qui ont assisté aux arrivées de Paris-Roubaix, les années précédentes, voudront encore les revoir dimanche prochain.

Mais, en attendant les coureurs, souhaitons-leur de bonnes routes, de machines indéraglables et un rayon de soleil pour réchauffer leur ardeur !

A. D.

PARIS-ROUBAIX RÉTROSPECTIF

Pour faire l'historique de la course Paris-Roubaix il faut remonter à la véritable origine. Celle-ci date de 1893, c'était le temps de Bordeaux-Paris, le mode d'aller aux courses sur route et on cherchait à en organiser. Ce fut, du reste, une des causes principales de l'extraordinaire et si rapide extension que prit le cyclisme car, rien ne parlait au masse populaire comme l'annonce des stupéfiantes performances de Terront, Jiel-Laval, Rivierre, etc... On comprit enfin quelle extraordinaire ressource la sapotite raine offrait à la locomotion moderne.

Roubaix ne pouvait rester en retard et un groupe cycliste « Le Sport Vélocipédique Roubaisien », eut l'idée d'organiser une course de Paris à Roubaix.

Des démarches furent aussitôt faites près des constructeurs, près des personnalités sportives pour obtenir des prix ; Mais le progrès n'avait pas encore accompli son œuvre, notre région était encore considérée comme réfractaire à la bicyclette — que les temps ont changé depuis ! — et on rencontra d'abord à la bicyclette aux demandes de nos concitoyens. Bref l'idée d'une course Paris-Roubaix fut abandonnée !

Cependant en 1894 et 1895, la vogue du cyclisme gagna notre région, le tourisme fit de nombreux

CHAMPION, vainqueur en 1899

adeptes et au point de vue sportif l'interminable rivalité des deux champions roubaisiens, Jules Delespierre et Adolphe Accou, fut également un gros stimulant. Une société se forma pour la construction d'un vélodrome et vélodrome et celui-ci fut inauguré le 9 juin 1895 ; on sait le succès qu'il obtint.

Dès lors, le premier Paris-Roubaix fut décidé et le projet qui avait pris naissance trois ans auparavant, fut mis à exécution. Le jour de Pâques, 19 avril 1896, fut choisi pour la première course Paris-Roubaix.

1896

En 1896, le départ fut donné de la Porte-Maillot à 5 h. et demie du matin. L'entraînement était fait avec toiles, l'entraînement était fait par machines multiples. La distance était de 280 kilomètres. Il y eut 54 partants. Le temps mis par le premier pour effectuer le courses fut de 9 h. 17. C'est Joseph Fischer gagna, suivi de Meyer, dont fut troisième.

Parmi les partants, il y avait Rivierre, Wuillamier, Linton, Ducom, le nègre Vendredi, Henri Desgrange, le directeur actuel de « l'Auto-Vélo », et comme régionaux : Baillot, Poiret, Assoman, Dubois, Quivy, Lisaron, Tébis, Delcambre, etc.

1897

En 1897, le départ se fit également de la Porte-Maillot, à 6 heures et demie du matin.

Deux catégories de coureurs se mirent en ligne : les professionnels et les amateurs. Ces derniers partirent à 6 heures et les « pros » à 6 heures et demie. Même parcours ; et même moyen d'entraînement qu'en 1896. Ce fut Maurice Garin qui sortit vainqueur de l'épreuve, battant Cordang... A l'arrivée sur la piste, après un duel émouvant.

58 partants se décomposant ainsi : 26 amateurs et 32 professionnels, qui partirent à 6 h. pour les amateurs et à 6 h. 43, pour accomplir le parcours.

Parmi les professionnels citons encore Rivierre, Vendredi, Frédérick, Borbin, Marius Thé... de Marseille, etc. Trousselier fut premier des amateurs, en 18 heures, devant les régionaux Ouvrier, Théo Carlane, Tébis, de Roubaix, Duquesne, de Hem, Hervynck, de Swevoghem, etc.

1898

En 1898, changement de tableau. C'est Chatou qui est choisi comme point de départ, afin d'éviter les traversées de Suresnes et de Rueil. La distance est ainsi ramenée à 255 kilomètres. Tous les modes d'entraînement sont admis, automobiles, motocycles, etc. Le starter abaisse son drapeau à 7 heures 45 du matin sur un lot de 63 partants, dont 31 coureurs professionnels cyclistes et 18 motocyclistes.

C'est encore Maurice Garin qui a pris la première place, dans le temps merveilleux de 8 heures 13 minutes sur Stéphane. Degrais est premier de la catégorie motocycle, en 17 heures 29 m. par un temps exécrable et des routes défoncées par la pluie.

1899

C'est encore à Chatou que les concurrents se mettent en ligne en 1899. Comme l'année précédente les moyens d'entraînement sont admis et la distance se retrouve la même. Le départ est donné à 7 heures 5 à 89 partants, 32 coureurs cyclistes profes-

---

sionnels et 57 motocyclistes. Champion est vainqueur de la première catégorie devant Bor, en 8 heures 22 minutes ; Maurice Garin a abandonné. Osmont sur un motocycle bat ses 56 adversaires dans le temps fantastique de 5 heures 35 minutes, devant Béconais et Girardot.

1900

En 1900, le lieu du départ est à nouveau reculé, et c'est Saint-Germain qui est choisi. La distance n'est donc plus que de 260 kilomètres. L'entraînement reste identique. 48 partants, 19 coureurs cyclistes professionnels et 29 motocyclistes s'alignent sous les ordres du starter à 9 heures du matin. Bouhours termine premier des cyclistes devant Joseph Fischer, et Barba bat 56 concurrents à motocycle. Le temps de 7 heures 10 m. 30 s. est le meilleur qui ait été fait, même en tenant compte de la différence de distance.

Maurice Garin victime d'accidents, se classe troisième, Itsweire, 4e, Lepoutre, 5e, Simon, 6e.

1901

L'an dernier, les amateurs rentrent en ligne ; par contre les motocyclistes sont remplacés par les Paris-Roubaix à l'abord dont on se rappelle le succès. Le départ est donné de la Porte-Maillot à 6 h. 7 aux amateurs et à 6 heures 17 aux professionnels. L'entraînement est fait par bicyclettes, par des suiveurs ou automobiles. Soixante-quatre coureurs dont 39 professionnels et 21 amateurs. Lesna est vainqueur de Ambroise Garin. Itsweire est troisième, Says, 4e.

L'ARRIVÉE DE LESNA EN 1901

Schuller, en débutant Roubaisien, est cinquième. Le temps de Lesna est de 10 heures 49 minutes 37 secondes pour les 277 kilomètres.

Dans la catégorie des amateurs, Chapparon, devenu depuis professionnel, est premier dans le temps remarquable de 11 heures 16 minutes. Guérin, deuxième, en 13 heures 10 minutes.

Telle est rapidement esquissée l'histoire de la grande épreuve dont nous aurons dimanche la septième édition !

Paris-Roubaix 1902

Après avoir fait valoir ce qu'ont été les précédentes courses Paris-Roubaix, il nous faut maintenant dire ce que sera Paris-Roubaix 1902 et vous donner

BOUHOURS, vainqueur en 1900

tous les détails d'organisation que nous classerons par nature :

Le Règlement

Des courses ont été organisées par nos confrères spéciaux de « l'Auto-Vélo » et le « Nord-Sportif ».

Les règlements de course adoptés sont ceux de l'Union Vélocipédique de France.

Le droit de l'engagement est fixé à cinq francs, remboursables aux partants.

La course est internationale.

Les coureurs seront placés au départ tirage au sort d'inscription au programme.

Les changements de machines sont autorisés.

Tous les genres de bicyclettes seront admis, pourvu que la force musculaire soit le seul moyen de les actionner.

L'entraînement humain à bicyclette sera seul permis. Tout coureur surpris ou convaincu d'avoir employé un autre système d'entraînement sera disqualifié.

Il est interdit aux concurrents de se faire précéder, accompagner ou suivre par des automobiles. Cette défense s'applique également aux motocycles et aux bicyclettes.

Tout coureur qui se sera fait tirer ou pousser, ou bien encore remplacer sur une partie du parcours, aussi petite soit-elle, qui aura certes employé un moyen illicité pour frauder les règlements habituels des courses, sera également disqualifié.

Ce sont MM. Hewo, Martin et Ruinart, Leurs décisions seront sans appel.

La durée maxima des courses sera de vingt-quatre heures.

Les réclamations, pour être valables, devront être posées par écrit, accompagnées d'une somme de 5 francs, avant le 14 avril, minuit. Passé ce délai, aucune réclamation ne sera plus admise.

Les responsabilités civiles et pénales resteront à

---

la charge des concurrents et elles incombent, étant bien entendu que les organisateurs déclinent toute responsabilité de quelque nature qu'elle soit. Toute infraction au présent règlement entraînera la disqualification.

Les Prix

Voici la liste des prix dont la dotée la course Paris-Roubaix 1902 :

1ᵉʳ prix, offert par « l'Auto-Vélo » et le « Nord-Sportif »	1000 fr.
2ᵉ	»	600 »
3ᵉ	»	400 »
4ᵉ	»	200 »
5ᵉ	»	100 »
6ᵉ, offert par M. Eug. Motte, député	100 »
7ᵉ, offert par M. de Montalembert, député	100 »
8ᵉ, offert par le « Journal de Roubaix »	100 »
9ᵉ, offert par les commerçants d'Hem	60 »
10ᵉ	»	60 »

Comme on le voit, nos représentants ont tenu à encourager par des prix généreusement offerts, la populaire manifestation sportive. Signalons particulièrement les 9e et 10e prix supplémentaires offerts à la suite d'une souscription entre les commerçants d'Hem. C'est là de gracieux encouragements aux organisateurs.

L'Itinéraire

L'itinéraire de la course Paris-Roubaix a, cette année, son point de départ à Chatou ; il ne comprend donc qu'un total de 265 kilomètres au lieu de 280 kilomètres qu'on avait en 1901, avec le départ à la Porte-Maillot, soit 15 kilomètres de moins. En voici le détail :

Localités traversées	Distance entre les localités	Distances totales km.
Chatou	0 kil. 000	0 000
Saint-Germain	4 kil. 000	4 000
Croix-de-Noailles	6 kil. 000	10 000
Achères passage à niveau	4 kil. 500	14 500
Pont de Conflans	2 kil. 000	16 500
Conflans	2 kil. 500	19 000
Franoy	2 kil. 000	21 000
Pontoise	3 kil. 000	24 000
Ennery	7 kil. 000	31 000
Héroville (embranchement)	2 kil. 000	33 000
Vasvangourland	7 kil. 000	40 000
Andeluville	7 kil. 000	47 000
Méru	4 kil. 000	51 000
Corbeil-Cerf	6 kil. 000	57 000
Beauvais-Palllsey	3 kil. 000	60 000
Bois-de-Milla	2 kil. 000	62 000
Saint-Quentin d'Anneull	8 kil. 000	70 000
Beauvais (bifurcation)	7 kil. 000	72 000
Bonneuil	6 kil. 000	73 000
Traversée de Beauvais	2 kil. 000	77 000
Villa	4 kil. 000	80 000
Encaria Saint-Martin	4 kil. 400	90 000
Noirmont	2 kil. 000	97 000
Froissy	6 kil. 000	102 000
Quiry	5 kil. 000	100 000
Breteuil	7 kil. 000	114 000
Folie-le-Bonnetil	6 kil. 000	120 000
Flers	7 kil. 000	122 000
Saint-Souffier	4 kil. 000	126 000
Dury	6 kil. 000	132 000
Amiens	8 kil. 000	140 000
Villers-Bocage	2 kil. 000	150 000
Talmas	3 kil. 000	160 000
Beauval	2 kil. 000	168 000
Doullens	10 kil. 000	174 000
Mondicourt	7 kil. 000	181 000
Arbret	4 kil. 000	181 000

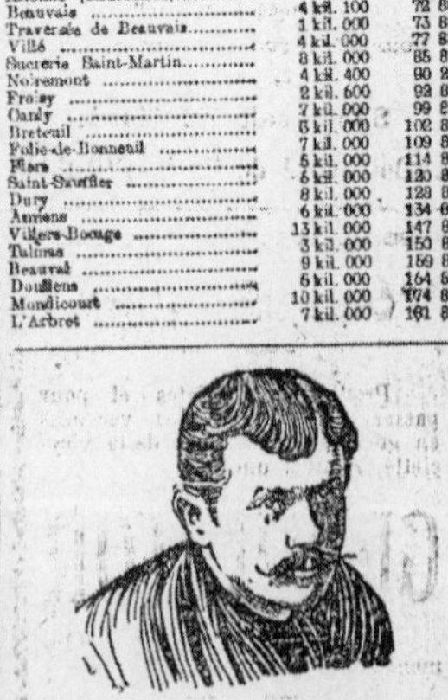

LESNA, vainqueur en 1901

Beaumetz-les-Loges	11 kil. 000	192 000
Arras	9 kil. 000	201 000
Henin-Liétard	13 kil. 000	214 000
Carvin	6 kil. 000	231 000
Seclin	6 kil. 000	237 000
Wattignies	4 kil. 000	245 000
Lille	4 kil. 000	249 000
Hellemmes	4 kil. 000	253 000
Annoy	2 kil. 000	255 000
Croix	6 kil. 000	261 000
Roubaix	4 kil. 000	265 000

Les Contrôles

Deux sortes de contrôles seront installés : les contrôles fixes où les coureurs devront s'arrêter et signer une feuille de passage et les contrôles volants

---

M. GARIN, vainqueur en 1897 et 1898

Attention, Messieurs ! Son doigt presse la détente ! Pan ! le peloton s'ébranle et on le voit s'égrener à l'horizon. Voilà les vaillants routiers lancés, vers Roubaix ! Dans les campagnes comme dans les villes qu'ils traversent, la foule sympathique se range à leur passage et les encourage ; s'arrêtent pour un motif quelconque, chacun s'empresse autour d'eux, leur prodigue les soins nécessaires, leur aide s'il s'agit d'une réparation. Les braves paysans de la route seront fiers de lire le soir, au cabaret, qu'ils ont rendu le moindre petit service aux coureurs de Paris-Roubaix !... On réconforte le coureur et en s'éloignant, on ne pense et il est blessé, des groupes de cyclistes l'escortent jusqu'à ce qu'il soit sorti de la ville ! Et plus les coureurs approchent du but, plus la foule se presse et plus les encouragements sont nourris. Il semble que l'intérêt va « crescendo » jusqu'au terme du parcours.

Mais cet enthousiasme atteint son paroxysme, c'est autour des barrières du Vélodrome Roubaisien. Là, se pressent 10.000 personnes attendant les arrivées, et il faut avoir assisté à ce spectacle pour en apprécier l'impressionnant intérêt !

Quel de plus curieux que l'effet produit par ces milliers de spectateurs qui lisent avidement les télégrammes provenant des différents contrôles et inscrits sur le tableau de la pelouse.

Ces conversations sont animées, on commente la marche des coureurs, on remarque que l'un gagne du terrain, l'autre en perd, les fanatiques changent de paris !... Toute cette foule qui s'écrase suit dans une pensée unique les énergiques coureurs dans leur marche et le but tardie de les voir, de leur prouver l'enthousiasme qu'ils provoquent.

Chacun devine le combat auquel se livrent les adversaires de quelques lieues de là. On les voit se passer, se rejoindre, tour à tour, s'épuiser en efforts décisifs, activer leurs entraîneurs... Hélas ! on les voit aussi luttant contre les éléments, contre les accidents de la route...

Mais voici un télégramme émanant du dernier contrôle, les premiers dont il indique les noms doivent être bien proches !... Roubaix, les phares grandits résonnent, un frison s'empare autour de la foule attentive. Un coureur arrive !... Il est là, on l'aperçoit débouchant à la piste ! Une première acclamation s'élève de cette foule compacte ! le voilà !...

L'arrivant, au moment même il a la vue de ce public qui n'a des yeux que pour lui, accueilli sa

Lesna wins Paris-Roubaix by way of good-bye

The seventh Paris-Roubaix was disputed on 30th March 1902. The event still opened the cycling road season but the riders no longer only considered it as a repetition of Bordeaux-Paris. The race had become, for the riders something particularly special to add to their list of victories. Thus far the French, with the exception of the initial event, had remained the masters of the race. However, it must be said that the Belgians were still looking for their first champion of any consequence, while in Holland, apart from the track competition, cycling was virtually unknown. In Italy bike racing was only in its early stages.

The beginning of Spring and in the bars and cafes Maurice Garin was often the centre of the discussions. The champion had just left the town to establish his permanent home at Lens. Rumour had it that he had given up the sport and that he was to write a novel entitled, 'The Mysterious Cyclist'. As the little chimney sweep had not sent in his entry for the Easter race, everyone believed that he had been lost to cycling. Those in charge of L'Auto were to receive seventy seven entries, all accompanied by the required five francs, which would be reimbursed to all starters. This edition was to be disputed not only without motorised pacers but controlled by commissaires comfortably mounted in various following vehicles. This innovation came into effect at Arras for the strategic sections of the race. All was ready, apart from the rain which had been falling for several days. The start had been moved to the establishment of "Monsieur Bouché" at 47 Route de St Germain at Chatou.

While the 'Aces' slept at the 'Hotel of the Golden Sun', the more enthusiastic riders and their pacers prepared their plans of campaign. Lesna, who had the best team of pacers

1902

Lucien Lesna enters the velodrome.

at his disposal, appeared to be very confident as he signed on. Henri Desgrange believed that Lesna was strong enough to do the double. Then after him were Paul Bor, Jean Fischer, Ambroise Garin, Edouard Wattelier and the rest of the peloton. Oscar Lepoutre, the man from Lille certainly believed in his star. After hard training sessions over the Northern roads he always finished the day with twenty fast kilometres over the velodrome track. Ambroise Garin was also determined to make Lensa crack: "I have never in my life felt stronger. If I don't win Paris-Roubaix this year then I will never be able to understand anything any more."

Under a light rain, at precisely 5.05am the fifty starters listened attentively to the final instructions. Several hundred people applauded for the last time as the procession slowly pulled away. In the front of The Great Stag Hotel at Pontoise, where the first control was situated, a huge crowd was spilling across the road. The commissaires had difficulty in keeping open a passage for the arrival of the nine riders who comprised the leading group. Under a menacing sky Beauvais was crossed at great speed by Lensa with only Wattelier able to hold his wheel. Three men were involved in a serious pursuit; Chapperon competing under the pseudonym of Daudon, Sales and Pagie. The bunch followed further behind and then came the various dropped riders. The last one, a certain Perrin after only seventy kilometres of racing was already two hours down. Having taken note of his deficit he lost heart and took off his armband. His race was over. It was still a long way to go to the strategic sectors but the gaps were already considerable. The St Roch esplanade at Amiens was dense with people. The inseparable Lensa and Wattelier signed the control sheet before plunging their heads into buckets of water and sharing a cup of hot chocolate. At this point a determined Ambroise Garin arrived a mere three minutes later. At Café Thulliez at Doullens the tension rose as the news arrived. Garin's fight back caused the beer to flow freely. On the hill where the roadside gutters had become two streams of water, spectators were fighting for the high ground. Now, Wattelier and Lensa had relegated Garin to four minutes while the fourth man Daudon was at sixteen minutes, the astonishing Leroux at eighteen and behind them it was chaos !

As Arras approached, Wattelier gradually showed signs of weakness and suddenly Lesna was two hundred metres in front and then five hundred metres. Rapidly the gap was to be measured in minutes, as it was for everyone else. As the race went through the mining region the roads were lined solid banks of vociferous spectators. The velodrome was crowded, mainly with Frenchmen, but there was also a considerable number of Belgians. For the first time the Cycling Club of the Antwerp Docks had organised an excursion to Roubaix.

At 2.48pm and the clarions gave way to the Marseillaise. The rain had stopped for a few moments to salute the arrival of the champion. Lucien Lensa had beaten the elements for a second time. He lapped the track with a huge smile on his face. His famous 'Cleveland' bike was covered in mud as he slowly completed the last three laps of the velodrome, savouring the cheers of the crowd. An exhausted Wattelier arrived eight minutes down, then Ambroise Garin at nearly twelve and then the others. Lensa was already in his fortieth year. After a few days rest he took the train to Marseilles to prepare for one of his last races; Marseilles-Paris, the event that by way of a good-bye, he added to his list of victories.

1902

LA VIE AU GRAND AIR

LA COURSE PARIS-ROUBAIX — DANS LA CÔTE DE DOULLENS

left:
1902 atmosphere at the velodrome.

1. Lucien LESNA (France)
2. Edouard WATTELIER (France)
3. Ambroise GARIN (France)
4. P. DAUDON (France)
5. Oscar LEPOUTRE (France)
6. Jean FISCHER (France)
7. Philippe LEROUX (France)
8. Emile PAGIE (France)
9. Georges PASQUIER (France)
10. BARBE (France)

Paris-Roubaix 1903

NOTES D'UN NÉOPHYTE

Nous avons trouvé dans la boîte du journal les curieuses notes que l'on va lire et qui, dues à une plume absolument anonyme, encadreront à merveille les curieuses photographies prises à l'intention de nos lecteurs sur les diverses péripéties de Paris-Roubaix 1903.

Lundi 13 avril. — Je rentre à Paris, fourbu, esquinté, bon à jeter au panier, comme une loque.

Manque d'entraînement, c'est certain.

Au contrôle de départ, à Chatou, 5 heures du matin.

Une grande pancarte annonce :

« Paris-Roubaix, organisé par l'*Auto* ».

Ah oui! l'*Auto*: je connais, mes fils le lisent.

C'est là le contrôle. Et le contrôle s'éveille.

Le jour paraît. De grands gars, de petits, mais tous bien râblés, attachent un brassard rouge sur leur maillot, et patiemment ils attendent. Les uns mangent, les autres causent, se racontent leurs prouesses passées, leurs espérances présentes.

L'appel! Mon ami, très compétent me fait voir les favoris. Un gaulois roux, Pasquier; un grand diable, solidement charpenté, Aucouturier; puis des jeunes « pur-sang », Lorgeou, Trousselier, Chapperon, Forestier; de vieux routiers, Jean Fischer, Barroy, Ambroise Garin, Lepoutre.

Trousselier.   Lorgeou.   Wattelier.

Le peloton des coureurs traversant Le Pecq.

Samedi soir, à la sortie du théâtre, je soupais dans un cabaret dont le nom importe peu. J'entends trépider une automobile. Entre un chauffeur, en tenue de route, de grande route même.

C'est un ami.

— Viens-tu avec moi?

— Où çà!

— À Chatou, assister au départ de Paris-Roubaix.

— ? ? ?

— Oui, une grande course cycliste, c'est très curieux. Viens voir cela.

— Mais j'ai un chapeau haut de forme. Ce n'est pas pratique pour aller en automobile.

— Viens donc tout de même.

Et j'y vais.

Délicieuse traversée du Bois de Boulogne à 3 heures et demie du matin. La nuit est violette, un violet clair.

Je passe pour la première fois de ma vie à Suresnes et à Rueil à cette heure là.

Chatou! Arrêt, buffet

Le passage sur la place Jeanne Hachette, à Beauvais.

J'ai acheté l'*Auto* que des camelots crient à tue-tête et je relève maintenant tous ces noms pointés dimanche matin.

— Allez! Qu'est-ce que tu attends?

— Monte donc?

J'obéis et grimpe dans la voiture.

Hop! les coureurs viennent de filer dans un grand nuage de poussière.

Et mon ami met sa voiture en marche.

— Où me mènes-tu? Nous ne revenons pas à Paris? J'ai envie de dormir.

— Non, viens jusqu'à Pontoise.

Je ne vais pas souvent en automobile, et cela m'amuse. Je me laisse donc faire.

Que c'est joli la forêt de Saint-Germain et que la route y est unie!

Je me prends pour une bille de billard qui « prise en tête » file à toute vitesse sur le fin tapis vert rigoureusement horizontal.

Et ces diables de coureurs se sauvent, dos courbé, mains crispées sur le guidon.

Hippolyte's year

The route of the following years remained unchanged. The little town of Chatou became the traditional starting point for numerous editions of the event. This usually peaceful place woke up a few days before the start of the classic. The bike shop, where the riders came to sign on, was run by Monsieur Bouché who became the local hero for several hours.

For the manufacturers, a victory was worth it's weight in gold. Following a success on these difficult roads, the make of bicycle became as well known as its rider. It was a label of quality and of resistance recognised by everyone. Sponsors were prepared to pay large sums in order to get the best pacers. A recognised trackman was able to earn more money hiring his services in this way than by winning a Grand Prix, even though the prizes in the latter were far from negligible.

The eighth Paris-Roubaix represented a new era. Many of the pioneers of the early editions had taken a well earned retirement.. New names appeared. The conflict between the generations began to make itself felt and this edition confirmed it.

On Sunday 11th April 1903, fifty one participants answered the call of the starter, the faithful Mercier. The best of them pushed their way through to the front line: Lorgou, Aucouturier, Georget, Wattelier...All of them knew from experience that the start was of capital importance and that the unskilled beginners could sometimes cause crashes.

Louis Trousselier was the pre-race favourite, ahead of Lorgeou and Wattelier. The group started at a lively pace. The St Germain hill, which had previously broken up the bunch, this time only caused some off-form competitors to be dropped off the back.

A little further on, the hill of Ennery already caused the decisive break to be formed. Lorgeou attacked. Aucouturier, Trousselier, Chapperon, Forestier and Wattelier, sensed that this was the right move and got onto the heels of the fugitive. The fate of the race was sealed, or nearly, for five of them occupied the first places eight hours later at the velodrome.

Until Amiens they rode well together, then Lorgeou and Chapperon, unable to follow the pace and close to exhaustion, dropped off.

Trousselier confirmed his role of favourite but the menace from Aucouturier started to take shape. For several years he had been held back by bad luck. Typhoid fever, for example, had wiped out his 1902 season.

Nicknamed 'the Terrible', Aucouturier multiplied his attacks as Doullens approached. The champion would no longer leave the head of the race, even when Chapperon, in a sudden astonishing burst, rejoined him a little later.

Chapperon did his share of the work and as the velodrome came into sight managed to drop Aucouturier who followed him fifty yards behind. There then remained three laps of the track to be completed.

Tradition had it that the riders changed their machines at the entrance to the stadium. Generally this did not lead to any particular problem, except today, for Chapperon in his haste seized...Trousselier's bicycle!

Rapidly he stopped, went back and changed machines. Furiously he accused an official. In the confusion Aucouturier went past him and now had a lead of one hundred metres. Chapperon realised he might never have another opportunity to enter

1903

Hippolyte AUCOUTURIER
(France, 1876 -1944)

Nicknamed "The Terrible". One of the most resilient champions of the heroic era of cycle racing.

1901 : Brussels-Roubaix,
2nd Bordeaux-Paris,
3rd Paris-Brest-Paris
1902 : 3rd Paris-Rennes
1903 : Paris-Roubaix, Bordeaux-Paris,
2nd Paris-Valenciennes
1904 : Paris-Roubaix
1905 : Bordeaux-Paris, 2nd Tour de France

LA VIE AU GRAND AIR

ABONNEMENTS

Paris.... Un an 14 fr.   ÉDITION DE LUXE
Départem^{ts}. — 15 fr.   France. Un an . 30 fr.
Etranger . — 20 fr.   Etranger . 40 fr.

18 Avril 1903. — N° 240.
Rédaction et Administration : 9, Avenue de l'Opéra, PARIS (1er Arr^t)

PUBLICITÉ

Pages de Couverture, la ligne . . 1 fr 50
La Page . . . . 600 fr.
Encartage . . . . 500 fr.

(Temps couvert.)

Aucouturier.   Chapperon.

LA COURSE PARIS-ROUBAIX. — UNE ARRIVÉE DISPUTÉE

Notre photographie représente l'arrivée au vélodrome du Parc Barbieux, où ils terminaient le parcours par trois tours de piste, d'Aucouturier et de Chapperon. Ce dernier, entré le premier dans l'enceinte, à 50 mètres devant son rival, est descendu de sa machine pour en prendre une autre qu'il croit préparée pour lui et qui est, en réalité, destinée à Trousselier. Tandis qu'il reprend sa bicyclette de route, Aucouturier a pu, lui, changer de machine, passer et prendre 100 mètres. Il finit avec la même avance, en 9 h. 12 m.30 s., battant le record de Joseph Fischer par 4 m. 30 s.

(Voir l'article pages 248 et suiv.)

into history. He fought with all his strength, pulling back ninety metres. But the last ones, the most difficult ones, remained impossible to regain.

Hippolyte was over the moon. For once luck was on his side! Quite exceptionally two other riders arrived within the same minute; a frustrated Trousselier at forty seconds and Wattelier fourth at one minute.

Behind them, the gaps were much more significant., Lorgeou to whom belonged the merit of launching the race, finished fifth at almost half an hour. As for Jean Fischer, for this his last Paris-Roubaix, he was placed sixth, just as had been the previous year.

After this success Aucouturier dominated the beginning of the season. In the image of Lesna in 1901, he carried off Bordeaux-Paris a few weeks later.

No member of the 'Garin tribe' was at the finish his time. On the 19th January, the newspaper 'L'Auto' had announced the creation of a new type of event. A stage race called 'Tour de France' joining Paris to Paris, with ports of call at Lyons, Marseille, Toulouse, Bordeaux and Nantes. A race that was said to be a little mad with an uncertain future !

Maurice Garin, already winner of some of the great classic one-day races, took up the challenge. He renounced Paris-Roubaix and dedicated himself exclusively to preparation for the Tour de France. His reasoning seemed to be correct, for in the Tour he outstripped Lucien Pothier by nearly three hours, winning three stages in the process. Hippolyte Aucouturier, seemingly insatiable in this year of 1903, picked up two stages, first at Marseille, then Toulouse.

1903

| 1. Hippolyte AUCOUTURIER (France) |
| 2. Claude CHAPPERON (France) |
| 3. Louis TROUSSELIER (France) |
| 4. Edouard WATTELIER (France) |
| 5. Georges LORGEOU (France) |
| 6. Jean FISCHER (France) |
| 7. Arthur PASQUIER (France) |
| 8. Paul TRIPPIER (France) |
| 9. Léon GEORGET (France) |
| 10. Oscar LEPOUTRE (France) |

AUCOUTURIER,
vainqueur de Paris-Roubaix 1903.

Course Paris-Roubaix

Dimanche 3 Avril 1904

(9me ANNÉE)

Simples Réflexions

—x—

Roubaix, 2 avril.

Neuvième année !... Savez-vous que c'est toute une existence pour une course sur route !... Et cependant « Paris-Roubaix » ne vieillit pas et retrouve toujours le même enthousiasme, chaque année, dans la région du Nord de la France...

Pourquoi diront les profanes ? D'abord parce que c'est « Paris-Roubaix » et que ces deux mots dans leur union annuelle ont sur la foule une sorte d'influence magique, ensuite parce que l'épreuve du jour de Pâques marque avec l'ouverture d'une nouvelle saison le commencement d'une série de courses sur route qui — qu'on le veuille ou non — retiennent l'attention du public initié ou non, enfin parce que chacun des « Paris-Roubaix » successifs apporte des changements soit dans les conditions de la course, soit dans la présence de concurrents encore inconnus...

Cette grande bataille sportive qui va dérouler demain ses péripéties le long du ruban de route qui sépare notre ville de la capitale — et qui est, comme les années précédentes, organisée avec soin par notre confrère l'*Auto* de concert avec l'Administration du Vélodrome Roubaisien — a vu son intérêt s'accroître encore cette année par la suppression des entraîneurs et soigneurs... C'est une sage décision à laquelle on a applaudi dans le Nord... Ce sera donc la lutte à armes égales entre tous les vaillants routiers n'ayant que « leurs propres moyens » pour se mesurer, c'est-à-dire l'homme et sa frêle machine, en butte aux péripéties du long parcours.

Et cette lutte sera d'autant plus ardente que les circonstances sont défavorables : les routes sont boueuses, les pavés sont gluants, peu importe aux valeureux champions ! La victoire ne sera que plus méritante et lorsqu'ils viendront sur le ciment du Vélodrome Roubaisien, au milieu de la foule enthousiaste qui s'y pressera, recueillir des ovations bien méritées, leur visage couvert de boue reflétera une inoubliable impression de bonheur et de gloire...

On peut ne pas partager les émotions sincères qu'éprouvent les véritables sportsmen à la vue de semblables spectacles mais une épreuve du genre de Paris-Roubaix est de celles qui en imposent, même aux indifférents et aux profanes, parce qu'elles constituent d'éclatantes manifestations de l'énergie humaine...

Souhaitons donc aux organisateurs tout le succès que mérite une telle entreprise et aux vaillants coureurs beaucoup de soleil pour stimuler leur ardeur et un peu de gloire pour récompenser leurs efforts...

A. D.

Les Impressions d'un "Paris-Roubaix"

—x—

On se plaît trop souvent à dire que le coureur qui lutte avec tant d'énergie dans ces grandes batailles de la route est dépourvu de sentiments, que devant l'effort physique produit, il n'éprouve pas de sensations morales, que ses impressions disparaissent devant la préoccupation d'arriver parmi les premiers pour toucher la forte allocation, etc.... Ce sont là des préjugés devant lesquels nous tenons à nous élever : Il y a au fond de tout coureur un sportsman que la récompense morale intéresse souvent plus que la satisfaction matérielle. Pour ceux qui en doutent, nous allons citer l'exemple de Valpic — de son nom véritable : Vallée-Picaud — qui a conquis tant de sympathies dans notre sportive région. Qui ne connaît ce jeune coureur au maillot rayé noir et blanc, qui sous une apparence chétive cache une

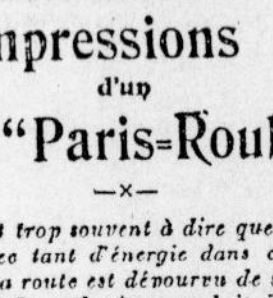

Marcel VALLÉE-PICAUD (*alias VALPIC*)

énergie extraordinaire !... Valpic est le type du coureur qui d'ancien amateur est devenu professionnel par amour du sport, par passion, pour pouvoir disputer aux grands cracks les lauriers qui lui faisait tant envie, envisageant plus la gloire que le « vil métal »... Tout jeune encore — 19 printemps — Valpic issu d'une excellente famille a le tempérament du coureur avec la délicatesse du garçon bien élevé; son visage doux, expressif, éclairé par deux grands yeux où brillent l'intelligence, la bonté, lui attire à première vue des sympathies... et il a droit à celles-ci...

Il nous a donc semblé intéressant pour nos lecteurs de demander au jeune Valpic de nous conter dans ce supplément spécial ses impressions recueillies le long du parcours de Paris-Roubaix... Il l'a fait de fort bonne grâce et, ce qui est plus, avec un réel talent... Tous les sportsmen, et même les profanes, liront avec plaisir les lignes ci-dessous, c'est le récit vécu des impressions de route d'un des acteurs du grand « event » annuel... et nos lecteurs se joindront à nous pour remercier le journaliste-coureur et lui souhaiter de trouver sur la piste comme dans la presse, tout le succès qu'il mérite...

—x—

Non, je ne courrai pas Paris-Roubaix cette année, et mon cœur en est rempli de tristesse !

J'ai en effet dit adieu aux longues courses sur route pour goûter des émotions plus violentes, mais combien plus monotones aussi, des courses de demi-fond.

Si je ne suis pas au nombre des vaillants qui partiront de Paris, les uns remplis de confiance, les autres d'appréhension, je veux tout au moins revivre par la pensée les heures heureuses et trop

PARIS-ROUBAIX 1903
Vue prise au départ à Chatou

courtes, que j'ai passées sur le long ruban de route qui sépare les deux capitales du sport.

Et cette revue d'un passé plein de joies me sera d'autant plus agréable, chers lecteurs, que vous voudrez bien m'accompagner.

Ce sera pour moi encore participer à la course, d'une manière indirecte il est vrai, mais qui n'en est pas moins réelle; les heures, les choses, et les distances auront de l'importance d'après les souvenirs qui s'y attachent; je verrai toujours le passage à niveau d'Eragny fermé et escaladé ; une automobile en panne m'empêchera de prendre à mon aise le tournant au bas de la descente de Vallangoujard; la traversée d'Amiens me sera

PARIS-ROUBAIX 1903
Un groupe de coureurs et entraîneurs sur la route

pénible et me fera la sensation d'un vide absolu dans l'estomac; le clocher de l'église de Doullens marquera toujours 12 heures 55 comme en 1901 ; et dans le chemin du Vélodrome la petite voiture d'un marchand d'oranges me barrera la route, et j'aurai envie d'en voler une.

Mes impressions, les voici telles quelles, en bloc, comment elles se présentent à mon souvenir.

—x—

4 heures du matin. — Marcel, réveille-toi et mon dévoué manager me secouant doucement me tire de mon sommeil, où plutôt de ma torpeur, car les appels de cyclistes, les rumeurs et les coups de trompes des autos ont contribué à rendre agité le repos que la simple idée du combat à venir troublait déjà suffisamment.

Lentement je revêts mon habit de course, habit léger, que la pluie qui tombe sans cesse fait paraître encore plus dérisoire. Mon Dieu ! quel temps ! De la pluie, encore de la pluie, toujours de la pluie. De par sa position précoce dans la saison, le jour de Pâques est fort souvent contrarié et gâté par cette infernale pluie qui vous glace, vous annihile, vous enlève toute ardeur.

Bien agité le repas du matin ! D'abord à cinq heures, au saut du lit, l'appétit n'a pas eu le temps de se manifester, et puis, un je ne sais quoi un peu nerveux me resserre l'estomac.

— Allons, mange, songe un peu à la dépense que va nécessiter l'effort. Tout à l'heure il sera trop tard, la faim se fera sentir et l'estomac vide, tu ressentirais les effets de la défaillance,

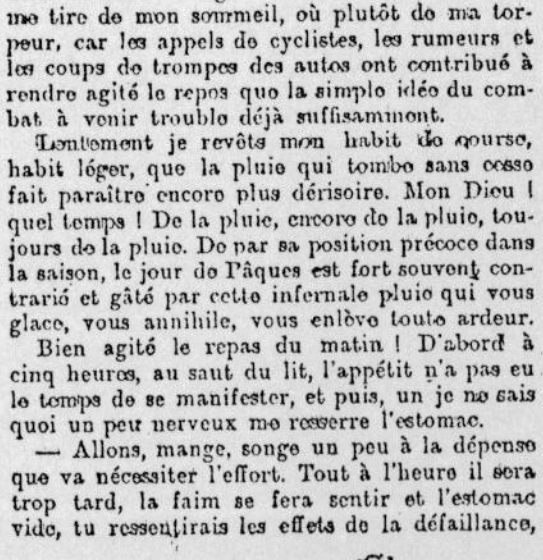

PARIS-ROUBAIX 1903
Valpic traversant la place Jeanne-Hachette, à Beauvais

etc., etc. Les exhortations se multiplient. Que ce bifteck est énorme ! Que ce chocolat est épais ! Enfin à force de temps, le repas est consommé, non sans peine.

— Eh bien ! Valpic, vous sentez-vous en jambes ? Croyez-vous que cela va aller ? — Ah, Monsieur Géo Lefèvre, je voudrais bien être arrivé là-bas, et pourtant je ne donnerais pas ma place au départ pour tout l'or du monde. — Allons tâchez de bien figurer, vous êtes un vaillant, la pluie ne vous effraie pas. Tenez, voici votre brassard.

— Ben mon vieux, t'en as de l'audace. T'en aller sur la route avec une chaîne de trois. Tu risques rien d'rester en panne en haut de la côte du Pecq. Avec la boue, elle va rien sauter ! A toi tout le bonheur ! — Eh ! Pige-moi cette tête de fourche ! Tu parles de c'qu'elle va prendre sur les pavés du Nord' ! — Merci, Messieurs, des avis autorisés comme les vôtres me sont précieux, et vos encouragements me touchent ! — Il n'empêche que ma chaîne ne s'est pas tendue malgré la boue, et que ma tête de fourche est encore de ce monde.

Le temps de donner un coup de clef aux écrous, de vérifier l'action du frein, de tâter si le pneu n'est pas trop dur ni trop mou, et vous voilà rangé. Pendant l'appel, on cause avec son voisin ; on calcule, on cherche quel chemin se frayer à travers le peloton pour sortir indemne de la bagarre qui va se produire inévitablement.

— Vous êtes prêts, Messieurs ? — Un silence de mort ; chacun est trop anxieux pour pouvoir desserrer les dents, ne fût-ce que pour laisser sortir un : oui.

— Partez ! Et le drapeau s'abaisse.

Dans une brusque détente j'ai démarré, je suis parti. J'emballe sans me soucier de mes concurrents, comme si le but de ma course était à 30 mètres de là. Une chute, juste le temps de faire un crochet et d'éviter l'homme maladroit ou guignard qui vient de tomber ; une seconde, une troisième chute, je ne les compte plus, et miracle, je parviens à passer librement.

La côte du Pecq. Penser à prendre le trottoir, le pavé trop gras ne permettant pas de se tenir en équilibre. — Avance donc, feignant ! A droite, à droite ! — Misère, j'ai pris le trottoir de droite qui m'allonge davantage.

Enfin, nous voilà en haut. Je traverse Saint-Germain en faisant un détour de ma façon qui me permet d'éviter deux virages brusques et encombrés. La forêt. Ici l'allure est plus régulière, il fait à peine jour. Où suis-je, avec qui, quelle position occupé-je ?

Un coup d'œil devant et derrière, quelques questions me renseignent. Il s'agit de coller sagement au peloton, dans lequel je suis. Il faut ruser pour prendre une bonne position mener le moins possible, s'échapper si un échappage se produit. Mais non, tout est calme, nous filons silencieusement, mes jambes tricotent éperdûment, nous faisons 40 à 45 à l'heure certainement.

PARIS-ROUBAIX 1903
Aucouturier à sa descente de machine ayant reçu le traditionnel bouquet

La pluie a cessé, la boue reste. Nous sommes six ensemble. Qui arrivera premier de nous six ? Sera-ce moi ? Je ne suis pas assez outrecuidant pour le penser, mais je l'espère. Qui décollera le premier ? Sera-ce moi ? Rien que cette idée me donne des ailes.

Une côte, démarrage, lâchage. Pédalez, mes amis, ce n'est pas dans les côtes que vous m'aurez, nous restons quatre ; tant mieux, on est moins serré.

J'ai faim ; déjà ! Oui, déjà, je voudrais encore être devant le repas près duquel je boudais tout à l'heure.

Un concurrent vide une bouteille. — Passe m'en un peu ? — Tu peux crever ! — Merci.

Pavé, tournant, applaudissements. — Vos numéros ? — Méru, plus que 215 kilomètres ; ça se tire comme on dit, ou plutôt, on dira, à la caserne.

Oh ! que j'ai froid aux pieds ! Le reste du corps, passe encore, il y a mouvement ; mais les pieds à plat sur les pédales prennent un bain de boue dans les souliers ! Je n'ose proposer à un de mes concurrents de battre la semelle ; les minutes sont des siècles, les secondes des heures.

Menons le train chacun notre tour, on va en rattrapper un. — Effectivement on le rattrape. — T'as décollé du peloton. — Siou-plait ? — Tu t'es fait lâcher. — Ça file, sais-tu, et puis dans les côtes, ils montent ! — C'est un belge, on va le lâcher dans la descente du Bois de Molle !

Beauvais. Emballage sur le pavé. Que pense Jeanne Hachette de voir une troupe d'hommes demi-vêtus se précipiter vers une table criant : 2. 27. 18.59, etc., etc.

Sitôt signé, sitôt parti ; celui qui signe le dernier est un homme lâché. On ne s'arrête pas à Beauvais, à quoi bon ? Les soigneurs attendent leur homme au haut de la côte qui est à la sortie de la ville.

— Le voilà, le voilà ! — C'est toi ? — Oui, c'est moi ! — Mais non, c'est pas lui. — Pourtant, moi, c'est moi ! Il paraît que non !

Mon petit sac est vidé. Et moi qui le trouvais lourd au départ, que n'était-il deux fois plus chargé ! Enfin voici mon entraîneur. — Vous voilà, j'ai vos provisions ! Bien, collez au peloton, je les prendrai un peu plus loin.

Hélas, mille fois hélas ! Je me retourne peu après, mon entraîneur est décollé, lâché au train et, ce qui est pire, mes provisions avec lui. — Que faire ? l'attendre ? Mille fois non ma faim redouble, mais la rage s'en met, j'irai jusqu'à Amiens, là je me referai.

Je commence à me réchauffer, le temps est potable, la circulation reprend son cours dans les extrémités. Le jour est complètement venu, et nous montre la campagne picarde, terne, monotone avec ses grands champs encore incultes.

Mon estomac gronde, moi aussi ! Bonheur, je viens de retrouver une tablette de chocolat au fond de mon sac. Comme elle est bonne et succulente ! La vérité est qu'elle m'empâta la bouche ! Mais je ne peux ni ne veux faire le difficile.

Encore une côte. Mettez-en, les amis, vous ne me tenez pas encore. Le fait est qu'il s'en est fallu de peu.

PARIS-ROUBAIX 1903
Fischer, le « Grimpeur », sur la pelouse du Vélodrome Roubaisien explique pourquoi il n'est pas arrivé premier.

Amiens 5 kilomètres, dit la borne. Amiens 50 kilomètres lisent mes yeux qui, ainsi que le dit La Fontaine, sont serviteurs indirects de l'estomac.

C'est en plat que j'ai été lâché ; car je suis lâché. J'ai la défaillance, une belle et bonne défaillance. La route descend heureusement jusqu'à Amiens, et quelques amis sont venus au devant de moi.

A la vue des provisions les forces me sont revenues. — Là, dans mon sac, et vivement. — Je me précipite sur le porte-plume et signe. Quelques poignées de mains et me voilà en route.

— Tiens, bois ! — Merci. — Tiens, mange. — Je mange sans remercier. J'interroge mon entraîneur. — Combien suis-je ? — A quelle distance ? — Qui est le premier ? — Qui est devant moi ? — Loin ! — Allons du train, il faut rattrapper le temps que cette diable de défaillance m'a fait perdre. Ah ! mon soigneur de Beauvais ! J'aurai un compte à régler avec toi au retour.

Bien collé à la roue de mon entraîneur, digérant les provisions que j'ai englouties à Amiens, je me repose moralement et réfléchis.

J'avais tant envie de faire Paris-Roubaix ! Eh bien, mon opinion sur la course est qu'il y fait joliment faim — car malheureusement je ne peux vivre sur mes réserves, la graisse étant pour moi un objet de luxe tout à fait inconnu. Et pourtant savoir que par mes propres forces j'ai déjà parcouru un long ruban de route à travers la France, que j'ai traversé les deux grandes villes qui ont nom Beauvais et Amiens, que dans quelques heures je serai à la frontière, dans ce Nord dont on parle tant, que je connais si

Joseph FISCHER
Vainqueur de Paris-Roubaix 1896

peu ; cela me ragaillardit, et je me trouve un tout autre homme. Que les kilomètres filent vite tout en étant si longs.

Doullens et sa côte, sa fameuse côte ! Je viens de rattrapper deux concurrents, deux hommes du Nord.

Les forces me sont revenues et avec elles du courage et de l'aplomb. J'ai déjà couvert facilement la moitié de la route, le reste sera vite fait.

— Bonjour, camarades, on va faire route ensemble ? Oui, répondent-ils à l'unisson. — Comptez-y ! Chacun son tour, j'ai été lâché, je vais prendre ma revanche. Pendant que vous allez monter la côte de Doullens à pied, je vais la grimper allègrement à vélo, on se reverra à Roubaix ; bon voyage ! — Il est fou ! — S'il croit nous lâcher comme ça !

La fameuse côte. — Au revoir les amis ! — Et je m'en vais, poussant régulièrement, montant la côte doucement sans effort. A mes côtés les gamins trottinent. — T'esquinte donc pas, Eh ! tu ne la monteras pas. — Mon vieux, il n'y en a que quatre qui l'ont montée. — Vise donc les petits pneus. — Regarde son bonnet, s'il est laid. — Il la montera tout de même ! n'avait pourtant pas l'air. Enfin me voilà en haut. Cristi, elle n'a pas volé son renom. Je me retourne, mes deux adversaires la montent à pied. Avant qu'ils soient en haut, je serai loin.

La route est belle et plate, l'estomac garni, pédalons, c'est le moment. Et l'on file. Tâchons de rattrapper quelques minutes, et si possible, quelques places.

Maurice GARIN
Premier dans Paris-Roubaix 1897-1898

Arras, 200 kilomètres. Plus que 65, qu'est-ce que cela ? Une promenade. — Eh bien, ouiche ! j'ai changé d'avis en cours de route, si jamais je suis tant secoué, abimé et endolori que ce jour-là, j'en serai étonné. Je n'avais jamais imaginé qu'on eût pu mettre tant de pavés à la suite les uns des autres, et dans quel état ! Sans compter que cela active votre digestion et que la faim revient vous talonner.

Heureusement que les trottoirs sont là.

Que de monde ! Que de monde !

Si la fin de la course est la plus difficile, c'est bien aussi la partie où l'on est le plus encouragé. Les entraîneurs et les suiveurs ne manquent pas. Les applaudissements non plus. Je n'ai jamais vu population aussi sportive se déranger en aussi grand nombre pour une course que sur le parcours Arras-Roubaix pour la grande épreuve annuelle. Cela vous fait oublier nombre de moments de fatigue, ces encouragements que tout ce peuple prodigue au premier comme au dernier, reconnaissant que l'effort s'il est moins beau est tout aussi méritoire chez ceux-ci.

Enfin voici Hem.

Hem, pour moi, c'est le nom de la dernière localité avant Roubaix, c'est la cloche pour le dernier tour, c'est le village donateur de la prime de 50 francs, dénommée : Prix d'Hem. Et je regarde avec plaisir l'auberge dont le patron prit l'initiative de la création de ce prix. Brave homme, sais-tu que cela console de bien des déboires de voir que s'il est trop tard pour passer à la caisse directoriale, on n'en sera pas moins indemnisé de ses frais, surtout quand cet argent est dû à la générosité de sportsmen.

Et le patron pointe avec un soin jaloux les coureurs, tout joyeux de savoir le nom de l'heureux gagnant du prix d'Hem. A celui-là, une ovation est faite aussi grande qu'au vainqueur. N'est-ce pas Pasquier ? N'est-ce pas Georget ?

Roubaix ! Dernière montée, dernier pavé. Foule, gendarmes, barrière, et le ciment du vélodrome.

Les acclamations retentissent nombreuses. L'avouerai-je ? Je ne les entends pas ; je ne vois pas les milliers de spectateurs qui bondent le vélodrome. Je suis tout entier en moi-même. Je suis fier et un peu orgueilleux. Je suis heureux du résultat acquis. J'ai fait Paris-Roubaix, et j'ai beau l'avoir recommencé, je suis aussi satisfait que la première fois.

Me voilà à mon avis sacré grand coureur de fond, je viens de passer mon brevet, j'ai monté de plusieurs degrés dans ma propre estime.

—x—

Sans avoir la portée d'un Bordeaux-Paris, qui est bien le véritable critérium de la route Paris-Roubaix est de par sa longévité, et sa date, une épreuve importante et décisive.

Au début de la saison, elle donne une ligne précise entre les anciens concurrents, les vétérans, et les jeunes. Déjà l'on peut prévoir quel sera l'homme de la saison, car toujours Paris-Roubaix fut l'apanage d'un grand coureur, les

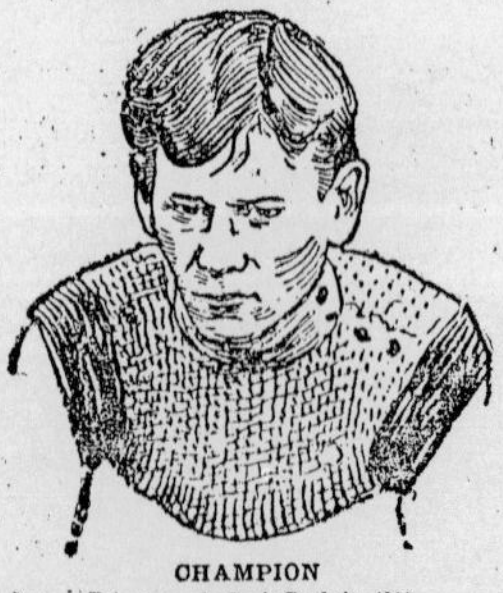

CHAMPION
Vainqueur de Paris-Roubaix 1899

victoires de Garin, Bouhours, Lesna et Aucouturier en sont une preuve.

Sa distance, son parcours, lui impriment un cachet spécial qui la caractérise et la distingue nettement des autres épreuves.

Relativement courte, c'est une course essentiellement de vitesse. Le parcours souvent côtueux, le sol tantôt propice aux grandes vitesses, tantôt rugueux et détestable, la rendent très dure et demandent une réelle qualité, un grand courage et un moral solide pour arriver non seulement à se bien classer, mais encore à la terminer.

Hippolyte, again

Twelve months later, in 1904, Paris-Roubaix underwent an important change. From now on pacers were forbidden. Those strange processions of cyclists preceded by tandems, triplets and even motorcycles, would no longer be seen.

The organisers stipulated that race conditions were to be the same for all competitors. This was easier said that done. In fact numerous deplorable incidents took place. One competitor, Pagie, furious at the finish in Roubaix, claimed: "Handfuls of nails were strewn in the road by followers, and even, it appeared, by the riders themselves"

Even more serious, certain riders had covered part of the course comfortably installed in motor cars! This last accusation was never confirmed but the doubt remains.

It must be remembered that the beginning of the century was a period when cheating was widespread in cycle sport. Victories were very important and the competitions attracted unscrupulous people. Moreover the commissaires and organisers were not yet in a position to verify that the race was properly run. The rare following vehicles were unable to control a bunch of riders spread over many kilometres. Paris-Roubaix was not the only event affected. That year's Bordeaux-Paris too, was also afflicted by this curse, as the first four finishers were disqualified a month and a half later.

The second edition of the Tour de France was also stained by irregularities, with the disqualification of the first four riders overall.

On the 3rd April 1904 at Chatou, the early morning spectators had the surprise of seeing a new type of roadman. The end of the paced era obliged riders to carry their own emergency equipment; spare tubulars worn as bandoliers around their shoulders, a bag attached to the machine containing a spanner, a sponge, several bottles and some food to help sustain them in their long effort.

Sixty four riders came to pick up their armbands. Maurice Garin, officially suffering from flu, was one of the last minute defectors. His detractors accused him of not wanting to put his prestige at risk after his outstanding success in the first Tour de France.

Aucouturier was surrounded by other pretenders. Jean Fischer, René Pottier, Petit-Breton, Beaugendre, Georget and a young man by the name of Eugène Christophe, who would regularly return to the Northern roads up until ...1926.

Several local men helped to make up the field such as Proy, Lobsten and Charles Crupelandt from Roubaix, who was the new terror of the peloton in the region, but this was his first race at this level.

According to the sporting press, notably 'L'Auto' and 'La Vie Sportive', Aucouturier was the race favourite, followed by Pagie and Georget. Hippolyte seemed confident. A few minutes before the start he told the journalists: "Last year you forgot me in your forecasts and I won. Today you have named me as favourite and this time you are right, for I am going to win again".

A few feet away Georget had different ideas: "Aucouturier can try to be smart. I only ask him not to have an accident and then we will see."

On the other side of the road, Samson with his Brussels accent was sure of himself: "I am very happy you know, for out of these sixty four entrants, few of them will be in front of

1904

me at Roubaix."

The white line painted outside Monsieur Bouché's shop was only waiting for the champions to start. As usual the race started fast. At Pontoise, thirteen riders formed the leading group, among them was Ambroise, César, Pagie, Lepoutre, Christophe and...Aucouturier. One by one the others dropped

'Hippolyte' - Mahdjoub Ben Bella's painting of 1995.

back until a certain Octave Doury came through half an hour down, which was to say that was scarcely going faster than if he was on foot!

On the outskirts of Breteuil, four men went clear; Aucouturier, César, Georget and Pagie. Shortly after, Pagie disappeared with a puncture. The battle started to rage. At Amiens Pothier replaced César Garin in the front group which had a lead of a minute over Wattelier and Trippier, then at two minutes were Christophe and several others.

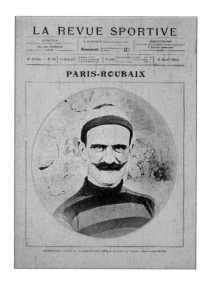

LA REVUE SPORTIVE

PARIS-ROUBAIX

Doullens appeared on the horizon. Spectators were surprised that the contestants were so far ahead of schedule but the wind had been blowing at their backs since the start. At the foot of the famous climb Aucouturier was slightly clear of the others. Pothier went through at two minutes and Georget at three. Opposite the Garage Delansorne, the traditional control point at Arras, the man at the head of the race had increased his lead to three minutes. A confident César Garin, in second place, cried out that nevertheless he would be first to the velodrome. His brother Maurice who was following the race confirmed: "It's no problem for Cesar. He will beat Aucouturier on the cobbles."

Lens was waiting for the riders under the rain. The roads had become dangerous. As well as the cobblestones, the riders were confronted with mud containing large quantities of coal dust. Crossing the mining town, Garin came through just one minute behind Aucouturier and at the entrance to Carvin he caught the fugitive. The kilometres flew by before the deserted pavements as the race speed was so high. Suddenly at Ascq, not far from the finish, an accident intervened. The 'La Vie au Grand Air' car was following too closely and knocked Garin off. He crashed heavily but instinctively got straight back on his bike.

For the first time since its creation the race arrived in an almost empty velodrome. Only about twenty spectators had taken their seats. Legend has it that there was no commissaire at the finish. Yet the truth is that a few kilometres before Roubaix the 'L'Auto' car went in front of them to open the gates of the velodrome. The correspondent of the newspaper just had time to unfold the result sheet and get to the finishing line to see the sprint for victory.

During the three laps of the track the two champions watched each other. Aucouturier went for a long sprint. Garin could not get past him. Two lengths separated them after 268 kilometres of racing! Lucien Pothier arrived three minutes down, then in front of about thirty spectators Wattelier and Léon Georget spilled onto the track. Charles Crupelandt, the champion from Roubaix confirmed his talent. At seventeen and a half, he finished thirteenth. Forty two men finished the event. The Dutchman Piechnik, next to last, had come by bicycle from Arnhem to Paris for the race. The following day he was to return to his native country in the same fashion, a total of 1200 kilometres in a couple of days! For this eighth edition Hippolyte Aucouturier achieved the third double after Maurice Garin in 1897-1898 and Lucien Lesna in 1901-1902. Astonishingly, a second Paris-Roubaix took place on the 15th May on the Roubaix velodrome.

In fact the organisers had the curious idea of organising a 'Paris-Roubaix' on the track - 265 kilometres with intermediate sprints, imitating the control points on the road. Among the entrants were Petit-Breton, Léon Georget and Emile Paige, who had married the day before and arrived at the velodrome in a frock coat, top hat and tie which he hastily exchanged for his racing clothes! Petit-Breton, who was never successful over the cobbles, won the sprint from Vanderstuyft and Charles Crupelandt whose star was beginning to rise in the firmament.

1904

1. Hippolyte AUCOUTURIER (France)
2. César GARIN (France)
3. Lucien POTHIER (France)
4. Edouard WATTELIER (France)
5. Léon GEORGET (France)
6. Aloïs CATTEAU (France)
7. Eugène CHRISTOPHE (France)
8. Paul TRIPPIER (France)
9. Emile PAGIE (France)
10. SAMSON (Belgium)

LA VIE AU GRAND AIR

La Course Paris-Roubaix
Petit-Breton et Pottier à la sortie de Pontoise

Publications Pierre Lafitte
La Vie au Grand Air - Femina - Musica

9, avenue de l'Opéra, Paris
Je sais tout — La Joie des Enfants

The exploit of "Trou-Trou"

'Trou-Trou.....it's Trou-Trou. Come on 'Trou-Trou'. In this year of 1905, Louis Trousselier appeared on the scene at the very highest level and there was no lack of encouragement for him. Coming from a sporting family - his eldest brother Léopold had finished ninth in Paris-Roubaix in 1897 - Trousselier was in the middle of his military service. In spite of his training being restricted, he accumulated successes: Paris-Roubaix as we shall see, but also the Tour de France with five stage victories. He was able then to achieve the first Paris-Roubaix and Tour de France double. It should be said that his participation in the Tour remained uncertain for a very long time. Private Trousselier started the race with a leave of just 24 hours!

When he returned to the barracks, 21 days later, his triumph had appeased the wrath of the military authorities.

The 1905 edition of Paris-Roubaix was an unprecedented success. One hundred and ten contenders for victory had sent their entries to the newspaper L'Auto. Never before had such a figure been approached. Certainly the number of non-starters was very high, but 63 courageous men finally presented themselves at the back of Monsieur Bouche's shop. From Aucouturier, the natural favourite, to René Pottier passing by way of Petit-Breton, Wattlier, Cornet, Christophe and Trousselier, the best of them stepped forward to sign the start sheet.

From seven o'clock onwards the riders warmed up and exchanged a few words. Petit-Breton, perhaps because he was anxious, had not been able to sleep. He decided to spend most of the night playing billiards with friends.

Aucouturier was, as he often used to say, "in peak condition," as was René Pottier in his fine white jersey. Several latecomers finally came to the line. The Dutchman De Groote was one of them. He had left the day before from the Porte Maillot and ridden all night to arrive at Chatou. Some mischievous people had misdirected him around the other side of Paris!

The control had just closed when the German Carl Todt also arrived late. He was reproached, but he did not speak a word of French so they could not make him understand. This would later help to take him off course in a mining village near Carvin.

The start was imminent ; gendarmes cleared the road. Among the spectators was a nostalgic Lucien Lesna. He had hung up his wheels but still enjoyed the cycling atmosphere. The public had not forgotten his exploits and applauded him. He was offered the starter's flag and told that it was high time for him to start the others!

The first attack worthy of the name was the work of Henri Cornet at Amblainville. He raced through Beauvais at 73 kilometres, with a lead of two minutes on his first pursuers, fifty five minutes up on Carl Todt and ...3 hours 15 minutes on a certain Riehl who, exhausted, arrived at the start on foot!

At Breteuil two riders tangled in the pleoton, causing a mass pile-up. Only Trousselier and Pottier were spared, to the great despair of Aucouturier whose machine was damaged.

However Henri Cornet, perhaps too presumptuous, saw his lead start to diminish. His hopes of finishing alone evaporated when Pottier and Trousselier caught him near Amiens.

In the capital of Picardy the three men signed the control sheet with a three-minute lead on a high-powered pair: Wattelier and Aucouturier.
The outcome of the race was going to be decided between them, for the others led by Chapperon were already eight minutes

1905

110. - L. TROUSSELIER
Vainqueur de Bordeaux-Paris 1908, sur bicyclette " Alcyon ", pneus Dunlop.

Louis TROUSSELIER
(France, 1881-1939)

"Trou-Trou" achieved immense popularity during a career which was highlighted by victory in the 1905 Tour de France.

1903 : Paris-Roubaix-Anvers
        3rd Paris-Roubaix
1905 : Paris-Roubaix, Tour de France,
        Brussels-Roubaix
1906 : 2nd Paris Tours, 3rd Tour de France,
        3rd Bordeaux-Paris
1907 : 3rd Paris-Roubaix
1908 : Bordeaux-Paris,
        2nd French Championship,
        3rd Paris-Brussels
1909 : 2nd Paris-Roubaix,
        2nd Bordeaux-Paris,
        3rd Tour of Lombardy,
        3rd French Championship,
1910 : 2nd Paris-Tours, 2nd Bordeaux-Paris
1911 : 2nd Milan-San Remo

adrift. It was here that the really serious moves started and where the weaknesses became evident.

The strong men were clearly in front and now started to tear each other apart without mercy. It was René Pottier, the King of the Mountains in the Tour de France, who this time proved to be the best. Pottier attacked, Cornet was able to hold his wheel, but then broke a toe strap and was dropped.

Trousselier smelt the trap and rapidly got up to René Pottier. There was a clear passage through the town of Arras, there was no control sheet to sign. Trousselier went through thirty seconds before Pottier and one minute before Cornet.

Near Carvin, the heart of the mining country, there were about forty kilometres of cobblestones to go. Pottier started to struggle, a fact which did not escape 'Trou-Trou' who attacked hard. Pottier resisted but lost 10 metres, then 15, then 20. It was the point of rupture and the gap continued to grow.

TROUSSELIER sur sa Bicyclette Alcyon

BRETEUIL — " Paris-Roubaix " qui passe

Libr. C. Dubois Breteuil

Sure of himself Trousselier reached the last points on the course - Seclin, Asqc, Forest and Hem. At the velodrome the fanfare of trumpets rang out. Thousands of people chanted 'Trou-Trou'. During the last laps of the track the winner was virtually carried along by the public. The Parisian, astonishingly fresh, did not hide his joy. He rode round with his pale blue jersey covered with dust, brandishing his bouquet in all directions. The winner assured those few journalists who were present : "Paris-Roubaix was my main objective for the year. In spite of the constraints of my military service I have been training three months especially for the race. This success is a just recompense."
Seven minutes later René Pottier arrived and admitted when he got off his machine: "There was nothing I could do. Trousselier was by far the best. He is a strong man and I am the eternal second."
In one month's time, René Pottier would be first in Bordeaux-Paris behind Aucouturier!
As Cornet finished in third place at Roubaix, the rain began to fall. He had ridden a superb race but seemed disappointed with his result: "I rode badly. If only I had waited for Arras or Seclin before attacking... I was beating my head against the wall for nothing. I really rode like a beginner. I'll take notice of it next time."
Twenty six minutes after Trousselier arrived, a new ovation shook the velodrome : Aucouturier appeared on the damp track. He was not happy. After his crash at Breteuil he had been the victim of several punctures. Contrary to his usual habit he stayed dumb and, with Bordeaux-Paris looming on the horizon, was planning his revenge. About half past six the police evacuated the crowd. The most passionate among them went to the night control at the Café Loquet, at the junction of the Boulevard de Paris and the Boulevard Gambetta.
At that precise moment, Maurand Delcambre, the last man in the race was still two and a half hours from Roubaix.

1905

1. Louis TROUSSELIER (France)
2. René POTTIER (France)
3. Henri CORNET (France)
4. Hippolyte AUCOUTURIER (France)
5. Edouard WATTELIER (France)
6. Claude CHAPPERON (France)
7. Aloïs CATTEAU (France)
8. Paul CHAUVET (France)
9. Lazare BRAULT (France)
10. Louis COLSAET (France)

CORNET GAGNE PARIS=ROUBAIX

1. *Le peloton de tête très compact, mené par Gougoltz, Pottier et Aucouturier ne s'est disloqué qu'à la côte de Doullens où Cornet et Cadolle ont pu prendre la tête. Cornet, jusqu'à ce moment était resté volontairement à la queue du peloton.* — 2. *Dans les rues de Méru, César Garin essaie vainement de s'échapper sur le pavé.* — 3. *Cornet, gagnant de Paris-Roubaix 1906 en 10 heures 2 secondes 1/5, sur pneus Michelin. Le gagnant de Paris-Roubaix avait été classé premier il y a deux ans dans le Tour de France, après la disqualification du premier. Le jeune coureur est très énergique, et derrière tandems humains, sur piste, s'est déjà prouvé l'égal des meilleurs. Sa victoire d'hier montre qu'il ne leur est pas inférieur sur route.* — 4. *La voiture automobile de la « Vie au Grand Air ». Mise à la disposition de la « Vie au Grand Air » par l'excellent mécanicien et réputé conducteur Paul Faure, la Mercédès 24 HP a permis à nos collaborateurs de suivre la plus grande partie de la course.* — 5. *Devant le contrôle volant de Breteuil. Sans se soucier des virages à angle droit, Trousselier qui vient de rattraper le peloton passe en tête à toute allure, suivi de César Garin, de Decaup et de Gougoltz.*

Henri Cornet confirms

In 1906 the Paris-Roubaix was overshadowed by a mining disaster at one of the northern pits. On the 10th March the Courrières coal mine suffered a firedamp explosion, the phenomenon so much feared by the miners. The rescuers counted 1,200 victims...

Following this catastrophe a revolt rumbled round the mining region. Serious accusations of neglected safety measures were levelled at the mining company. Orders to strike caused an unprecedented agitation among the population.

These troubles would perhaps force the organisers of Paris-Roubaix to modify the classic itinerary from Arras onwards. The General Director of L'Auto, Abran estimated that it would be dangerous to let the contestants pass through Hénin-Liétard and Carvin saying: "They will throw stones in their faces." Rumour had it that several motorists had been attacked in this delicate sector. Prudently, Henri Desgrange decided to change the end of the route. After Arras the riders diverted to St Laury-Blangy, Vitry, Corbehem, Douai, Râches, Faumont, Bersee and Pont-à-Marcq to return to the original roads at Lesquin. The distance of the race was slightly increased, nevertheless the roads were of better quality, for those of Hénin-Liétard and Carvin were quite appalling!

At Roubaix, the finish of the event announced the beginning of festivities of a whole series of sports meeting. The velodrome had been renovated, The special edition of the 'Journal of Roubaix', printed on the day before the race, sold like hot cakes. The Northern Railway Company joined the spirit of the occasion by offering half-price fares for those competitors wanting to get back to Paris.

On the 15th April, the stars were rubbing shoulders: Louis Trousselier but also César Garin, the young Marcel Cadolle with an impressive amateur record, René Pottier, Georges Passerieu, Dortignac the revelation of the Tour de France and the "old ones" Emile Georget and a revengeful Hippolyte Aucouturier, who wanted to show his critics that he still able to beat the young ones!

In spite of the opposition, one name stood out, that of Henri Cornet. Surprise winner of the 1904 Tour de France after the disqualification of the first four, he was late confirming the feat. The man was nevertheless on form as was proved by his victory on the 18th March in a paced event over fifty kilometres at the Buffalo track. This was the day that he left Marcel Cadolle and the world champion Bobby Walthour far behind. Since then Cornet had been training over distances of 250 kilometres between Orleans and Paris in company with his friend Beaugendre.

At the rendezvous at Chatou, by now the traditional starting place, a fine rain froze the spectators. Only the arrival at the signing-on sheet of Aucouturier warmed things up a bit. He was the first to sign saying he hoped to do the same thing at the Roubaix velodrome. The Peugeot "armada" with its leaders Trousselier, Pottier and Passerieu, fitted in well together.

A few minutes before the start a few rays of sunshine poked timidly through the clouds. As soon as the flag dropped, a crash shook the bunch. Flauvel with the number 13 armband had to immediately retire.

Beauvais saw a first peloton of eleven riders pass through, among whom were Aucouturier, Cadolle Cornet, Cesar Garin, Georget, Pottier and Passerieu. Trousselier, a puncture victim followed at two minutes. There were eight of them at Amiens comprising the

1906

176. Cyclisme — CORNET, routier Français   C. M.

Henri CORNET
(France, 1884-1941)

The surprise winner of the 1904 Tour de France when the first four riders were disqualified. Cornet went on to confirm his worth in events such as Paris-Roubaix.

1904 : Tour de France
1905 : 3rd Paris-Roubaix
        3rd Bordeaux-Paris
1906 : Paris-Roubaix, 2nd Bordeaux-Paris,
        3rd Paris-Tours
1910 : Paris-Alencon
1911 : 3rd Bol d'Or

9ᵉ Année ⌀ N° 398   50 centimes.   4 Mai 1906 ⌀ Tous les Vendredis

LA VIE AU GRAND AIR

Voir

dans ce numéro :

l'Entraînement
en Amérique
par Geo ORTON

CORNET
le vainqueur de Paris-Roubaix, est le grand favori des épreuves
de longue distance sur route
pour la saison qui vient de commencer

Abonnements :
Paris et Départements,, ,, ,, 24 francs
Etranger,, ,, ,, ,, 28
Téléphones 280-52, 280-56, 254-88

Publications Pierre Lafitte & Cⁱᵉ
Je sais tout ⌀ Fermes & Châteaux ⌀ Femina
Musica ⌀ Jeunesse ⌀ La Vie au Grand Air
9 et 11, Avenue de l'Opéra ⌀ Paris

above riders plus Trousselier who after a terrible effort over twenty four kilometres had just rejoined the head of the race.

The rhythm was sustained. On the hill of Doullens, Henri Cornet, who appeared to be the freshest of them all, attacked. The group came apart as Trousselier, then Passerieu and César Garin lost ground. Only Cadolle and Aucouturier, and he only for a short time managed to keep contact with the favourite.

The lead of the two champions kept growing; four minutes at Arras, seven at Douai. After the difficult sectors the velodrome came into sight. Cornet was the fastest but he hoped to arrive alone at the stadium where there was not a single seat left. He attacked unremittingly but Cadolle resisted.

The sprint was a formality. The spectators were delirious with joy, for Cornet was a popular champion who the crowd admired. The winner was beaming: "What a race, never in my life have I swallowed so much dust. I attacked at Doullens, and that was it.."

Pottier was third, Trousselier fourth, César Garin fifth and Aucouturier, disappointed by his heavy defeat, sixth.

Following his triumph Cornet passed the night in a Roubaix hotel. The next day after his arrival in Paris, he confided in Robert Coquelle, the eminent journalist of L'Auto: "At the start I was afraid of crashing but up until Beauvais nothing happened to me. I redoubled my efforts on the hill at Doullens and only Cadolle was able to stay on my wheel. The sprint was no problem, I would have beaten Kramer (the American sprinter, twice winner of the Paris Grand Prix).

Several of the riders who finished behind him were to be marked by destiny. Certainly Marcel Cadolle was, as he triumphed in Bordeaux-Paris a month later, beating Cornet and Trousselier. But Cadolle was to see his career come to a sudden end when he had a serious crash at Nimes in the Tour de France of 1907.

René Pottier second at Roubaix in 1905, third this year and winner, a few months later, of the Tour de France, would however, never return to these Northern cobblestones. He was found hanged on the 25th January of the following year in the Peugeot workshops at Levallois-Perret. A drama of passion according to his brother André. Finally for Hippolyte Aucouturier and César Garin, this Paris-Roubaix of 1906 would mark their last performances of any note.

1906

1. Henri CORNET (France)
2. Marcel CADOLLE (France)
3. René POTTIER (France)
4. Louis TROUSSELIER (France)
5. César GARIN (France)
6. Hippolyte AUCOUTURIER (France)
7. Georges PASSERIEU (France)
8. Marceau NARCY (France)
9. Emile GEORGET (France)
10. SAIN (France)

CORNET

Vainqueur du Tour de France 1904
(2.397 kil. en 96 h. 5 m. 55 s.)

Passerieu, vainqueur de Paris-Roubaix 1907.

Le jeune stayer a conquis ses galons de grand stayer en remportant avec beaucoup de brio l'épreuve classique de Paris-Roubaix. Il a fait les 270 kilomètres du parcours en 8 h. 45 m., battant d'une minute le Belge Vanhouwaert, la révélation de la course.

Passerieu
and the zealous gendarme !

In March 1907 the English government refused once again to envisage the project of a tunnel under the Channel. It appeared to them that national security would be seriously compromised !

As far as cycling was concerned, the Anglo-Saxon domination of the heroic days was now a thing of the past. The British were absent from the main European events. In the peloton however, they were talking more and more in glowing terms of 'The Englishman of Paris' - George Passerieu. He was thought to have British nationality. In fact, although he was certainly born in London in October 1885 , of an English mother, his real country was France. For most of the public the doubt was lifted when, after having been a professional for just a few months, he finished second in the Tour de France 1906. After this performance he became one of the "protected riders"of the Peugeot team, the same as Cornet and Garrigou.

Paris-Roubaix 1907 marked the beginning of the epic battles between the trades teams.

Up until then they placed all their hopes on a single rider. This strategy changed, especially for the powerful teams who had two, three or even four men capable of winning. Directed by Norbert Peugeot in person, Peugeot was the team to beat at the start of each event. The preparation for each rider was carefully planned So on this occasion Alibert had arranged a number of training sessions over the Paris-Roubaix route.

With the Alcyon team the main opposition, training took place in secret. Bourotte, the former sprinter who supervised the team would only say that Cadolle rode every day behind his pacer.

The enthusiastic welcome from the people of Douai in 1906 persuaded the organisers to keep to the same route. Monsieur Jobart, the treasurer of L'Auto newspaper had received ninety one requests to take part in the race. Among them were the favourites Cornet and Cadolle, then Passerieu, Trousselier, Emile Georget, Petit-Breton, Pothier, Garrigou, and also a young man of twenty, who in his first year as a professional in 1906 had shown signs of enormous possibilities, a Luxembourger living at Colombes by the name of François Faber...

Finally, a rather strange rider also made his first appearance. He was called Cyrille Van Hauwaert and came from a country where the cycling tradition did not exist: Belgium. Van Hauwaert was feared by the stars of the road, not because he was strong but because he was dangerous!

In fact, Trousselier and Georget remember their first meeting with him very well. At the finish of an edition of Brussels-Roubaix, emerging in the lead onto the Roubaix track, the Belgian, ignoring the direction to take, provoked a general crash!

Much later his directeur sportif, Pierre Pierrard, remembered his arrival in France: "I have seen many riders come and go since I first started in cycling, many of them champions, but none of them impressed me as much as Van Hauwaert. A big rough Fleming, thickset with an almost frightening face and who the French sportsmen were quick to

1907

Georges PASSERIEU
(France, 1885-1928)

A valiant competitor in the one-day classics, Passerieu also shone in the Tour de France.

1906 : 2nd Tour de France
1907 : Paris-Roubaix, Paris-Tours
1908 : 3rd Tour de France
1909 : Paris-Dijon
1913 : 2nd Paris-Tours

10ᵉ Année — N° 446   50 centimes   6 Avril 1907 — Tous les Samedis

LA VIE AU GRAND AIR

Publications Pierre Lafitte & Cⁱᵉ
Je sais tout ⚬ Fermes et Châteaux ⚬ Femina
Musica ⚬ Jeunesse ⚬ L'Art et les Artistes ⚬ ⚬
90, Av. des Champs-Elysées ⚬ Paris

LA COURSE PARIS-ROUBAIX
Une voiture d'entraîneurs
Dans ce numéro : UN HORS-TEXTE
La première Course Bordeaux-Paris

Abonnements :
Paris et Départements,, .. » 24 francs
Etranger .. ,, .. » .. 28 —
Changements d'adresse 0 fr. 75

nickname of "Open Belly".

He was a tremendous roadman, a man carved out of rock. Never will I forget his arrival in Paris, when he left his job as farm labourer at Moorslede, in order to come and dispute his first big race. It was in 1907, two days before Paris-Roubaix and I was in my office at 'La Francaise' when this huge fellow came in dressed as a peasant, with large hobnailed boots. His only luggage was a cardboard box containing some clothes and in his hand he had a letter from our agent in Ypres. Of course this colossus did not speak one word of French. Paris-Roubaix at the time was ridden with pacers from start to finish and the Georget brothers had all our available pacers. But the letter of recommendation spoke of him in glowing terms and I did not have the heart to send this timid and humble man back home. He would start without pacers.

So I took Van Hauwaert to the workshops and asked the mechanics to assemble a bicycle for him, then I went back down to my office. The Belgian stayed in one corner of the workshop. A few minutes later, Monsieur Harmon, boss of 'La Francaise' passed through the room and seeing the Flandrian asked "who is that man over there?"

"A new rider" the mechanics replied..."A new rider? I've had quite enough of them. Get rid of him, throw him out" and he was pushed out of the door.

A quarter of an hour later I found my Fleming sitting on the pavement..I arranged things with the boss and took Van Hauwaert to a hotel where we dined together. It was obviously the first time that he had eaten in a restaurant. Incapable of saying what he wanted he looked at what others were eating and pointing with his finger he said: 'that, that'!

So I saw him gobble up, in the following order, a huge cheese, roast beef, asparagus and sardines, all washed down with milk and then with wine.

So it was without any faith in him that I saw him start this Paris-Roubaix."

A total 56 men finally started. At the control of Beauvais ten riders went through in the lead among them Petit-Breton, Cadolle, Trousselier and Passerieu. The hill at Doullens did not settle things as some riders rejoined the front group.

At Arras, Passerieu, Petit-Breton, Trousselier, Emile Georget and Garrigou were one minute in front of Léon Georget and two minutes in front of the astonishing Van Hauwaert. Passerieu who was an intelligent rider but with a poor sprint understood that if he wanted to win the race he had to arrive alone. Just before Douai he went clear for good.

While everyone was waiting for Trousselier or Cornet to reply to him it was Van Hauwaert who pulled out all the stops on the cobblestones. The Belgian maintained the pressure, and the tension in the velodrome became unbearable.

The trumpets played their fanfare but, the public still had to wait because the leader was stopped at the entrance to the velodrome by a gendarme who wanted to make absolutely sure that the little plate attached to his bicycle proved that he had paid his road tax!

Passerieu who had spent the day suffering became very agitated before finally escaping again.

He came onto the track to be greeted by the bravos of the crowd. Passerieu had not crossed the finishing line when Van Hauwaert came into the stadium. The little colony of Belgians were beside themselves. It was an historic moment: for the first time ever one of their compatriots climbed onto the podium at Roubaix.

Trousselier finished third in front of Garrigou who distinguished himself for the first time. It was not to be the last, as in his first professional year he became champion of France and won Paris-Brussels, the Tour of Lombardy and two stages in the Tour de France.

Two months later, Van Hauwaert, the real revelation of the day, lined up for Bordeaux- Paris. At the start the novice assured Pierre Pierrard: "Me, first Bordeaux-Paris." At the finish this was exactly what happened.

1907

1. Georges PASSERIEU (France)
2. Cyrille VAN HAUWAERT (Belgium)
3. Louis TROUSSELIER (France)
4. Gustave GARRIGOU (France)
5. Auguste RINGEVAL (France)
6. Emile GEORGET (France)
7. Léon GEORGET France)
8. Henri CORNET (France)
9. François FABER (Luxembourg)
10. Pierre PRIVAT (France)

Journal de Roubaix

CHOCOLAT DELESPAUL-HAVEZ Universellement reconnu le meilleur

Cinquante-troisième année. — N° 112 | DIRECTEUR-PROPRIÉTAIRE : ALFRED REBOUX PÈRE | MARDI 21 AVRIL 1908.

TARIF D'ABONNEMENTS
Roubaix-Tourcoing, le Nord et les Départements limitrophes : Trois mois...... 5 francs ; Six mois...... 9 — ; Un an...... 18 —
Les autres Départements et l'Etranger le port en sus.
Agence particulière à Paris, 26, rue Feydeau

5 Centimes

BUREAUX ET RÉDACTION :
ROUBAIX : 71, Grande-Rue ‡ TOURCOING : 5, rue Carnot
ÉDITION DU MATIN

5 Centimes

ABONNEMENTS & ANNONCES
A Roubaix.......... Aux bureaux du journal, Grande-Rue, 71
A Tourcoing.......... Aux bureaux du journal, rue Carnot, 5.
A Mouscron.......... Chez M. Henri Lerouge, rue de la Station
A Tournai.......... Chez M. Verdière, 23, rue Bourdon Saint-Jacques
A Paris et à Bruxelles Dans les agences de publicité.
En vente à Paris dans toutes les Bibliothèques des gares et dans les principaux kiosques

LA COURSE PARIS-ROUBAIX

OPINIONS

L'immoralité en action

Quelques-uns des directeurs de ces petits théâtres parisiens, qui poussent un peu partout, comme des champignons peu sains, n'ont rien trouvé de mieux, pour peupler le désert de leurs salles, que d'exhiber chaque soir sur les tréteaux un bataillon de femmes qui gagneraient à être jolies et dont la plus décemment vêtue emprunte à Eve son costume d'avant le péché. Comme il n'en coûte rien d'appeler d'un nom honnête les choses qui le sont le moins, ils prétendent nous ramener, par ces exhibitions, au culte antique de la beauté. S'armant d'une vieille thèse qu'ils ne se donnent même pas la peine de rajeunir, ils dissertent à perte de vue sur la moralité relative du nu sur le retroussé. A les en croire ; — mais eux-mêmes ne croient point à cette mauvaise plaisanterie, — rien n'est plus chaste qu'une statue sans feuille de vigne ou une femme sans draperie.

Cependant, il y a mieux ou pire. A l'indécence de ces exhibitions, d'autres ajoutent, pour relever d'un fort piment ce mauvais poivre, l'obscénité d'une pantomine. Prudents, ils prennent une petite précaution pour se mettre, à tout hasard, en règle avec la police ; elle consiste à transformer des spectateurs, qui payent cependant leurs places et dont ils ne connaissent pas un seul, en invités, et leur spectacle, très public, en une soi-disant réunion privée. Moyennant quoi, le délit de droit commun dont ils se rendent coupables et qui s'appelle, de son vrai nom, attentat à la pudeur publique, se transforme comme par enchantement en une manifestation artistique, artistique et rien de plus. Ils abritent leur spéculation derrière cette enseigne menteuse : « Liberté de l'art ! » C'est de cette liberté et de cet art qu'ils se couvrent, comme d'un bouclier, contre les poursuites qu'ils redoutent et rendent ainsi, selon le mot du moraliste, un involontaire hommage à la vertu : c'est, du reste, le seul.

Encore ceux-ci et ceux-là peuvent-ils prétendre que les admirateurs d'un art dramatique si spécial ne s'effarouchent plus, depuis longtemps, de rien : que, sur le chapitre de la pudeur, la morale, avec eux, n'a plus quoi que ce soit à perdre : « Où il n'y a rien, dit un proverbe, le roi perd ses droits. » Mais cette excuse, d'ailleurs détestable, ne peut être invoquée par ces entrepreneurs de cinématographes qui font, en des matinées pourtant dédiées à la jeunesse, se dérouler une série de tableaux qu'un fils, même très nouveau jeu, hésiterait à placer devant les yeux de son père. L'honnête Lhomond nous enseignait autrefois, dans sa grammaire, qu'on doit aux enfants le plus entier respect, et c'était aussi le temps où l'on mettait entre leurs mains un petit livre qui tenait scrupuleusement les promesses de son titre : « La morale en action. » C'est l'immoralité en action que, maintenant, on leur sert.

Etonnez-vous, après cela, que le vice soit si précoce ! C'est pur miracle que cette gangrène morale dont, chaque jour, les faits-divers, la chronique des tribunaux nous permettent de mesurer les ravages, ne fasse pas de plus terribles progrès, de plus nombreuses victimes.

Le mal date d'une vingtaine d'années, et bien qu'il n'eût point alors la violence que nous déplorons aujourd'hui, d'honnêtes gens résolurent de substituer leur initiative à celle d'un parquet trop indulgent ou trop sceptique et leur action à celle d'une justice qui, de boiteuse qu'elle fut toujours, devenait cul-de-jatte aussitôt qu'il lui fallait se lancer à la poursuite de ceux qui semblent s'être donné pour mission de pervertir jusqu'au vice lui-même. Ils fondèrent la « *Société centrale de protestation contre la licence des rues* » et mirent à sa tête M. Bérenger. Ils ne pouvaient faire un meilleur choix ; ils vient d'acquérir un nouveau titre à leur confiance et à notre estime en signalant à l'attention d'une justice trop distraite les exploits de ces entrepreneurs de scandales. Tout permet de croire qu'ils apprendront à leurs dépens ce qu'il en coûte de se livrer à une aussi peu recommandable industrie.

Une certaine presse et de mauvais plaisants se sont beaucoup moqués de ce sénateur rugueux et noueux, à la figure réfrigérante de procureur, qui s'est donné pour mission de poursuivre et de traquer la pornographie, de défendre les oreilles, les yeux et les intelligences contre les sollicitations malsaines qui s'insinuent et s'étalent partout. Ils ont raillé, toujours avec injustice, parfois avec esprit, ce « papa la vertu ». Il a méprisé leurs quolibets ; il a, sans défaillance, rempli tout son devoir.

L'association qu'il préside a livré de nombreuses batailles ; elle en a gagné un grand nombre et perdu quelques-unes ; mais, dans l'une et l'autre fortune, elle ne fut pas lâchée, par le ministère public trop sensible aux sarcasmes.

Elle est, en cela, moins favorisée que sa sœur anglaise, cette « National Vigilance Association » devant laquelle pâlissent et tremblent les pornographes d'Outre-Manche, car ils en ont aussi, en Angleterre. C'est que celle-ci est armée du droit de poursuite directe, tandis que celle-là en est réduite au seul droit de dénonciation, qui est peu de chose, et dont elle ne tirerait rien du tout si elle n'avait pour président un sénateur. Lorsque M. Bérenger se heurte à une inertie systématique et prolongée, il lui suffit de prononcer ce petit mot : interpellation, pour que procureurs et substituts deviennent singulièrement actifs.

De là, dans la répression, une inégalité qui déconcerte. Quand le Sénat est en vacances, l'impunité semble acquise ; elle ne l'est que relativement lorsqu'il siège. On frappe Pierre ; mais on a épargné Paul, alors que, cependant, Pierre n'est pas le plus coupable des deux. Il en irait autrement si, comme la « National Vigilance Association », notre « Société centrale de protestation contre la licence des rues » avait le droit de poursuite directe au lieu de ne pouvoir agir qu'au nom des personnes lésées. Ce sont de braves personnes ; rarement des personnes braves. Elles s'indignent, elles protestent, mais dans l'intimité. Aussitôt qu'on les met en demeure de joindre les actes aux paroles, de donner simplement leurs signatures, une insurmontable timidité glace leur indignation et paralyse leur courage. Elles ont pris pour devise et comme règle de conduite : C'est le moment de nous montrer, cachons-nous.

Le jour où la société que M. Bérenger préside pourra se passer du concours de ces héros, le parquet, soutenu, poussé par elle ; la police, mise en demeure de remplir son devoir, cesseront de se modeler sur ces idoles qui ont des yeux et ne voient rien, qui ont des oreilles et n'entendent pas.

Paul Bosq.

BULLETIN

Dimanche, 19 avril 1908.

Les mineurs de la Loire ont décidé de se mettre en grève le 1er mai prochain.

***

Le Congrès des instituteurs a été clos à Lyon par un discours syndicaliste de M. Nègre, instituteur révoqué.

***

L'antimilitariste Collongy a été arrêté à Nancy pour outrages publics dans une réunion, au commissaire de police.

***

Un incident russo-japonais vient de surgir au sujet des pêcheries d'Extrême-Orient.

***

L'escadre italienne a reçu l'ordre d'occuper une île turque de la mer Egée.

***

La grève des mineurs américains est terminée.

***

Les Etats-Unis ont envoyé deux navires de guerre au Venezuela.

DANS LE SUD-ORANAIS

A LA POURSUITE DES HARKAS MAROCAINES

Oran, 19 avril. — On n'a reçu aucun renseignements sur la marche des quatre colonnes volantes lancées par le général Vigy, à la poursuite des troupes de Moulaï-Lhassan. Les deux partis doivent avoir pris contact et l'on attend avec impatience des détails sur ce nouveau combat.

Le général Vigy a adressé un ordre du jour de félicitations à la colonne Pierron qui a vaillamment fait son devoir le 16 avril dernier.

Cet ordre du jour a produit sur les troupes une excellente impression.

De nouveaux renforts sont partis pour Talzaza et Colomb-Béchar, menacés par les incursions marocaines.

LES OPÉRATIONS AUTOUR DE SETTAT

Paris, 19 avril. — Le général d'Amade télégraphie de la Kasba des Ouled Saïd, que les colonnes, pour rassurer les populations et confirmer les soumissions déjà recueillies se sont portées sur le territoire des Ouled Saïd.

Le général a recueilli la soumission d'une fraction des Mzamza — les Gdava — tribu enclavée entre l'Oued oum Rebia et les Ouled Saïd.

L'état sanitaire est satisfaisant.

INFORMATIONS

Arrestation d'un antimilitariste

Nancy, 19 avril. — M. Louis Collongy, antimilitariste, anarchiste, ancien gérant du journal le *Cri du Peuple*, à Nancy, condamné par la Cour d'assises de Meurthe-et-Moselle, le 13 février dernier, pour reproduction d'un article invitant des militaires à la désobéissance, à deux années d'emprisonnement, avait bénéficié récemment de l'amnistie.

Dans une réunion politique, ayant outragé le commissaire de police présent et dans l'exercice de ses fonctions, il a été arrêté et écroué.

Un incident russo-japonais

Saint-Pétersbourg, 19 avril. — Le baron Motono, ministre du Japon à Saint-Pétersbourg, avait demandé la révision de la Convention russo-japonaise pour les pêcheries.

Le Conseil des ministres a catégoriquement refusé d'examiner cette proposition.

Cette décision, due à l'initiative de M. Stolypine, le premier ministre russe, a été hautement approuvée par l'opinion publique.

Contre le pirates du golfe Persique

Aden, 19 avril. — Deux vaisseaux de guerre anglais ont jeté l'ancre dans le golfe de Koweit pour réprimer la piraterie dans le golfe Persique.

Grève monstre terminée

New-York, 19 avril. — Les deux cent mille mineurs de Toledo (Ohio), en grève depuis plusieurs semaines, ont décidé de reprendre le travail.

LE CONGRÈS DES INSTITUTEURS

La séance de clôture

Lyon, 19 avril. — La Fédération nationale des syndicats d'instituteurs a clos, son Congrès par un meeting de nuit, tenu à la Bourse du travail.

Le meeting a débuté par un discours de M. Guerry, secrétaire général de la Bourse du travail de Lyon, qui a félicité les instituteurs syndiqués de leur action et critiqué l'enseignement de nos écoles primaires.

M. Nègre, instituteur syndiqué a prononcé un long discours en faveur des syndicats de fonctionnaires.

Voici les principaux passages de son discours :

« Nous voulons rapprocher les délégués des instituteurs des délégués ouvriers. Le gouvernement veut empêcher ce rapprochement, nous voulons qu'il se produise.

Ce n'est pas parce que nous n'aurons pas envoyé une adhésion formelle à la Confédération générale du travail que nous ne marcherons pas d'accord avec elle, pour travailler ensemble à l'émancipation des prolétariats manuel et intellectuel.

» D'autre part, comme les instituteurs ont été jusqu'ici des agents politiques, le gouvernement a compris qu'une force allait lui échapper. Nous ne comprenons pas que l'instituteur soit assujetti à l'influence néfaste d'une homme politique ».

Il a terminé son discours par cette déclaration : « Si j'avais à choisir entre la réaction de M. de Mun et celle de M. Clémenceau, je choisirais la première, parce qu'alors je serais massacré par des adversaires francs et loyaux, tandis qu'au contraire, avec la réaction de M. Clémenceau, c'est au nom des grands principes qu'on nous ravit nos libertés. »

Après l'intervention de deux anarchistes qui prennent violemment à partie le gouvernement et les parlementaires, l'assemblée vote un ordre du jour félicitant les congressistes d'être résolus à fonder des écoles nouvelles et invitant les instituteurs à venir nombreux aux syndicats.

La sortie s'est effectuée sans incident.

LA VIANDE A SOLDAT

Nancy, 19 avril. — Le boucher-charcutier Krich, fournisseur de la garnison de Lunéville, inculpé de livraison de viandes malsaines a reconnu devant le juge d'instruction que les saucisses préparées et livrées par lui contenaient du cœur de bœuf.

Krich va être traduit devant le tribunal correctionnel.

M. Chéron va enquêter à Toulon

Toulon, 19 avril. — M. Chéron, sous-secrétaire d'Etat à la Guerre, est attendu à Toulon, où il procédera à l'inspection des casernes de la 2e division coloniale, et surtout des viandes et de la charcuterie livrées à la troupe.

La marine se plaint

Brest, 19 avril. — Une enquête va être incessamment ouverte sur la qualité de la viande livrée par les bouchers de Brest aux équipages de la flotte.

Il paraît en effet que les viandes livrées aux marins, tant à terre qu'à bord des navires, sont avariées à ce point que les hommes ne peuvent en manger.

LE PRIX du Président de la République

VICTOIRE DE DANDOLA

Paris, 19 avril. — *(Par dépêche).* — Le prix du président de la République s'est couru dimanche à Auteuil par un temps incertain, devant une assistance considérable et élégante et où les personnages officiels ne manquaient pas.

Le président de la République, accompagné de Mme Fallières et de Mlle Fallières, de M. Jean Lanes, secrétaire général, et des officiers de sa maison militaire, est arrivé en voiture fermée à l'affichage du Prix Le Gourzy, qui servait, avec le Prix du Bois, de lever de rideau à la grande pièce de la journée. Reçu avec le cérémonial habituel par le président et les commissaires de la Société des steeple-chases, il a été conduit à la tribune réservée où se trouvaient la plupart des ministres.

LE DÉPART

Les concurrents sortent du paddock et sont très admirés.

Ils défilent, selon la coutume, dans l'ordre du programme et prennent leur canter, se dirigeant vers le poteau de départ. Le silence règne à ce moment. Mais, tout à coup, des clameurs se font entendre : les concurrents sont partis ; pendant qu'on entend la sonnerie confirmant leur départ.

Austral s'élance rapidement en tête et mène à bonne allure devant Rosita III et Pincette. Au mur en pierres, Pimlico culbute. Pour sauter la rivière, Austral, Coquet, Dandolo, Pincette et Salomon sont à peu près ensemble. Tous les concurrents franchissent l'obstacle sans encombre. Au huit, Austral est serré de près par En Avant Marche, Dandolo et Adonis II. Ces quatre chevaux prennent entre les tournants une assez bonne avance sur leurs adversaires et après le bull-finch la course se dessine entre En Avant Marche et Dandolo. Mais celui-ci domine son adversaire et sur le plat il prend un avantage décisif. Il gagne de dix longueurs devant En Avant Marche, Adonis II et Rosita III qui finissent dans cet ordre.

LE VAINQUEUR

La course a été très régulière, à part la chute de Pimlico, il ne s'est produit aucun incident. Les chevaux âgés ont pris leur revanche et c'est le vieux Dandolo qui a été l'heureux vainqueur. L'ancien gagnant du grand steeple bénéficiait d'un avantage important. Sa condition parfaite qui attirait l'attention de beaucoup de personnes dans le paddock ne s'est jamais démentie un instant pendant la course, qu'il a gagnée en somme avec une grande désinvolture. Il est juste de dire que la pluie avait rendu élastique le terrain et ainsi augmenté sa chance, tandis qu'au contraire, elle avait diminué celle de En Avant Marche. On doit enfin associer Parfrement à la victoire de Dandolo, car il l'a piloté avec sa maîtrise habituelle.

A l'issue de la course, le prince Murat et le baron de Neuflize ont présenté M. Fischhof au président de la République, qui l'a chaleureusement félicité sur la victoire de son cheval.

Voici les résultats des différentes épreuves :

Prix du Bois (course de haies, à réclamer, 3.000 fr., 3.100 m.) : 1er, Toute Bonne II, à M. G. Kousnetzoff, pes. 106.00, pl. 33.00, pel. 68.50, pl. 18.50 ; 2e, Callista, à M. Pascaud, pes. 67.00, pel. 23.00 ; 3e, Lavandier II, à M. H. de Mumm, pes. 35.00, pel. 19.50. — Non placés : Rossignol II, Comète, Bastion, Andréas, Rosy Letty, Good News, Souveraine III, Saint-Eloi III.

Prix Le-Gourzy (course de haies, 20.000 fr., 4.000 m.) : 1er, Ingénu, à M. A. Coblentz, pes. 33.00, pl. 31.00, pel. 17.50, pl. 17.00 ; 1er, Sosthène, à M. Jean Stern, pes. 20.00, pl. 16.50, pel. 8.50, pl. 9.50 ; 3e, Agrippa II, au comte de Fitz-James, pes. 49.50, pel. 17.50. Non placés : Kimolo, Endymion, Bol, Chemulpo, Camisard, Bigourdane, Rossinante.

PRIX DU PRÉSIDENT DE LA RÉPUBLIQUE (steeple-chase, handicap, 50.000 fr., 4.200 m.) : 1er, Dandolo, à M. Fischhof, pes. 118.00, pl. 37.50, pel. 62.50, pl. 21.00 ; 2e, En Avant Marche, à M. Ch. Liénart, pes. 58.50, pel. 28.00 ; 3e, Adonis II, à M. Gaston-Dreyfus, pes. 33.50, pel. 17.00. — Non placés : Rosita III, Dynamo III, Salomon, Hayashi, Matsouyé, Coquet, Pincette, Sans Souci IV, Austral, Matelot, Taxamètre, Bessborough, Pimlico.

Prix Louis de Turenne (steeple-chase militaire, hors série, objets d'art, 4.000 m.) : 1er, Mount Prospect's Pr., à M. de Goualine, pes. 57.50, pl. 20.50, pel. 45.00, pl. 12.00 ; 2e, Baudré, à M. de Lozé, pes. 30.50, pel. 14.00 ; 3e, Drink, à M. C. de Sugny, pes. 30.50, pel. 27.00. — Non placés : Cérès V, Bambina, Zéphir II, Cythère II, Clarinette IV, Girandole III, Rikiki, Ravissante, Ratagan, La Suippe.

Prix d'Apremont (steeple-chase, 3e série, 6.000 francs, 4.000 m.) : Ecurie Liénart, gag. pes. 35.50, pel. 19.00 ; 1er, Le Connétable III, à M. Ch. Liénart, pes. 36.00, pel. 19.00 ; 2e, Marquis de Carabas, à M. E. Balsan, pes. 24.50, pel. 13.50 ; 3e, Pharaon. — Non placé : Quille.

Prix du Pont d'Iéna (course de haies, handicap, 4.000 francs, 3.100 m.) : 1er, Sirius II, à M. Ch. Liénart, pes. 26.50, pl. 21.00, pel. 13.00, pl. 10.00 ; 2e, Evohé II, à M. Olry Rœderer, pes. 32.00, pel. 22.00 ; 3e, Pont d'Eragny. — Non placés : Novio, rBaganza, Nourrice, Le Connétable II.

Les conflits du travail

LA GRÈVE DES JARDINIERS PARISIENS

Paris, 19 avril. — La grève des ouvriers jardiniers semble toucher à sa fin. Une tentative de médiation est sur le point d'aboutir. Les patrons ont accepté les revendications suivantes :

1° Suppression du couchage, sauf pour les garçons maraîchers ; 2° journée moyennes de dix heures et un franc pour les heures supplémentaires.

UN MEETING DES TERRASSIERS

Paris, 19 avril. — Les ouvriers terrassiers ont tenu dimanche une réunion syndicale à laquelle assistaient près de 4000 personnes, et qui a duré plus de trois heures.

Les divers orateurs ont demandé à la corporation d'accomplir un acte de solidarité, en faisant cause commune avec les ouvriers maçons, frappés par le lock-out.

Un ordre du jour en ce sens a été voté.

La Course Paris=Roubaix

(13e Année) Organisée par « l'Auto »

VICTOIRE DU BELGE VAN HOUWAERT ; 2e Faber, battu à l'arrivée ; 3e Lorgeou

Un gros succès... malgré la pluie et la grêle. -- 90 partants. -- Dans les contrôles et sur la route. - La foule brave le mauvais temps. - Faber en tête, tombe et se blesse. -- Les arrivées au Vélodrome. -- Le triomphe de Van Houwaert. - Les courses de vitesse. - Le classement général

La treizième course cycliste Paris-Roubaix est courue... Par un temps détestable, sous des rafales de neige, 90 concurrents n'ont pas craint de s'élancer sur les routes boueuses, donnant un bel exemple d'endurance et d'énergie... Bravant les intempéries, la foule habituelle des « Paris-Roubaix » est venue les acclamer au passage sur la route ou à l'arrivée au Vélodrome Roubaisien, affirmant une fois de plus l'extraordinaire popularité de la grande épreuve sportive du jour de Pâques.

Le coureur belge Van Houwaert, de Moorslede, confirmant son récent succès dans la course Milan-San Remo et se classant définitivement parmi les grands champions de la route, est sorti vainqueur... Mais si le vaillant belge a droit à de vives félicitations pour cette glorieuse victoire, il convient d'y associer aussi le jeune coureur parisien, Fabert, qui a fait également une course admirable, perdant juste à l'arrivée le fruit de ses efforts... Les Lorgeou, Ringeval, Trousselier, Passerieu, Plateau et autres, doivent être aussi félicités et cités comme des exemples d'énergie et de valeur athlétique, car ceux qui, dans ces conditions, sont parvenus jusqu'au bout ont bien mérité du sport.

Notre confrère spécial l'*Auto*, et la direction du Vélodrome Roubaisien ont droit, eux aussi, à la reconnaissance des sportsmen, car ils ont su assurer la parfaite organisation d'une grande et passionnante manifestation sportive dont le succès a résisté aux éléments déchaînés...

Mais passons aux détails de cette journée.

LE DÉPART

Suivant la coutume le départ de la grande course annuelle Paris-Roubaix a été donné à Chatou et, malgré l'heure matinale, de nombreux cyclistes, automobilistes se trouvaient présents pour assister à l'envolée de ces vaillants champions.

Le contrôle était tenu par nos confrères : MM. Ravaud et Mercier, de l' « Auto ». A partir de 5 heures un quart, les concurrents viennent retirer leur brassard et poser leur signature sur le registre spécial. Voici le team Alcyon d'abord au grand complet, puis c'est ensuite le team Peugeot qui fait sensation. Comme les commissaires nous annoncent que le départ est reculé d'une demi-heure, la plupart des concurrents retournent se reposer dans leurs quartiers généraux.

Le contrôle est fermé à 6 heures et l'on dirige les coureurs sur la ligne de départ. Il fait froid et les concurrents se réchauffent comme ils peuvent. Le champion belge Van Houwaert déclare à Petit-Breton qu'il est en « pleine forme » ; les Italiens Ganna et Pavesi sont aussi très entourés.

Enfin, à 6 h. 34 minutes, le sacremental « Partez » se fait entendre et 90 coureurs suivant s'élancent à la conquête de la victoire :

Les partants

1. Georges Passerieu, Neuilly-sur-Seine.
2 Gustave Garrigou, Bondy.
3. Emile Georget, Courbevoie.
4. Lucien Petit-Breton, Paris.
5. L. Beaugendre, Salbris.
6. Laurent, Brest.
7. Ganna, Milan.
8. Henri Cornet, Choisy-le-Roi.
10. Brocco, Fismes.
11. Paulmier, Paris.
12. Henri Allegoedt, Roubaix.
13. Alcide Vivier, Paris.
14. Eugène Libeaud, Paris.
15. Isidore Audebert, Saumoussay.
18. Rettich, Paris.
19. Léon Georget, Châtellerault.
20. Chauvet, Paris.
21. Cruchon, Paris.
22. Lorgeou, Paris.
23 Fabert, Paris.
24. Louis Trousselier, Levallois.
25. André Pothier, Paris.
26. Cyrille Van Houwaert, Morslède.
27. Henri Lignon, Choisy-le-Roi.
28. Augustin Ringeval, Maisons-Alfort.
29. Georges Landrieux, Mantes.
31. Henri Stoffel, Lyon.
32. Marcel Godivier, Versailles.
33. Marcel Duboc, Rouen.
34. Eugène Plateau, Tourcoing.
35. Aloïs Catteau, Tourcoing.
38. Masselis, Ledeghem (Belgique).
40. Verstraeten, Bruxelles.
41. Vincent Dhulst, Wattrelos.
45. Eugène Forestier, Saint-Ouen.
49. Jean Alavoine, Paris.
50. Pierre Langlade, Paris.
51. Albert Dupont, Estaimpuis (Belgique).
52. Guido Devogelaere, Uccle (Belgique).
53. Georges Ryon, Paris.
54. Gaston Dutilleul, Lille.
56. Joseph Merle, Marseille.
57. Maurice Pellerin, Nanterre.
58. Pierre Proy, Roubaix.
62. François Lafourcade, Boulogne-sur-Seine.
63. Ferdinand Lafourcade, Boulogne-sur-Seine.
64. Emile Boudry, Paris.
65. Moïse Ghellinck, Marcq-en-Barœul.
66. Gaston Vereecke, Lille.
67. L. Soulier, Bagnols-sur-Cèze.
69. Gabriel Guidez, Paris.
73. Octave Doury, Mouzay.
74. Auguste Dufour, Grenoble.
76. Charles Rousselot, Anvers-sur-Oise.
77 Paul Didier, Belfort.
78. Joseph Ponthieu, Forest.
79. Henri Serrier, Brest.
80. Chrétien, Paris.
81. Chaudron, Paris.
82. Hubert Baert, Croix.
83. Eugène Dubois, Neuilly.
86. François Vanzura, Paris.
87. Antony Wattelier, Paris.
88. Lucien Dumoutier, Paris.
89. René Pilte, Orléans.
91 Georges Boisdenghien, Amiens.
92. Léon Mopin, Fatouville-Grestain.
93. Constant Ménager, Amiens.
99. Maurice Loit, Paris.
102. Jules Deloffre, Le Cateau.
103. Piochnich, Arnheim.
104. Marcel Lejeune, Chantilly.
105. Edouard Tondu, Pré-Saint-Gervais.
108. Jean Lousberg, Aix-la-Chapelle.
109. Edouard Wattelier, Paris.
110. Auguste Cousin, Paris.
111. Henri Moity, Caudry.
112. Léon Priche, Aubervilliers.
113. Georges Avenet, Paris.
114. Raoul Dumont, Paris.
115. Louis Tartas, Genève.
116. G. Privat, Anvers-sur-Oise.
117. M. Lequatre, Genève.
118 Maurand Delcambre, Douai.
119. Christophe, Courbevoie.
120. Joseph Vachter, Paris.
121. Aucouturier, Paris.
122. Eberardo Pavesi, Milan.
124. Anderson, Paris.

De suite après le départ, un peloton composé de Trousselier, Petit-Breton, Garrigou, Van Houwaert, Brocco, Passerieu se forme et s'élance vers Saint-Germain. La terrible côte est escaladée à toute allure. Un second peloton suit d'assez près les leaders.

Dans la forêt de Saint-Germain, le coup d'œil est très pittoresque. De très nombreuses voitures automobiles ayant à bord des machines de rechange, suivent les coureurs. A la Croix-de-Noailles, malgré l'heure matinale, des centaines de spectateurs acclament les concurrents.

DANS LES CONTROLES

Pontoise (24 kilomètres). — Un peloton compacte passe à 7 heures 20, emmené par Passerieu suivi de tous les favoris.

Beauvais (72 kil. 800). — C'est par un temps épouvantable que les coureurs sont arrivés ici : la pluie, la grêle et la neige tombaient avec violence. Le contrôle était assuré par le Véloce Club Beauvaisien.

Le peloton de tête est passé à 8 h. 57, légèrement en retard sur l'horaire prévu. Il était composé de Privat, Baert, Lorgeou, Dufour, Landrieux, Petit-Breton, Paulmier, Vanhouwaert, Menager, E. Wattelier, Trousselier, Emile Georget, Passerieu, Ringeval, Pothier, Catteau, Verstraeten, Fabert, Cornet et Beaugendre.

Breteuil (102 kil. 900). — A dix heures 05 passent Masselis, Van Houwaert, Christophe, Trousselier, Brocco, Fabert, Garrigou, Lorgeou, Passerieux, etc...

Amiens (134 kil. 900). — A 11 h. 22 passent ensemble Brocco, Van Houwaert, Passerieu, Plateau, Garrigou, Trousselier, Lorgeou, Ringeval, Godivier, Paulmier, Cornet, Alavoine, Fabert, Privat, Georget Emile, Masselis, Petit-Breton.

Doullens (164 kil. 900). — A 12 h. 40 passent : Petit-Breton, Van Houwaert, Plateau, E. Georget, Passerieu, Masselis, Cornet, Trousselier, Lorgeou, etc.

Arras (202 kil. 900). — Passent à 2 h. 07 : Trousselier, Fabert, Garrigou, Lorgeou, Van Houwaert, Ringeval.

Passerieux, Masselis, 2 h. 15 ; Plateau, Georget, 2 h. 18 ; Pottier, 2 h. 19 ; Godivier, 2 h. 20 ; Brocco, 2 h. 22 ; Baert, Ganna, Aucouturier, 2 h. 35 ; Guido, Vincent, Wattelier, Ryon, Lombret, 2 h. 47 ; Lafonnade, et Catteau, qui abandonne, à 2 h. 53.

Douai (228 kil. 700). — Faber passe à Douai, à 3 h. 05 ; Van Houwaert, à 3 h. 08.

SUR LA ROUTE

Par la lecture des télégrammes qui nous sont parvenus des contrôles, on peut avoir déjà une physionomie de l'épreuve.

Comme les années précédentes, la course s'est surtout dessinée après la fameuse côte de Doullens. A la sortie de celle-ci, Garrigou part seul, prend 200 mètres d'avance sur tout le lot, mais après une poursuite de 10 kilomètres, il est rattrapé par le peloton de tête qui est pourtant quelque peu disloqué à Arras. C'est à la sortie d'Arras que Fabert, dans un effort superbe, lâche le peloton de tête et, seul, se sauve à travers la campagne... à Douai il a trois minutes d'avance sur Van Houwaert, qui a aussi lâché ses concurrents, et il augmente encore son avance, poursuivi par le redoutable Belge... Mais ce long effort a probablement épuisé ses forces, car à Ascq et à Forest on le signale comme paraissant fatigué — on le serait à moins — et voici que près du Vélodrome, Van Houwaert l'atteint alors qu'il croyait avoir course gagnée, ainsi qu'on le verra plus loin... C'est là le fait saillant de l'épreuve.

D'ASCQ A FOREST

Le succès de la course classique a paru ici un peu compromis par le mauvais temps. Les averses intermittentes de pluie, de neige et de grêle avaient éloigné une partie des amateurs de cette récréation annuelle. Les cyclistes et attelages de toutes sortes que l'on rencontrait habituellement sur le parcours des coureurs, en files compactes, étaient relativement clairsemés. Les cabarets, échelonnés de chaque côté de la route, ne présentent pas non plus cette animation bruyante des années précédentes. Néanmoins, les consommateurs s'intéressent à la course, et le sort des coureurs, en raison de ce temps abominable, les inquiète tout particulièrement. Les uns et les autres plaignent ou louangent

Cyrille, king of the Belgians at Roubaix

For the first time in this year of 1908 an international road race preceded Paris-Roubaix. The second edition of Milan-San Remo was disputed on the 5th April, three weeks before 'la Pascale'. Van Hauwaert, by now irresistible had already won his first bouquet of the season at San Remo.

In order to better prepare for the Paris-Roubaix, the powerful Peugeot team came up with an idea which, at the time most thought was preposterous. They organised a training camp in the South of France. On the other hand Van Hauwaert and the Alcyon team remained faithful to their usual training over the Northern roads.

In the week preceding the 19th April the day of the race, the weather took a turn for the worse and the North was certainly not spared. The state of the roads became pitiful. A number of entrants drew back when faced with these difficulties did not started the race.

Impassive as usual, Van Hauwaert was anxious to confirm his Italian success. He wanted, moreover to be the first Belgian to win Paris-Roubaix. He would nevertheless have to be strong, for the French, the masters of the event so far, had decided that they were going to remain so.

In spite of the last minute defections the field for the race was an exceptional one. To those used to competing in the event such as Passerieu, Garrigou, Georget, Petit-Breton, Cornet, Brocco, Lorgeou, Trousselier, Alavoine and Faber, were added several Italians such as Luigi Ganna and Eberardo Pavesi!

From 5.15 am onwards the Alcyon champions came to pick up their armbands. Van Hauwaert arrived first, before Lignon who did not stop joking about his chances.

The cold and the sleet had not deterred the hundreds of spectators. Calm reigned as everyone waited for the starters signal,except in the front ranks of the bunch where an argument broke out between the Englishman Anderson and Luigi Ganna who insulted each other in...French.

At 6.35 am the start was given. Rapidly the favourites took control.

Trousselier, Petit-Breton, Garrigou and Van Hauwaert monopolised the first few places. At Meru, while the "crack" Italian Pavesi had already retired, a crash broke up the rest of the peloton.

As Beauvais approached the weather got even worse. The rain gave way to sleet and snow. In these appalling conditions a "royal escape" formed at the front. Trousselier led through the Jean Hachette square in front of Petit-Breton, Masselis, Van Hauwaert, Christophe, Brocco, Faber, Garrigou, Passerieu, Emile Georget and several others.

The group roared through Breteuil and Amiens. Doullens came into sight. At the control, situated at the bottom of the hill, Van Hauwaert remained in the lead. Then Garrigou decided to give it everything. He managed to stay clear for about ten kilometres before seeing five men come up to him: Trousselier, Faber, Lorgeou, Ringeval and...Van Hauwaert. Their lead was considerable: eight minutes on Plateau and their closest pursuers.

Before Douai, while Trousselier was crashing, the great Faber launched an offensive. He went through the town three minutes before Van Hauwaert and Garrigou, and twenty before the

C. Van Houwaert, belge
Vainqueur de Bordeaux-Paris 1907-1909 San-Remo Milan 1908
Paris-Roubaix 1908, sur bicyclette Alcyon

Cyrille VAN HAUWAERT
(Belgium, 1883-1974)

Belgium's first great cycling champion, Van Hauwaert's record was one of the finest of his era.

1907 : Bordeaux-Paris
1908 : Paris-Roubaix, Milan-San Remo
　　　　2nd Belgian Championship,
　　　　2nd Paris-Brussels,
　　　　2nd Bordeaux-Paris
1909 : Belgian Champion, Bordeaux-Paris,
　　　　3rd Tour of Belgium
1910 : Paris-Menin, 2nd Paris-Roubaix,
　　　　3rd Paris-Brussels
1911 : 2nd Paris-Tours,
　　　　3rd Belgium Championship,
　　　　3rd Paris-Roubaix,
　　　　3rd Tour of Lombardy
1913 : 2nd Paris-Brussels,
　　　　2nd Bordeaux-Paris
1914 : 3rd Bordeaux-Paris

1908

120. Cyclisme
VAN HOUWAERT, *roulier Belge*

popular 'Trou- Trou'.

Riding with superb ease, Faber - the Giant of Colombes - continued to increase his lead, but the effort proved to be too hard for a 21 year old.

At Forest, not far from Roubaix, he collapsed. Van Hauwaert , showing his usual great resolve, came back inexorably to him. In just a few kilometres the Belgian wiped out a lead of five minutes!

At Hempempont, Faber would still not give in but eventually fatigue overcame courage. At a mere one hundred and fifty metres from the velodrome, the Luxembourger crashed and the blood started to flow freely from his head.

At the velodrome when the spectators were already applauding, perhaps to warm themselves up, a fanfare announced the arrival of the first man. No one was certain of his identity. As a black mass, some sort of apparition came into sight. The Belgians rejoiced; without any doubt it was Van Hauwaert. In fact, Van Hauwaert on entering the stadium collided with a groundsman and crashed. He instantly got back up to finish the required six laps. Then Faber arrived. Exhausted by his lone break of sixty five kilometres, he took another tumble on the track!

Lorgeou was still pedalling with ease, he managed to take advantage of the incident to catch and then pass Faber before the finishing line.

The large Belgian contingent surrounded their champion who told them: "I wanted to prove that I was not afraid of Paris-Roubaix The weather, the cold and

the snow, naturally suited me. Now, the only thing I haven't won is the Tour de France and I'll try to take that this year."

Van Hauwaert did not succeed in the Tour de France. Nevertheless his 1908 season would be exceptional with victories in Milan-San Remo, and Paris-Roubaix and then his second places in Bordeaux-Paris, Paris-Brussels and the championship of Belgium.

François Faber too was satisfied with his race, in spite of his troubles at the finish: "I was disappointed with my rotten luck. I had the conviction that I could win The crash knocked the stuffing out of me for the final struggle."

Far from these considerations, on this 19th April the beer was flowing freely in the bars in and around Moorslède.

However people were beginning to say very nice things indeed about Octave Lapize, a former French amateur champion who came back from the Games in London with an Olympic medal.

They would certainly speak more about him in the future.

1908

1. Cyrille VAN HAUWAERT ((Beglium)
2. Georges LORGEOU (France)
3. François FABER (Luxembourg)
4. Edouard LEONARD (France)
5. Louis TROUSSELIER (France)
6. Georges PASSERIEU (France)
7. André POTTIER (France)
8. Gustave GARRIGOU (France)
9. Emile GEORGET (France)
10. Jules MASSELIS (Belgium)

Edition J. Boldo, 100, Avenue Kléber, Paris

308. - **VAN HOUWAERT et MASSELIS** (Routiers)
sur bicyclettes '' Alcyon '', pneus Dunlop

CYCLES

O.LAPIZE

ROUTE

CHAMPION DE FRANCE
amateurs (2 fois)

CHAMPION DE FRANCE
professionnels (2 fois)

Vainqueur de PARIS-ROUBAIX (3 fois)

PARIS-TOURS

PARIS-BRUXELLES

DU TOUR DE FRANCE

etc., etc.

PISTE

RECORDMAN du MONDE
amateurs derrière grosses motos
Vainqueur du "BOL D'OR"
amateurs et de nombreuses courses
derrière tandems :

6 heures Bruxelles
12   -   Bruxelles
Recordman 100 kilomètres
derrière tandem 1910.
Recordman du monde des
50 kilomètres professionnels 1911
6 heures à l'américaine. Paris 1912

IMP. MARCIAL GOFFIN & Cie PARIS.

Octave Lapize,
an unknown at Roubaix !

Then Octave Lapize appeared. Quickly nicknamed "Curly", the Parisian celebrated his twenty first birthday. He had not been a professional for very long but he had a very flattering amateur record.

However, at the start of the 1909 Paris-Roubaix few knew him. That did not stop Lapize from winning on the Roubaix track to the detriment of Trousselier. On this day in the month of April, one of the greatest champions in cycling emerged on these Northern roads.

However, at Chatou his 165 centimetres provoked several sniggers. Why had a kid like this come to take part in such a demanding event?

Following the example of Maurice Garin, who was the same size, Lapize was aggressive, courageous and a strategist. Moreover during the race he remained always concentrated and was never distracted by the encouragement of the crowd - because he was deaf...

'Curly' was also to carry off the following two editions of Paris-Roubaix, realising the first consecutive triple, that up until the present time has only been equalled by Francesco Moser, 70 years later.

He was to manage other important triples such as the French championship in 1911, 1912, 1913 and Paris-Brussels in the same years. On top of which he won Paris-Tours in 1911 but above all the Tour de France in 1910. So the winner over the cobblestones would be first over the Pyrenean climbs of the Aspin, Peyresourde and the Tourmalet, all climbed for the first time.

Like a lot of champions of his generation, his career would be affected by the war. When the conflict broke out, he was twenty seven. Declared unfit for military service in 1907 due to his deafness, this time he joined up to defend his country. Sadly, on the 14th July 1917 he was killed in an aerial combat over Pont-à-Mousson. This very sombre day which commemorated the founding of the French Republic, also marked the disappearance of the greatest champion of the heroic years along with François Faber.

Milan-San Remo once again preceded Paris-Roubaix. For its third edition, Luigi Ganna chalked up the first Italian success in front of Emile Georget.

At the beginning of this new season Henri Desgrange remarked, apparently not without some regret, the way cycling was perpetually changing. He noted as well that since 1896 and the beginnings of Paris-Roubaix it had become considerably more commercialised. He thought that it was a matter of regret that the end of the race always belonged to the riders who were defending the colours of the major bicycle companies.

However cycling had also become international, as was proved by the appearance of such riders as Van Hauwaert and Ganna, real pioneers in their own countries. With the success of the Tour de France, the craze for cycle sport had never been so strong. It was in this atmosphere of euphoria that the Paris-Roubaix was run. The race was the main target of the powerful Alcyon team. Monsieur Gentil, its director and a veritable "PR agent" before his time, never hesitated to claim that: "Alcyon never backs away from a struggle, it has proved this many times...It must be said that it would be out of place and even improper to play the waiting game with men in his team of the calibre of Van Hauwaert, Garrigou, Trousselier and Faber...

On the 11th April 1909, opposing them, the little Lapize had only the modest role of outsider to play in his little Biguet team...

Octave Lapize
**Overwinnaar van Paris-Roubaix
1909.**

Octave LAPIZE
(France, 1887-1917)

The incomparable 'curly' was one of cycling's greatest champions.

1909 : Paris-Roubaix
1910 : Paris-Roubaix, Tour de France,
       2nd Paris-Brussels
1911 : Paris Roubaix, French Champion,
       Paris-Brussels, Paris-Tours,
       2nd Paris-Brest-Paris
1912 : French Champion, Paris-Brussels
1913 : French Champion, Paris-Brussels

1909

PARIS - ROUBAIX 1909
le peloton de tête à la Croix Renard

At 6.45 am, Ravaud lowered L'Auto flag and liberated one hundred and four men. Towards Pontoise, a first group of about thirty was formed. The leading group had been reduced to fifteen by the time the race went through Beauvais. Among them were Faber, Van Hauwaert... and Octave Lapize. There remained only twelve of them when they reached the famous hill of Doullens. Masselis and his friend Van Hauwaert, then the traditional cohort of Frenchmen: Trousselier, Leonard Charpiot, Dochain, Cruchon, Ménager, Duboc, Pagès, Passerieu, and Lapize with whom the stars were becoming increasingly intrigued.

Inexorably they were eliminated, one by one. Passerieu, the victim of an accident had to retire, several of the others could not match the speed and were obliged to revise their ambitions...

At Douai six men prepared to tear each other apart: Van Hauwaert, Masselis, Trousselier, Godivier, Faber and Lapize, the only intruder among the greats.

At the Roubaix velodrome, where record receipts had been recorded, three champions arrived on each other's wheels in front of ten thousand spectators: Trousselier, Masselis and Lapize. The disappointment showed on the faces of the Belgian supporters for Van Hauwaert, victim of a crash, entered the track on the lap down.

Trousselier felt strong. Opposed to Masselis, who was a poor sprinter, he was sure of winning. The novice Lapize was not worth considering.

"Trou-Trou' went for a long sprint, ignoring the youth who stayed glued to his wheel. But against all expectations Lapize pipped a dumbfounded Trousselier to the post. In the stadium everyone was totally surprised: who was this who was able to beat the popular Trou-Trou?

For his part, Lapize was enjoying his success and replying to the journalists avid to know a little more about him: "I made my debut in the small races in the Paris

region," he told them," to the great despair of my father who was convinced that things would turn out badly. After I had prepared seriously for Paris-Rouibaix, I presented myself at Chatou confident of myself, fearing only a crash or a series of punctures. I was riding easily up to Doullens, where I was dropped but I rejoined on the flat. Then riders were eliminated right up until here where I was riding with all my strength, animated by an irresistible desire to win."

Lapize had not wanted to make it clear that his strong character was forged during the time when he was working for his father from five in the morning to seven in the evening, and that in the summer he was allowed a few hours off for training. While he was trianing, the young Lapize was obliged to pay someone to take his place in the family enterprise.

After the finish the grievances were aired. Trousselier was especially disappointed. "I had the race in my pocket, but my handlebars became loose before the final sprint." Van Hauwaert was still angry after his crash. The only one, apart, from Lapize, to be satisfied was Garrigou. His performance mattered little to him as that time he was thinking only of his imminent wedding!

1909

1. Octave LAPIZE (France)
2. Louis TROUSSELIER (France)
3. Jules MASSELIS (Belgium)
4. Cyrille VAN HAUWAERT (Belgium)
5. François FABER (Luxembourg)
6. Marcel GODIVIER (France)
7. Gustave GARRIGOU (France)
8. Henri HANLET (Belgium)
9. Edouard LEONARD (France)
10. Paul DUBOC (France)

La Course Paris=Roubaix

VICTOIRE DE LAPIZE EN 9 H. 03'
TROUSSELIER SECOND - MASSELIS TROISIÈME

Les trois premiers coureurs arrivent en peloton au Vélodrome Roubaisien. — Sur tout le parcours, une foule considérable applaudit les concurrents. — La réunion au Vélodrome Roubaisien. — Un triomphal succès

Octave LAPIZE, gagnant de Paris-Roubaix 1909

Octave Lapize confirms...

The second part in Lapize's victorious trilogy took place in 1910. Henri Desgrange was always on the look out for some new novelty. Having decided to do away with the pacers, he cancelled all the feeding stations as well.

At Roubaix in the week preceding the event the enthusiasm mounted all the more as the riders were going to arrive at a brand new velodrome. It was the masterpiece of Kersten from Brussels who had designed a superb modern track with bankings of 45 degrees. Moreover the stands had been changed to receive more than ten thousand spectators.

Genoa-Nice, run on the 20th March and won by Omer Beaugendre, began the season. However the best professionals, following the example of the Alcyon team led by François Faber, preferred to train over the route of the Northern classic. The La Francaise team followed the same programme and spent some time in the area, while at the same time singing the praises of the new '"Continental" tyre.

The record of the number of participants was beaten as 145 men presented themselves at Chatou. Lapize was favourite in spite of the presence of Van Hauwaert, Trousselier, Faber and the two men from Roubaix, Crupelandt and Leturgie.

At seven o'clock precisely the start was given. In spite of the rapid rhythm eighty riders were still together at Beauvais where Van Hauwaert won the sprint to be first to sign the control sheet. In their haste the machines were thrown to the ground. It was confusion as everyone tried to gain some advantage by being among the first to sign the register. The pen was fought for and sometimes deliberately disappeared in the turmoil. Then the bunch restarted, minus a few tired riders or those who were simply too slow...

It was surprising to see a bunch of about fifty riders emerge unscathed from the hill at Doullens. Then François Faber decided to attack. Under his impulsion a dozen men went clear. Naturally Lapize was among them but there was also Van Hauwaert, Georget and Garrigou.

After Arras where Lapize was the first man through, the race really came alive. Lapize always at the head of things, was joined by Van Hauwaert, then Leonard and Crupelandt. But the latter was to loose contact at Hénin-Liétard following two punctures in rapid succession.

At Carvin he was replaced at the front by Faber and Christophe. A few kilometres further on Faber showed the first signs of weakening before riding into the ditch. Exhausted he was put back in the saddle but any hopes of victory had disappeared..

The duel between Van Hauwaert and Lapize, often to be repeated during the classic races of this period, reached its height as they crossed the difficult roads through the mining sectors. The two men did not cease attacking each other but neither were able to gain the advantage. The race would be decided by a sprint.

Twelve thousand people were waiting for the champions at the velodrome. Just before four o'clock several motor cars arrived in the track centre, just in front of the four inseparable leaders; Van Hauwaert followed by Lapize, Leonard and Christophe. They were greeted by a tremendous ovation.

The Belgian led for five laps, but at the exit of the last bend the still rapid Lapize passed him without a glance. Van Hauwaert kept his second place but two clear lengths behind "Curly". During this turbulent sprint, Leonard had been balked. A crash left him bleeding on the track. He finished only fourth behind Christophe.

1910

LES COURSES FRANCO-BELGES

Lapize appeared to be satisfied with his day's work. As he got off his machine he insisted that this victory was much easier than the previous year's had been, while making it clear that: "I tried hard to get rid of my opponents at Doullens, and then at Arras. but then gave up and co-operated with them. On top of which, I was the victim of two crashes and one puncture. But that's quite normal in this type of race. From now on my main objective is the Tour de France."

Scarcely had he finished the sentence that a thunder of applause shook the velodrome; the Roubaisan Crupelandt arrived together with the Belgian Vanenberghe. Fifth, he would have arrived with the leading quartet if he had not been dogged with such bad luck. "Having finished my military service last September," Charles said, "I decided to train without saying any thing. In this way I could not be criticised if I did not do well. Frankly I don't have a lot of confidence in myself...but now that has all changed and I am optimistic about the rest of the season."

The 1910 season would effectively be the real start of his international career, for several months later he was to win the first stage of the Tour de France run between Paris and Roubaix, over the same route as the famous classic.

Seventy four riders finished this Paris-Roubaix. Louis Trousselier, one of the favourites did not. Trou-Trou retired on the outskirts of Amiens. It seems that he was having trouble with his eyes. It was one of the few disappointments of the day.

As for Lapize, he won "his" Tour de France, picking up four stages in the process, including the prestigious ones at Grenoble and Luchon.

1910

1. Octave LAPIZE (France)
2. Cyrille VAN HAUWAERT (Belgium)
3. Eugène CHRISTOPHE (France)
4. Edouard LEONARD (France)
5. Charles CRUPELANDT (France)
6. René VANDENBERGHE (Belgium)
7. Léon GEORGET (France)
8. Jules MASSELIS (Belgium)
9. Gustave GARRIGOU (France)
10. Joseph VAN DAELE (Belgium)

106. ROUBAIX — Vélodrome du Parc Barbieux, le jour de la course Paris-Roubaix
Arrivée des deux premiers Van Houwaert et Lapize

LA VIE SPORTIVE

LES GRANDES ÉPREUVES CYCLISTES
PARIS-ROUBAIX 1911

Demain, dimanche 16 avril, se disputera pour la 16e fois
la grande épreuve organisée par notre confrère "l'Auto"

TOUS LES CHAMPIONS DE LA ROUTE SONT ENGAGÉS

Lapize, Van Houwaert, Garrigou et Faber sont grands favoris

A l'occasion de Paris-Roubaix, le Vélodrome du Parc Barbieux, où se feront
les arrivées, a organisé de sensationnelles réunions

La Grande Journée

Paris-Roubaix est comme le bon vin qui s'améliore en vieillissant... Nous voici, pour la seizième fois, à la veille de la grande course classique et il semble que les émotions que réserve aux sportsmen la journée de demain doivent être plus intenses encore que celles des années précédentes.

Jamais le lot des concurrents n'a été aussi formidable, jamais la lutte à laquelle vont se livrer tous les « rois de la route » n'est apparue plus acharnée. Il y a là, dans cette interminable liste de concurrents, tous les meilleurs champions tels que : Lapize, Vanhouwaert, Garrigou, Faber, etc., etc.

Quel est celui qui va inscrire son nom au glorieux palmarès de la classique épreuve? Ce problème passionne les sportsmen, mais dans la masse du public aussi, chaque année, se presse le long du parcours, notamment dans la dernière partie, peu importe le vainqueur!... Ce qu'on applaudit, c'est le courage dont font preuve tous ces vaillants routiers, jusqu'à la belle leçon d'énergie qu'ils donnent à la jeunesse qui les acclame au passage... Depuis le premier jusqu'au dernier, ils provoquent la même admiration et si la foule a parfois des préférences pour les favoris, elle sait aussi encourager et réconforter les déshérités, ceux que la guigne a poursuivis et qui ne trouvent pas la juste récompense de leurs efforts.

C'est l'âme du peuple qui vibre ainsi le long du ruban de route qui sépare Roubaix de la capitale et si un jour Paris-Roubaix devait disparaître, ce serait un grand vide...

OCTAVE LAPIZE

CYRIEL VANHOUWAERT

mense dans nos manifestations athlétiques et dans les réjouissances populaires de... région.

Mais Paris-Roubaix ne saurait disparaître, c'est la grande journée classique qui marche, chaque année, le retour de la saison cycliste et dont la popularité grandit sans cesse... C'est pourquoi, demain, les valeureux routiers retrouveront aux acclamations d'un dernier et les dévoués organisateurs ajouteront un succès de plus à la liste des grandes batailles sportives...

A. D.

Les Engagements

Voici la liste complète des engagés :

1. O. Lapize (Paris).
2. C. Vanhouwaert (Moorslede).
3. E. Georges (Châtellerault).
4. G. Passerieu (Levallois-Perret).
5. Crupelandt (Roubaix).
6. L. Georget (Châtellerault).
7. Crisilou (Paris).
8. Maitron (Nevers).
9. Dubos (Rouen).
10. Charpiat (Lyon).
11. Plistean (Roubaix).
12. G. Lorgeou (Levallois-Perret).
13. F. Buitier (Nevers).
14. Ricoux (Paris).
15. L. Pothier (Sens).
16. Niedergang (Paris).
17. Dhers (Seine).
18. Meulet (Paris).

19. Ryon (Paris).
20. F. Faber (Colombes).
21. G. Garrigou (Pantin).
22. E. Paul (Colombes).
23. L. Trousselier (Paris).

24. J. Alavoine (Versailles).
25. J. Masselis (Moorslede).
26. Blaise (Boumagne).
27. Vandenberghe (Bruxelles).
28. Delisya (Bruxelles).
29. Verschoore (Moorslede).
30. Depauw (Moorslede).
31. Vaaleberge (Moorslede).
32. Ch. Christophe (Malakoff).
33. Godivier (Versailles).
34. Tribouillard (Paris).
35. L. Poyet (Paris).
36. G. Verbelen (Roubaix).
37. H. Olivier (Buffet).
38. J. Bruers (Paris).
39. Ed. Léonard (La Garenne-Colombes).
40. Fr. Ruinart (Paris).
41. Létargie (Roubaix).
42. Colsaet (Battries).
43. Germain (La Plaine).
44. R. Schiller (Fontenay-sous-Bois).
45. P. Mercier (Paris).
46. A. Faure (Saint-Étienne).
47. J. Mosaur (Saint-Étienne).
48. J. Leblanc (Châteaux-Gontier).
49. Tibal (Kremlin-Bicêtre).
50. D'Annunzio (Saint-Maurice).
51. M. Buysse (Eecloo).
52. R. d'Awans (Jemeppe-sur-Meuse).
53. V. Dekker (Jemeppe-sur-Meuse).
54. N. Dubois (Rennes).
55. P. d'Aben (Louvain).
56. M. Corbière (Paris).
57. P. Dasnoys (Paris).
58. C. Mus (Dadizeele).
59. C. Liseljou (Marcq-en-Baroeul).
60. J. Lesschaeve (Marcq-en-Baroeul).
61. L. Spieranza (Bruxelles).
62. Ramackers (Fexhe).
63. L. Heughen (Bruxelles).
64. Van Booth (Schaelfen-Niel).
65. L. Charlier (Cousdre).
66. H. Devroye Mons-Croiteux-lez-Liège).
67. F. Delcampe (Jupille).
68. Pichon (Châtellerault).
69. H. Buet (Paris-Nord).
70. F. Griffon (Mareuil).
71. M. Perilleux (Maubeuge).
72. L. Ganna (Milan).
73. P. Albini (Milan).
74. O. Brambilla (Milan).
75. O. Sacks (Marseille).
76. T. Haulet (Oise).
77. R. Chaud (Magny-en-Vexin).
78. G. Decuype (Fives-Lille).
79. R. Knecht (Évreux).
80. Ph. Thys (Anderlecht-Bruxelles).
81. Vital Dorne (Barthenon-au-Pont).
82. B. Dejonghe (Baythem).
83. J. Demaeghere (Ledeghem).
84. P. Pautrat (Pantin).
85. L. Nuessens (Saint-Denis).

87. V. Reychler (Eecloo).
88. A. Lauwers (Woesmael-lez-Louvain).
89. C. Olifager (Amiens).
90. R. Saïfot (Le Perreux).
91. L. Lannoy (Calais).
92. M. Pardon (Paris).
93. A. Cognat (Nevers).
94. E. Dorvillers (Amburg).
95. A. de Smet (Lierre).
96. A. Bottini (Milan).
97. A. Bottini (Milan).
98. R. Latouroube (Paris).
99. J. Mora (Nice).
100. O. Melotte (Bruxelles).
101. A. Govaert (Bruges).
102. Gadin (Saint-Brieuc).
103. G. Weirus (Vincennes).
104. W. Reed (Paris).
105. P. Gérard (Lille).
106. H. Durche (Paris).
107. W. de Mara (New-York).
108. G. Ginisty (Paris).
109. Dupont (Estaminet).
110. G. Paulmier (Thiais).
111. O. Beaugendre (Salbris).
112. R. Beaugendre (Salbris).
113. A. Azrini (Milan).
114. L. Azani (Milan).
115. V. Borgarello (Milan).
116. G. Canepari (Milan).
117. U. Gittara (Milan).
118. H. Pélut (Argenteuil).
119. F. Verstraeten (Bruxelles).
120. J. Beyens (Genval).
121. Roche (Troyes).
122. J. Vandenhoueck (Louvain).
123. A. Billet (Staden, Belgique).
124. Loit (Juvisy).
125. G. Schmacke (Lomme).
126. D. Verstraete (Comines).
127. B. Mortier (Coucklaere).
128. A. Ringeval (Maisons-Alfort).
129. F. Bardiu (Paris).
130. H. Pélissier (Paris).
131. A. Verstraeten (Cruyshautem).
132. P. Prisson (Seilly).
133. P. Delange (Lille).
134. P. Copeaux (Plessis-Bouchard).
135. P. Vandereldo (Lovendeghem).
136. A. Vandaele (Moorslede).
137. R. Fercourths (Oosken-Roulers).
138. A. Vandecke (Oosken-Roulers).

139. A. Peeveyn (Nazareth).
140. R. Anxa (Bentegem).
141. J. Coursemont (Humbeke).
142. J. Nempou (Paris).
143. A. Marion (Paris).
144. Petit-Breton (Périgueux).
145. M. Marchaisou (Vincennes).
146. P. Haughem (Renaix).
147. R. Harquet (Paris).
148. A. Devaux (Paris).
149. J. Sauvage (Marcinelle).
150. F. Lambot (Marcinelle).
151. F. Brouzeira (Saint-Gilles-lez-Bruxelles).
152. P. Sutter (Paris).
153. O. Doury (Paris).
154. J. Declerco (Schlaghem).
155. J. Mistiaen (Vormezeele).
156. De Kopf (Dalhem).
157. E. Lachaise (Gentilly).
158. Dairieu (Paris).
159. O. Perenui (Paris).
160. F. Descos (Paris).
161. G. Romet (Paris).
162. H. Alacoine (Paris).
163. J. Vandenstollen (Valenciennes).
164. C. Sigala (Milan).
165. A. Agostini (Milan).
166. P. Nabaulet (Périgueux).
167. P. Gibbolti (Argenteuil).
168. L. Gilles (Paris).
169. L. Theuriaut (Paris).
170. Mervilte (Nogent-sur-Marne).
171. R. Barret (Paris).
172. L. Leman (Poudre).
173. Delafre (La Chapelle).
174. A. Malaye (Chantilly).
175. A. Tibilletti (Varese).

Les coureurs régionaux français ou belges sont indiqués en italiques.

COLSAET

L'itinéraire

Voici l'itinéraire officiel et le kilométrage :

LOCALITÉS TRAVERSÉES   K. M.

Chatou	—
Saint-Ouen (4 kil. 600)	6 600
Croix-de-Noailles (4 kil. 600)	10 600
Achères (passage à niveau (2 kil.))	12 600
Pont du Confians (3 kil. 600)	16 400
Conflans (600 m.)	17 000
Eragny (4 kil.)	21 000
Pontoise (3 kil.)	24 000
Ennery (3 kil. 700)	27 700
Hérouville, embranchement (3 kil. 900)	31 900
Valangoujard (11 kil. 800)	43 800
Méru (4 kil. 200)	47 200
Corbeil-Cerf (3 kil. 500)	50 700
Ressons-l'Abbaye (4 kil.)	54 700
Bois de Molle (2 kil. 300)	57 000
Saint-Quentin-d'Armeuil (3 kil. 500)	60 500
Allonne, bifurcation (7 kil. 500)	68 700
Beauvais (4 kil. 100)	72 800
Troissereux de Beauvais (1 kil.)	73 800
Villé (4 kil.)	77 800
Snarerie Saint-Martin (8 kil.)	85 800
Noirémont (4 kil. 400)	90 200
Froisy (11 kil. 800)	102 000
Crèvecoeur (7 kil.)	109 000
Breteuil (7 kil.)	116 000
Folie-de-Bonneuil (7 kil.)	123 000
Flers-sur-Noye (6 kil.)	129 000
Saint-Sauflieur (5 kil.)	134 000
Dury (8 kil. 500)	142 500
Amiens (6 kil.)	148 500
Villers-Bocage (13 kil.)	161 500
Talmas (6 kil.)	167 500
Doullens (9 kil.)	176 500
Mondicourt (10 kil.)	186 500
Beaumetz-les-Loges (11 kil.)	197 500
Arras (6 kil.)	203 500
Saint-Nicolas (3 kil.)	206 500
Bailleul-Sire-Berthould (7 kil.)	213 500
Arleux (3 kil.)	216 500
Bois-Bernard (4 kil.)	220 500

FRANÇAIS

DEPAUW

Drocourt (3 kil.)	222 500
Hénin-Liétard (3 kil.)	225 500
Courrières (4 kil.)	229 500
Carvin (6 kil.)	235 500
Wattignies (4 kil.)	240 000
Fretin (5 kil.)	245 000
Lesquin (5 kil.)	251 000
Ascq (5 kil.)	256 000
Forest (3 kil.)	261 000
Hem (2 kil.)	264 000
Croix (3 kil.)	267 000
Vélod. du Parc Barbieux (2 k.)	269 000

Il est interdit aux coureurs de changer leur machine de route, pour une machine de piste, dans l'enceinte du Vélodrome du Parc Barbieux.

Les Contrôles

CHATOU (contrôle de départ), chez M. Ch. Bocché, 47, route de Saint-Germain. Contrôleurs : Rédaction de l'Auto.

SAINT-OUEN-L'AUMONE-PONTOISE (contrôle volant), maison Chapelle frères, mécaniciens, rue du Pont. Contrôleurs : M. Denage, correspondant de l'Auto et les membres de l'Union Sportive Pontoisienne, et du Cercle Athlétique d'Enghien.

BEAUVAIS (contrôle fixe), Café Polard, place Jeanne-Hachette. Contrôleurs : M. Bernier, correspondant de l'Auto, assisté du Véloce-Club Beauvaisien et de la société de trompettes l'Étendard.

BRETEUIL (contrôle volant), Hôtel du Commerce, place de l'Hôtel-de-Ville. Contrôleur : M. Prevost, correspondant de l'Auto.

AMIENS (contrôle fixe), Café Pâ, esplanade Saint-Roch, au coin de l'avenue du Général Foy. Contrôleur : M. Georges Sens, correspondant de l'Auto.

DOULLENS (contrôle volant), Taverne Moderne. Contrôleur : M. Picourt-Lermechin.

ARRAS (contrôle fixe), Café Gérard, place de la Cité. Contrôleur : M. D. Delamorre, correspondant de l'Auto.

HÉNIN-LIÉTARD (contrôle fixe), maison Bernard, correspondant de l'Auto, assisté des membres des sociétés cyclistes de Hénin-Liétard, Lens, Airon et Billy-Montigny.

SECLIN (contrôle volant), Auberge du Forgeron, 17, rue d'Arras. Contrôleur : M. H. Smaghe, correspondant de l'Auto.

ROUBAIX (contrôle d'arrivée), Vélodrome du Parc Barbieux, correspondant de l'Auto : M. A. Vanneste, correspondant de l'Auto et la direction du Vélodrome.

A partir de sept heures du soir, le contrôle sera transporté au Café Wagram-Rozé, 2, boulevard Gambetta, à Roubaix.

L'Horaire probable

Kilom	Heures de passage	Heures de fermeture des contrôles
Chatou	—	7 h	7
Pontoise	24	7 35	10
Beauvais	72 800	9 30	4
Breteuil	102 800	10 30	3
Amiens	134 800	11 35	7
Doullens	161 800	12 50	9
Arras	203	2 15	1 m 1e 28
Hénin-Liétard	223	2 40	2 10
Seclin	241	3 15	4
Roubaix	269	—	—

Les Favoris

Qui gagnera le seizième Paris-Roubaix?

Avec une semblable liste d'engagés, tout pronostic semble bien fragile et, pour ce qui nous concerne, nous nous bornerons à indiquer « la route » qui circule à Paris :

Lapize, Garrigou, 4/1 ; Faber, Vanhouwaert, 4/1 ; Trousselier, Ganna, Brocco, ...

LÉON GEORGET

Petit-Breton, Émile Georget, 8/1 ; les autres, 16 et 33/1.

Il semble, cependant, qu'on ait fait peu de cas des coureurs régionaux français et belges qui seront en grand nombre au départ.

Il est évident que l'absence de Crupelandt est des plus regrettable, mais avec Colsaet, Létargie, Dupont, Niédergang, Dhulst, Platteau, Dorvillers, Masselis, Depauw, Verschoore, etc., nos sportsmen peuvent encore garder l'espoir d'applaudir parmi les premiers arrivants un coureur de la région.

Le Palmarès de Paris-Roubaix

		H. M. S.
1896.	1. Jos. Fischer ; 2. Meyer ; 3. M. Garin.	9 17 »
1897.	1. Maurice Garin ; 2. Cordang ; 3. Frederik.	10 4 »
1898.	1. Maurice Garin ; 2. Stéphane ; 3. E. Wattelier.	8 13 16
1899.	1. Champion ; 2. Bor ; 3. Maurice Garin.	8 23 33
1900.	1. Bouhours ; 2. Jos. Fischer ; 3. Maur. Garin.	7 10 30
1901.	1. Lesna ; 2. Ambroine Garin ; 3. Itsweire.	10 49 37
1902.	1. Lesna ; 2. E. Wattelier ; 3. Ambroise Garin.	9 37 29
1903.	1. Aucouturier ; 2. Chaperon ; 3. L. Trousselier.	9 12 30
1904.	1. Aucouturier ; 2. César Garin ; 3. Pothier.	8 14 30
1905.	1. L. Trousselier ; 2. R. Pottier ; 3. Cornet.	9 59 15
1906.	1. Cornet ; 2. Marc. Cadolle ; 3. R. Pottier.	8 4 »
1907.	1. Passerieu ; 2. Vanhouwaert ; 3. L. Trousselier.	8 45 »

TROUSSELIER

1908.	1. Vanhouwaert ; 2. Lorgeou ; 3. François Faber	10 34 25
1909.	1. O. Lapize ; 2. L. Trousselier ; 3. Masselis.	9 3 30
1910.	1. O. Lapize ; 2. Vanhouwaert ; 3. Christophe.	9 5 12

Comme répartition de victoires au point de vue international, les coureurs français ont remporté treize fois Paris-Roubaix, les Allemands une fois et les Belges une fois.

En 1896 et 1897, l'entraînement s'est effectué à bicyclette ; de 1898, 1899 à 1900 on est revenu à l'entraînement à cyclette, et en 1908 et 1909 cet entraînement n'a plus été autorisé que jusqu'à Beauvais. Le reste de la course ayant lieu sans entraîneurs, ni suiveurs, ni soigneurs. En 1910, la course a eu lieu sans entraîneurs, ni suiveurs, ni soigneurs.

Il en sera d'ailleurs de même cette année.

2. Course d'amateurs, U.V.F. (1,000 mètres).
3. Régionale contre-montre (1,000 mètres).
4. Grand Prix de Pâques (scratch pl. deb.).
5. Course de tandems (séries).
6. Deuxième internationale (réservée aux... classés du Prix de Pâques).

LES ENGAGÉS

Cette réunion sensationnelle a réuni les engagements suivants :

Fédéraux : L. Bouchard, Dubélat, Chaux Georges, Walbizgarger, Jacquelin, Eschrher, Iemain, Léons Goets, Bonsoumat.

Professionnels : Dupuy, Hoizquek, Boothé, Morilhot et Denis et de Paris, Michaels, Lavie..., no mois, J. Zimmermann, Catolie, Otto, Delou Walmots, de Bruxelles, P. Guadefroy et Dame de Rouen, Legrand, Carpentier, Delahaye revecka et Provest, de Lille ; Girardin, de Bourg ; Meuger et Pérée, d'Amiens ; Danselie Louvrel ; Martel, de Baltimore ; Bertrand, le coiffé et The Piat, de Roubaix.

Doutremepuich, E. Pottier, F. L..., hoste, Blondel, Guadefroy, A. Dupoux, M. 7... leinando.

Tandems : Legraud Marcelli, Delahaye Carpentier, Meuger-Bertraud, Otto-Catolle, Wilson-leu, Guadefroy-Hugot.

Jamais, une semblable réunion n'a été amisée à l'occasion de Paris-Roubaix et toute des spectateurs de la course de dimanche, où des pédestriers Bouchard, Dubélat, Walbizgare, des sprinters Dupuy (qui battit tout dernier resment Friol et Dupré), Hatquek, Boothé, Otto, Meuger, Delahaye, Legrand, les coureurs Doutremepuich, Blondel, Guadefroy, permet des luttes émouvantes sur la piste de ... bieux alors que sur la route se poursuivra, bravo jours plus ardente, la bataille des routiers, bataille dont le public acclamera l'émotionte sur les 333 mètres du Vélodrome du Parc Barbieux.

La réunion commencera à 3 heures précises. Les portes seront ouvertes à midi.

LUNDI 17 AVRIL

Le lendemain, lundi, nouvelle réunion attrayante comportant, «entre une course d'une heure (sans entraîneur), réservée aux routiers ayant accompli Paris-Roubaix, une heure lustre, les finales du Grand Prix de Pâques.»

Nous reviendrons plus longuement sur le programme de cette seconde réunion, mais d'ores et déjà disons que nous venons de donner ci... que détails que nous venons de donner ci-dessus, l'accrochement intérêt et sans aucun doute tous ceux qui auront assisté au spectacle du matin, retourneront lundi au Vélodrome applaudir les vaillants Paris-Roubaix, et les rivalités des coureurs les plus importantes de ces premières journées du beau sport.

— Aujourd'hui, samedi, à 8 heures et demie du soir, réunion des contrôleurs à l'estaminet du « Convoyeur », rangée des rues des Champs et du Chemin-de-Fer.

LAFOURCADE

la course de tandems, une course de primes surpassée pour donner sérieuse, deviendra la course de motocyclettes. Cette dernière épreuve n'a pas réuni moins de cinq engagés parmi lesquels le fameux Raoulbégnou, dont sportsmen régionaux connaissent l'incomparable valeur.

Nous reviendrons plus longuement sur le programme de cette seconde réunion...

COLSAET

Lapize - the first trilogy

The rumour of another war between Germany and France spread following various incidents in Morocco where the interests of the two countries clashed. Other events shook France such as the riots of the wine producers in Champagne, the accidental death of the Minister of War, Berteaux, at an air show and the theft of the Mona Lisa from the Louvre...

Roubaix, meanwhile, was preparing for its International Exhibition when thousands of visitors would fill the town for several months.

Paris-Roubaix, in the same way as the passage of the Circuit of European Aviation, the inauguration of the new Town Hall, or even the European Championships (sprint and motor-paced) organised at the two velodromes of the 'City of the Mills' were all part of the great events of that year.

Octave Lapize at the height of his glory was the logical favourite of the 16th Paris-Roubaix. In his 24th year, Curly' already had a prestigious record (one vicotry in the Tour de France and two in Paris-Roubaix), to which would be added this year a French championship, Paris-Tours, Paris-Brussels and a third Paris-Roubaix. If you please.

At the start at Chatou the man seemed to be as motivated as he had been a fortnight before in Paris-Tours. Moreover he desired to confound several critics who had always minimised his two previous victories. Lapize decided not only to achieve a first and extraordinary triple, but to make it an unforgettable one by finishing alone, clear of the rest of the field.

This was easier said than done, as he was up against the elite of the cycling world, from Faber to Garrigou passing by Van Hauwaert, Trousselier, Ganna, Petit-Breton, Georget and Passerieu. Also, in the shape of Deman, Pélissier, Thys and Defraye, a new generation was appearing on the horizon.

César Garin who had become a garage owner at Roubaix had even come back to reimmerse himself in this familiar atmosphere. On this 16th April, the former champion was driving the Journal of Roubaix car over these roads of which it was said that he knew even the smallest pothole.

The only one missing was the local hero Charles Crupelandt who had crashed heavily in Paris-Tours.

Once the race had started, it was obvious the favourites were all waiting for the hill at Doullens to make their big attack. But they were all curtailed by an avalanche of punctures. In a few kilometres about twenty men and even a motorist fell victim.

Nine men arrived in a group at Arras. Among them were Lapize, Garrigou and Van Hauwaert. Passerieu was trailing at seven minutes, Pelissier, Faber and Trousselier at nine minutes!

In the mining sector, Lapize and Van Hauwaert decided to go to the front. From then nobody was able to match them. Followers were predicting that the race would end with another sprint between the two riders when, at Ascq just a few kilometres from the Velodrome, the Belgian's back tyre gave up the ghost. Givong a big gesture of despair he was obliged to watch the Parisian disappear.

The village of Forest was under siege from the crowds. At 3.30 pm the official vehicles announced the arrival of the champions. The man wearing a No 1 armband emerged from

1911

1909

1910

LAPIZE

a cloud of dust . The crowd was jubilant.

Behind him, but at a respectable distance, Charpiot the man from Lyons had just rejoined Van Hauwaert, then to a huge ovation Vandenberghe, Garrigou and Faber trailed through, contorted over their machines.

The Belgian fans were unaware of the misfortune of their man from Moorslede. When the fanfare rang out, all eyes were fixed on the entrance to the track. As the first rider appeared the spectators thought they recognised Van Hauwaert and chanted his name.

Their disappointment was considerable when the man was identified — it was Octave Lapize.

The champion had time to cover four laps of the track before the news arrived: Cyrille had punctured. The Belgians were devastated. The Frenchman's lead of the race was so great that he had time to sign the register and ride a lap of honour to the strains of the Marseillaise before the next man, Charpiot, appeared.

While Charpiot completed the required distance to polite applause, Van Hauwaert entered the stadium. The place exploded.

A QUI LE PARIS-ROUBAIX 1911 ?

BLAISE.   MASSELIS.   VAN HOUWAERT.   VAN DEN BERGHE.   DUPONT.

SPIESSENS.   GARRIGOU.   LAPIZE.   TROUSSELIER.   HANLET.

MAITRON.   PAULMIER.   CRUPPELANDT.   FABER.   GEORGET.

NOS GRANDS CHAMPIONS CYCLISTES

VAN HOUWAERT

ÉMILE GEORGET

SUR
BICYCLETTES "LA FRANÇAISE DIAMANT"
PNEUMATIQUES "HUTCHINSON"

His nerves got the better of him: he cried. His disappointment was so great that the organisers had the greatest of difficulty in getting him accept his bouquet of flowers.

At more than seven minutes, Garrigou finished fourth in front of the Belgium Vandenberghe who crashed on the track.

In the absence of Crupelandt, Roubaisan honour was saved by Consant Nierdgang and Maurice Leturgie in eighth and ninth places.

The day after the race two cycle companies announced that a reward of three thousand Francs would be paid to the person who supplied the information that would lead to the arrest of individuals who had spread nails on the road at Doullens. In spite of this the "bandits" were never found..

For his part Octave Lapize had taken a liking to this region of the North. The following Sunday he was the main star at a meeting at the Velodrome of Croise-Laroche, a few kilometres from Roubaix. A little later, Curly would put on his first red white and blue French champion's jersey, the first step towards another superb treble.

1911

1. Octave LAPIZE (France)
2. André CHARPIOT (France)
3. Cyrille VAN HAUWAERT (Belgium)
4. Gustave GARRIGOU (France)
5. René VANDENBERGHE (Belgium)
6. Georges PASSERIEU (France)
7. Georges TRIBOUILLARD (France)
8. Constant NIEDERGANG (France)
9. Maurice LETURGIE (France)
10. Eugène DHERS (France)

Charles Crupelandt
brings the title home

The 1912 season started well for the French. Milan-San Remo run on the 31st of March was dominated by Henri Pélissier and Gustave Garrigou who took the first two places. The two champions promised their rivals that they would be in at the showdown of Paris-Roubaix.

In spite of bad weather, the champions prepared assiduously for the Easter confrontation. As well as Pélissier and Garrigou all of the other "giants of the road" were present: Petit-Breton, Lapize, Trousslier, Faber, Georget, Passerieu, Cornet, the Belgians: Thys, Deman, Defraye, Masselis and Van Hauwaert. However, the man to beat was Charles Crupelandt. He not only knew the race but also the route. He trained every day at the Roubaix velodrome where the public had taken him to their hearts.

At the age twenty five the Roubaisan had reached the peak of his career. The previous year a crash in Paris-Tours had spoilt the start of his season, but he went on to ride an excellent Tour de France. On top of his two stage

Riders on the hill at Doullens.

The feeding station at Arras.

wins at Chamonix and Marseilles, when he demonstrated his considerable climbing ability, the Northerner finished fourth overall in Paris behind Garrigou, Duboc and Emile Georget. Henri Desgrange saw in him a future winner of his event.

The 17th Paris-Roubaix was the sole objective of the beginning of his season.

Against all expectations Easter Sunday was bathed in sunshine. This splendid weather encouraged a mass of spectators to witness the start at Chatou. The throng was such that police reinforcements were needed to control the crowd. The riders were set free in an atmosphere of euphoria. The race took off too quickly - a crash just after the start resulted in about ten riders hitting the ground. However the main item of note at the beginning of the race was the retirement, before Bretreuil, of Lucien Petit-Breton, who was suffering with his eyes.

By Amiens the high speed had caused numerous riders to retire; the favourites watched each other very closely. Van Hauwaert was the first to reveal his ambitions. He hoped to get rid of several rivals before tackling the hill at Doullens. In fact there were still forty of them at the bottom of the climb. At the top it was Garrigou and Verschoore who were first over, slightly detached from the others.

On the road to Arras a man went clear and entered the town alone, to the surprise of the spectators. This front runner was Maurice Leturgie, certainly a good rider but not the sort of star that the people of the town were expecting to be first at the

1912

4e Année. — N° 8   Le Numéro : 30 centimes   15 Avril 1912

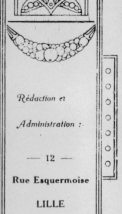

LE NORD-ILLUSTRÉ

MAGAZINE
BI-MENSUEL
d'Actualité Régionale
o o

Direction :
Émile Lante et André Fage

Rédaction et
Administration :
— 12 —
Rue Esquermoise
LILLE

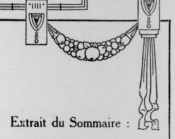

Extrait du Sommaire :

Le Numéro : 30 centimes
(Etranger : 0,40 centimes)

ABONNEMENTS

France : 7 fr. 50 - Étranger : 10 francs

L'abonnement continue, sauf avis contraire.

PUBLICITÉ :

M. Eugène FRANCHOMME,
52, Rue du Faubourg-de-Roubaix, LILLE

DÉPOSITAIRES GÉNÉRAUX :

Nord, Pas-de-Calais, Somme, Ardennes et Aisne :
Messageries de L'Echo du Nord, Lille.

Paris et Bibliothèques des Gares :
Messageries Hachette, 113, rue Réaumur, Paris.

Bruxelles et la Belgique :
Agence Dechenne & Cie, 20, rue du Persil, Bruxelles.

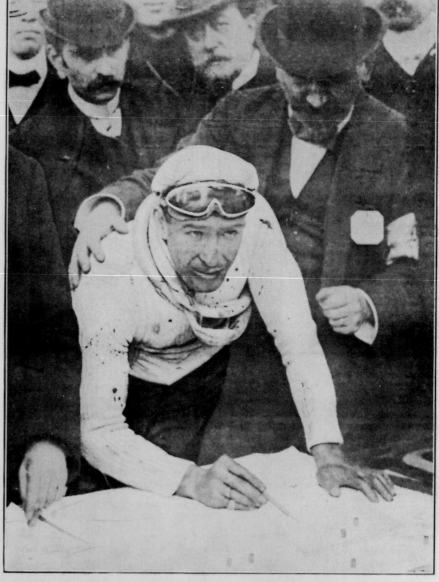

Ch. Cruppeland signe au contrôle d'arrivée. *(Photo J. Bauchart, plaque Lumière).*

Un Roubaisien a gagné la course cycliste Paris-Roubaix

La victoire de Ch. Cruppelandt, notre vaillant compatriote, dans Paris-Roubaix, a eu un
énorme retentissement dans notre région, où il est si populaire. Cruppelandt est en effet roubaisien et habite Roubaix, où il est ajusteur-mécanicien.

Déjà, à dix-huit ans, en 1904, dans cette même course, il se classait onzième. Mais c'est
surtout depuis deux ans qu'il connaît la grande célébrité : 6e dans le Tour de France (1910) ;
1er dans l'étape Paris-Roubaix du « Tour » ; 3e dans Paris-Bruxelles (1911) ; 1er dans Paris-
Menin (1911).

control. The man himself was a little worried and asked: "Has anybody else been through yet?" After being reassured he quickly set off for Hénin-Liétard.

The "aces" Lapize, Trousselier, Faber, Heusghem, Deman, Masselis, Crupelandt and several others formed the framework of the peloton hot on his heels.

The mining villages of Courrières and Carvin were crossed in front of an imposing crowd. The main cheers were for the man at the head of the race. In spite of his determination, Leturgie was caught just before Seclin by Deruyter, Garrigou, Masselis, Crupelandt and Defraye. Rapidly Lapize realised the danger of letting such a group go without him. After a brief and intense effort he latched on to the leaders.

So the battle for victory was about to begin. As the enthusiastic public spilled onto the road the riders had difficulty in getting through. A figure of one hundred thousand spectators was claimed.

In the overheated atmosphere of the velodrome, one name was on everybody's lips - Charles Crupelandt. When the first race vehicles appeared the public rose to its feet, then a rider entered the stadium. The crowd exploded, for the ten thousand spectators had recognised Crupelandt coming first onto the wooden track. The Roubaisan was followed by Garrigou. The two men had scarcely covered two hundred metres when the third man spilled onto the track. It was Maurice Leturgie who had crashed at the entrance to the stadium. The public did not know who to encourage most.

However it was not over, as a few seconds later Lapize, Masselis, Defraye and Deruyter arrived. There were seven on the same lap for an extraordinary finish!

In front, Garrigou, followed like a shadow by Crupelandt, led so strongly that he caught Lapize and Defraye. Crupelandt was obviously faster but also crafty, for he intelligently took the wheel of his friend Lapize who led out the sprint. On the finishing line there was no surprise. Garrigou in spite of his efforts was only second and Leturgie third.

Crupelandt was delighted. Everyone wanted to congratulate him, but as soon as he got off his bike, he could think only of washing the dust from his face and eyes.

His wife arrived by his side. She confided to journalists that Paris-Roubaix had haunted the nights of her husband, and that he had always dreamed of winning on "his" velodrome. As for his father, a normally undemonstrative man, he shouted to whoever wanted to hear: "Isn't Charles terrific? Ah, he really deserves to win Paris-Roubaix." Garrigou had little to say but Leturgie, surrounded by his friends from the Lion Velo Club, proclaimed: "I gave it all I had. I was at the front of the race for so long that I could see myself winning but a car knocked me off just before the velodrome. But I'm third and that's not so bad."

As for François Faber, he was once again disappointed with his Paris-Roubaix. After six punctures he finished seventeenth, on foot and more than a quarter of an hour after Crupelandt.

The "Giant of Colombes", normally so calm, was very upset this time. As he went away he lifted his arms to heaven and swore to return and wipe out this affront.

1912

Charles CRUPELANDT
(France, 1886-1955)

The only Roubaix-born rider to win the 'Queen of the Classics', Crupelandt was one of the outstanding champions of the pre first World War era.

1907 : 2nd Paris-Brussels
1911 : Paris-Menin, 3rd Paris-Brussels, 4th Tour de France
1912 : Paris-Roubaix
1913 : Paris-Tours, 3rd French Championship, 3rd Paris-Roubaix, 3rd Paris-Brussels
1914 : Paris-Roubaix, French Champion 3rd Milan-San Remo

1. Charles CRUPELANDT (France)
2. Gustave GARRIGOU (France)
3. Maurice LETURGIE (France)
4. Octave LAPIZE (France)
5. Odile DEFRAYE (France)
6. Jules MASSELIS (Belgium)
7. Charles DERUYTER (Belgium)
8. Joseph VAN DAELE (Belgium)
9. Eugène PLATTEAU (Belgium)
10. Paul DEMAN (Belgium)

Faber takes his revenge

March 1913. The storm rumbles over Amiens. Paris-Roubaix is at the centre of a debate in this normally peaceful town. For reasons that only he knew, the Mayor of the City decided to modify the part of the route which went through his town. The organisers opposed the move and threatened to remove Amiens from the route altogether.

A large number of supporters demonstrated their discontent. Faced with this veritable revolt, the Municipal Council distanced themselves from the decision and confusion reigned as they overruled the unfortunate decision of their chief.

Crupelandt's success in the 1912 edition had led to such enthusiasm in the North that all the track meetings held on the Roubaix velodrome had been sold out. This would of course once again be the case for the arrival of the 18th Paris-Roubaix.

All the class roadmen were present in the 165-man peloton - Lapize, Faber, Crupelandt, Garrigou, Trousselier, Georget, Petit-Breton, Masselis, Defraye, Deman, Heusghem and many more.

The only important absentee was Van Hauwaert, who had crashed heavily in the recent Paris Six-Day. Crupelandt, on the other hand, was in tremendous form and had finished fourth in his first Paris Six in company with Godivier. More than a few journalists presented the Roubaisan as the man to beat on the Northern cobbles.

On the 23rd March the weather was ideal. The "Maison Fromentin" a new starting point, had replaced Monsieur Bouché's shop.

As soon as they were released by the starter, Brocco and Lapize went to the front of the race behind the official cars. An attentive Faber took over from them at the head of things.

As the race approached Beauvais several crashes scattered the bunch. Crupelandt was one of the fallers. In spite of intense pain in the knee he got back on his bike crying: "you can't retire in Paris-Roubaix."

A 'motorised' lap of honour for Faber and Deruyter.

François Faber surrounded at the finish.

The town was crossed by a "royal escape" comprising Philippe Thys, the world hour record holder Oscar Egg, Henri Pélissier, Paul Deman the recent winner of the Tour of Flanders and Octave Lapize. As for Tribouillard, Engel, Luguet Hepest and Deruyter, who accompanied them, they were much more than minor figures.

Many supporters predicted that this was the "right" break. But the entente cordial just was not present in the midst of the group. The fact that nobody would work properly, led to the failure of the offensive. All it did was to eliminate some of the weaker men at the back.

At the Amiens control 23 men formed the leading bunch and they started to watch each other closely as the hill of Doullens was approaching. This time however this strategic climb did not make its traditional selection. Certainly the group was dislocated a little, but those who had been delayed were later able to rejoin the leaders.

Tiredness was having its effect however, and eight riders made up the scouting party at Arras: Masselis, Maertens, Crupelandt, Luguet, Mottiat, Deruyter, Vandaele and Benoit. The latter was rapidly eliminated by a puncture. At this moment three men seemed to be dominating the event: the Belgian from Tourcoing, Deruyter, young Luguet, who at eighteen astonished everyone with his resilience and Crupelandt, in spite of his crash and his usual punctures.

However a "bolide" came up from behind, François Faber. After having a bad time on the hill at Doullens the 'Giant of Colombes' had recovered some of his lively energy. Sitting snugly on his wheel, Oscar Egg made the most of the opportunity and also rejoined the escapees.

On the cobblestones of Hénin-Liétard, Crupelandt, Luguet, Masselis, Deruyter and Faber remained inseparable. Only Mottiat and Vandaele were able to come back to them at Seclin.

All eyes were focused on Crupelandt who seemed to be the best of them. By the sides of the road the encouragement was mostly directed at the Roubaisan. But there were also many Flemish voices.

As the velodrome approached a sudden fall of sleet dampened their spirits. In spite of this the seven riders

1913

François FABER, Vainqueur de Paris-Roubaix 1913, sur sa bicyclette Peugeot

François FABER
(Luxembourg, 1887-1915)

Luxembourg's first superstar of ycling. Before the first World War intervened he had many great victories.

1908 : Tour of Lombardy,
2nd Tour de France,
3rd Paris-Roubaix,
3rd Paris-Tours
1909 : Tour de France, Paris-Brussels,
Paris-Tours
1910 : Paris-Tours, 2nd Tour de France
1911 : Bordeaux-Paris, 2nd Paris-Brussels
1913 : Paris-Roubaix

14e ANNÉE. — 4.542. — QUOTIDIEN

Le Numéro : 5 Centimes

DIMANCHE 23 MARS 1913.

L'Auto

AUTOMOBILE — AÉRONAUTIQUE — CYCLISME

ATHLÉTISME, YACHTING, ESCRIME, POIDS & HALTÈRES, HIPPISME, GYMNASTIQUE, ALPINISME

Rédaction, Administration, Publicité :
10, Rue du Faubourg-Montmartre, Paris (9e).

TÉLÉPHONE { 1re LIGNE . . . 227-68
{ 2e LIGNE . . . 228-12
{ 3e LIGNE . . . 228-56

Adresse Télégraphique : VÉLAUTO-PARIS

Directeur-Rédacteur en chef :
Henri DESGRANGE

ABONNEMENTS :
SIX MOIS   UN AN
SEINE et SEINE-ET-OISE . . . 10.50   20 »
DÉPARTEMENTS et ALGÉRIE . . 12 »   24 »
ÉTRANGER (Union postale) . . 20 »   40 »

On s'abonne sans frais dans tous les Bureaux de poste.

AU PARC DES PRINCES

UNE SENSATIONNELLE RÉOUVERTURE

La plus belle piste de monde fait aujourd'hui sa réouverture. — La première du Meeting Pascal. — Kramer, Hourlier, Ellegaard, Dupré, Perchicot, Moretti, Pouchois, Dupuy, Polledri, etc. dans le Grand Prix de Pâques. — Un grand match de demi-fond : les deux hommes de l'hiver contre le roi du Parc des Princes.

EN CAS DE PLUIE

ELLEGAARD   KRAMER   HOURLIER

DUPRE   PERCHICOT

Allô ! Allô !

AUJOURD'HUI

Cyclistes, allumez vos lanternes à 6 h. 30.

LE CIRCUIT DE PARIS

(Motocyclettes, cyclecars, voiturettes)
23-24 mars
Organisé par l'Autocycle Club de France, sous les règlements de l'U.M.F.

AUJOURD'HUI, PREMIÈRE ÉTAPE : 266 KILOMÈTRES

Une intéressante épreuve. — Les grandes lignes du règlement. Vingt et un concurrents seront au départ. — L'itinéraire de l'étape d'aujourd'hui.

UN ESSAI

LES GRANDES ÉPREUVES CYCLISTES

PARIS-ROUBAIX

(XVIIIe ANNÉE)

Organisé par l'AUTO le dimanche 23 mars 1913

LA PREMIÈRE ÉPREUVE SUR ROUTE

Une course triomphale ! — La lutte s'annonce comme devant être des plus âpres. — Les détails d'organisation. — Quelques concurrents étrangers n'ont pas encore montré leurs licences. — Au Vélodrome du Parc Barbieux à Roubaix.

DIX-HUIT ANS !

Dix-huit ans d'âge et d'un étourdissant succès ininterrompu n'ont pas terni le prestige de Paris-Roubaix.

UNE BELLE LUTTE

1. Faber, 2. Garrigou, 3. Crupelandt, 4. Lapize, 5. E. Georget, 6. J. Alavoine, 7. Petit-Breton.

François Faber signs the finishing sheet.

continued their inexorable progress towards the tumult that was waiting for them in the stadium.

In theory, and the spectators knew it well, Crupelandt had the sharpest sprint. From their perspective the Belgians looked to Masselis to avenge Van Hauwaert. They screamed that the Fleming deserved to carry it off after having finished the last five editions among the first ten.

The three laps of the track were ridden very fast. Deruyter led, then was passed by Faber, who in one last burst of energy pipped them all at the finishing post Deruyter even snatched second place from a totally dumbfounded Crupelandt.

The Giant of Colombes was overcome. Cornered by the cameramen of Gaumont, he remained simple and unaffected. He smiled and embraced his friends in the centre of the track in front of the film-makers.

Until then Paris-Roubaix had been cruelly missing from his prestigious record which already included the Tour de France, the Tour of Lombardy, Paris-Brussels, two Paris-Tours, Bordeaux-Paris and many others.

Crupelandt was not too disappointed, considering that his crash in Beauvais could have prevented him from even finishing. He was moreover very happy at the victory of his friend Faber who he slapped on the back in front of the eyes of the cameras.

This Paris-Roubaix marked the last important success of the Luxembourger. Following the example of Octave Lapize, he joined up as a volunteer at the start of the World War One.

The champion died at the age of twenty eight, on the 9th May 1915 on the battlefield of Artois.

1913

1. François FABER (Luxembourg)
2. Charles DERUYTER (Belgium)
3. Charles CRUPELANDT (France)
4. Louis MOTTIAT (Belgium)
5. Louis LUGUET (France)
6. Joseph VAN DAELE (Belgium)
7. Jules MASSELIS (Belgium)
8. Georges PASSERIEU (France)
9. Adelin BENOIT (Belgium)
10. André BLAISE (Belgium)

Crupelandt before the storm

At the start of the 1914 season, the sporting calendar was starting to fill out. In Belgium, the Carolorégienne Star, disputed on the 15th March and the second Tour of Flanders saw the successes of Victor Doms and Marcel Buysse respectively. On the other hand serious floods in the Tours region caused Paris-Tours to be postponed. So once again Paris-Roubaix marked the beginning of the French road season. Just as in the "heroic times" the start of the event was in Paris. The finish would be in the renovated velodrome with seats for an extra of fifteen hundred people.

Among the one hundred and fifty three starters for this nineteenth edition, the observers were curious to see at work on the cobbles, not only the usual Lapize, Van Hauwaert and Faber, but five Australians who had come to ride the great European events. One, named Kirkham, had been widely talked about after finishing ninth in the Milan-San Remo.

This Milan-San Remo was to remain in the memories of the people of Roubaix for another reason. A week before "La Pascale", Crupelandt should have opened his score for 1914 at San Remo. In fact the Frenchman, intrinsically the fastest, saw himself neatly pushed into the crowd in the final sprint by his two remaining adversaries Galetti and Agostoni!

Crupelandt returned to his native soil consumed with a desire for revenge.

He had reached an age when he was perfectly able to combine his remarkable athletic qualities with an exceptional energy and considerable will-power.

Thanks to his exploits the "Bull of the North", as his numerous supporters called him, was able to escape from the miserable conditions of the working man.

His strength allowed him to push an enormous gear of 24 x7. His name always

Charles Crupelandt and his friend Octave Lapize at the Roubaix velodrome.

CRUPELANDT. CHAMPION DE FRANCE

1914   1922.1923

figured prominently on most forecasts.

On the 12th April the superb weather encouraged everyone to take things easy. The crowds witnessed a wonderful race.......... in which nothing happened in the first few hours! In this connection the article which appeared in "La Vie au Grand Air" seems enlightening: "The victory was unfortunately contested in a sprint and it is to be regretted that the roadmen of today give the impression that they consider road races as sprint events: 153 at the start, 125 at Beauvais, 100 at Amiens, 50 at Arras, 21 with 10 kilometres to go and seven for the final sprint.

The waiting race for the old and the young. The young deliberately do not go to the front because they are afraid, they are not sure of themselves and are scared of the records of their rivals. The old watch each other trying not to expend too much energy in efforts that may be useless. Ah, what has happened to the old times? Where are the Kings of the Road? When the Garins, the Pottiers, the Petit-Bretons, the Georgets came through alone well in front of the rest. When the public shook with excitement and discussed the riders' chances. The man who achieved a great exploit became immediately famous. He was a hero. Today times have changed.

We must face up to the facts, if we do not remedy the present state of affairs, cycling on the road will go through a period of crisis and this must be avoided at all cost."

Even the hill at Doullens only had the effect of eliminating a few second-rate riders. Nevertheless, and this was the big surprise of the day, François Faber came through a quarter of an hour down!

A large peloton of fifty riders went through Arras, then the mining towns of Hénin-Liétard and Carvin were reached before Seclin, Ascq and Hem were crossed. At this point there was still fifteen of them left, all black with dust and at the head were Luguet, Van Hauwaert, Oscar Egg and Crupelandt. The second group, who were now at five minutes, had given up all hope.

At the velodrome, while the sprinter Meurger had just carried

1914

TWEEDE JAARGANG. — N° 242

ABONNEMENTSPRIJS :
BELGIE
Voor 50 nummers . . . . fr. 2.50
» 100 » . . . . » 4.50
BUITENLAND
Voor 50 nummers . . . . fr. 5.00
» 100 » . . . . » 9.00

AANKONDIGINGEN :
4e en 3e bladzijde : fr. 0.50 per regel
4e bladzijde : bij overeenkomst

BEHEER- EN OPSTELRAAD :
Boekstraat, 3, BRUSSEL.
TELEFOON B 5574
Telegram-adres : SPORTWERELD BRUSSEL

De schrijvers alleen zijn verantwoordelijk voor hunne artikelen.

MAANDAG 13 APRIL 1914

ABONNEMENTSPRIJS :
BELGIE
Voor 50 nummers . . . . fr. 2.50
» 100 » . . . . » 4.50
BUITENLAND
Voor 50 nummers . . . . fr. 5.00
» 100 » . . . . » 9.00

AANKONDIGINGEN :
2e en 3e bladzijde : fr. 0.50 per regel
4e bladzijde : bij overeenkomst

BEHEER- EN OPSTELRAAD :
Boekstraat, 3, BRUSSEL.
TELEFOON B 5574
Telegram-adres : SPORTWERELD BRUSSEL

De schrijvers alleen zijn verantwoordelijk voor hunne artikelen.

SPORTWERELD

ORGAAN ALLER SPORTEN

5 Centiemen per nummer   5 Centiemen per nummer

PARIJS-ROBAAIS

EENE FRANSCHE OVERWINNING !!

De belgen doen niettemin 'nen prachtigen koers ! - Van Houwaert, Rossius, Mottiat, Van Lerberghe, Marcel Buysse en Pierke Vandevelde verdedigen zich als echte wilden. — Vanlerberghe en Marcel Buysse worden omverregereden aan de poorten van den velodrom. — Pierke Vandevelde verdient eene bijzondere melding ! - Defraeye, Masson, Faber, Engel en Thys waren de ongelukkigsten.

Parijs-Robaais

KAREL CRUPELANDT, van Robaais
die voor den tweeden keer Parijs-Robaais komt te winnen

HET VERTREK

ZIJ DIE VERTROKKEN

1. O. LAPIZE, Parijs;
2. K. CRUPELANDT, Robaais;
3. VAN HOUWAERT, Brussel;
4. MONSEUR, Gentbr.;
5. LAUTHELEMY, Parijs;
6. TIEBAGHI, Parijs;
7. EGISELT, Parijs;
8. VAN DAELE, Meerbeem;
9. CRUNEL, Parijs;
10. MOTTIAT, Brussel;
11. SPIESSENS, Robaais;
12. DEMAY, Luna;
13. VANLERBERGHE, Antwerpen;
14. VANDENBERGHE, Brussel;

LANGS DE BAAN

PIERKE VANDEVELDE, van Lovendegem
die eene streepen als groote baanrenner kreeg om te winnen. Rijdt heden in den velodrom van Evergem.

DE BELGEN WORDEN HARD BEPROEFD!

PONTOISE (33 km. 100 meters)

NIEUWE SLACHTOFFERS

EMIEL ENGEL GEEFT OP

VASTE KONTROL VAN BEAUVAIS (81 km. 300 m.)

WEINIG VERANDERING

VLIEGENDE KONTROL VAN BRETEUIL

FRANS FABER MOET LOSSEN

VASTE KONTROL VAN AMIENS (143 km. 900)

THYS IS ZIEK

MAURITS GARIN
de kies der vroegere baankoersen

EMIEL BOUHOURS
die even goed was op de baan als op straat

off the Easter Grand Prix, the fanfare announced the arrival of the first riders. At 4.46 pm seven men swept into the entrance to the stadium. Enthusiasm was at its peak in the stands stuffed with Belgians and Roubaisians, for their respective favourites Van Hauwaert and Crupelandt were going to dispute the victory.

There remained three laps of the track, just what was needed for Crupelandt to get his huge gear turning effectively. Thanks to an electrifying sprint, which only he was able to produce, he won to an indescribable ovation. Luguet, Mottiat, Egg, Rossius, Van Hauwaert and Vanvervelde could in no way match his speed.

Ninety eight riders finished at Roubaix where the complaints and excuses were as numerous as ever: Lapize had two punctures and was obliged to retire just before the finish. Leturgie, in nineteenth place, raged that two tyres had let him down. Petit-Breton, Buysse, Garrigou and several others crashed several times.

However, shortly after, new battles and much more bloody ones were going to turn the world upside down. On the 28th June, the assassination at Sarajevo of the Archduke of Austria Franz-Ferdinand was going to upset the fragile balance of Europe. Philippe Thys was busy winning his second Tour de France but attention was elsewhere as the pace of events began to accelerate.

On the day following the murder of Jean Jaures, the socialist leader, the order for a general mobilisation went out in France, then Germany officially declared war.

The champions put their bikes to one side in order to put on their uniforms.

Crupelandt, who had won the French Championship on the 21st June, found himself on the 4th August, the day war was declared, at Berlin where he was honouring a contract on the Olympia track!

The man from Roubaix had to use all his cunning to get back, for the Germans had closed their frontiers. On the train which took him back to France, via Cologne, Aix-la-Chapelle, Amsterdam and Brussels, he passed himself off as a Dutchman by hiding his military papers. Afraid of being recognised he spent a large part of the time locked in the toilet.

Posted on the 52nd Motorcycle Division he was seriously wounded in March 1915 and was decorated with the Croix de Guerre for his bravery at the front. Then, in these difficult times, he was curiously found guilty of minor offences in 1917.

After the war he applied for a new racing licences with the UFV. It was not only refused but he was banned from racing for life because of his "criminal" record. Eighty years later witnesses are almost as rare as the censored records. The reasons for his condemnation remain uncertain as does the intransigent and incomprehensible position of the Federation. At the time certain people insisted that it was due to pressure brought by the Pélissiers, bitter rivals of the Northerner who wanted to rid themselves of a dangerous opponent!

The scandal caused a lot of ink to flow up until 1923 when several newspapers demanded in vain the re-establishment of the champion. But the UVF remained inflexible.

His career broken he took out a licence with a dissident federation: The Society of the Races. Crupelandt accumulated victories, including two other titles of French Champion, but the "spring" was manifestly "broken".

He continued to ride for pleasure up until the beginning of the 1950's before succumbing in February 1955 close to destitution, practically blind and with two legs amputated.

After World War One the golden age of Roubaix cycling came to an end, with not only the demolition of the 'Roubaix Velodrome' by the Germans but also the end of the career of Charles Crupelandt, its most prestigious champion.

VIE AU GRAND AIR

1914

1. Charles CRUPELANDT (France)
2. Louis LUGUET (France)
3. Louis MOTTIAT (Belgium)
4. Oscar EGG (Switzerland)
5. Jean ROSSIUS (Belgium)
6. Cyrille VAN HAUWAERT (Belgium)
7. Petrus VANDEVELDE (Belgium)
8. Jules MASSELIS (Belgium)
9. Dieudonné GAUTHY (Belgium)
10. Emile AERTS (Belgium)

20ᵉ ANNÉE. — Nº 6.582. — QUOTIDIEN   Le Numéro : 10 Centimes   Le Numéro : 10 Centimes   MERCREDI 29 JANVIER 1919

Rédaction, Administration, Publicité :
10, Rue du Faubourg-Montmartre
PARIS (9ᵉ)

Téléphone Central : 28-12
— 27-68

Adresse Télégraphique : VÉLAUTO-PARIS

Directeur-Rédacteur en chef :
HENRI DESGRANGE

ABONNEMENTS :

L'Auto

AUTOMOBILE — AERONAUTIQUE — CYCLISME
ATHLÉTISME, ALPINISME, BOXE, ESCRIME, GYMNASTIQUE, HIPPISME, POIDS & HALTÈRES, YACHTING

Rédaction, Administration, Publicité :
10, Rue du Faubourg-Montmartre
PARIS (9ᵉ)

Téléphone Central : 28-12
— 27-68

Adresse Télégraphique : VÉLAUTO-PARIS

Directeur-Rédacteur en chef :
HENRI DESGRANGE

ABONNEMENTS :

On s'abonne sans frais dans tous les Bureaux de poste.

TOTO
chien de guerre

— Tiens, Julot ! Comment qu'ça va, vieille cloche ?

— Pas mal... Très bien même : j'viens d'être déliberé.

— Alors, j'comprends qu'ça peut coller... Toi on t'a d'avancé parce que t'avais quatre gosses. Moi qui compte pas un seul salé à l'effectif j'suis en train de limer une combine qui va me mettre au même niveau que toi : ma mère est veuve et cultivatrice !

— Mais tu n'sais même pas comment qu'c'est fait un' herse.

— J'occupe pas... Chacun son pain et son oharrue... A propos, qu'qu'un fabriques dans l'quartier rupin ?

— J'attends l'vicomte !

— Pas possib'! L'est déliberé aussi, naturellement ?...

...

ROBERT OUDOT.

LA SOUSCRIPTION FONCK

Maximum par souscription : 50 fr.

...

NOS EDILES SPORTIFS

FRANÇOIS FABER

Le regretté recordman de Paris-Roubaix nous entrainera en 1 h. 15 m.

LES GRANDES EPREUVES CYCLISTES DE L'AUTO

PARIS-ROUBAIX
20ᵉ année. — Organisé par l'AUTO, le 20 avril 1919

Le 20ᵉ Paris-Roubaix. — Après une interruption de 5 années, la grande course pascale va constituer un admirable début de saison. — Le règlement. — Les engagements sont ouverts.

...

Le Règlement

...

Les engagements sont ouverts

...

AUTOMOBILE

UNE PROTESTATION

...

Henri PÉLISSIER
GAGNANT DU TOUR DE FRANCE 1923
sur Bicyclette

AUTOMOTO

Henri Pélissier winner of "The hell of the North"

March 1919. Paris-Roubaix seemed so distant, so futile. In the news the names of Verdun, Douaumont or of Ypres had replaced those of Doullens and of Hénin-Liétard. The regions of the North and of the Somme, where the battles were so bloody, had suffered terribly. Most of the roads were unusable. The vegetation had been replaced by bomb craters and the blood-stained trenches dismally decorated the devastated countryside.

Octave Lapize, Lucien Petit-Breton, François Faber, Frank Henry, Emile Engel, Edouard Wattelier, Marius Thé and many others would not come back from the fighting, they were among the nine million victims of war.

After the Armistice, life slowly returned to normal. Once again the Paris-Roubaix and even the Tour de France were organised. Many young men were still wearing uniform and bicycle manufacturers were finding it difficult to reform their teams of riders.

The face of the peloton had changed. In spite of the disappearance of some of the old lions, such as Van Hauwaert, Trousselier or Passerieu who had all retired, there were still some indomitable ones left such as Eugène Christophe or Jules Masselis who were still prepared to answer the call.

The renewed Paris-Roubaix was organised on the 20th April over abominable roads. The route had suffered so much that after Doullens the riders were obliged to switch to another itinerary, leading towards St Pol and Bethune. After inspecting these roads a Parisian journalist, appalled by the state of the countryside, went so far as to say the race was going across "the Hell of the North".

One hundred and thirty cyclists came to the start. The spectators, braving the rain and cold, recognised some of the riders whose faces had been furrowed by time and by suffering - Thys, Mottiat, Deruyter, Rossius, Barthélemy, Christophe, Masson, Defraye and Henri Pélissier.

The riders started out over the roads after a minute's silence. The images of Faber, of the Lapize phenomenon, of Petit-Breton's striped jersey were fixed in everyone's memory.

For many of the competitors, this Paris-Roubaix constituted a return to racing after a very long period of inactivity. Nobody really dared to enter into the battle too early for fear of having nothing left for the finish. The bunch remained intact until eighty kilometres from Roubaix.

As they crossed through La Bassée, whose town centre had been devastated by the conflict, two men tried a first attack: Henri Pélissier and his brother Francis who had just joined the ranks of the professionals.

Rapidly the two Parisians increased their lead to two minutes over a perished bunch. Three successive punctures handicapped Francis, who in addition was the victim of the most terrible "Fringale" , the infamous hunger knock. On these roads taking your hands off the bars for an instant could lead to disaster.

Henri Pélissier, who wanted to finish with his brother, slowed the pace but this enabled Philippe Thys to catch them.

The astute Belgian quickly noticed the fact that Francis Pélissier was "cooked" and immediately attacked. Henri could not risk letting a man like Thys get away so had no choice but to jump on his

1919

Henri PELISSIER
(France, 1889-1935)

One of the great cyclists of the early era. Oldest of a famous cycling family, he was also the most gifted of three brothers.
His name remains linked to the "convicts of the road affair", a famous report by Albert Londres.

1911 : Tour of Lombardy
1912 : Milan-San Remo,
      2nd Tour of Belgium
1913 : Tour of Lombardy
1914 : 2nd Tour de France
1917 : 2nd Tour of Lombardy
1919 : Paris-Roubaix, French Champion,
      Bordeaux-Paris
1920 : Tour of Lombardy, Paris-Brussels,
      2nd French Championship,
      2nd Milan-San Remo
1921 : Paris-Roubaix,
      2nd French Championship
1922 : Paris-Tours
1923 : Tour de France,
      3rd French Championship

195. Cyclisme — PÉLISSIER, *routier Français*   C. M.

wheel leaving Francis to his fate.

Henri Pélissier thought that he was going to arrive with Philippe Thys on the new finish in the Barbieux Park, but at Lesquin a closed level-crossing level held up the two men.

Pélissier first saw Honore Barthélemy rejoin them after a few minutes. Fuming with impatience, he could stand it no more. He jumped over the barrier, opened one of the doors of the stationary train and crossed through the compartment with his bike on his shoulder, pushing several passengers out of the way in the process.

Following his example, Thys and Barthélemy did the same before the train was able to restart.

All three men wanted to finish alone so the attacks came fast and furious. First Thys tried several times and then Pélissier attempted to go clear but eventually they all had to accept that the race was going to be decided by a sprint.

The elder of the Pélissiers had no trouble with Thys at the finish. The first words of the winner were for his brother Francis: "I am of course happy with my win, however it is incomplete as I had hoped to complete a double with my brother. Before the war I dreamed of carrying off this victory but luck never smiled on me. This time I managed it."

Eighty riders finished. The last one, classified an hour and fourteen minutes behind the winner was Albert Dejonghe. The young Belgian was making his debut in the event. He learned the lesson very quickly.

Following his victory Henri Pélissier, a soldier, until the following August, in the General Automobile Reserve of the military government of Paris, returned to his barracks in the Avenue de Clichy.

His undemanding superiors, allowed him to train as much as he wanted. They were not to regret it as Henri also carried off, in this same year, the French Championship and Bordeaux-Paris.

1919

1. Henri PELISSIER (France)
2. Philippe THYS (Belgium)
3. Honoré BARTHELEMY (France)
4. Louis HEUSGHEM (Belgium)
5. Alexi MICHIELS (Belgium)
6. Francis PELISSIER (France)
7. Jean ROSSIUS (Belgium)
8. Emile MASSON (Belgium)
9. Eugène CHRISTOPHE (France)
10. Alfred STEUX (Belgium)

"Hel van het Noorden" door TEEL...

TEEL.95

Deman, twelve years after Van Hauwaert

Cyrille Van Hauwaert, the first star of Belgian cycling, blazed a trail that others quickly followed. Odile Defraye the first Belgian winner of the Tour de France in 1912, was succeeded in the two following years by Philippe Thys. From the restart of racing in 1919 Firmin Lambot in his turn inscribed his name on the list of winners of the Tour.

Strangely the cyclists of Flanders were still waiting for a successor to Van Hauwaert, the 1908 winner, on the roads of Paris-Roubaix.

Paul Deman, by carrying off this 21st edition of the Queen of the Classics, made up for this deficiency. However his victory did not stir up a lot of enthusiasm, even in Belgium, for the man was too modest and discrete to really move the crowds. The Fleming, a roadman of great class, expressed himself solely on a bicycle and his reputation, unjustly, did not reflect his superb record.

Originally from Rekkem, a few kilometres from Roubaix and just a stone's throw away from the French border, he was in a family tradition, a carpet weaver. His career took a decisive turn in 1909 when he won the amateur Tour of Belgium and reportedly received a staggering 41 bicycles as prizes!

His success persuaded him to give up his job as a textile worker for good.

In 1911, at the age of twenty one, Paul Deman rode his first Tour de France. He finished thirteenth but took the important individual classification. After that he

Pélissier and Deman
on the cobbled roads of Pontoise.

The finish at the 'stadium'.

was naturally seen as a stage race rider, but he was never able to follow up this fine performance. In fact he suffered from gastric problems and his performances in this type of race became very irregular.

So Deman successfully specialised in one-day events. Before the first world conflict he had already won the first Tour of Flanders in 1913 as well as a famous Bordeaux-Paris the following year ahead of his compatriots Marcel Buysse and Cyrille Van Hauwaert.

The war naturally stopped his career. He was only able to escape from it with a lot of luck for in 1918 he was condemned to death by the Germans. Deman had in fact been surprised at the Dutch frontier carrying messages hidden in a gold tooth!

He should have been shot when at the last minute the Armistice intervened and he was released from a sordid cell in a Louvain prison.

After a difficult year of resumption in 1919, he was perplexed as to what course his career should follow. At the beginning of 1920 he started training again but his condition did not seem good enough to ride the Tour of Flanders, the event in which he had proved his class seven years previously.

A week later he entered Paris-Roubaix with the sole ambition of finishing in the "City of Mills".

At the start, among the ninety three contestants, he appeared insignificant alongside the favourites such as Pélissier, Christophe, Heusghem, Masselis, the Buysses and Jules Van Hevel who had just won the Tour of Flanders. Moreover, for the first time, the Italians had come in force with the illustrious Constante Girardengo, the very first "Campionissimo" and Gaetano Belloni, recent winner of Milan-San Remo.

From the start the riders, as in 1919, had to contend with icy rain as well as the atrocious roads. Nevertheless the tempo of the race was very fast, although mechanical mishaps rapidly eliminated Belloni and Francis Pélissier.

On the hill of Doullens, Girardengo, who had carefully studied

LES GLOIRES DU CYCLISME
PAUL DEMAN

Paul DEMAN
(Belgium, 1889-1961)

The first ever winner of the Tour de Flanders, famously added the 1920 Paris-Roubaix to his list of honours, which also included medals for bravery for his exploits in the first World War.

1913 : Tour of Flanders,
Etolie Carolorégienne
1914 : Bordeaux-Paris,
3rd Tour of Belgium
1920 : Paris-Roubaix
1923 : Paris-Tours

1920

the course, threw down the first challenge, but Henri Pélissier considered that this man from the other side of the Alps was too dangerous and quickly latched onto his back wheel in company with seven others.

In the space of just a few kilometres as the race crossed through Lens fate first overcame Girardengo who broke his bike, then his compatriot Azzini and the Belgian Jules Van Hevel were puncture victims. Gerbaud and Christophe were dropped so that there were four champions in command of things, two Frenchmen against two Belgians: Pélissier and Barthélemy versus Deman and Lucien Buysse. The real duel was about to begin.

The men worked well together until two kilometres from Roubaix when Deman found himself alone in the lead.

In fact while Pélissier had seen his back tyre give up the ghost the other two had been delayed by mechanical problems!

Deman was astonished to experience all his old sensations of victory. The Belgian surpassed himself. Despite his lack of form, by dint of courage, he finally preserved fifty three seconds lead at Roubaix over the "Old Gaulois" Eugène Christophe, who finished in front of Buysse and Honoré Barthélemy.

Poor Pélissier arrived more than seven minutes down. The champion of France would not accept defeat and swore to all and sundry that he was already

Paul Deman arrives at Roubaix.

preparing his revenge. As was his custom he kept his word by winning Paris-Brussels and a third Tour of Lombardy.

As for Paul Deman, twelve years after Van Hauwaert, he gave Belgium a second Paris-Roubaix in the town where he came to often consult the reputed Professor Fauverghe, a specialist in gastric complaints!

Two years later he completed his "palmares" with another classic success in Paris-Tours. In spite of all these victories, the man that Philippe Thys called "the finest stylist that I have ever seen", never really emerged from the semi-anonymity which suited him so well.

1920

1. Paul DEMAN (Belgium)
2. Eugène CHRISTOPHE (France)
3. Lucien BUYSSE (Belgium)
4. Honoré BARTHELEMEY (France)
5. Jules VAN HEVEL (Belgium)
6. Henri PELISSIER (France)
7. Robert GERBAUD (France)
8. Giuseppe AZZINI (Italy)
9. Félix GOETHALS (France)
10. Marcel BUYSSE (Belgium)

CYCLISTES N'OUBLIEZ PAS QUE
DEPUIS VINGT ANS
LABOR
CRÉE
LES
CHAMPIONS

The Pélissiers as if in a dream

Henri PÉLISSIER

On the 27th March 1921 not less than one hundred and thirty riders appeared at Le Vésinet, the new start point for Paris-Roubaix.

The weather was superb. A favourable wind pointed to a very fast race. The first few kilometres were dominated by the veteran Jules Masselis. At 35 the Belgian wanted to finish his career with a bang in this race which had given him so much satisfaction. He managed to gain a lead of nine minutes but was obliged to relinquish it near Breteuil.

At this point of the race, Eugène Christophe, Romain Bellenger and the Pélissiers were monopolising the first few places.

The hill at Doullens was approaching. This was quite clearly the place that had been chosen by Henri Pélissier to mount his first attack which he hoped would be decisive. Just before the start he had taken Francis to one side and said to him: "We'll attack at Doullens. I'll take off, you take my wheel and ignore everyone else. When we get to Arras we'll see who is still with us."

The Pélissier plan was carried out to the letter. At the top of the of the famous climb, the bunch was scattered over a considerable distance. Henri and Francis were naturally the first ones over followed by Romain Bellenger and then the Belgians René Vermandel and Emile Masson who were determined not to be caught in any trap. A few hundred metres later only two men were able to latch on to them: Léon Scieur and Hector Tiberghien.

As they raced through mining country, punctures eliminated Bellenger, Masson and then Tiberghien.

The weather was excellent, but this brought another hazard - dust raised by the following cars. For several kilometres, up to the outskirts of Carvin, Scieur was dropped, blinded by dust and coughing badly. However, a magnificent pursuit enabled him to rejoin his three adversaries at Seclin.

The Pélissiers were nevertheless worried, for they still had to get rid of René Vermandel. The former apprentice butcher from Anderlecht, who was already known as the "Belgian Lapize", was very fast, as he had proved in the recent Tour of Flanders. Even a Pélissier, as the two brothers well knew, could not beat him in the final run-in.

From then on the Frenchmen, multiplied their attacks but

1921

CHAQUE ROMAN COMPLET

LES ROMANS SPORTIFS

0f60

PARIS-ROUBAIX

(Nouvelle Série) — 3me Année — N° 14 — Dimanche 3 Avril 1921

LE GRAND
Hebdomadaire Illustré
DE LA RÉGION DU NORD DE LA FRANCE

25 CENTIMES le Numéro

Bureaux : 77, Rue Nationale, LILLE

Les annonces sont reçues au Bureau du Journal, à Lille, et à l'Agence Parisienne
au Printemps, 18, rue Drouot, Paris.
ABONNEMENTS (Nord et Limitrophes), **12 francs** par an.
Autres départements français, **13 francs.** — Étranger, **15 franc.**

LA COURSE PARIS-ROUBAIX

LES VAINQUEURS DE L'ÉPREUVE — A GAUCHE, HENRI PÉLISSIER, CLASSÉ PREMIER, A CÔTE DE LUI SON FRÈRE FRANCIS, CLASSÉ SECOND

were each time totally unsuccessful in achieving their object, for Vermandel proved to be a real leech, totally invulnerable!

But after many kilometres of tireless battering, he began to weaken and pleaded: "Don't drop me, I'd very much like to finish with you." Unfortunately for him, the Pélissiers were not naive and were certainly much stronger.

At Hem, the last difficulty of the day, Henri delivered the coup de grace to Vermandel. Francis stayed on René's wheel and allowed himself to be dropped as well. From then on neither Vermandel nor Scieur could catch an inspired Henri Pélissier flying towards his second victory bouquet at Roubaix.

The gap rapidly opened then Francis, in a fine tactical move, attacked. Secretly he hoped to rejoin his elder brother in order to cross the line together, their arms linked.

But a flint decided otherwise. Francis punctured. Vermandel caught him and went past him before he too suffered the same fate. It was too late to change tyres, so the two of them went on to finish the race riding on their thick wooden rims!

Henri arrived to the applause of a delirious public. As he got off his machine he waited for Francis to appear. Then his happiness was complete as Francis kept his second place in front of Scieur and Vermandel.

Next day the daily newspaper L'Auto told the story of the exploit under the headline: "The Thoroughbred Triumphs, The Victory Of The Best". Its owner Henri Desgrange had grudgingly agreed to this as he had only recently confided to his associates that: "these Pélissiers are beginning to exasperate me. Never again will their names appear on the front page of the newspaper."

This was just one among a number of quarrels between the powerful newspaper proprietor and organiser and the Pélissiers. The most notable was without question the retirement of the Pélissiers on the Cherbourg-Brest stage of the 1924 Tour de France. This episode especially stood out in people's minds after the reporter Albert Londres amplified the complaints of the two champions, describing them as "convicts of the road".

This domination in Paris-Roubaix marked the pinnacle of the Pélissier clan. It remained for a long time engraved on the memory of Henri who often repeated : "Just once in my career I have experienced the sort of Paris-Roubaix that you can only normally dream about. Superb weather, a following wind and not a single puncture. On days like that it's all such fun."

As for Francis, just before his death in 1959, he too recalled that the 27th March 1921 was one of the best days of his life. However, he too knew many other successes by winning three national championship jerseys, Paris-Tours in the same year of 1921, Bordeaux-Paris in 1922 and 1924, the Criterium des As in 1926 as well as many other events.

1921

1. Henri PELISSIER (France)
2. Francis PELISSIER (France)
3. Léon SCIEUR (Belgium)
4. René VERMANDEL (Belgium)
5. Hector TIBERGHIEN (Belgium)
6. Emile MASSON (Belgium)
7. Romain BELLENGER (France)

The Belgians come to power

In 1922 the balance of power swung to Belgium and the whole face of Paris-Roubaix changed. A talented new generation of Belgian riders emerged. The podiums of the Tours de France and the classics were monopolised by riders such as Thys, Lambot, Scieur, Sellier, Van Hevel, Vermandel, Masson and Mottiat to mention only the most famous of them.

The French who had had things their own way for such a long time, had no other choice than to accept this domination. The reality was that in the face of this Flemish armada only the Pélissiers could hope to do anything about it.

After a Tour of Flanders won by Léon Devos, the crack Belgians came to Chatou with the object of dominating the racing over these Northern roads.

From the start, by way of provocation, Henri Pélissier "sounded the charge". A closed level crossing at Achères hardly delayed him as, sticking to his usual custom, he was quickly through the foot gate and across the line, followed by his team-mates Lacquehay, Brunier, Detreille, his brother Francis and Léon Devos.

It was only as the town of Meru was reached that the front of the bunch was able to rejoin the escapees. Pélissier had achieved both of his objectives - not only had he demonstrated that he was the one to beat but had also forced the others to make excessive efforts. Even before they had reached Beauvais many riders had already lost all hope of final victory.

Emile Masson and Jean Rossius at Roubaix.

On the road to Amiens the high pace imposed by Pélissier, proved unsustainable and provoked several retirements. By the time the front group hit Amiens it had been reduced to a mere eleven riders.

Henri Pélissier was expending his energy without counting the cost and formed a new break as he crossed the top of the Doullens hill in the lead, but suddenly his pedalling lost its smooth rhythm. He started to pay a heavy price for the mighty efforts he had been making since the start.

On the plateau of Arras the Parisian was hit by a terrible weakness due to not taking sufficient food. He begged spectators for a scrap of bread but it was too late, the damage had been done. Victory slipped away from him and he finally arrived at Roubaix suffering terribly, a quarter of an hour behind the winner.

As the race passed through Arras only Lacquehay and Brunier attempted to resist the attacks of five Belgians: Dejonghe, Scieur, Rossius, Masson and Steux. Most forecasts were for Emile Masson or Jean Rossius but, against all expectations, it was Albert Dejonghe who progressively stepped up the pace. Nobody was able to follow him and he quickly demonstrated that he was the master of the situation as his lead came to be measured in minutes.

At Seclin, where the pavements were deserted, he was so far in advance of the predicted timetable, and of his rivals, that in order to reassure himself he slowed down to ask a passer-by if he was still on course!

1922

Albert DEJONGHE
(Belgium, 1894-1981)

One of Belgium's finest roadmen in the period between the wars.

1919 : 3rd Bordeaux-Paris
1920 : 2nd Tour of Flanders,
2nd Tour of Belgium, 3rd Paris-Tours
1922 : Paris-Roubaix
1923 : 3rd Tour of Flanders
1926 : Paris-Angers

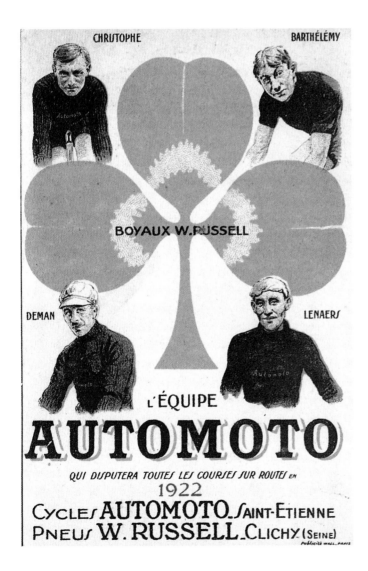

CHRISTOPHE

BARTHÉLÉMY

BOYAUX W. RUSSELL

DEMAN

LENAERS

L'ÉQUIPE
AUTOMOTO
QUI DISPUTERA TOUTES LES COURSES SUR ROUTES EN
1922
CYCLES AUTOMOTO SAINT-ETIENNE
PNEUS W. RUSSELL CLICHY (SEINE)

The journalists question Paul Deman.

The outcome of the race had definitely been decided, the others were merely contesting the minor placings. In spite of the efforts of Jean Brunier and Charles Lacquehay, still a bit young and inexperienced in the face of these tough neighbours, the Belgians showed themselves to be so strong at the finish that they took four of the first six places.

Six minutes after Dejonghe, Jean Rossius took second place in front of Emile Masson and Paul Deman. For Albert Dejonghe the victory was unexpected. A serious chill had stopped him taking part in the Tour of Flanders. It was only on orders of his short-tempered team manager Alphonse Bauge that he was even at the start of Paris-Roubaix. Without training he hoped to go, like Deman the previous year, as far as possible.

Most of the public were astonished by his victory, even in Belgium. Nevertheless the observers were forced to recognise the fact that he had turned professional in 1914 for Ludovic Feuillet's team which was a reference in itself.

From 1919 he should have attracted attention when he finished third behind Henri Pélissier and Louis Heusghem. Following this he produced a whole series of good performances but his poor sprint robbed him of numerous well deserved victories which went to others, simply because they were much faster at the finish.

1922

1. Albert DEJONGHE (Belgium)
2. Jean ROSSIUS (Belgium)
3. Emile MASSON (Belgium)
4. Paul DEMAN (Belgium)
5. Charles LACQUEHAY (France)
6. Gaetano BELLONI (Italy)
7. Alfons VAN HECKE (Belgium)
8. Léon SCIEUR (Belgium)
9. Marcel GODARD (France)
10. Henri PELISSIER (France)

Albert Dejonghe,
Avenue des Villas.

(Nouvelle Série) — 5me Année — N° 14 — Dimanche 8 Avril 1923

LE GRAND

25 CENTIMES
le Numéro

Hebdomadaire Illustré

DE LA RÉGION DU NORD DE LA FRANCE

Bureaux : 77, Rue Nationale, LILLE

Les annonces sont reçues au Bureau du Journal, à Lille, et dans les Agences
en Publicité, à Paris.

ABONNEMENTS (Nord et Limitrophes), **12 francs** par an.
Autres départements français, **13 francs**. — Étranger, **15 francs**.

LA COURSE PARIS-ROUBAIX

L'ARRIVÉE DE HENRI SUTER, VAINQUEUR DE LA COURSE

Heiri in the face of the Flemish horde

At the beginning of 1923, the Swiss champion Oscar Egg was approaching the end of his career, and tended to avoid the more difficult road events as he slowly progressed towards a well deserved retirement. Near to his home in the Canton of Argovie, the Suter dynasty, six brothers, all racing cyclists, had already been widely talked about for some time, but this year marked the arrival at the very highest level of the youngest of the family: Heiri.

Oscar Egg saw Heiri Suter as a worthy successor capable of winning everything thanks to his incredible sprint.

Heiri was national champion but few people outside Switzerland knew anything about this stocky man. In his twenty fourth year Heiri decided to follow the advice of his brothers and to show himself in the great classics.

At the end of March he dared to take on the Belgians on their favourite home ground: the Tour of Flanders. At the start he felt a little isolated among all these robust Flemings. In spite of his red jersey with the white cross which marked him out as the Swiss champion, nobody really paid any attention to him. Certainly as the kilometres went by people were astonished at his resistance but how could anyone imagine that this little Swiss could make these mighty Flemings look ridiculous?

In the final straight there were only three left to dispute the victory in this seventh Tour of Flanders - Charles Deruyter, Albert Dejonghe and...Heiri Suter. The sprint was only a formality for Heiri as Deruyter finished several lengths down. Flanders was plunged into a deep consternation. The spectators were devastated for, sacrilege, it was the first time a foreigner had won their "Ronde van Vlaanderen".

A week later, Sunday 1st April, Heiri was at the start of Paris-Roubaix, confident of himself. However there was the small matter of two hundred and fifty other riders, a record figure, to be taken into account before he could think of victory on the Avenue des Villas at Roubaix.

The superb weather caused everyone to feel more like relaxing than making an effort. Nevertheless as soon as the starter's pistol was fired the whole rhythm of the race was very quick. Escape attempts were rare and the elimination of the riders was at the back of the field. The various mechanical problems which delayed some of the strongest of them did not hinder the progress of the race and Henri Pélissier in particular was easily able to regain the head of the field.

The initial difficulties reduced the principal group to about a hundred riders but the favourites were awaiting the traditional hill at Doullens before joining in the action. At the bottom of the slope, inevitably, Henri and Francis Pélissier attacked. On the plateau of Arras six men rejoined them: Deruyter, Lacquehay, Vermandel, Tiberghien, and Charles Pélissier, the last of the family..

It seemed for most of the followers that this initiative was the right one. The eight riders were not only the best but also among the most experienced of the bunch. Unfortunately for

Cliché Meurisse

9. SUTER, Champion Suisse

Heiri SUTER
(Switzerland, 1899-1978)

Before Kübler and Koblet, there was Suter. A dynamic sprinter, he dominated his native country's top races after the first World war, before crossing the borders to win ...Paris-Roubaix, and the Tour of Flanders, the only Swiss rider to have done so.

1919 : Zurich Championship
         3rd Tour of Lombardy
1920 : Swiss Champion,
         Zurich Championship
1921 : Swiss Champion
1922 : Swiss Champion,
         Zurich Champion,
         2nd Paris-Tours
1923 : Paris-Roubaix, Tour of Flanders,
         2nd Zurich Championship
1924 : Zurich Championship
1925 : Bordeaux-Paris
1926 : Swiss Champion, Paris-Tours
1927 : Paris-Tours
1928 : Zurich Championship
1929 : Swiss Champion,
         Zurich Championship

1923

them, Heiri Suter who had been trapped in a second group, was filled with a desire to win. The Swiss wanted to confirm his success in Flanders. Under his impulsion and to the great surprise of the Pélissiers, a partial regrouping was effected before Arras.

In spite of the difficult passage through the mining sector, always tricky to negotiate, the major moves were over almost before they had started.

The leading group of twenty three riders remained compact.

The victory was going to be decided in a sprint on the superb Avenue des Villas. As in the heroic times at the Roubaix Velodrome, the spectators were impatiently waiting for the riders and warmly applauded the musicians who were waiting to salute the winner.

The band was getting ready to play the "Marseillaise" for as the conductor said to his men, "with the Pélissiers in the group you never know."

Towards three o'clock the Avenue was cleared for the finish. The officials had the greatest of difficulty in containing the excited crowd.

As they entered the final straight, Marcel Huot launched the sprint, quickly relayed by the powerful Charles Deruyter. Francis Pélissier came up to his shoulder but finally Heiri Suter went clear of them all.

The Swiss was well in front of Vermandel, whose tyre exploded once he was over the line. Next to finish were Sellier, Beeckman and Lacquehay.

The public were disappointed once again, nevertheless the spectators politely applauded the winner without realising the importance of the event: for the first time a rider had achieved the double of the Tour of Flanders and Paris-Roubaix.

Suter, assailed by the reporters proclaimed: "It was not really too hard and I felt very confident. I was sure I would be able to win."

Meanwhile, the town band, not knowing the Swiss national anthem, had to satisfy themselves with playing the "Marseillaise". It meant that for once it was not a Belgian who won.

1923

1. Heiri SUTER (Switzerland)
2. René VERMANDEL (Belgium)
3. Félix SELLIER (Belgium)
4. Théo BEECKMAN (Belgium)
5. Charles LACQUEHAY (France)
6. Marcel HUOT (France)

(Nouvelle Série) — 6me Année — Nº 15 — Dimanche 13 Avril 1924

LE GRAND

Bureaux : 77, Rue Nationale, LILLE

Les annonces sont reçues au Bureau du Journal, à Lille, et dans les Agences de Publicité, à Paris.
ABONNEMENTS (Nord et Limitrophes), **12 francs** par an.
Autres départements français, **13 francs**. — Belgique, **15 francs**.

Hebdomadaire Illustré

DE LA RÉGION DU NORD DE LA FRANCE

25 CENTIMES le Numéro

LA COURSE CYCLISTE PARIS-ROUBAIX

LE BELGE VAN HEVEL, VAINQUEUR DE L'ÉPREUVE

Van Hevel
fortifies the Belgians

In 1924 for the first time Paris-Roubaix deserted its traditional Easter Sunday spot. Nevertheless the race looked like being an exciting one as all the stars were present at the start.

In spite of wintry temperatures a huge crowd turned out at Le Vésinet. As usual the riders were surrounded by the public. Italian supporters encircled the compatriots. Costante Girardengo, dressed in his fine tricolour jersey with a Basque beret screwed on his head seemed calm. After three successes in Milan-San Remo and the Tour of Lombardy the 'Campionissimo' wanted to add to his record by winning this Northern event at least once. His team-mates Pietro Linari recent winner of Milan-San Remo, and Federico Gay tried to shield him but could do little to restrain the enthusiastic Italian fans.

The first hours of the race were calm and gave no pointers to the form of the various riders. Only punctures and the usual mechanical incidents troubled the tranquillity of the followers and team managers.

At the front of the bunch Girardengo was chatting to Linari while Henri Pélissier was looking after his young brother Charles. As for the Belgians Deman, Sellier, Van Hevel and Vermandel, they stayed together and watched Heiri Suter. The Flemings had not got over the affront that the Swiss inflicted on them in the Tour of Flanders the previous year.

Beauvais was approaching and the race started to come alive. Two men tired to escape, the modest Italian Arduino and Charles Pélissier. Everything came together again at the exit to the town but this insignificant move had the merit of arousing the offensive spirit a little.

Marcel Gobillot, then Arsene Alancourt followed by Van Hevel, Huyvaert, Vermandel and Arduino went away. Not for long however, for it was a compact bunch which crossed through Amiens a good hour down on schedule.

As was so the often the case, it was the strategic hill at Doullens which brought the race to life. Three men had just attacked and were clear at the top of the climb, the hard-wearing Hector Tiberghien, a cheerful 36 year old, Federico Gay and Heiri Suter.

Only Adelin Benoit, a young professional was able to get up to them after a superb and intensive effort.

Only a second bunch put up any resistance to the runaways, for at the back it was a complete disorder. Linari had already retired and Girardengo, who was clearly in difficulty, would shortly do the same.

Under the impulsion of Henri Pélissier eight men managed to rejoin the leaders. Then the north wind gathered strength until it reached violent proportions. This had the effect of bringing the race together again and the leading group now contained thirty men. In the face of these conditions it was impossible for anyone to escape although there was no shortage of attempts.

A sprint was inevitable. The group contained a lot of specialists so the result was especially difficult to predict. As the kilometres went past, most people were fighting to get on Heiri Suter's wheel. However he did not seem to be in the same form as he had been in 1923.

The Belgians were backing Jules Van Hevel and Félix Sellier. Van Hevel, the former, double champion of Belgium and winner of a memorable Tour of Flanders in 1920, was an adept track rider well used to turning very big gears. Ultra-powerful he was always difficult to beat when he went for a long sprint, sometimes as much as one kilometre from the line!

43. Jules VAN HEVEL
Gagnant du Critérium des Aiglons 1923

Jules VAN HEVEL
(Belgium, 1895-1969)

A brilliant rider who was capable of winning major victories on both road and track.

1919 : 3rd Tour of Flanders,
       3rd Tour of Belgium
1920 : Belgian Champion,
       Tour of Flanders
1921 : Belgian Champion,
       2nd Tour of Flanders,
       3rd Tour of Belgium
1924 : Paris-Roubaix
1925 : 3rd Paris-Roubaix
1928 : Tour of Belgium

1924

The front of the peloton at the hell of Doullene.

The peloton passes through the feeding zone of Amiens

Félix Sellier, the other favourite who was just as fast, was the current Belgian champion and winner of the previous two Paris-Brussels, an impressive reference.

The finishing straight was slightly uphill and being one thousand metres long it enabled the best of them to go clear. As expected, Van Hevel gave a perfect demonstration of his power and was the clear winner in front of Maurice Ville, Félix Sellier, Nicholas Frantz and Henri Pélissier, while Heiri Suter was much further back.

After the arrival of their favourite, the Belgians celebrated. To them it was no surprise that one of their men had triumphed in the City of the Mills. For them, quite obviously, Heiri Suter's success could only have been an unfortunate accident.

1924

1. Jules VAN HEVEL (Belgium)
2. Maurice VILLE (France)
3. Félix SELLIER (Belgium)
4. Nicolas FRANTZ (Luxembourg)
5. Henri PELISSIER (France)
6. Robert GERBAUD (France)
7. Gaston DEGY (France)
8. Robert JACQUINOT (France)
9. Théo BEECKMAN (Belgium)
10. Romain BELLENGER (France)

MERCREDI 15 AVRIL 1925   Prix : 0 fr. 75   TROISIÈME ANNÉE. — N° 80

La Pédale

SOUS LA PLUME DES MEILLEURS SPECIALISTES

REVUE HEBDOMADAIRE DE LA BICYCLETTE
a DES INDUSTRIES QUI S'Y RATTACHENT

PARAISSANT LE MERCREDI   **SPORT. INDUSTRIE. TOURISME**   PARAISSANT LE MERCREDI

REDACTION, ADMINISTRATION	FRANCE ABONNEMENTS ETRANGER		PUBLICITE
17, Faubourg Montmartre PARIS (9°)	Un an .... 33 fr. Six mois .... 18 fr. Trois mois ...... 11 fr.	Un an .... 41 fr. Six mois .... 23 fr. Trois mois ...... 14 fr.	17, Faubourg Montmartre Téléphone : BERGERE . 40-44

LE 26ᵉ PARIS-ROUBAIX

Une amusante photo du « troupeau » des concurrents de Paris-Roubaix, gagné par F. SELLIER.
sur bicyclette ALCYON, pneus DUNLOP.

Sellier
in spite of the Italians

Paris-Roubaix 1925 returned to its traditional spot - Easter Sunday, 12th April - and as usual it attracted most of the top international riders. Once again the Italians came in force. Their national champion Costante Girardengo who had just picked up his fourth Milan-San Remo hoped to shine at last on the Northern roads where he was normally so unlucky. He was surrounded by a group of stars, including Ottavio Bottecchia, winner of the previous year's Tour de France, Pietro Linari, Piero Bestetti, Giovanni Brinero, Federico Gay and Bartolomeo Aymo.

Finally the Italian journalists were expecting the appearance of one of their young compatriots living in Nice, who was beginning to make a name for himself in the South of France - Alfredo Binda.

There was no question that the Italians were the men to beat. Suter, Sellier, Van Hevel and others such as Gérard Debaets, recent winner of the Tour of Flanders were all aware of the danger. As for the chances of the French, they rested as usual on the shoulders of the Pélissiers.

The first part of the race was so like the preceding editions that it was difficult to tell them apart. The compact bunch rode as far as the feeding station at Amiens where ninety riders went through together. Even the hill of Doullens, unquestionably the most famous in the region, had for several years lost the magic power that it had known in the heroic times.

Certainly the pace was faster in the kilometres which had preceded it, the attacks had been quite frequent on the climb and the bunch had broken up. But, as was so often the case, the peloton reformed on the plateau of Arras before tackling the principal difficulties of the mining sector together.

Alfredo Binda decided to make his presence felt and tried to get away alone. However, Henri and Francis Pélissier were not far away as well as the Belgian Adelin Benoit.

After the regrouping, the outsider Emile Hardy tried to grab some glory. Unknown to most of the stars in the bunch, he went clear, pushing an enormous gear.

At Arras his lead had stabilised at 2mins 30sec. The favourites were still not taking this initiative too seriously. Finally, the veteran Eugène Christophe, forty years old and the most experienced of them all, realised that something had to be done to avoid a disaster. According to the "Old Gaulois" they could not allow the event to be won by an unknown.

Under his impulsion the bunch slowly reeled Hardy in. He resisted them as far as the outskirts of Seclin where about

1925

41. SELLIER routier Belge
Vainqueur de Paris-Bruxelles 1922, 1923

Félix SELLIER
(Belgium, 1893-1965)

A winner of Paris-Roubaix and like the famous Lapize a three time winner of Paris-Brussels.

1922 : Paris-Brussels,
3rd Belgian Championship
1923 : Belgian Champion
Paris-Brussels, 2nd Paris-Tours,
2nd Tour of Belgium,
3rd Paris-Roubaix
3rd Liège-Bastogne-Liège
1924 : Paris-Brussels, Tour of Belgium,
2nd Belgian Championship,
3rd Paris-Roubaix,
3rd Tour of Flanders
1925 : Paris-Roubaix
1926 : Belgian Champion,
2nd Tour of Belgium,
3rd Paris-Brussels
1928 : 2nd Belgian Championship

FÉLIX SELLIER
VAINQUEUR DE PARIS-ROUBAIX 1925

Gagnant de PARIS-BRUXELLES 1922-1923-1924

Sur BICYCLETTE *Alcyon*

(PNEUS DUNLOP)

fifty men went past him without even a glance as he capitulated after a lone break of sixty kilometres.

Once again it seemed as if the finish would be decided by a big sprint on the wide Avenue des Villas at Roubaix.

The team men started their difficult job of trying to get their leaders to the front. The sprinters started to watch each other and after a few kilometres began to become very nervous. Jules Van Hevel was obviously after the double, Heiri Suter too wanted to renew his past exploits. Among the favourites there remained men of the calibre of Gérard Debaets, René Vermandel as well as the Italians Girardengo and Binda.

The pace became so fast that about fifteen riders were dropped in the last few kilometres.

Nevertheless it was a group of thirty seven riders which turned onto the long finishing straight. Van Hevel was at the front and looked unbeatable but at the last moment Félix Sellier drew alongside.

It was a fabulous sprint and the former Walloon coal miner proved unbeatable. The Italian Bestetti finished second a good length down, Van Hevel, Linari and Suter even farther back.

Sellier's effort was so violent that he collapsed after crossing the finishing line. His loss of consciousness was only temporary and he fully came round when he heard the first sound of the Belgian national anthem.

To the public of Roubaix his victory was hardly a surprise, as for the two previous years he had finished third on this very same spot just a few metres down on Heiri Suter and Jules Van Hevel.

This triple consecutive winner of Paris-Brussels cheerfully completed a record already containing a national title and the prestigious Tour of Belgium.

Sellier was not only fast and strong but also particularly crafty. At his request a mechanic had made him a thirteen- toothed sprocket. When he was on form he cautiously and discreetly took it out of the pocket of his jersey to screw it onto his rear hub. From then on the others could normally only hope to contest the minor places...

1925

1. Félix SELLIER (Belgium)
2. Piero BESTETTI (Italy)
3. Jules VAN HEVEL (Belgium)
4. Pietro LINARI (Italy)
5. Heiri SUTER (Switzerland)
6. Adelin BENOIT (Belgium)
7. Jean DEBUSSCHERE (Belgium)
8. Denis VERSCHUEREN (Belgium)
9. Gérard DEBAETS (Belgium)
10. Eugène CHRISTOPHE (France)

Delbecque underlines the Belgian domination

From the very first events of the 1926 season, it was obvious that a new generation was appearing. Certainly the "old ones", such as Lucien Buysse, who was to win the Tour de France a few months later, Henri Pélissier or Eugène Christophe were by no means finished, but they were up against a handful of young, talented and ambitious riders who were determined to overturn the established hierarchy.

These young ones, among whom were Gaston Rebry, George Ronsse and Julien Delbecque, were incontestably to leave their mark on the 1930's. Paris-Roubaix 1926 was to be the theatre for a tremendous showdown between the generations.

All of these riders came to the starting line in a very determined mood. The cloudburst which had made the road wet did not cool the aggressive ardour, for the race shot off at top speed.

It took less than the quarter of an hour for Henri, Francis and Charles Pélissier, accompanied by Depauw, Sausin and Notter, to leave the main bunch at five hundred metres.

The stars of the peloton such as Christophe, Verschueren, Souchard,

Amiens, 4 April 1926 Paris-Roubaix.
A general view of the feeding zone of Amiens.

4 April 1926,
Paris-Roubaix on the road to Amiens

Bottechia, Frantz and Debaets all worked hard, but they were incapable of pulling back one second on the runaways.

Several incidents hampered the progress of the small leading group: Francis punctured at Conflans, as did Sausin at Balincourt, then the Swiss Notter weakened and the enterprise was condemned as the numbers had become so unequal. The main bunch quickly rejoined Henri, Francis and Depauw.

This display of force by the Pélissiers nevertheless had the merit of thinning out the leading bunch - there were no more than thirty eight of them together at Breteuil.

Entering Amiens Henri Pélissier attacked again. Only ten men were able to go with him. With the exception of the puncture victims Debaets and Benoit, they were still together on the hill of Doullens.

Henri Pélissier seemed to be really motivated. For a long time the flag-carrier of the Automoto team, a difference with his boss Mr Montet during the winter made him decide to change teams. Moving to 'Dilecta' with his brothers, he had a strong desire to prove that his former employer was wrong in thinking that he was finished. In such circumstances a third success at Roubaix would have the greatest impact.

The Frenchmen led the dance on the hill of Doullens with Marcel Colleu and four Belgians stuck to his wheel: Delbecque, Van Slembrouck, Eelen and a young professional

1926

(Nouvelle Série) — 8me ANNÉE — N° 15 — Dimanche 11 Avril 1926

LE GRAND

40 CENTIMES le Numéro

Bureaux : 77, Rue Nationale, LILLE

Les annonces sont reçues au Bureau du Journal, à Lille, et dans les Agences de Publicité, à Paris.

ABONNEMENTS (Nord et Limitrophes), **18 francs** par an.
Autres départements français, **20 francs**. — Belgique, **22 francs**.

Hebdomadaire Illustré
DE LA RÉGION DU NORD DE LA FRANCE

LA COURSE CYCLISTE PARIS-ROUBAIX

LE VAINQUEUR DE L'ÉPREUVE, LE BELGE JULIEN DELEBECQUE, PHOTOGRAPHIÉ A SON ARRIVÉE A ROUBAIX

of twenty one, Gaston Rebry.

Pélissier was driving the leading group along as far as Pont-de-Courrières where a puncture prevented him from playing a leading role any more. He would never again see the front of the race.

While those in the bunch saw all hope disappearing, Julien Delbecque seemed to be the freshest of the leaders.

The Belgian increased his attacks and by Seclin had got rid of Colleu, Eelen and the astonishing Rebry.

There was only one more young man on his wheel, Gustave Van Slembrouck, already second in the recent Tour of Flanders.

The last few kilometres were only a formality for Julien Delbecque who was able to cross the finishing line with his arms raised to the sky.

His victory was certainly very well applauded, but the people of Roubaix were becoming a little disappointed at the Belgian domination. Henri Pélissier was sixth and Marcel Colleu eighth but the Belgians monopolised the first four places.

For Delbecque it was ample confirmation of his success in the Tour of Flanders the previous year. 1926 was to prove to be an excellent year for this slim champion, weighing only sixty five kilos, as he was to win the difficult Circuit of Champagne before finishing second in the Belgian Championship and in Bordeaux-Paris.

Following the example of Paul Deman his career would be held back by gastric problems which forced him to give up racing in 1930 at the age of twenty seven.

As for Eugène Christophe, the most faithful of the faithful he had just completed his fourteenth and last Paris-Roubaix. Present on the roads of this Northern classic since 1904, he decided at the age of 41 it was time to hang up his wheels.

The "Old Gaulois" could hand over to the young ones, notably to Gaston Rebry, who by finishing third in his first participation had dazzled the public and the followers. Without any doubt a rider with a future.

1926

LES GLOIRES DU CYCLISME
DELBECQUE

Julien DELBECQUE
(Belgium, 1903-1977)

A typical hard working Flandrian, he achieved success early in his career with victories in the Tour of Flanders and.....Paris-Roubaix.

1925 : Tour of Flanders
1926 : Paris-Roubaix,
       Circuit de Champagne,
       2nd Belgian Championship,
       2nd Bordeaux-Paris
1927 : Circuit de Champagne,
       2nd Belgian Championship
1928 : 2nd Tour of Belgium

QUELQUES CHAMPIONS ET QUELQUES VICTOIRES
TOUR DE BELGIQUE 1927
PARIS-ROUBAIX 1926
CIRCUIT DE CHAMPAGNE 1926
ETOILES DE FRANCE 1926
TOUR DE FRANCE 1927
(16e Etape)
1er

à'ARMOR

L. MATTON. MAUCLAIR DELBECQUE VERVAEKE

CYCLES & MOTOS "ARMOR" 23, Avene Trudaine, PARIS.

GAILLARD _ PARIS-AMIENS

1. Julien DELBECQUE (Belgium)
2. Gustave VAN SLEMBROUCK (Belgium)
3. Gaston REBRY (Belgium)
4. Lode EELEN (Belgium)
5. Kastor NOTTER (Belgium)
6. Henri PELISSIER (France)
7. Félix SELLIER (Belgium)
8. Marcel COLLEU (France)
9. Camille VANDECASTEELE (Belgium)
10. Adelin BENOIT (Belgium)

MERCREDI 20 AVRIL 1927.   PRIX : UN FRANC   CINQUIEME ANNEE. — N° 185

La Pédale

REVUE HEBDOMADAIRE DU CYCLE

32 PAGES

17, Faubourg Montmartre, PARIS (9°)
Téléphone : GUTENBERG 45-13

RONSSE, qui fournira le vainqueur du 28° Paris-Roubaix *(sur Bicyclette AUTOMOTO)*, est premier en haut de Doullens, devant Ch. PÉLISSIER.

George Ronsse
makes a name for himself

Paris-Roubaix 1927 was not the most memorable edition of the great race. There were too many abstentions - Henri Pélissier was injured and a non-starter for the first time in many a long year - other withdrawals, more or less justified, were Bottecchia, hardly at home on the cobbles, Debaets and the Swiss brothers Heiri and Max Suter.

Another surprising fact was that Doullens hill no longer played any part in the final selection of the race. This was confirmation of the impression so many people had had over the previous few years. The only ones who had any misgivings about it were those who were without any form. Most of the race followers and journalists regretted the lack of aggressive spirit in the bunch.

The 1927 race kept the spectators waiting a long time before any real action took place. Beautiful Spring weather certainly toned down the aggressiveness of the riders. The crowds at St Germain, Pontoise and Méru saw a compact bunch of one hundred and twenty three riders dawdle past.

Any action was due solely to punctures, notably those suffered by former winners Van Hevel and Delbecque, and more seriously the crash of the Belgian Standaert who was forced to retire.

At Amiens the leading group was one hundred strong. Before the passage to Doullens, the race seemed deadlocked.

At the foot of the slope, Belgium's George Ronsse "led the train" in front of Charles Pélissier. The two men crossed over the top of the hill with a small lead. They quickly decided to pursue their adventure. The presence of the youngest of the Pélissiers surprised no one. Charles was of the calibre of his two brothers, but even the Belgian followers were surprised to see Ronsse in the lead.

The young man, in his second year as a professional had only just celebrated his twenty first birthday. Certainly in 1926 he had shown his winner's temperament on several occasions but being in the lead of the Paris-Roubaix was really a giant step forward for him.

His pace was fluid although this hardly worried his companion. Behind them the tempo was whipped up by Gaston Rebry. After a pursuit match of twenty six kilometres the two runaways were caught at Beaumetz-les-Loges. It was back to square one.

The feeding station at Arras was getting close. The riders only stopped for a brief moment and grabbed the supplies that were necessary to negotiate the difficult cobbled sectors of the mining area.

Against all expectations the restless Ronsse refused his bag of food and his bottle in order to get away again. In the confusion he rapidly gained several hundred metres. The young rider from Antwerp was skilled, he made light of the difficulties, jumping from one pavement to another and like an old veteran he weaved his way through the cars to gain more of a lead!

In addition to which he was cunning for, he allowed himself to be rejoined before Hénin-Liétard. Ronsse saw about twenty riders get up to him, his attack had thinned out the ranks of the peloton. A number of favourites were no longer there: an off-colour Francis Pélissier, but also Achille Souchard, Toto Grassin and several others. Nevertheless several stars escaped the trap such as Charles Pélissier, Julien Delbecque, Adelin Benoit, Julien Vervaecke and this devil Gaston Rebry.

In the last few kilometres the pace quickened considerably and finally it was sixteen men who arrived together at the bottom

1927

Georges RONSSE
(Belgium, 1906-1969)

The first Belgian winner of the World road championship in 1928, he also won it the following year. Ronsse also took many of the calendars top classics.

1927 : Paris-Roubaix, Bordeaux-Paris,
       3rd Paris-Tours
1928 : World Champion, Paris-Brussels,
       2nd Paris-Roubaix
1929 : World Champion,
       Bordeaux-Paris,
       2nd Belgian Championship,
       2nd Paris-Roubaix,
       2nd Tour of Flanders,
       3rd Paris-Tours
1930 : Bordeaux-Paris,
       3rd World Championships
1932 : 2nd Paris-Roubaix,
       3rd Paris-Brussels
1933 : 3rd Tour of Belgium

9me Année — N° 17 — Dimanche 24 Avril 1927

LE GRAND

Bureaux : 77, Rue Nationale, LILLE

Les annonces sont reçues au Bureau du Journal, à Lille, et dans les Agences de Publicité, à Paris.

ABONNEMENTS (Nord et Limitrophes), **18 francs** par an. Autres départements français, **20 francs**. — Belgique, **22 francs**.

40 CENTIMES le Numéro

Hebdomadaire Illustré

DE LA RÉGION DU NORD DE LA FRANCE

LE 28ᵉ PARIS-ROUBAIX

RONSSE, LE VAINQUEUR DE L'ÉPREUVE, PORTÉ EN TRIOMPHE A SON ARRIVÉE A ROUBAIX

of the Avenue des Villas. Most people fancied Charles Pélissier's chances. Unfortunately for the Parisian two riders opened a small gap in the last kilometre; the man from Marseilles Joseph Curtel, who, it has to be said did not often shine in top events and the untiring George Ronsse!

The battle over the last few metres was terrific. Witnesses saw Curtel apparently win by the width of a tyre. A few seconds later the 'fanfare' played the French national anthem, an event that had been waited for here since 1921!

At last a Frenchman had won, six years after Henri Pélissier, Curtel was carried in triumph - but then came the official announcement of the result.

The finishing judge announced: First George Ronsse, Belgium, second Curtel, France.

There was almost a riot. The incident provoked several fights between supporters and some people even threatened to lynch the officials.

Ronsse and his powerful team manager, Pierrard, were filled with joy. Rumour had it that Pierrard had played a part in this amazing reversal of fortune.

Ronsse was savouring a success that was totally deserved. This victory was to mark the start of a superb career which was to be crowned with two world titles.

Several weeks later, Ronsse started the Bordeaux-Paris. At the Parc des Princes six men contested the sprint finish. Ronsse was convincingly first by several lengths to pick up the first of his three victories in the paced classic.

1927

1. Georges RONSSE (Belgium)
2. Joseph CURTEL (France)
3. Charles PELISSIER (France)
4. Julien DELBECQUE (Belgium)
5. Adelin BENOIT (Belgium)
6. Romain BELLENGER (France)
7. René HAMEL (France)
8. André VERBIST (Belgium)
9. Léopold MATTON (Belgium)
10. Alexandre MAES (Belgium)

PARIS-ROUBAIX (260 kil.) 1ᵉʳ Georges RONSSE

sur Bicyclette

AUTOMOTO

JANTES BOSTON
FREIN/BOWDEN

152 Avenue Malakoff.
–PARIS–

AUTOMOTO a remporté les Tours de France 1923-24-25-26 et les Championnats de France 1923-24-25-26

The peloton chats at the start.

The feed at Amiens. Rebry and Lucien Buysse.

"Dede" in paradise

For several years the Belgians had completely dominated this Northern event. The memory of Henri Pélissier's victory in 1921 was fading fast. Faced with the talented new young Flemish generation led by George Ronsse and Gaston Rebry, the French champions seemed to have an inferiority complex.

Against all expectations, French cycling was going to lift its head again in this 29th Paris-Roubaix. No less than six riders from the hexagon of France would achieve the exploit of finishing among the first fifteen!

The triumph belonged to André Leducq who confirmed the talent which had been revealed in the 1927 Tour de France when he finished fourth.

Leducq had already taken part in two Paris-Roubaix, in 1926 and 1927. The first time, due to lack of experience he had retired at Amiens. The following year he was in the leading group when a puncture destroyed his chances. He finished frustrated in seventeenth position, riding the fixed wheel which had been imposed on him as an economy measure by Ludovic Feuillet his team manager!

The popular "Dede" had carefully prepared for his revenge. After a first success in Paris-Le Havre, a week before this Northern rendezvous, he went to the severe and famous training camp of the Velo Club Levallois directed by the "Father Ruinart".

Physically but above all psychologically well prepared, he came to the start full of confidence. This public joker surprised even his companions on the road as this time he was totally serious the whole day long.

Nevertheless, to win the event he had to overcome several other serious contenders such as the Belgians led by Georges Ronsse, Gaston Rebry, Julien Vervaecke and Jules Van Hevel, as well as others, such as Kastor Notter, Nicholas Frantz and the Frenchmen Antonin Magne, Marcel Bidot and the evergreen Pélissiers.

Right from the start the race was lively. Before Doullens the attacks were too numerous to count. However, the first really serious offensive started at Arras. Ronsse wanted to test the water and went away in the streets of the town.

Charles Pélissier and the astonishing Belgian Meunier understood the danger and latched onto his wheel before they reached Hénin-Liétard. Rebry and the attentive Leducq also made the junction a little later.

The right break was launched. Leducq's plan was working marvellously. A puncture twenty five kilometres from the finish did nothing to dent his confidence. Instead of panicking he changed his tyre and turned his wheel round, thus taking advantage of a 17-tooth sprocket in place of his 18-tooth one. He restarted with a big gear of 47 x17!

It seemed that the five champions were going to arrive together at the Avenue des Villas. However two men were dropped just a few kilometres from Roubaix. First of all Charles Pélissier had not consumed enough food and suddenly "blew up" in a big way just five kilometres from the line. He was totally unable to cover them and took refuge in a cafe. The youngest of the Pélissier brothers was perhaps the fastest of the five men and had just lost his best chance of winning Paris-Roubaix.

The other victim, Rebry, was overcome with stomach cramps.

André LEDUCQ
(France, 1904-1980)

Known as "Dédé" he was one of the most popular professionals of the 1930's. A double winner of the Tour de France - winning over twenty stages - he was a "complete" rider with a fine record in the classics.

1924 : World Amateur Champion
1928 : Paris-Roubaix, 2nd Tour de France,
2nd French Championship
1929 : 3rd French Championship
1930 : Tour de France
1931 : Paris-Tours,
3rd French Championship
1932 : Tour de France
1933 : Criterium National
1935 : 2nd Paris-Roubaix

1928

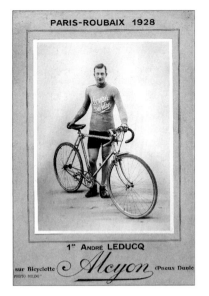

PARIS-ROUBAIX 1928

1ᵉʳ André LEDUCQ
sur Bicyclette *Alcyon* (Pneus Dunlo)

Three men remained in command: Ronsse in his purple Automoto jersey, André and Meunier. The latter, a professional since 1926, had never really achieved anything of note before. Race followers were intrigued to see how he followed the established stars over the cobbles without apparently suffering at all. Nobody knew how fast he was in a sprint. This lack of information was going to affect the way the final sprint took place as Ronsse mistrusted Leducq but felt obliged to keep an eye on Meunier.

It was a worried Ronsse who started the sprint too early. Leducq could never have asked for so much. Stuck to the Belgian's wheel he had absolutely no trouble in coming past him in the last fifty metres. Ronsse was several lengths down and Meunier even farther back. Rebry finished fourth at twenty seconds.

The popular Leducq was carried aloft in triumph. At last a "tricolour" had won at Roubaix. His success was so clear-cut that even the Belgians applauded. At twenty eight years, Paris-Roubaix had opened the gates of paradise to him. He confirmed the hopes placed on him since 1924, the year when the Parisian had won the world amateur championship in Paris.

This first important success was to herald many others as for example two Tours de France in 1930 and 1932 and Paris-Tours in 1931. His simplicity and his kindness were to make him the most popular rider of them all in the 1930's.

Among the first fifteen, other than Leducq, the French finished in positions of honour. Achille Souchard was fifth, Bonney eighth, Cuvelier tenth, Bidot eleventh and Magne fourteenth.

This success made up for the poor performance of the Pélissiers. Charles missed out on the chance of a lifetime. Henri made his last appearance in the race and Francis did not finish.

If that was not enough the latter two were victims of a road accident on the way back to Roubaix. Their car hit a tree and finished upside down in a ditch. For the first time since 1919 there was no Pélissier was at the finish.

1928

1. André LEDUCQ (France)
2. Georges RONSSE (Belgium)
3. Charles MEUNIER (Belgium)
4. Gaston REBRY (Belgium)
5. Achille SOUCHARD (France)
6. Jules VAN HEVEL (Belgium)
7. Louis DELANNOY (Belgium)
8. Maurice BONNEY (France)
9. Hector MARTIN (Belgium)
10. Georges CUVELIER (France)

QUELQUES VICTOIRES D' *Alcyon* EN 1928

TOUR DE FRANCE
1ᵉʳ FRANTZ — 2ᵉ LEDUCQ
TOUR DES PAYS BASQUES
1ᵉʳ DEWAELE — 2ᵉ LEDUCQ
PARIS - ROUBAIX
1ᵉʳ LEDUCQ
PARIS - RENNES
1ᵉʳ FRANTZ
PARIS - LE HAVRE
1ᵉʳ LEDUCQ

Tous sur Bicyclette type super Tour de France autogène
PNEUS "DUNLOP"

FRANTZ   LEDUCQ

10me Année — N° 16 — Dimanche 15 Avril 1928

LE GRAND

Bureaux : 77, Rue Nationale, LILLE

Les annonces sont reçues au Bureau du Journal, à Lille, et dans les Agences de Publicité, à Paris

ABONNEMENTS (Nord et Limitrophes), **18 francs** par an.
Autres départements français, **20 francs**. — Belgique, **22 francs**.

40 Centimes le Numéro

Hebdomadaire Illustré

DE LA RÉGION DU NORD DE LA FRANCE

LE 29e PARIS-ROUBAIX

LEDUCQ, LE VAINQUEUR DE L'ÉPREUVE, PHOTOGRAPHIÉ A L'ARRIVÉE A ROUBAIX

(Voir texte page 253)

Charles Meunier
in spite of Georges Ronsse

The 31st March remains engraved in the memory of Georges Ronsse. He was clearly the strongest man on that day during the Paris-Roubaix. He failed completely by only taking a second place that was to remain a very bad memory. It was the day on which he learnt the lesson that in sport, as in another things, it is sometimes not enough to be the best in order to win.

At the start at Le Vésinet, the Belgians had decided to wipe out the snub inflicted on them by Leducq the previous year. With this object in mind, the Tour of Flanders disputed a fortnight before, helped them to polish up their form. Joseph Dervaes won it but the man who had dominated it was Ronsse. However the latter dressed in his rainbow jersey had suffered more than his share of bad luck - a crash just before the finish had robbed him of all hope of winning.

Faced with Ronsse and his compatriots, the chances of the French on the Northern roads seemed rather slim once again.

Leducq was not in devastating form and it seemed that Paul Le Drogo had not yet recovered from the efforts that he had made in the Paris-Le Havre. As for the young prodigy Jean Maréchal, he was only nineteen.

From the start it was an icy wind which blew in to the faces of the riders who, for the first and the last time, would arrive at the Amédée-Prouvost stadium at Wattrelos. In their own self interest, the organisers had abandoned the Avenue des Villas. It was much easier to demand an entrance fee to a sports arena. As expected the stands were crowded and the receipts excellent.

Passing through Pontoise

Up to Doullens, the bunch..... of followers, apart from punctures and crashes, had nothing to get excited about. The Belgians seemed to have the situation perfectly in hand, for no break was allowed to form without one of them. At the start of the Doullens climb Julien Vervaecke and Van Rossem decided to launch a big attack. After a dazzling acceleration they went clear of the bunch. Mauclair and Foucaux, two Frenchmen latched on to their wheels.

At the top of the climb Vervaecke had thirty seconds on Mauclair, forty on Van Rossem, fifty on Foucaux and more than two minutes on the bunch.

On the plateau of Arras there was little cooperation between the escapees. So, by the feeding station in the town, they were joined by a bunch of twenty five men.

World champion Ronsse could no longer restrain himself. Along with his La Française team-mates Aimé Déolet and Charles Meunier he attacked. Only Alfred Hamerlinck, another Belgian could follow them.

Ronsse was crafty. He knew that as they crossed through the mining area the road became narrow, that the thick suffocating dust was raised above head height. The man from Antwerp also knew that the spectators formed two ranks which only left a small passage for the champions of the road. In short all these conditions were extremely favourable to a breakaway.

The four men devoured the cobblestones at more than forty kilometres an hour. Behind them in the thick barrier of dust there was panic.

While the rapid Hamerlinck was eliminated from the contest with a puncture at Hénin-Liétard, the leading trio increased their lead.

Of the three, just as in the Tour of Flanders, Ronsse was clearly the strongest. He did not flinch at doing most of the work. Meunier occasionally did his turn. As for the young Déolet, he seemed quite happy just to be able to stay with his team-mates.

In everybody's minds, riders and followers alike, the finishing order could only be: First Ronsse, second Meunier and third Déolet.

A puncture to Ronsse sixteen kilometres from Roubaix delayed his progress a little but he rejoined without difficulty and his superiority was such that he made no attempt to drop

1929

Charles MEUNIER
(Belgium, 1903-1971)

He made his name as an "independent", a semi-professional rider and enjoyed a brief professional career with a victory in a classic ...Paris-Roubaix.

1928 : 3rd Paris-Roubaix
4th Belgian Championship,
5th Bordeaux-Paris
1929 : Paris-Roubaix, 2nd Paris-Lille
4th Brussels-Paris

the two men, as the result of the sprint was so obvious.

As they approached the Amédée Prouvost-stadium, as expected Ronsse was leading in front of Meunier and Déolet. It was in this order that the men entered the arena. On the cinder track in order to avoid crashing they were only riding at walking pace. Ronsse had a lead of several metres and could not be beaten when - catastrophe, he slid on the last bend. Déolet could not avoid him.

By the time Ronsse was on his feet he realised that his front wheel was broken. His bicycle was unrideable. He got up just in time to see the victory of Meunier.

He was totally disillusioned as he painfully crossed the line in second position with his bike on his shoulder. Once across this line he threw the machine down in a rage and collapsed in tears.

Paris-Roubaix after the Tour of Flanders, was the rest of his season to be cursed with bad luck?

The irritation, the crowd, the defective organisation and the inadequate security all led to the inevitable: the public invaded the track. A few minutes later the bunch arrived but it was stopped at the entrance to the stadium by officials who cancelled the sprint for fourth place.

This turbulent finish would cause a lot of ink to flow. The question came fast and furious: "How can you finish such a prestigious classic such as the Paris-Roubaix on a cinder track? It is unacceptable. What would have happened if a big group was sprinting for first place? "

The outcome was regrettable but the Belgians, as expected had shown themselves to be unbeatable. The French who were hardly brilliant at the start of the race had later fallen apart. Certainly some of them were unlucky but in the final analysis it was a bitter failure.

In the days that followed, certain journalists, perhaps a little facetiously, were going to ask another question: "Why do the French still insist in taking part in this race made for the Belgians ?"

1929

left:
Georges Ronsse at the entrance
to the stadium in front of Meunier and Déolet.

1. Charles MEUNIER (Belgium)
2. Georges RONSSE (Belgium)
3. Aimé DEOLET (Belgium)
4. Armand VAN BRUANE (Belgium)
5. Gaston REBRY (Belgium)
6. Alfred HAMERLINCK (Belgium)
7. Joseph MAUCLAIR (France)
   Camille FOUCAUX (France)
   Julien VERVAECKE (Belgium)

Charles is first across the finishing line.

The peloton advances.

Maréchal declassified after "the affair"

The finish of the 1927 Paris-Roubaix had provoked several disputes, that of 1929 a lot of rumblings. However, up until that time injustice had not been flagrant. The outcome of the 1930 edition was to leave a lot of regrets as much to the spectators as to poor Jean Maréchal who claimed up until the end of his life that a prestigious victory had been stolen from him.

On the 20th April 1930, there were only a few minutes left before the finish of the thirty first Paris-Roubaix. Two men had been in the lead for nearly sixty five kilometres. By dint of obstinacy and of courage they had been able to withstand pressure from the bunch. There was the magnificent Jean Maréchal, bursting with health and the Belgian Vervaecke. The latter stayed desperately glued to the wheel of the French champion. The orders of his team manager Ludovic Feuillet were: "I forbid you to work." As it was scarcely conceivable to disobey Feuillet, the Belgian complied.

Suddenly, to the great astonishment of Maréchal, Vervaecke attacked!

He jumped onto the pavement in front of the Parisian who, totally surprised, lost fifteen metres. Maréchal enraged to see what he called "the wheel-sucker" take off, got back on to his wheel and wanted to get in front of him. But at this spot the passage was narrow, the champions touched elbows: a collision was inevitable. Vervaecke lost his balance and somersaulted into the ditch. Promptly he got back on his machine. Maréchal only possessed a few metres lead but he was unleashed.

Liberated, he was assured of his victory, Vervaecke was dropped for good. For this young man of twenty, the Avenue des Villas seemed like a triumphal way. He rode the last few metres to the acclaim of the public not knowing whether to laugh

or cry.

Twenty four seconds later, Vervaecke arrived. Immediately he wanted to remonstrate with Maréchal who was slowly coming round after the terrific effort he had made. Ludovic Feuillet protested. He lodged a complaint and demanded that Maréchal be declassified.

The Belgian supporters protested claiming that "Vervaecke had been pushed into a ditch full of water".

In an atmosphere of extreme tension the commissaires came together to listen to the different versions of the accident. Romain Bellenger explained: "Our car was alongside the two riders. Vervaecke was on the pavement and attacked. Maréchal was riding on the cobbles and he too jumped onto the pavement. As he tried to restablish his balance he touched elbows with Vervaecke who fell. It was as simple as that." For his part Maréchal swore that it was a simple collision. Feuillet's version was different of course.

It seemed to be agreed that Maréchal's action was involuntary. Therefore he could not be disqualified. But it also appeared that Vervaecke had been wronged. After long discussions Maréchal was demoted to second place. This punishment was surprising, for according to the rules if Maréchal was guilty then he should have been disqualified and if he was not then the protest should have been simply rejected.

However, it seemed that the other interests already had an influence on the results that were purely sporting. A few observers noted that Vervaecke and Feuillet both worked for Alcyon Cycles who would be in a position to pay for entire pages of advertising in all of the dailies. The young Maréchal, equipped by Mr Colin, a modest Parisian constructor, would never be able to do this. For many this was the real reason for the official result.

However the day promised to be a good one. Another Belgian victory seemed inevitable. From the start the eighty six contestants followed the "Vivasix" Renault of the young race director, Jacques Goddet, and were already getting ready for the climb to the top of the hill of Cormeilles where Jean Maréchal went through in the lead.

1930

Julien VERVAECKE.

Julien VERVAECKE
(Belgium, 1899-1940)

Brother of Félicien, the King of the Mountains in the Tour de France, Julien specialised in the single-day classics.

1924 : Circuit France-Belgium
1926 : Circuit France-Belgium
1927 : 3rd Tour de France
1928 : Grand Prix of Wolber
1930 : Paris-Roubaix
1931 : 4th Bordeaux-Paris
1932 : Paris-Brussels
1933 : 2nd Paris-Roubaix

The crowd at the finish.

All day long the race was lively, one attack followed another. At Doullens Jules Merviel and the Austrian Max Bulla preceded Antonin Magne by a minute and a half, with the peloton at three minutes. As the race went through Arras the positions had changed, Julien Vervaecke, Leander Gyssels and Maréchal had a lead of three minutes on a small group of survivors. There remained sixty five kilometres but the race was over.

Gyssels could not sustain the pace imposed by his two adversaries. Maréchal kept attacking and as they passed through Hénin-Liétard Vervaecke found it difficult to stay with him. For several kilometres the "Maréchal kid" led the race but a puncture at Carvin stopped him in his tracks. Vervaecke went past him but not for long. Maréchal "tickled" the pedals and came back to him in just a few hundreds metres. But soon the dream would turn into a nightmare.

A fortnight after the demonstration at Roubaix, Paris-Tours was run. There were no more pavements to jump, no more ditches and this time Maréchal was the undisputed winner. On that day once again he proved himself to be the best.

Sunday the 20th April 1930 would remain engraved on his memory.

For his part, Julien Vervaecke was to win Paris-Brussels 1932 and would often return to the roads of this Northern classic.

The Belgian had a sad end when in May 1940 he was shot by Polish soldiers (*) of the British army. He was firmly opposed to the requisitioning of his furniture. During a war such things are not forgiven.

(*) Translator's note: An enquiry by a certain Jean-Paul Delcroix argued that Vervaecke was shot by soldiers of the Middlesex Regiment.

1930

left: Julien Vervaecke hopes for victory.   Jean Maréchal believes that he has won.

The finish on the Avenue des Villas at Roubaix.

Entry of the "bulldog"

Since the revival in 1919, Paris-Roubaix had been dominated by Belgian champions. Certainly, several exceptional riders such as Henri Pélissier, André Leducq and Heiri Suter figured among the records, but the little world of cycling from now on was forced to recognise the domination of the riders of the kingdom of Belgium over these Northern cobbles.

The thirty second edition of the classic, disputed on the 5th April 1931 was to confirm the supremacy and amplify the rout of the tricolours. In fact, at the finish, there were nine Belgians in the first ten. Only Charles Pélissier, an excellent second was able to compete at the same level for practically the whole day.

The honours were taken by Gaston Rebry, nicknamed the "Bulldog" because of his small size and his crouched appearance on a bicycle. This champion rapidly became the first "Mr Paris-Roubaix" four decades before Roger De Vlaeminck.

From 1926, at the age of twenty one, Rebry had already shown his class by finishing third in the City of the Mills. Since then he had actively participated in each edition with some success by being classed 14th in 1927, fourth in 1928 and fifth the following year.

He was the type of roadman perfectly suited to this legendary event, but Rebry had nevertheless to overcome a terrible handicap, for his lack of sprinting ability

meant that he had to finish alone in order to win.

On the 5th April 1931 Easter Sunday was flooded. The rain froze the one hundred and two starters who crowded towards the control pint at Luna Park.

The forty eight Belgians formed nearly half of the peloton. Opposing them were thirty eight Frenchmen as well as two Luxembourgers, one Swiss, one Austrian and, surprisingly, no less than a dozen Germans. The riders from the other side of the Rhine had came for the unique purpose of familiarising themselves with the French roads ready for the next Tour de France.

Under the rain Gaston Rebry kept his smile, unlike many others, and at the start he perfectly expressed the confidence of his compatriots: "Today will be a 'fete' day for us." The fete was going to effectively become a national holiday for the Belgians.

From the start at Argenteuil the race went off like a rocket. Jean Maréchal wanted to avoid the worst and took the first prime of two thousand francs at the top of Cormeilles Hill .

The fast pace discouraged all escape attempts and it was compact bunch that crossed Beauvais, then Amiens, where the only incident of note was the retirement of André Leducq.

The outcome of the race was to be sealed a little before Doullens hill. The storm obliged the riders to form several echelons. The best riders were to be found in the first of these: Gaston Rebry, Emile Joly, Georges Ronsse, Emile Decroix and Charles Pélissier. The second group comprising Maréchal, Loncke, Van Slembrouck, Félicien Vervaecke and Martin followed twenty metres behind.

Behind these men the bunch had exploded and only Marcel Bidot, Jean Aerts and the German Buse looked as if they might be able to get back.

1931

Just before the opening of the Cafe 'Au Paris-Roubaix' belonging to Gaston Rebry

For a few kilometres the gaps remained the same, but Rebry wanted a more comfortable lead. He turned up the wick. At the back both Jean Maréchal and Gérard Loncke understood the danger and after an intensive effort they managed to latch on to the leading group at the foot of Doullens hill.

At the top of the climb, Rebry who was increasing the pressure, was first over in front of Ronsse and Joly and then came Charles and Decroix.

Maréchal and Loncke who had not recovered from their efforts, lost one hundred metres. They would no longer see the front of the race, as was to be the case of the trio comprising Van Slembrouck, Vervaecke and Dervaes who went through with a deficit of five hundred metres.

Rebry now had the bit between his teeth and led the runaways tirelessly. Their lead over the survivors never stopped growing.

In the mining sector the followers already started to speculate on the chances of Charles Pélissier in the sprint. The odds on the talented Parisian went even higher when surprisingly Ronsse was the first to be dropped twenty kilometres from Roubaix!

As the rain lashed down, Rebry decided to take things in hand. He attacked at Vendeville. With the greatest of difficulty only Emile Joly could go with him. Emile Decroix and Charles Pélissier had reached their limit.

The "Bulldog" was hardly happy - he knew what a good sprinter his compatriot was. He wanted to get rid of him as quickly as possible. The task was made easy for him when Joly punctured at Lesquin.

The way was open to Rebry who went on to win "his" Paris-Roubaix.

To the acclaim of a public who had forgotten all about the bad weather he finished on the Avenue des Villas. 1min. 42sec late, Charles Pélissier had no trouble disposing of Emile Decroix. Georges Ronsse and the unfortunate Emile Joly both finished at four minutes.

While Rebry was carried off in triumph, the youngest of the Pélissiers told the story of his race to the journalists: "For several months I have kept to a diet which has been so strict that I hoped it would one day pay off. I have been known as a good trackman. Now they will be forced to admit that I am nor a bad roadman either. Today I had the will to win and I suffered. My popularity has been criticised, but today nobody can say that I have not done all I can to justify it."

This performance was relatively unexpected as a few days beforehand he was still riding on the track at the Velodrome d'Hiver in the Paris Six-Day.

Unfortunately, Pélissier was the exception that confirmed the rule as you had to go down to twentieth place to find one of his compatriots, the young professional Albert Barthélemy.

In 1931, even the Germans did better on these Northern roads.

1931

Gaston REBRY
(Belgium, 1905-1953)

The first "Mr Paris-Roubaix" long before the appearance of Roger De Vlaeminck. The "Bulldog" possessed all the qualities to succeed in Paris-Roubaix, which he won three times.

1924 : 2nd Paris-Menin
1925 : Paris-Nantes, 3rd Paris-Roubaix
1928 : 4th Paris-Roubaix
1929 : 5th Paris-Roubaix
1931 : Paris-Roubaix, 4th Tour de France
1934 : Paris-Roubaix, Tour of Flanders, Paris-Nice
1935 : Paris-Roubaix
1936 : 3rd Paris-Roubaix

1. Gaston REBRY (Belgium)
2. Charles PELISSIER (France)
3. Emile DECROIX (Belgium)
4. Georges RONSSE (Belgium)
5. Emile JOLY (Belgium)
6. Josef DEMUYSERE (Belgium)
7. Alfons SCHEPERS (Belgium)
8. Gustave VAN SLEMBROUCK (Belgium)
9. Romain GIJSSELS (Belgium)
10. Armand VAN BRUANE (Belgium)

DEMAIN SE COURT LA PREMIERE GRANDE EPREUVE INTERNATIONALE SUR ROUTE

LE XXXIIᵉ PARIS=ROUBAIX

Tous les " As " belges, allemands et français au départ. -- Nos routiers auront, cette année encore, beaucoup de peine à décrocher la victoire.

BEHEER EN PUBLICITEIT
Nieuwbrug, 13, Brussel
Telefoon : 17.27.08

OPSTEL
Em. Jacqmainlaan, 127, Brussel
Telefoon : 17.2796 — 17.2797

Telegramadr.: Sportwereld-Brussel

BESTUURDER :
KAREL VAN WYNENDAELE

SPORTWERELD

EN
HET ALGEMEEN NIEUWS
DAGBLAD

Stichter : LEON VAN DEN HAUTE

40 CENTIEM 40 CENTIEM

19e JAAR   Nr 3146

MAANDAG
28
MAART 1932

ABONNEMENTEN
          Binnenland Buitenland
3 maand   30 fr.   45 fr.
6 maand   55 fr.   90 fr.
12 maand   110 fr.   170 fr.

Postcheckrekening 3256

ROMAIN GIJSSELS, beslist een der beste baanrijders van de gansche wereld, wint, aan meer dan 37 km. per uur,

PARIJS-ROBAAIS

HET REKORD VAN DE KOERS GEKLOPT; MET WIND IN HET VOORDEEL WORDEN DE 255 KM. AFGELEGD IN 6.49 UUR. — NA 58 KM. ONTSNAPPEN DE FRANSCHEN MERVIEL EN MAUCLAIR, EN WORDEN EERST 60 KM. VERDER INGELOOPEN DOOR ROOSEMONT EN LE DROGO. — VANAF DOULLENS BEGON HET GROOTE OFFENSIEF. — DE WEGLOOPERS WERDEN BIJGEHAALD EN OVERSTOKEN DOOR PEGLION EN MARCEL BIDOT MET DEN DUITSCHER SIRONSKY. — DANK AAN RONSSE, ROMAIN GIJSSELS, SCHEPERS EN JAN AERTS WERD HET TEN SLOTTE TOCH EEN BELGISCHE ZEGE, ALS WIJ OP 25 KM. VAN DE AANKOMST MEENDEN DAT WIJ NIET MEER KONDEN WINNEN. — DEMUYSERE, MARTIN EN REBRY LEVERDEN PUIK WERK, MAAR HADDEN, SPIJTIG GENOEG MET TEGENSLAG AF TE REKENEN

Eene moeilijke maar geestdriftig bevochten Belgische overwinning

De rapste en misschien wel de schoonste Parijs-Robaais, die wij ooit mochten volgen, is gisteren geëindigd met een algemeen verwachte maar daarom niet minder achterwaartsche Belgische overwinning. Want die overwinning werd moeilijk, uiterst moeilijk behaald en bevochten met de meest zooals misschien nooit voordien.

De heele koers door hebben de Franschen, eerst met Merviel, Mauclair en F. Le Drogo,

GIJSSELS   RONSSE

De orde der aankomsten

1. ROMAIN GIJSSELS (Belg) 255 Km. 700 m. in 6 u. 49 m. 58 s. (rekord) (gem. 37 Km. 400 m.) op « Dilecta Wolber ».
2. Georges Ronsse (Belg), op 3 l.
3. Sironski (Duitscher), op 10 meter.
4. Jan Aerts (Belg), op 20 meter.
5. Fons Schepers (Belg), in 6 u. 50 m. 40 s.
6. Demuysere (Belg), in 6 u. 51 m. 13 s.
7. Ghesquière (Belg), in 6 u. 52 m.
8. Decroix (B.), op 1 lengte; 9. J. Vervaecke (Fr.) 8 u. 52 m. 56 s.; 12 Tommies (B.), s u. 53 m. 10 s.; 13. Maréchal; 14. H. Martin; 15. Rebry; 16. F. Vervaecke, 6 u. 54 m.; 17. Peglion 6 u. 55 m.; 18. M. Bidot 6 u. 56 m.; 19. Roosemont; 20. Careyn; 21. Buse; 22. Leducq 6u.58m; 20; 23. A. Magne; 24. John 6 u. 59 m.; 25. Berremans; 26. Deudon; 27. P. Magne 7 u. 2d; Stoepel 7 u 01 s.; 29. Verdijck; 30. Moineau 7 u. 2 m.; 31. Neuhard; 32. Morceis; 33. Olboeter; 34. Blattman; 35. Speicher; 36. Bernard; 37. Perrain; 38. Gevre; 39. Geyer; 40. Kuisbach; 41. Marcaloux; 42. Meerschaut; 43. Loncke; 44. Bonduel; 45. Van Rysselberghe; 46. Reyns; 47. Jan Wauters; 48. Naert; 49. Aumerie; Robitaille; 51.V. Tricht; 52. Bouillet; 53. Buttafochi; 54. Frantz; 55. Goosens; 56. Cornez; 57. Rijaud; 58. Devecht; 59. Balser; 60. Nietschke; 61. Hamerlinck; 62. Louyet; 63. Vivene; 64. Van Hee; 65. Koch; 66. Mertens; 67. Van Hee; 68. Baud; 69. Morelle.

Het regent van het vertrek...

Parijs, het sportieve Parijs, beleefde bij het

Met hen langs de baan

We drukken op de versneller van de « Dodge », die trouwe bewaker en de moeilijkheden...

AERTS

SCHEPERS

MARECHAL IN MOEILIJKHEDEN

DE ZWARTE REEKS...

Morgen komt het hoofdopstel op dit alles terug.

WILLEM VAN WYNENDAELE.

HET STROOVUUR

MERVIEL EN MAUCLAIR BEGEVEN NIET

DE KOERS BEGINT

SYMPATHIE UIT DE WOLKEN

IN DEN ACHTERGROND...

DE HANDEN UIT DE MOUWEN

ROOSEMONT EN FERD. LE DROGO LOOPEN DE LEIDERS IN

DE GROEP STOPT

VOOR DEN BERG VAN DOULLENS

DEMUYSERE

GHESQUIERE

DE BEKLIMMING VAN DOULLENS

WE ACHTERHALEN...

DE KLASSIEKE VLUCHT NAAR ARRAS

WE ZIEN DE KLASSIEKE RONSSE

DECROIX

J. VERVAECKE

VIJF LEIDERS

Romain Gijssels snatches it

At the beginning of the 1930's, the cycling calendar was beginning to expand. In 1932, as well as the traditional Tour of Flanders won by Romain Gijssels and the Mont Faron hill-climb, the French had a new opportunity to prepare for the classics thanks to a new event, the National Criterium. Léon Le Calvez achieved the first of his many wins by beating Pierre Magne and Maurice Archambaud. Up to this time the Italians had never won Paris-Roubaix. Over the years, after the failure of Binda, Linari, and Girardengo there were very few of them to be seen at the start. This tendency was confirmed in the 1932 edition. On the Northern roads they were progressively replaced by the Germans and a handful of Austrians. As was often the case, the first few hours of the race were dominated by the French. On the other hand, and this was much rarer, two of them should have been able to win on the Avenue des Villas.

The race was late in coming alive. The hill of Cormeilles however put paid to the chances of several of them, such as the Algerian Ali Areski, Van Rossem and more surprisingly the former French champion, Bisseron.

At Pontoise an incident was to change the whole face of the event. Gijssels broke his freewheel and was obliged to use a huge gear of 47 x 16. Several times he implored his team manager to change his wheel but the latter, rightly, remained inflexible.

The first movement worthy of any interest was launched near Beauvais by two Frenchman, the man from the South, Jules Merviel and Joseph Mauclair. There remained almost two hundred kilometres to cover and the Belgians preferred to wait patiently for the right moment. For a long time the two men were expecting reinforcements to join the from behind. It was a vain hope, for although both Jean Aerts and Ghesquieres tried, neither of them were able to stay clear from the bunch for very long.

The feeding station at Amiens witnessed indescribable confusion. The two escapees were only a few seconds in front. In the crush, Fernand Le Drogo and the Belgian Roosemont caught Merviel and Mauclair. The movement was relaunched for a few kilometres before Le Drogo punctured and Mauclair weakened, surrendering on the hill of Doullens.

At the top of the climb, the hard working Roosemont and Merviel preceded Mauclair by thirty seconds and were one and a half minutes in front of Louviot who was leading the bunch. The two leaders were unable to resist the pressure from the pursuers for very long. Marcel Bidot took advantage of the regrouping to escape off the front. The Frenchman was the man on form at the beginning of the season. Moreover he was helped in his initiative by the German Herbert Sieronski who was here confirming the talent already seen in the Tour de France.

As they passed through Arras the duo had fifty seconds on Péglion from Marseilles and a little more on a group of sixteen men led by Charles Pélissier and Romain Gijssels.

Over the cobbles, the gap kept growing and for the followers there was no doubt that Bidot was going to win it five years after André Leducq. However, destiny overwhelmed the man from Troyes, for just after Lesquin he was victim of an accursed puncture. For him the race was finished, especially when a second tyre went flat just before the finish.

At the front, Sieronski could not stay clear unaided and saw four men come onto his wheel, four Belgians: Roman Gijssels, Jean

Romain GIJSSELS
(Belgium, 1907-1978)

In 1932 he achieved an incredible treble, with victories in three long distance classics, the Tour of the Flanders, Paris-Roubaix and Bordeaux-Paris.

1931 : Tour of Flanders,
2nd Bordeaux-Paris,
3rd Paris-Brussels
1932 : Paris-Roubaix, Tour of Flanders,
Bordeaux-Paris
1933 : 3rd Tour of Flanders,
3rd Bordeaux-Paris
1934 : Paris-Belfort, 2nd Paris-Tours

1932

14ᵉ ANNÉE. — Nᵒ 14. — Dimanche 3 Avril 1932

LE GRAND

40 CENTIMES le Numéro

Bureaux : 77, Rue Nationale, LILLE

Les annonces sont reçues au Bureau du Journal, à Lille
et dans les Agences de Publicité, à Paris

ABONNEMENTS (Nord et limitrophes), 18 francs par an
Autres départements français, 20 francs Belgique, 22 francs

Hebdomadaire Illustré

DE LA RÉGION DU NORD DE LA FRANCE

LA COURSE CYCLISTE PARIS-ROUBAIX

LE COUREUR BELGE GYSSELS, LE VAINQUEUR DE L'ÉPREUVE, PHOTOGRAPHIÉ A SON ARRIVÉE A ROUBAIX

Aerts, Alfons Schepers and the formidable Georges Ronsse.

On the Avenue des Villas, when the composition of the group was announced, a big cheer went up from the Flemish. Once again they had not come for nothing! Forecasting was tricky. Certainly Romain Gijssels was not only very fast but also in excellent condition as was proved by his recent success in the Tour of Flanders. But it was hardly thinkable that Ronsse could be distanced as Paris-Roubaix was incontestably his race, and even less so the elegant sprinter Jean Aerts from Brussels. Also, how could anybody forget Schepers, a one time Belgian champion and winner of the Liège-Bastogne-Liège.

The sprint was started very early. Ronsse seemed to have the advantage and then Gijssels started to turn his big gear perfectly and in an impressive rush pipped his four adversaries on the line.

The finishing judge took a full twenty five minutes to establish the correct order. He officially declared Romain Gijssels as the winner of the 33rd Paris-Roubaix in front of Ronsse, Sieronski, Aerts and Schepers. 1932 was to mark the peak of Romain Gijssels' career, for after the Tour of Flanders and Paris-Roubaix he would inscribe Bordeaux-Paris on his record a few months later. The French had admirably enlivened the race, but once again the Belgians had been allowed to monopolise the finish. If the French were successful in the stage races, with for example André Leducq and Antonin Magne winning the Tour de France, the results in the classics, and notably Paris-Roubaix, were not coming to them at all.

1932

1. Romain GIJSSELS (Belgium)
2. Georges RONSSE (Belgium)
3. Herbert SIERONSKI (Germany)
4. Jean AERTS (Belgium)
5. Alfons SCHEPERS (Belgium)
6. Josef DEMUYSERE (Belgium)
7. Alfons GHESQUIERE (Belgium)
8. Emile DECROIX (Belgium)
9. Julien VERVAECKE (Belgium)
10. Alfons DELOOR (Belgium)

The peloton on the hill at Cormeilles just after the start.

Sylvère Maes emerges on the scene

By 16th April 1933 the cycling season was already well under way; the Belgian Alfons Schepers had just won the very first Paris-Nice, beating his compatriot Louis Hardiquest. Many other events had also been disputed, whereas ten years previously the riders had to be content with grinding out the training kilometres. Popular André Leducq had carried off the second National Criterium of the Road and the young René Le Grevès had outsprinted Léon Le Calvez in Paris-Caen. Finally, it is hardly necessary to say that the Belgians had remained the masters of the Tour of Flanders: first Schepers, second Tommies, third Gijssels, fourth Alfons Deloor. Reading the classification makes all comment superfluous. This year the organisers of Paris-Roubaix noted with satisfaction the return, led by Domenico Piemontesi, of several notable Italian riders. The Germans, for who cycling was flourishing, were also present led by their best man, the powerful Ludwig Geyer, often seen at the front of the recent Paris-Nice. Finally, the specialised press did not forget in its forecasts the Austrian Max Bulla, the revelation of the 1931 Tour de France.

Cazalis assembled the troupe at the Porte Maillot for the symbolic start. The riders rode slowly as far as Argenteuil where the world boxing champion Marcel Thil officially released the peloton.

After the hill of Cormeilles, where Raymond Louviot snaffled the prime of two thousand francs, the serious work began. On the road to Pontoise five men took command: the elegant Georges Speicher, the Belgians Sylvère Maes and

After Arras, Sylvère Maes leads in front of Magne, Vervaecke and Thallinger.

Félicien Vervaecke and finally the modest Italians Abondi and Caimi. For a number of kilometres the runaways resisted the pressure of the bunch, but before Beauvais everything came together again.

This was the moment chosen by Sylvère Maes to go again in company with the eldest of the Vervaeckes, Julien, plus Antonin Magne and Karl Thallinger. At the Amiens control the quartet had a lead of more than four minutes. In spite of the ever-growing gap the peloton was dawdling a little. This relaxation was to cause several crashes and the retirement of several riders of which the most unlucky was Leducq.

The outline of Doullens appeared on the horizon. Julien Vervaecke, who knew the event well, attacked the slope in first position and went over the top in company with Sylvère Maes, while Magne and Thallinger were dropped!

It seemed that the Belgian pair were the masters of the race. The presence of Vervaecke was hardly surprising. The man had already won the event in 1930. More than that, since 1926, he was regularly at the front of most of the one-day classics. On the other hand, Sylvère Maes was a surprise. Certainly he had turned professional at the beginning of the year and had immediately made his mark by winning the prestigious International Criterium of Cross-Cyclo-Pedestre, but from there to seeing him at the head of Paris-Roubaix was a step which few of his number would dare to take.

In the streets of Arras the gap over the peloton, which was

1933

Sylvère MAES
(Belgium, 1909-1966)

Double Tour de France winner - one of only four riders to have won both the overall and the points prize in the same Tour which he did in 1939 - Maes honours include a ... Paris-Roubaix.

1933 : Paris-Roubaix
1935 : 4th Tour de France
1936 : Tour de France
1938 : 2nd Tour of Flanders,
       2nd Flèche Wallonne
1939 : Tour de France, Circuit of Morbihan

beginning to wake up, was still four minutes.

As was so often the case the race was going to be decided in the strategic mining sector. The cobbles, riders constantly jumping the pavements and the dust were slowly to have their effects. Thallinger showed that he was no expert in this kind of racing. Suffering from cramps, he was dropped on the outskirts of Hénin-Liétard. Antonin Magne crashed while jumping up a pavement and was left behind. Now, only the two Belgians remained in the lead, both from the powerful Alcyon team. In his following car their team manager Ludovic Feuillet was jubilant. At Carvin, he drew alongside Julien Vervaecke to ask him if he needed anything. Vervaecke assured him that everything was fine. Maes, who had the disadvantage of not understanding any French, asked him what had been said. Vervaecke thinking he could take advantage of the situation answered: "Mr Ludo came to tell me that you must let me win, your turn will come next year." Maes could not understand the reason for this, and so was not taken in.

Behind them the opposition was starting to organise itself. Gijssels, Rebry and Charles Pélissier shook up the bunch and started chasing in earnest. The pursuit would continue up to the streets of Roubaix where the escapees had a lead of no more than eight hundred metres. It proved to be enough, for the bunch, so long concerned with watching each other, was sprinting only for third place.

On Avenue des Villas, Sylvère Maes had no trouble in disposing of Julien Vervaecke. Almost two minutes later, Léon Le Calvez was third in front of Geyer, Archambaud, Deloor, Rebry, Charles and the rest of the peloton. With this Paris-Roubaix, Sylvère Maes really started his career. However, in spite of this success in a single-day race he quickly became a stage race specialist, as his wins in the 1936 and 1937 Tours de France proved.

1933

1. Sylvère MAES (Belgium)
2. Julien VERVAECKE (Belgium)
3. Léon LE CALVEZ (France)
4. Ludwig GEYER (Germany)
5. Maurice ARCHAMBAUD (France)
6. Alfons DELOOR (Belgium)
7. Gaston REBRY (Belgium)
8. Charles PELISSIER (France)
9. Emile DECROIX (Belgium)
10. Roger BERNARD (France)

Sylvère Maes leaves Julien Vervaecke several lengths behind.

Rebry and Lapébie lead on the hill of Doullens.

Rebry on the "green carpet"

Roubaix, Sunday 1st April 1934. At the other end of the Avenue des Villas the crowd was excited. At the apparition of the silhouette of the first rider the cries broke out, it was delirium. Just think, since 1928 no French rider had succeeded in taming the Belgians on the Northern cobblestones. This time Roger Lapébie, wearing the French champion's jersey was arriving and no one could stop his success. Everyone was full of joy. The last few hundred metres were the most difficult, he zig-zagged before crossing the finishing line and collapsed.

The champion from Bordeaux quickly recovered from his great effort and was carried in triumph to the strains of the Marseillaise. Unfortunately his name was never to appear in the records of the Queen of the Classics. The rules and the rules alone unjustly prevented the name of Lapébie from figuring among the list of winners.

In fact, ten kilometres from Roubaix four men were alone in the lead; two Frenchmen René Le Grevès and Roger Lapébie and two Belgians Gaston Rebry and Jean Wauters. Logic pointed to the fact that the first two of them, both very good sprinters would take the best two places on the podium. However, in an instant the race was turned upside down. First René Le Grevès had to stop when he broke his handlebars. Then Roger Lapébie was the victim of a puncture. His team manager's car had been held up behind in a traffic jam.

While the two Belgians disappeared, the French champion rode a few hundred metres on the rim. His eyes were fixed on the cloud of dust thrown up by the passage of his last adversaries. Certainly he knew the rules which forbade him changing machines but suddenly he decided not to adhere to them. He saw by the side of the road a ladies bike, quickly grabbed it and set off at top speed. A little later he changed again and borrowed another bike with "racing" handlebars,

Louviot, Le Grevès and Lapébie lead at Arras.

more suited to the occasion. In spite of the time he had lost and a bike not really his size, Roger Lapébie in one of the best rides of his life, caught Rebry and Wauters and dropped them just before the finish.

A few moments after the finish, Francis Pélissier lodged a complaint with the officials, holding the bike in question in his hand. Those concerned could see that the seal of the organiser which had been fixed to all the bikes on the day before the start was missing; so it was not the bike on which Lapébie had started the race that same morning at Argenteuil !

The heavy sanction fell immediately: Roger Lapébie was disqualified. The victory was handed to Gaston Rebry as he had finished second.

The man from Bordeaux did not contest the verdict even if he thought it was unjust, for he had demonstrated the whole day that he was the best, and that he had won the sprint on the Avenue des Villas.

French cycling had found in the twenty three-year-old rider, a leader in the classics a few years before his success in the 1937 Tour de France. Before this dramatic outcome the race had been lively. Right from the start one attack succeeded another. Those of Louviot then Merviel, Noret, Le Calvez, Leducq, Mithouard or Chocque enlivened the progress of the event. But it was one big bunch which arrived at the feeding station at Amiens.

At this spot Félicien Vervaecke and Noterman refused their traditional musettes and escaped. The two men saw another four riders join them: Roger Lapébie, René Le Grevès, Gaston Rebry and the recent winner of the Milan-San Remo, Joseph Demuysère. Just before the town of Doullens was reached it was back to square one again as the bunch caught the leaders. Doullens hill, nine hundred metres long and an average

1934

Lapébie, Rebry, Hardiquest, Godinat,
Le Grevès and Maes before Seclin

1. Gaston REBRY (Belgium)
2. Jef WAUTERS (Belgium)
3. Frans BONDUEL (Belgium)
4. René LE GREVES (Belgium)
5. André GODINAT (France)
6. Alfons SCHEPERS (Belgium)
7. Romain MAES (Belgium)
8. Louis HARDIQUEST (Belgium)
9. Raymond LOUVIOT (France)
10. Alfred HAMERLINCK (Belgium)

gradient of eight per cent, suited the talents of Rebry who led over the top. Lapébie and Le Grevès were on his heels. The others were about fifteen metres down. On the plateau of Arras the headwind facilitated a regrouping. A group of thirty arrived at Arras where the followers were waiting for the traditional Belgian attack. Against all expectations, Roger Lapébie, dropped them all. Immediately René Le Grevès followed him like a shadow. Rebry smelt the danger and in his turn got up to him in company with Bonduel, Hardiquest, Wauters and Godinat. While flat tyres eliminated Hardiquest and Bonduel, Godinat could not follow the pace imposed by Rebry and Lapébie. So just four of them remained for the result which we already know.

The winner from Menin did not blush after his success, for following the example of Lapébie he had shown himself to be one of the best on the day in "his" race. Lapébie had prepared well for the 1934 season and with his national champion's jersey on his shoulders everyone was expecting him to do something. He had established his training camp under the Italian sun but a crash stopped him from performing well in Milan-San Remo. On returning to his own country he finished second in Paris-Nice behind Rebry. Finally eight days before "La Pascale" he won the National Criterium, the final competition before the Northern rendezvous.

Roger Lapébie, in spite of a long list of victories -1937 Tour de France, Paris-Nice, another Criterium in 1937, Paris-Angers 1933 - was never able to win another Roubaix. Although "officially" he had broken the rules, it was without question a sporting injustice.

1934

right: Rebry finishes.

Gaston Rebry
enters into the legend
with Octave Lapize

"The thirty sixth Paris-Roubaix will go down in history as the most fiercely contested since the war. " This was the way that the majority of sports writers summed up the event that was disputed on the 21st April 1935. The unanimous opinion was that this edition and its winner would enter the annals of cycle sport. The elite of the roadmen were present at the start. Predictions were difficult, several names were put forward, those of the world champion Georges Speicher, of Maurice Archambaud and of Roger Lapébie. Then there were the Belgians; Rebry, Kaers, Meulenberg, Aerts

The riders passing through Pontoise.

The leading group close to Arras is lead by Rebry.

and De Caluwe.

This was not an exhaustive list however for it was hardly reasonable to exclude Magne, Vietto, who had just won Paris-Nice, Bidot, Merviel, Leducq, Maréchal, Charles Pélissier, Félicien Vervaecke, Duerloo, Sylvère Maes or even Demuysere and Danneels. For the first time the finish would be at the Flanders race course at Marcq-en-Baroeul where more than forty thousand spectators could enjoy the traditional horse races in addition to the arrival of the Queen of Classics.

Nine o'clock at Argenteuil. One hundred and sixty competitors are released by the boxer Marcel Thil who appreciated the duels between cyclists. The early kilometres were disrupted by an incredible number of crashes and incidents. Luckily nothing serious happened but several of the favourites, including Pélissier, Maréchal and Gijssels lost time.

In the rain several attempts to escape by Danneels, Rebry, Rigaux and Speicher obliged the field to maintain a fast pace. A compact group crossed Beauvais where René Le Grevès took the prime before being knocked over by a following car. Suffering with an injured knee he sadly had to retire.

Over the years the dominant role played by the hill of Doullens had diminished. No longer was this place that was so full of history the decisive point of the race. However the spectators were always there in great numbers to applaud the champions of the road.

The first to the top, the mighty Gaston Rebry had the greatest difficulty in finding a passage through the dense crowd at the summit. As was often the case, after Doullens, the first

1935

GASTON REBRY
Vainqueur de Paris-Roubaix
Paris-Nice
du Tour des Flandres 1934
sur
Alcyon
1935

17ᵐᵉ Année. — Nᵒ 17. :.: Le numéro : **20 CENTIMES** :.: Dimanche 28 Avril 1935.

LE DIMANCHE
de Roubaix-Tourcoing

DIRECTRICE : MADAME VEUVE ALFRED REBOUX

| RÉDACTION et BUREAUX | ROUBAIX : 71, Grand-Rue. - Tél. 327-51 à 327-54. TOURCOING : 26, rue Carnot. - Tél. 37. LILLE : 3, rue Faidherbe. - Tél. 539-31. PARIS : 13, Bd des Italiens. - Tél. Richelieu 65-73. | ABONNEMENTS | France .... Belgique .... Union Postale ...... Chèques postaux : 87 Lille |

LE 36ᵐᵉ PARIS-ROUBAIX CYCLISTE

LE BELGE GASTON REBRY, DU V.C. TOURQUENNOIS, EST VAINQUEUR DE LA GRANDE EPREUVE PASCALE

En médaillon : Gaston Rebry, vainqueur pour la troisième fois de la grande épreuve pascale. — *A gauche : en haut :* Le peloton, quelques instants après le départ, à Argenteuil ; — *en bas :* Le passage de la course à Beauvais.
A droite : de haut en bas : Deux groupes de coureurs sur le Grand Boulevard et au Croisé-Laroche ; — Les deux premiers, Gaston Rebry et André Leducq, confiant leurs impressions au micro.

serious moves came from the Flemish riders. An attack from the tireless Rebry took twenty men clear. The Bulldog was accompanied by his compatriots Aerts, Roels, Bonduel, Spiessens, Decroix, Danneels, Taverne and Herckenrath, the Frenchmen Le Grevès, Vietto, Buttafocchi, Krauss, Speicher, Godinat, Leducq, Le Calvez, Archambaud, Noret and Charles Pélissier.

Punctures thinned the group down. Pélissier was the first to suffer one at Arleux-en-Gohelle before being followed in misfortune by Speicher, Vietto, Le Grevès and Danneels. As for Archambaud, a broken pedal put paid to his chances on the cobbles.

At Carvin after two hundred and twenty kilometres had been covered at a fast pace, eight men remained in the lead: Rebry, Noret, Leducq, Aerts, Le Calvez, Decroix, Hackenrath and Taverne. Just before entering the streets of Seclin, Rebry's long hard turns at the front saw Noret, Hackenrath and Decroix drop off. As the kilometres went by, the elimination continued as Taverne crashed and Le Calvez punctured. At the front there were only three riders left, three champions: Gaston Rebry, André Leducq and Jean Aerts. The Frenchman that nobody expected to be there, was opposed by two Belgians of the..... same team!

From then on he was spared nothing, neither attacks, nor sprints. But suddenly to the general surprise, just after Wattignies, Aerts was the first to be dropped! Leducq had refound his legs of former years and from now on found himself alone with the Bulldog. As the news was announced at the finish the French went wild. They knew that if it went to a sprint, the Parisian would eat the little "Bulldog" from Menin. But less than fifteen kilometres from the line Leducq felt his back tyre going down. He exchanged a furtive glance with his team manager Francis Pélissier who analysed the situation. It was too late to change wheels. The only solution was pump the tyre up quickly. It took only a few seconds. But it was enough for Rebry to fly away over the cobbles for good. The gap stabilised at three hundred metres but nobody could have regained any ground on the Belgian on his favourite cobblestones, especially Leducq as he was forced to stop a second time.

The Hippodrome of Flanders was waiting for its champion who arrived exhausted but victorious. Leducq was second at 2min 34sec, Jean Aerts at 4min 44sec, Vietto, Bonduel and the others much further back.

Several days later, Félix Levitan, at that time a young journalist with "Match L'Intran" paid tribute to the Belgian: "Since he has achieved glory, Rebry has not changed. He always arrives in Paris on the day before the start of the race, neat and tidy, but no more, his hat pulled down over his eyes. At Menin where he was born, he has bought houses as he has gone along, thanks to the fortune he has made on the road. Rebry leads the wise and healthy life of the villagers. In the summer he is seen and applauded just about everywhere, in the winter he rarely leaves Menin at least not to race, for several times a week he scours the countryside in order to buy flax. Yes, Rebry is a linen merchant. They say he earns as much if not more than he does from cycle sport."

As for André Leducq, he summed him up simply: "Rebry, he's a good chap."

A fortnight later, terrible news hit the cycling world and brought back memories of previous Paris-Roubaix. On the evening of the 1st May, following an argument Henri Pélissier was killed by his mistress in his house at Dampierre.

1935

1. Gaston REBRY (Belgium)
2. André LEDUCQ (France)
3. Jean AERTS (Belgium)
4. René VIETTO (France)
5. Frans BONDUEL (Belgium)
6. Maurice KRAUSS (France)
7. Omer TAVERNE (Belgium)
8. Maurice ARCHAMBAUD (France)
9. Antoine DIGNEF (Belgium)
10. Adrien BUTTAFOCCHI (France)

Georges Speicher
in a turmoil

1936. The crisis had become widespread. Europe slowly witnessed the beginning of a new major conflict. Civil war broke out in Spain. Hitler used the Olympic Games at Berlin as a propaganda exercise for Nazism. A winner of the Nobel Prize was interned in a camp in Germany.

France for its part was paralysed by strikes. These events came in the wake of the introduction of the forty hour week and the granting of two weeks paid holiday.

In spite of all these torments Paris-Roubaix remained untouched. For the moment sport apparently remained the best means of eclipsing the bad news which came from everywhere.

Unfortunately the arrival of this thirty seventh edition meant a new injustice. Three men arrived together at the entrance to the Flanders Racecourse: the French champion Georges Speicher and the two Belgians, the little Romain Maes and the "Bulldog" Gaston Rebry. The French were delighted for they knew Speicher to be much faster than his two final rivals.

But to everyone's surprise Romain Maes was threatening the Frenchman only fifty metres from the white line traced on the cinders of the racecourse. The large Flemish contingent exploded: against all expectation Romain Maes had beaten the Frenchman!

A few minutes after the finish the judge announced the following order: first Georges Speicher, second Romain Maes!

A grumble of dissent went round the stands. The Belgians and several Frenchmen screamed that it was scandalous. A fight nearly broke out. But in spite of everything the verdict remained unchanged. It was a cruel disillusion. Some people remembered the episodes which involved Maréchal and Lapébie and found simply that for on once injustice had changed sides.

However at Argentueil no one gave much chance to the French in the race which for publicity purposes was known as the "Duralumin Trophy".

The terrific Flemings were unbeatable over the cobbles no matter what the weather.

Nothing discouraged them, neither the mud, nor the cold, nor the snow. so the forecasts remained immutable: Rebry, Gijssels, Wauters, Hardiquest, Sylvère and Romain Maes, Bonduel, Danneels and Hendrickx. The press also spoke about a few of the rare "tricolours" capable of doing something such as Lapébie, Archambaud and Speicher.

Right from the start the race proved to be exciting. Eight men led from Cormeilles to Beauvais: Félicien Vervaecke, Jules Rossi, Level, Buttafocchi, Vietto, Weiss, Moineau and Roger Lapébie. However it was one of the big peloton which passed through the feeding zone to Amiens. Accidents had already eliminated Meulenberg, Di Paco, Vervaecke and various others, such as the ever-unfortunate Mallet, knocked off by one of the one hundred and fifty following vehicles!

At the exit to Arras a little silhouette broke clear, that of Rebry who was entering his kingdom - the cobblestones. Another rider went after him, it was the French champion Georges Speicher. Very quickly he latched onto the wheels of the man from Menin. Seven men, six of them Belgians, caught them both: Romain Maes, Gijssels, Kaers, Verlinden, Hendrickx, Wauters and the elegant Italian of Paris Jules Rossi.

At close to fifty kilometres an hour the riders comprising this little group jumped from one pavement to another under the rain which had not stopped falling. Another ten men managed

Photo Europe ©
GEORGES SPEICHER.
Champion du Monde 1933 , Vainqueur du Tour de France 1933

Georges SPEICHER
(France, 1907-1978)

A fine all rounder, he was one of the pillars of the prestigious French national team in the Tour de France during the 1930's.

1933 : World Champion, Tour de France
       3rd French Championship
1935 : French Champion, Paris-Reims,
       Paris-Angers
1936 : Paris-Roubaix
1937 : French Champion,
       3rd Grand Prix des Nations
1939 : French Champion

1936

to join the front group, but as often the roads through Hénin-Liétard claimed numerous victims.

As they arrived at Carvin there only remained fourteen of them in command, Speicher and Rossi accompanied by twelve Belgians!

Gaston Rebry, with his poor sprint had no choice but to lead a "hellish" pace to wear down his companions.

At Camphin, his multiple accelerations started to bear fruit, for there remained only six men struck to his wheel, then three after Hendrickx punctured and Rossi, Wauters and Gijssels weakened.

But Speicher was riding incredibly smoothly. The Belgians quickly understood that they would not be able to get rid of the Parisian as he was riding the cobbles just as well as the specialists.

So there would be three to contest the sprint.

On the day after this victory the French did not put out too many flags. In this virtual "Belgium Championship" apart from Speicher, they hardly distinguished themselves. Level was tenth, Archambaud eleventh and Buttafocchi twentieth. A rather pathetic balance sheet.

For his part, Georges Speicher completed his record with this prestigious jewel, of which he already had several, like the Tour de France 1933 and the world championship the same year.

1936

1. Georges SPEICHER (France)
2. Romain MAES (Belgium)
3. Gaston REBRY (Belgium)
4. Romain GIJSSELS (Belgium)
5. Jules ROSSI (Italy)
6. Jef WAUTERS (Belgium)
7. Frans BONDUEL (Belgium)
8. Emile VAN DE PITTE (Belgium)
9. Sylvain GRYSOLLE (Belgium)
10. Léon LEVEL (France)

Romain Maes (left) and Georges Speicher.

Jules Rossi,
the first Italian

For the first time since the Paris-Roubaix started in 1896, an Italian inscribed his name on the roll of honour. Where Belloni, Girardengo, Bestetti and Binda failed, Jules Rossi, a young rider of only twenty three succeeded. An orphan at the age of six, Rossi came to Nogent-sur-Marne in 1920 with the rest of his family. He started slowly in 1928 and reached top amateur level in 1933 with the famous Velo Club de Levallois. Impressed by his performances, Ludovic Feuillet engaged him in his professional team the following year.

From then on Rossi produced a whole series of distinguished performances, such as his wins in the Circuit of the Allier 1935 and Paris-St Etienne 1936, the same year as he finished fifth in Paris-Roubaix.

The event took place on the 28th March 1937. As usual the Belgians were the men to beat even if Roger Lapébie, winner of both the Paris-Nice and the National Criterium of the Road had been the man on form that Spring.

For the first few hours of the race the stars remained hidden in the bunch of one hundred and fifty nine riders. Fernand Mithouard shook them up on the hill at Pontoise and went away shortly after in company with Moerenhout, Blin, Archambaud, Danneels, Passat and Van Schendel.

The runaways raced through Beauvais with a lead of more than four minutes before being caught first by a group of ten and then by the whole bunch just before Arras.

Under beating rain, Félicien Vervaecke decided to relaunch the attack. The Belgian was alone for about twenty kilometres and resisted the pressure of Danneels, Rossi and Marcel Kint who led a handful of pursuers over the rough cobbles of Hénin-Liétard and of Courrières.

Vervaecke hoped to see reinforcements come up to him but when they did arrive he was no longer able to stay with them! Seven men went past without even a glance: Danneels, Hendrickx, Declerq, Lievens, Van de Pitte, the isolated Frenchman Vergili and the astonishing Rossi.

A few kilometres farther on a single man came up after a superb effort, César Moretti.

For the followers it was an enormous surprise, for despite it being his first Paris-Roubaix he was negotiating the rough roads like a seasoned veteran. Sadly for him a crash followed by a puncture eliminated him from the contest.

Isolated in this Flemish speaking group, Rossi had no other choice than to keep attacking. In this way he dropped

1937

Jules ROSSI
(Italy, 1914-1968)

The first Italian to win Paris-Roubaix and the first of an illustrious list of "transalpins" to shine in the Northern classic.

1936 : Paris-St Etienne
        2nd Bordeaux-Paris
1937 : Paris-Roubaix
1938 : Paris-Tours, 3rd Bordeaux-Paris
1941 : Paris-Reims, Grand Prix des Nations
1942 : 3rd Paris-Tours
1943 : Paris-Reims,
        2nd Grand Prix des Nations
1944 : 2nd Paris-Roubaix,
        2nd Grand Prix des Nations

Left top:
Passing over the top of the hill of Doullens.

Bottom: Off the cobbles Jules Rossi, in second position is very attentive.

JULES ROSSI

DIRECTION
HENRI DESGRANGE FONDATEUR
MAURICE ET JACQUES GODDET
ADMINISTRATION — RÉDACTION
RUE DU FG. MONTMARTRE PARIS

L'Auto

VITESSE — SPORT — SANTÉ

Mardi 30 Mars 19..
38ᵉ ANNÉE
TÉLÉPHONE
TAIT. 70.80
0ʳ30
N° 13.2..
PETITES A..
TAIT. 73..
ADRESSE TÉLÉGRAPHIQUE VELAUTO-P..

UN REPORTAGE de L'Auto

RÊVEZ, POTACHES DE FRANCE

Voici les grands collèges britanniques et leur magnifique organisation sportive

*La sévère discipline du collège de Westminster
n'exclut pas la grande liberté du sport qui y est pratiqué
sous toutes ses formes... sauf le rugby
« pas assez dans la tradition » (sic)*

De notre envoyé spécial Robert PERRIER

Hors la Cité

LONDRES, mars. — Au pied de la cathédrale de Westminster, dans la poussière même de l'ancienne abbaye, a gardé intégralement le caractère bel oublié, au moyen âge, la fraseur Édouard, au collège de Westminster poursuit, au vingtième siècle, sportive carrière.

...

Rugby ? Connais pas...

L'entraînement britannique est proverbial. Quand ces messieurs se trouvaient mis dans la tête d'ignorer quelque chose, le diable n'y mettrait-il que rien ne serait changé à leurs.

...

Le Paris-Roubaix 37

TROPHÉE DURALUMIN

60 à Hénin-Liétard... 5 à Roubaix

LE "PARCOURS INFERNAL" EN 40 KILOMÈTRE.. ENCORE UNE FOIS, ACCOMPLIT SON ŒUVRE

Jules Rossi, l'homme qui monte régulièrement voue maintenant sa carrière au Tour de France

En Italie, après le succès de Rossi, on reconnaît indispensabl.. la participation au Tour de France

En Belgique, on escompte de grandes victoires prochain.. de Hendrickx et de Declercq.

CONSOLATION ?

L'échec d'un plan Lapébie-Le Grevès, la déroute de nos vedettes ont perm.. à quelques aspirants français de prendre conscience de leur valeur.

COQUIN DE PRINTEMPS !

par Jacques GODDET

On sort de ce Paris-Roubaix secoué court-vêtus. Et il faut peut-être trouver d'impression. Fidèle à sa tradition, im-...

... dans des conditions anormales une explication...

... sous l'impulsion d'un Jean Maréchal...

CONCLUSION D'UNE GRANDE ÉPREUVE

RUGBY PATRONNÉE PAR L'Auto

..anguedoc - Roussillon
..ère Coupe Nationale
(..ge Pierre-Failliot)

CÔTE BASQUE

..uarts furent défaillants

..bat Côte Basque : 10-5 (7-0)

..ON...

par Lucien DUBECH

LE GRAND
Hebdomadaire Illustré
DE LA RÉGION DU NORD DE LA FRANCE

19ᵉ ANNÉE. — N° 14. — Dimanche 4 Avril 1937.

Bureaux : 77, Rue Nationale, LILLE
Chèque postal 526. — Téléphone 222
PUBLICITÉ RÉGIONALE ET LOCALE
dans nos bureaux, à Lille

50 CENTIMES le Numéro

Le 38ᵉ Paris-Roubaix

L'Italien Rossi, vainqueur de l'épreuve, porté en triomphe à son arrivée à Roubaix

Le match de football France-Italie se déroulera normalement

Nous nous sommes fait l'écho de bruits selon lequel la Fédération italienne aurait écrit à la FFFA afin que celle-ci ne porte garantie que le match France-Italie, le 11 avril, au Parc des Princes, se déroulerait sans manifestation.

An easy sprint for Jules Rossi.

Danneels and Vergili but that still left four stuck to his back wheel.
However the "entente" was not "cordial" between the Belgians. A victory at Roubaix was far too prestigious to help somebody else win, even if he was a compatriot..
As for Rossi, he wanted to enter into history and surpass Binda and Girardengo, his glorious elders, on the cobbles of the North.
The Racecourse of Flanders had been abandoned for good, the finish was, as it used to be in the good old days, on the Avenue Gustave Delory, the new name given to the Avenue des Villas at Roubaix.
In the last two kilometres Rossi led the group so fast that any attempt to get away was impossible, and he started the sprint from a very long way out.
Hendrickx, Declerq, Van Pitte and Lievens were stuck on his wheel but were totally unable to draw alongside him, let alone pass him. They finished in that order...behind Jules Rossi who had just achieved an incredible exploit.
Behind the barriers there was consternation among some of the public. How could this young Italian get the better of four Belgians?
Rossi was not interested in such questions. Carried in triumph he was savouring this unique moment. The band, who had no copies of the score for the Italian national anthem, had no choice than to play a soft air vaguely resembling the Marseillaise!
This thirty eighth edition of Paris-Roubaix marked not only the failure of the favourites but also the confirmation of several new young talents. That of Jules Rossi of course, one of the youngest winners of the event. Then those of the new Flemish generation who were already operational at the highest level. This seemed more important than the fact that for once the evergreen Gaston Rebry remained in the bosom of the peloton, apparently incapable of changing the way the race was run.

1937

1. Jules ROSSI (Italy)
2. Albert HENDRICKX (Belgium)
3. Noël DECLERCQ (Belgium)
4. Emile VAN DE PITTE (Belgium)
5. Aimé LIEVENS (Belgium)
6. Gustave DANNEELS (Belgium)
7. Edgard DE CALUWE (Belgium)
8. Frans BONDUEL (Belgium)
9. Séverin VERGILI (France)
10. Georges SPEICHER (France)

Lucien Storme
overturns the hierarchy

In the week preceding the thirty ninth Paris-Roubaix, arranged for the 17th April 1938, a number of cyclists were to be seen on the route. Jean Leulliot, never short of ideas had even organised for the occasion an official reconnaissance of the roads on the Wednesday before the event...

Among the regulars, in spite of the bad weather conditions, were several Frenchmen such as Mallet, Ducazeaux, Galateau and Goujon, one of the young Olympic champions at Berlin, but also several Belgians like Vlaemynck and Lucien Storme, a new-professional at that time unknown.

Just a few minutes after they passed through, another group of seven men rode through the streets of Faches, headed by the familiar figure of Gaston Rebry...

For years his preparation had been identical. So he was in the middle of his last training ride of one hundred and eighty kilometres over the route of the race five days before the event. The "Bulldog" appeared to be in excellent form and was acting as guide for his young companions on the road.

Each bend, each pavement brought back glorious memories: "Look, it was there," he said, "that I won Paris-Roubaix 1931, by going away with Joly. If I'm still there on Sunday. I'll know when I have to attack..."

On the morning of the race the weather conditions were hardly any better. It was cold and the strong wind was from the North.

From the start, in order to warm themselves up, the peloton led by Roger Lapebie, wearing his eternal Basque beret, rode at a fast pace. At the first feeding zone at Breteuil, Lesueur went through in the lead before his brief escape with Fontenay and...Lapébie had become untenable. The wind played a major role and the adventure came to an end.

While the hill at Doullens caused several retirements, Jean Fontenay and the Belgian colossus Leopold Maes attacked and at the summit were just clear of the others. But after a few kilometres everything came together again...

As Arras was crossed, Jean Maréchal, who after several years devoted to the track and had come back to his first love, tried to escape.

Unfortunately for him, it was the traditional place where Gaston Rebry woke up. The Man from Menin was the first to join the runaway in company with Jules Rossi. The peloton was only at a few hundred metres.

At Bois-Bernard, at least fifty kilometres from Roubaix, Marcel Kint started the first serious offensive of the day. The Belgian was rapidly joined by a very attentive Rossi. Kint had however expended too much energy for he found it impossible to follow the Italian.

Rossi in his turn was unable to survive alone in the lead, Gamard and then the bunch came up to him fast.

The attacks became more frequent. That of Constant Lauwers and of Robert Oubron was doomed to failure after the former suffered from a puncture and the latter from hunger knock...

Seventeen kilometres from Roubaix it was back to square one. Fifteen riders could still win on the Avenue Gustave Delory. In this group, for the most part Belgian, two Frenchmen had slipped in, Jean Frechaut and Sylvain Marcaillou. Louis Hardiquest decided that his hour of glory had arrived. He attacked and in a few seconds had opened a considerable gap.

Just one man was able to rejoin him: Lucien Storme. On the outskirts of Carvin, he had already tried to escape but he quickly allowed himself to be caught for the conditions were

L. STORME VAINQUEUR DE PARIS-ROUBAIX 1938
sur Cycle A. Leducq, pneus Hutchinson, dérailleur Super Champion

Lucien STORME
(Belgium, 1916-1945)

A talented roadman who, like many others, ended his life as a casualty of war.

1938 : Paris-Roubaix
1939 : 2nd Paris-Tours,
      3rd Paris-Brussels,
      3rd Paris-St Etienne

1938

The peloton at the start.

to hardly favourable. This time it was too late for calculations and he gave maximum help to his compatriot Hardiquest.

The latter was sure of victory. For several years he had been one of the best Belgians in the classics as was proved by his success in the 1936 Tour of Flanders. Consequently he could hardly consider this young man who had only been professional for a couple of months as any real danger.

More than eight thousand metres from the finish Storme was immobilised by a puncture. He changed wheels, which left him at least two hundred metres down. It seemed that Hardiquest would be able to win with one leg but on this 17th April Storme was head and shoulders above them all. In just a few seconds he caught his adversary, and in the finishing straight launched the sprint from a long way out to win with disconcerting ease.

At less than 22, Lucien Storme came to the attention of the public at large. A few moments after the finish, before going to the showers, he took a beer with his parents and friends and explained his victory in simple terms: "Hardiquest attacked so I followed him. I had no further problems..."

The Belgians remained more than ever the masters of the cobbles. They monopolised the first six places, for behind Storme and Hardiquest were Marcel Van Houtte, Emile Masson junior, fourth in spite of a puncture fifteen kilometres from Roubaix, Gerard Desmedt and René Walschot. Jean Fréchaud, the first "non-Belgian" was seventh.

Paris-Roubaix constituted the jewel in the career of Lucien Storme. The following year he won a stage in the Tour de France at la Rochelle and finished second in Paris-Tours and third in Paris-Brussels.

Then the dark days arrived. Mobilised just before the world war conflict he was quickly taken prisoner. Interned in the camp of Siegburg in Germany he was inopportunely shot with the arrival of the Americans on the 10th April 1945.

1938

1. Lucien STORME (Belgium)
2. Louis HARDIQUEST (Belgium)
3. Marcel VAN HOUTTE (Belgium)
4. Emile MASSON (Belgium)
5. Aimé DEOLET (Belgium)
6. René WALSCHOT (Belgium)
7. Jean FRECHAUT (France)
8. Sylvain GRYSOLLE (Belgium)
9. Albertin DISSEAUX (Belgium)
10. Constant LAUWERS (Belgium)

Emile Masson
just before the conflict

At the start of the fortieth Paris-Roubaix on the 9th April 1939 at Le Vésinet the atmosphere was morose. For several years the international situation had gradually been getting worse. Hitler who had been worrying Europe since 1933 had this time gone as far as to invade Bohemia-Moldavia..

Sporting competitions were still taking up the front pages of the newspapers, although not for much longer. André Deforge (National Criterium), Louis Thiétard (Paris-Caen), Karel Kaers (Tour of Flanders), and the World champion Marcel Kint (Ghent-Antwerp-Ghent) were the principal winners at the beginning of the season. All these men would be disputing victory in the "Easter race".

From the start, given by the aviator Michel Detroyat, the race went off like a rocket. On the road to Pontoise Roger Lapébie launched the first attack. Among the ten men who went with him were: Marechal, Mithouard and Charles Pélissier. only Braeckeveldt represented Belgium.

Their lead was already more than a minute on the bunch by the time they reached Pontoise, then three and a half minutes at Breteuil. The first one hundred kilometres were covered at average speed of 38 kph and the race followers were beginning to wonder if the winner was going to come from this group.

In the bunch a counter attack formed when Gerrit Schulte, the "pedalling fool" launched himself, taking five Belgians with him - Defoordt, Somers, Beeckman, Moerenhout and Lansens.

After a frantic pursuit, Schulte and his companions managed to join the leaders in the suburbs of Amiens.

A group of sixteen men crossed the town. Lucien Storme and Yvan Marie went through one minute down, the bunch thirty seconds later. Gaston Rebry had been dropped from the back of the peloton and having absolutely no chance of winning decided to retire. The strong man of the 1930's said a discreet good-bye to the race which had brought him so much glory...

On the way to Doullens, where several more men had got up to the leading group, Lapébie, the instigator of the morning's break punctured a tyre when the battle was beginning in earnest.

Storme, riding with incredible facility, was first over the top of the climb which was fatal to ... Charles Pélissier!

On the Plateau of Arras the strong men found themselves at the front. There were twenty five of them, all potential winners among whom were De Caluwé, Sylvère and Romain Maes, Le Grèves, Magne, Schulte, Rossi, Storme Speicher, Kint and Archambaud. The elite were getting ready to fire their guns in the crossing of the mining sector.

Vanoverberghe was the first to open hostilities. Successively Romain Maes, Le Grèves, Speicher and Archambaud got onto his wheel. The latter attempted to go it alone for a short while before Carvin where about twenty riders came together again at the front. Roger Lapébie finally reintegrated into the group after a pursuit of seventy kilometres!

At Seclin, Romain Maes tried to go off the front. Rapidly he was joined by Emile Masson who recounted the following in his book "Free Masson of Belgian Cycling":

"There remained twenty six minutes to cover. Jean Majerus had a lead of two hundred metres. Roger Lapébie replied and launched himself into his pursuit. Without any shadow of hesitation I jumped onto his wheel. At the big bend at Wattignies the

Émile MASSON, VAINQUEUR DE PARIS-ROUBAIX 1939 sur Cycle Alcyon, pneus Dunlop, dérailleur Super Champion

Emile MASSON
(Belgium, 1915)

His career spanned the second World War and he survived four years in a German prisoner of war camp.

1938 : Flèche Wallonne,
         4th Paris-Roubaix
1939 : Paris-Roubaix
1946 : Belgian Champion,
         Bordeaux-Paris
1947 : Belgian Champion
1949 : 2nd Bordeaux-Paris

1939

84ᵐᵉ Année. -- N° 100.   50 CENTIMES   LUNDI 10 AVRIL 1939.

BUREAUX
ROUBAIX. -- 60-71, Grande-Rue. Tél. 327.32, 327.53 et 327.54.
TOURCOING. -- 22, rue Carnot. (Tél. 37.
LILLE. -- 3, rue Faidherbe (Tél. 536.31.
PARIS. -- 28, boulevard Poissonnière. Tél. Pro-vence, 77.84.
MOUSCRON. -- 105, rue de la Station. Tél. 5.44.

ANCIENS DIRECTEURS :
Jean Rebous
Alfred Rebous
Madame Alfred Rebous

Journal de Roubaix

Quotidien de Roubaix-Tourcoing et de la Région

Le coup de force italien en Albanie

ROME par son chargé d'affaires donne à LONDRES

l'assurance que l'action italienne sera strictement limitée à l'Albanie et que le statu quo méditerranéen sera respecté

Sur ce point, et particulièrement en ce qui concerne la Grèce et Corfou, lord Halifax avait fait connaître la volonté du gouvernement anglais

A PARIS, le comité permanent de la défense nationale a tenu une importante réunion

A LONDRES, Lord Halifax a conféré avec les chefs d'état-major de l'armée et de la marine

---

A LYON

L'Union fédérale des anciens combattants

RÉUNIE EN CONGRÈS

s'est placée devant les dures réalités de l'heure

« Le temps des déclarations généreuses et sans lendemain est passé ; il n'y a plus de place que pour l'action et ceux qui renâcleraient devant le commandement des événements seraient balayés comme indignes de la tâche devant laquelle ils auraient été défaillants », a déclaré M. PICHOT.

Lyon, 9 avril. — Dimanche, à 8 h., des offices religieux ont été célébrés à l'occasion du congrès national de l'Union fédérale des anciens combattants; l'un à la cathédrale primatiale Saint-Jean, en présence du cardinal Gerlier, archevêque de Lyon, qui a prononcé une allocution; l'autre, au nouveau temple, sous la présidence du pasteur Rivet, président du consistoire, ancien aumônier du 14ᵉ corps d'armée, et enfin à la synagogue, en présence du grand rabbin Sèches, ancien aumônier du 21ᵉ corps d'armée.

A 9 h., l'assemblée solennelle du congrès s'est tenue, en présence d'un très [...]

Sous un soleil éclatant, après une course animée et indécise, un outsider,

LE BELGE MASSON GAGNE LE 40ᵐᵉ PARIS-ROUBA[IX]

KINT TERMINE SECOND DEVANT ROGER LAPÉ[BIE]
qui fut le grand animateur du « trophée Duralumin »

Deux résurrections : celles de Romain Maes et de Vanoverberghe | Longtemps on put croire à une vi[ctoire] française avec Lapébie et Speic[her]

La foule après le passage des coureurs, avenue Gustave-Delory.   (Ph. J.)

beaucoup de ceux qui suivirent la course, sans doute surtout parce que d'autres avaient paru, tout le jour, plus capables de l'emporter et que leurs efforts s'étaient montrés plus spectaculaires.

que la sage course du bru[n] Celui-ci sut attendre son h[eure] Il sut aussi profiter de l'oc[casion] fortune aime qu'on la mérite.
(Lire la suite page 3.)

(Meurisse-Mondial-Rol.)
Emile Masson,
vainqueur du 40ᵐᵉ Paris-Roubaix

(DE NOTRE ENVOYÉ SPÉCIAL)

Tout fut vraiment neuf dans ce quarantième Paris-Roubaix, le temps, la course, et le vainqueur.

Peut-être est-ce parce que nous avons vu l'épreuve pascale se disputer sous un soleil plus que printanier, par une température qui nous changeait heureusement des rudes randonnées sous la pluie, contre un vent froid et maussade, qu'elle nous semblait un « profil » et une histoire bien peu semblables à celles que nous avons suivies ? Le fait est qu'on a rarement assisté à tant de généreux efforts, à tant de surprises, à tant d'« effondrements » et à tant de « résurrections ». Et jamais, peut-être aussi, n'a-t-on pu pouvoir aussi aisément désigner le vainqueur... qui n'était pas le véritable ! Ne nous en plaignons pas, Paris-Roubaix, quarantième du nom, de par sa diversité, de par l'indécision de son issue, dix kilomètres encore avant la ligne blanche de l'avenue Gustave-Delory, méritera une place particulière dans les souvenirs de bien des ses auteurs.

* *

Ce fut vraiment, dimanche, la course des surprises. En veut-on un exemple ?

A Seclin, moins de trente kilomètres avant l'arrivée, on pouvait chercher partout, sauf sur les tablettes des journalistes suiveurs, le nom du gagnant. Et ce pour l'excellente raison qu'on n'avait littéralement pas vu Masson — le fils du père — jusqu'alors. Il se trouvait noyé dans un peloton compact, où il avait besogné obscurément tout le jour, lancé à la poursuite d'audacieux dont on dira les noms tout à l'heure.

Dans la côte de Fâches, bien plus encore que de Roubaix, Masson cassait sa roue et l'on était encore aussi plus éloigné de croire qu'il pourrait gagner, tant on demeurait persuadé que la course se jouait, par ailleurs, entre deux hommes : Lapébie et Jean Majérus. Et pourtant Masson a vaincu. Il a vaincu en champion, parce qu'il a su se montrer le plus fort et surmonter la défaillance à l'heure où les autres l'éprouvaient durement.

Il est certain que le fils de l'ancien routier belge, l'équipier du Tour de France est un homme de classe et il [...]

La situation internatio[nale]

LA TENSION GERMANO-POLONAIS[E] VA-T-ELLE S'AGGRAVE[R]

La Pologne est comparée de plus en plus ouvertement par les n[azis] à l'ancienne Tchécoslovaquie

(Ph. France-Presse.)
M. Chamberlain arrivant dimanche matin à Downing-Street

Le général Vuillemin et le vi[ce-amiral] Darlan, respectivement chefs [d'état-] major de l'Air et de la M[arine]

Berlin, 9 avril. — Les déclarations qu'il est possible de recueillir dans les milieux diplomatiques étrangers de la capitale du Reich, ne peuvent, par ailleurs, que confirmer l'impression que la situation s'est tendue d'une façon notable depuis 48 heures. La Pologne est comparée de plus en plus ouvertement à l'ancienne Tchécoslovaquie. On l'accuse d'être devenue un instrument entre les mains de Londres et de Moscou.

Berlin comme le plus néces[saire] plus urgent. De là à penser q[ue le gou]vernement du Reich voudra n[...] sans perdre un instant, d'une f[açon] d'une autre, il n'y a qu'un pas[...]

Beaucoup d'observateurs [...] franchissent ce pas et tou[...] inquiétude leurs regards v[ers un] libre.

Quant au ministre des Affaires étran[gères]
(Lire la suite page 4)

Luxembourger was no longer more than a few dozen metres in front. The moment had come to go onto the attack. A hard acceleration had Lapébie gasping for breath. One hundred metres farther on, Majerus saw me go past like a whirlwind. I was alone in command of the race. I was certain of winning. I threw all caution to the wind. I realised I had picked up a flint when the tyre on my back wheel gave up the ghost.

Catastrophe! The Alcyon team car was not there to help me. Once again I had to change a tyre unaided. While I was doing this, Lapébie and Majerus went past. a few seconds later the first bunch of fourteen men did the same. "A first effort brought me up to the group of fourteen. A second took me clear of them. Only Speicher made any attempt to stay with me but could not do so before caught and dropped Lapébie and Majerus.

"There remained twelve kilometres to the finish and behind me chasing was a "Mercier" quartet: Marcel Kint, Maurice Archambaud, Roger Lapébie and Cyrille Vanoverberghe. In spite of their efforts I crossed the finishing line with a lead of a minute and a half..."

In the Masson family, joy was everywhere. The wish of Emile senior, who had never been able to do better than finish third in 1922, was that his son won the "Pascale". He never stopped repeating: "I really want to see you win Paris-Roubaix and die two hours later. If it did happen I would go in peace, saying: I have made a champion of my son. Now he no longer needs me."

For second place, Marcel Kint finished in front of Roger Lapébie and Maurice Archambaud.

International tension mounted even higher. After Sylvère Maes won the Tour de France, worry gave way to anguish. On the 3rd September, after the invasion of Poland by the Reich, France and Great Britain officially entered the war.

1939

1. Emile MASSON (Belgium)
2. Marcel KINT (Belgium)
3. Roger LAPEBIE (France)
4. Maurice ARCHAMBAUD (France)
5. Cyrille VANOVERBERGHE (Belgium)
6. Sylvain GRYSOLLE (Belgium)
7. Robert WIERINCKX (Belgium)
8. Albert HENDRICKX (Belgium)
9. Antonin MAGNE (France)
10. Noël DECLERCQ (Belgium)

The ""Duralumin" under the occupation

In May 1940, Hitler's troops first of all attacked the Low Countries and Belgium before flooding through France and turning, the famous and inviolable Maginot Line!

On the 24th May Roubaix fell into their hands without any difficulty. The Northerners lived through the shame of annexation of the region by the invaders. Reprisals after acts carried out by the Resistance and rationing became part of everyday life.

The sport of cycling was scarcely any better off. Most of the champions were mobilised, few of them had any chance to train. Numerous careers, some of which promised to be brilliant, were broken for ever.

Besides the rationing of food, there was always a shortage of material. Unearthing tubular tyres was almost impossible.

During the "phoney war", in 1940, not a single cycle race was organised in the North. The only recourse possible for the Northerners was to participate in Belgian competitions. In France itself, only the National Criterium of the Spring could take place under almost normal conditions.

In spite of these difficulties, the management of "L'Auto" persisted in their intention of organising a Paris-Roubaix in 1940. However, they were obliged to face facts; the Germans refused access to Roubaix as it was situated in an army zone. Then they came up with the idea of running it in the opposite direction, starting in the City of Mills and finishing in the capital.

Certainly this was a long way from the original concept of the race and certain purists were against it, but in view of the circumstances the sporting public would have been happy. Unfortunately the "Prefet" (governor) of the departement of the Somme forbade the passage of the race through his area. The final veto of the General Headquarters of the Army sounded the final death knoll for all hope of organising anything in the North...

A "Wartime Paris-Roubaix" nevertheless took place between - Le Mans and Paris Keeping the name "Duralumin trophy", as in the good old times.

The course naturally bore no resemblance to that of "La Pascale". The hills of Dourdan and Chateaufort could not replaced the legendary cobbles of Hénin-Liétard or the famous turning of Wattignies.

Sixty three cyclists turned up at the banner proclaiming "Paris-Roubaix - Start". Among them was just one Belgian, Van Cauwenberghe. The Italian Jules Rossi, winner of Paris-Roubaix 1937, was everybody's favourite. In fact he seemed to be the best but two successive punctures destroyed his hopes.

For a while it seemed that victory was going to a young Northerner, Van de Velde, but finally Joseph Sofietti picked up the bouquet at the Parc des Princes in front of Van de Velde and Rossi.

In this year of 1940, there was no question of any Tour de France. Moreover its founder, Henri Desgrange, died on the sixteenth of August at the age of seventy five in his villa at Cogolin...

The following year, in 1941, the cycling calendar in the North was hardly any more abundant. The first road race, the Grand Prix de Fourmies, was only organised on the 10th August and saw the victory of the young professional Maurice De Muer.

Since the defeat, France had been divided into different zones, and cycling was as well. So the two departments of the North and the Pas-de-Calais were attached to the German Military Command of Brussels.

Paris-Roubaix was always on the programme, but the presence of a frontier on the Somme (the North-East Line), prevented the passage of a bicycle race.

"L'Auto" persisted in its intention of organising Paris-Roubaix, this time between Paris and Rheims on the 14th April. Easter Monday!

Nothing nor nobody could this time prevent Jules Rossi winning ahead of Louis Thiétard and Raymond Louviot.

The Italian followed this up by winning the Grand Prix des Nations and, in the North, the International Criterium at Lille. He was without doubt the great winner in a very sad cycling season.

In 1942 things were a little better. The organisers were still faced with the problems of the "zones". So Paris-Rheims remained the official replacement, "the ersatz Paris- Roubaix", according to the sporting chronicler Marcel Peltier. It was another win for Emile Idée and it really confirmed him as the champion of the younger generation.

As well as Paris-Rheims, his successes in 1942 were: a first French championship, National Criterium, Grand Prix of Provence, and above all the Grand Prix des Nations. The "King of the Chevreuse", as he was nicknamed, was born.

1940-'42

LES CYCLES
ALCYON
SILLONNENT LE MONDE...
AGENT:

AFFICHE/ GAILLARD/ PARIS/ AMIENS/

The winner Marcel Kint, in front of a lapped rider, crosses the finishing line.

The "black eagle" spreads his wings over Roubaix

At the end of 1942 France was completely occupied. The one good thing about it was that the relaxing of the tension between the two zones made the organisation of the national sporting events a lot easier, especially cycle races.

But the press remained divided. On the one side there were the newspapers who collaborated with the Germans, such as: "The France Socialiste" and on the other those who tried to remain as independent as possible like "L'Auto".

In this troubled period, the main preoccupation of Jacques Goddet, its director, was to keep a distance between himself and his competitors and the paper did not attend the meetings of the Paris Press, organised by...the Germans.

This did not stop Goddet from preparing for the organisation of an eventual Paris-Roubaix. After lots of difficulties and problems, he was finally recompensed when the authorities came to the offices of "L'Auto" in the Rue de Faubourg-Montmartre. The event could be reborn after three long interrupted years.

In the Spring of 1943, one hundred and twenty riders, of whom thirty were

Belgian, were getting ready for the first wartime Paris-Roubaix. At St-Denis, the starting point, the task of the few sporting journalists was made that much more difficult as they had little indication of the current form of the participants. At the most they knew that the French champion Emile Idée, should be once again the man to beat. As for the other Frenchmen there was also Camille Danguillaume, Louis Thiétard, Fernand Mithouard and the "Azurian" René Vietto.

The Belgians were numerically much weaker but had the considerable advantage of having just disputed the Circuit of the Dag and the Tour of Flanders won by Achiel Buysse. The current world champion Marcel Kint seemed to be the best of them but close on his heels were Buysse, Odile Vanden Meerschaut, Albert Sercu and the young and talented Maurice De Simpelaere whose formidable sprint was beginning to worry the peloton.

The cloudy sky was threatening rain. First to attack was Serge Svoboda. A former amateur champion of France, he had just signed his first professional contract with Dilecta. He was just burning with desire to reveal his talent. The famous reporter Georges Briquet, who knew him well, had gone so far as to encourage him to attack from the gun, explaining that: "As a young professional you have little chance of getting a good placing. But I am going to make two radio broadcasts in the morning, if you attack early, I will be able to mention your name..."

1943

The lesson was learnt and as soon as the race started, he went away with Léon Level, then Thomas and Dubuisson.

Nine other riders, among whom were Urbain Caffi, Fermo Camellini and René Vietto, joined them before Laigneville at the fortieth kilometre.

Their advance did not stop growing but the first little misfortunes intervened. Caffi and Jezo lost contact while Svoboda was delayed by a puncture. There were eight of them when they arrived at Amiens with a lead of more than two minutes: Thomas Dubuisson, Level, Camellini, Galle, Martino, Vietto and the Northerner Blanckaert.

On the road to Doullens the peloton woke up and the runaways capitulated round about L'Abret, after a break of one hundred and sixty four kilometres.

Emile Idée was riding with disconcerting ease. The champion of France attacked accompanied by Thiétard, Bonnaventure, Mithouard, Thomas and the robust Belgian Jules Lowie.

On the cobblestones of Arras, the spectators were amazed - for once the French seemed to be dominating the event!

But the Belgians had no intention of being outclassed. Successively Kint, Vanden Meerschaut, Bonduel, Vlaemynck, Sercu, Van Overloop and De Simpelaere were leading a determined counter attack. The junction took place at the exit to Arras. As the area of the coal mines approached, Lucien Vlaemynck was the first to shake the pack.

Sixteen men managed to get up to him. The outcome of the race was being decided and the winner was obviously among this group. The strategic crossing of Hénin-Liétard fulfilled its role perfectly as in the space of just a few hundred metres four riders were dropped. Firstly Mithouard and Goutorbe suffered from mechanical problems, then Dubuisson crashed and finally Idee, who a umber of followers saw as the winner, was betrayed by a puncture. he lost almost two minutes, almost managed to rejoin the leading group before weakening and dropping back.

At the front, Kint who was leading for most of the time. Only six riders managed to follow him all the way to the velodrome, the new finish of the race. Jules Lowie was first on to the track. He was followed by Kint and Louis Thiétard. A super-powerful Kint had no trouble in grabbing the lead and easily won the sprint in front of Lowie and Thiétard.

Many years after this success the man nicknamed "The Black Eagle" remembered: "During the war it was very difficult. I was a part of the Mercier team at a race at Clermont-Ferrand and between us we did not have one single spare tyre. Moreover instead of prizes we often got just a piece of cheese!

"When I rode the French classics, like Paris-Roubaix, I left on the bike on Saturday morning with my bag on my back. I took the train at Tourcoing and in the afternoon we picked up our stuff for the race and had our bikes checked and sealed. On the Sunday evening I returned home again on my bike.

"I have always remembered one particular thing about Paris-Roubaix 1943. We arrived earlier than the anticipated time. After the finish I did not wait around but went straight back home to Zwevegen, on my bike as usual but without my bouquet of flowers which I left at Roubaix. Not far from home, one of my supporters asked me what I was doing there. I told him that I had just won Paris-Roubaix. He did not believe me and burst out laughing. My family and friends would not believe it either. They were only convinced when they read it in the papers the following day.

"Paris-Roubaix left me with a lot of memories. Above all you had to be an acrobat to jump from one pavement to another as well as pushing a gear of 49 x 17. Now the cobbled sections are much more difficult and the gears even more so.

It really was another era."

Marcel KINT
(Belgium, 1914)

Known as the "Black Eagle", he spread his wings over professional cycling with great authority from 1935 to 1951.

1937 : 2nd Flèche Wallonne
1938 : World Champion, Paris-Brussels,
2nd Liège-Bastogne-Liège,
3rd Tour of Flanders
1939 : Belgian Champion,
2nd Paris-Roubaix
1943 : Paris-Roubaix, Flèche Wallonne
1944 : Flèche Wallonne
1945 : Flèche Wallonne
1949 : Ghent-Wevelgem

1943

1. Marcel KINT (Belgium)
   GS.Mercier-Hutchinson
2. Jules LOWIE (Belgium)
3. Louis THIETARD (France)
4. Achille BUYSSE (Belgium)
5. Albert SERCU (Belgium)
6. Camille DANGUILLAUME (France)
7. Lucien LE GUEVEL (France)
8. Alberic SCHOTTE (Belgium)
9. Rene ADRIAENSSENS (Belgium)
10. Jo GOUTORBE (France)

Difficult times ...

Paris-Roubaix was certainly relaunched but everyday life for the French remained very hard. In April 1944, Northerners were filled with consternation by the terrible massacre at Ascq. During the night of the first and second of April two explosions derailed a German military train. By way of reprisal the troops surrounded the village and shot eighty six people...
It was with this painful memory that the sportsmen of the region followed the progress of the forty second Paris-Roubaix.
This time there were a lot of Belgians among the one hundred and seventy five starters.
In Belgium they were speaking most favourably of a young phenomenon of nineteen and a half who already had on his shoulders the jersey of the champion of Belgium. Moreover, he had just won the Tour of Flanders in front of Schotte and Moerenhout. The whole of Belgium was waiting to see how Rik Van Steenbergen, their great hope, would perform over the northern roads of France. Several writers had no hesitation in nominating him as favourite for the event which he knew only by reputation.
The race started with the traditional skirmishes, but the first attack worthy of the name came just before the hill at Doullens. It was the work of Lucien Vlaemynck who was quickly joined by Guegan and Desmoulins. The trio led the race until the top of the climb where Vlaemynck took off by himself into the teeth of the wind.
On the road to Arras the Belgian was hoping for reinforcements and his wishes were fulfilled a few kilometres later when Munier and Huguet joined him. The peloton followed more than a minute down. The stars were watching each other and nobody wanted to initiate the pursuit. The experienced Rossi understood that something had to be done. Under his impulsion a small group went clear. It comprised Camille Danguillaume, the Southerners Giorgetti and Amedee Rolland, the Belgian Faignaert and naturally Rossi who could foresee the possibility of picking up a second Paris-Roubaix. As they went through Hénin-Liétard Munier punctured, then Danguillaume lost contact.
About twenty kilometres from the end of the race there remained six riders left at the front, all determined to contest the sprint at the Roubaix velodrome. The followers were already speculating on the chances of Rossi or of Faignaert. However, the race was turned upside down when the level crossing at Lesquin was closed. Certainly the runaways were only held up for a mere twenty seconds but that was enough to allow the return of another five candidates for victory: Georges Claes, Maurice de Simpelaere, Raymond Goussot, the astonishing Belgian Celestin Riga and a little Louis Thiétard.
Rossi, confident of his sprint and fortified by the presence of his team-mate Lucien Vlaemynck, did the major part of the work. When the men went onto the track his victory seemed assured.
For Rossi, who was tight on Vlaemynck's wheel, the plan seemed to be working perfectly. On the first bend, the Italian moved with ease into the lead in front of Louis Thiétard. Suddenly, in a tremendous rush, just one man managed to come up to him from behind and finally pass a totally disconcerted Rossi - it was Maurice De Simpelaere.
This unexpected winner was not a total surprise for everyone. At twenty three this talented rider, originally from Ledegem near Courtrai, was at one time considered to be one of the best juniors in the country.
His first appearances in France, in 1942, were crowned with success. De Simpelaere won the prestigious Grand Prix de

Maurice DE SIMPELAERE
(Belgium, 1920)

A good roadman-sprinter who notched up an enviable list of victories.

1944 : Paris-Roubaix
1945 : 2nd Het Volk
1946 : 2nd Ghent-Wevelgem
1947 : Ghent-Wevelgem,
       Paris-Montceau-les Mines,
       2nd Flèche Wallonne,
       2nd Paris-Brussels
1949 : Paris-St Etienne

1944

De Simpelaere

gagne
Paris - Roubaix

Voici le Belge, à 15 km. de l'arrivée, tentant une ultime échappade, poursuivi par Huguet, sur les pavés de l'Enfer du Nord.

(Photo Graphopresse.)

Boulogne and took third place in the Criterium des Aiglons. He was to confirm his great success at Roubaix by winning Ghent-Wevelgem 1947 and Paris-St Etienne 1949.

After this Paris-Roubaix, the Belgians seemed satisfied. The only setback was the retirement after a crash of Van Steenbergen. Several French journalists remained sceptical about him...but not for long!

The tribulations of a puny man by the name of Robic passed unnoticed. However, the young rider who was not yet known as "Biquet" had a very difficult Paris-Roubaix. Brought down in a crash at the feeding zone at Amiens he got back on his machine to finish at Roubaix with severe head pains. When he returned to Paris in a lorry he could not stop vomiting. On arrival he lost consciousness. When the doctor arrived he diagnosed a fractured skull which led to three months in hospital.

Finally it must be noted that the lot of the follower was not always a happy one. In this year of 1944 in a tiny Simca 5, were crammed Francis Pélissier and the journalists Constantin Brive, Jean Leulliot and Serge Svoboda. Half way along the route the huge Pélissier, tired of being almost folded into four at the steering wheel, suddenly stopped the car and opened the sun roof. He had had enough and spent the rest of the race sitting on top of the seat back with his head through the roof.

The return to Paris was scarcely much better. As they started out from Lille the surrounding areas were bombed. They took shelter in the cellar of a hotel. Hardly had they restarted when the car swerved violently, Francis had just run over an exploded bomb...

1944

1. Maurice DE SIMPELAERE (Belgium) GS.Alcyon
2. Jules ROSSI (Italy)
3. Louis THIETARD (France)
4. Raymond GOUSSOT (France)
5. Emile FAIGNAERT (Belgium)
6. Georges CLAES (Belgium)
7. Alvaro GIORGETTI (France)
8. Amédée ROLLAND (France)
9. Manuel HUGUET (France)
10. Lucien VLAEMYNCK (Belgium)

Vlamynck et De Simpelaere, après l'arrivée, sont très entourés.

nord
FRANCE

Le sprint du vainqueur
de Paris-Roubaix :
P. MAYE.

A Basque at Roubaix !

By early 1945, the Germans had been pushed back over the Rhine. The French, now freed of the yoke of the oppressors, followed the progress of the Allies towards Berlin.

At Roubaix, liberated a few months previously, rationing was still in force. So far as sport was concerned, an excellent way of forgetting the difficult years, things were slowly returning to normal and it took up the front pages of the few newspapers which were appearing regularly.

As in the first world conflict, a generation of sportsmen in all disciplines had lost their best years or in the worst cases their lives...

At the start of Paris-Roubaix the atmosphere was nevertheless excellent. The numerous spectators wanted to enjoy the spectacle as free men...

Only fourteen Belgians were present to sign the start sheet. However the quality of riders such as De Simpelaere and Albert Sercu seriously worried the home riders. The latter was not only a very fast sprinter but was also in top form as his second place in the Tour of Flanders confirmed, behind Sylvain Grysolle.

Above all the French were hoping for a good performance from Louis Thiétard, always well placed in the important events and already third at Roubaix on the two previous years.

After a very calm start, it was the Parisian Kléber Piot who commenced hostilities just before the hill at Doullens. As the kilometres went by a few riders were successful in their attempts to rejoin him, Lucien Teisseire then Paul Maye, Louis Thiétard, Edouard Muller, Robert Renoncé, Maurice De Muer and Maurice De Simpelaere!

The strongest of them all was incontestably Piot. The instigator of the escape was for most of the time leading the group at a very hot pace. Understanding that his chances in the sprint were somewhat limited in the face of the opposition, he tried many times to get away by himself.

De Simpelaere who had the unique chance of realising the double, neutralised every attempt. Five hundred metres from the entrance to the velodrome eight men were getting ready for the sprint when suddenly Maurice De Muer was eliminated from the "debate". His chain had just broken, he had to finish on foot.

So it was a bunch of seven riders which entered the velodrome crammed with thousands of spectators. At that precise moment De Simpelaere was the favourite. he arrived in company with Paul Maye, Kléber Piot who was still strong, then Louis Thiétard, Lucien Teisseire, Edouard Muller and Robert Renoncé.

Against all expectations De Simpelaere was pushed back into fifth place. The rapid Maye had ridden an excellent last lap of the track and did not let the opportunity slip through his fingers. Without difficulty he strung out Lucien Teisseire and Piot...

At thirty one this Basque from Bayonne won the most important event of a distinguished career. Some critics did not hesitate to claim that he did not know how to suffer and that he only shone in championship races (he achieved the unique exploit of being French amateur champion in 1934, military champion in 1935 and professional champion

PAUL MAYE
Jur "Cycle/ ALCYON" Dérailleur "LE /IMPLEX"
(Type Champion du Monde)

Paul MAYE
(France, 1913)

Maye specialised in winning national titles - including a unique treble of French amateur, military and professional - but his finishing speed earned him many other victories.

1934 : French Amateur Champion
1935 : French Military Champion
1938 : French Champion,
       3rd Paris-Tours
1939 : Paris-Angers
1941 : Paris-Tours
1942 : Paris-Tours, Paris-Nantes
1943 : French Champion
1945 : Paris-Roubaix, Paris-Tours
       2nd French Championship

1945

Paul Maye, according to Cello.

in 1938 and 1943!). This time he entered into legend by winning the biggest classic.

As he got off his machine he told the journalists and officials surrounding him: "I won Paris-Roubaix because it was not run on Easter day. This time it took place eight days later and you see the result..."

It was true that since he had started riding against the professionals in 1936 he had always punctured on that particular day. A week earlier he had ridden the Spring criterium and naturally...had a flat tyre!

In fact, his day finished very much better than it had started, for at one point he was forbidden to start!

When he was picking up his race number, an official insisted that he first pay an outstanding fine of four hundred francs. At first the impulsive Maye refused and hotly argued his case before finally giving in.

The day's most unlucky man was Emile Idée. The rider who had figured high on the list of favourites broke his forks near Chantilly. He rode for a long time with one hand while the other was holding the blade of his broken fork.

The rules still prohibited changes of machine, so he welded his forks by the side of the road just as Eugène Christophe had done at St Marie-de-Campan in the 1913 Tour de France. But being delayed so much, he had no choice but to retire.

As for Paul Maye, he finished his season with a third success in Paris-Tours and at the end of the year, only Eloi Tassin was ahead of him in the French championship contested for the second time on a points basis.

1945

1. Paul MAYE (France)
   GS.Alcyon
2. Lucien TEISSEIRE (France)
3. Kléber PIOT (France)
4. Louis THIETARD (France)
5. Maurice DE SIMPELAERE (Belgium)
6. Edouard MULLER (France)
7. Robert RENONCE (France)
8. Maurice DE MUER (France)
9. Maurice QUENTIN (France)
10. Lucien MALFAIT (France)

L'ÉQUIPE
LE STADE — L'AIR — LA ROUTE

LUNDI 22 AVRIL 1946
13, Fg Montmartre
PARIS (9e)
PROvence 85-21
Abonnements :
3 mois : 140 fr.
6 mois : 260 fr.
Cte Postal 423-791
2 fr. 1re ANNÉE N° 30

FRANCIA
SPORTS
52 RUE DE CLICHY PARIS 9e

Dans l'antichambre de "l'Enfer du Nord" les méridionaux Pernac et Rémy, lancent, avec Muller, la bataille. Mais...

La tradition s'en va : un " lévrier ", Georges Claes
gagne PARIS-ROUBAIX

Trophée Duralumin

Le Belge de Rochet-Dunlop bat au sprint Gauthier et Vlaemynck

Une épreuve au déroulement trop classique pour être passionnante.
Les Français n'ont jamais été éliminés. — Le Nizerhy, routier de classe internationale.
Tei. viré; Mayo, Caffi, malchanceux.

Van Steenbergen, déçevant par sa conception de la course,
abandonne après sa seconde crevaison

(D'un de nos envoyés spéciaux Claude TILLET)

Calme, le visage décontracté, à peine décoiffé, Claes explique posément la raison de sa victoire (cliché de droite). — N'est-ce pas le Morvandiau Gauthier qu'on prendrait pour un rouleur flandrien ? A 5 kilomètres de l'arrivée, Claes et son rival (de gauche à droit.) roulent côte à côte. Vlaemynck ne les a pas encore rejoi...

(Photos France Press)

ROUBAIX. — Pendant près de 200 kilomètres, nous avons cru...

LE CLASSEMENT

1. Georges CLAES, les 244 km. en 6 h. 19' 18", sur bicyclette Rochet, pneus Dunlop ;
2. Gauthier, à 1 long. ; 3. Vlaemynck, m. t. ;

LA SÉRIE NOIRE

LES BELGES BATTENT LES FRANÇAIS DE PEU

Quelques noms

La meilleure partie du SCUF en polo !

Il bat le champion d'Angleterre Electric Swimming Club : 5-3

(De notre envoyé spécial Georges DUCHESNE)

NOUVEAU REBONDISSEMENT DANS LE CHAMPIONNAT

Saint-Etienne et rejoint Lille

Lille, Lens et Reims battus par Roubaix, RO...

Victoire éclair de Dauthuille qui bat Toniolo en 1' 13" par jet de l'éponge

Aanstrantuono en gros progrès, a battu Pankoviak dans les deux derniers rounds. — Krawzick toujours imbattu

(De notre envoyé spécial Georges PEETERS)

GRANDE REPRISE INTERNATIONALE EN RUGBY XV

IMPRÉCISION ET CRAINTE CHEZ LES SÉLECTIONNEURS FRANÇAIS

Rouffia à l'arrière, Terreau au centr
Alvarez à l'ouverture, Soro à peine remi

FRANCE-GALLES
au Stade de Colombes
à 15 heures

LE SPORT SUR L'ANTENNE

The bunch gets ready for the sprint.

The succession of Georges Claes

The history of cycling has not retained the name of Georges Claes in the way that it should have done. This is not only a great pity but also a grave injustice. During his sporting career, the champion from Lovenjoel believed that results spoke for themselves and anything else was unnecessary.

This elegant roadman-sprinter, the complete opposite to "the Bulldog" Gaston Rebry, was certainly not short of results, for he strung together two Paris-Roubaix! In his first appearance on the Northern roads in 1944, he finished sixth and his agility was noted by the observers. The following year there was no longer any question of Paris-Roubaix, because during the month of April he was busy doing his military service...in Ireland!

Kept away from competition in 1945, he could not reasonably figure among the favourites of the 1946 Paris-Roubaix where all the stars were present.

In light of the results at the start of the season several names stood out. Above all that of Rik Van Steenbergen. After his victory in the Tour of Flanders, the Belgian press claimed that Rik was unbeatable.

A violent headwind was to play a decisive role in the way the race was run for it paralysed all attempts to escape.

Once again the first important victim was... Van Steenbergen. First a puncture delayed him at Esquenoy. After a pursuit of forty kilometres he came up to the peloton then promptly disappeared again after a second mishap. The most serious

1946

Georges CLAES
(Belgium, 1920-1994)

A veritable "Hare" of the road, Claes achieved two superb Paris-Roubaix victories in the immediate post-war era.

1941 : Circuit of Belgium
1942 : 2nd Tour of Flanders
1943 : 2nd Belgian Championship
2nd Flèche Wallonne
1946 : Paris-Roubaix
1947 : Paris-Roubaix, Tour of Limbourg
1948 : 3rd Paris-Roubaix

George Claes in second position, there is five
hundred metres to cover...

attack had been unleashed at Luzarches at the seventeenth kilometre.
Pawlisiak, Dubuisson, Bourlon, Le Guevel and Delacotte went to the front,
soon followed by Georges Claes, Dolhats and Neri.

This little bunch gained a lead of three and a half minutes. At Doullens it was
down to Neri, who was first over the hill, Georges Claes and Albert Dolhats.
But with only three of them to fight the wind, they could not resist for long.
Inevitably the regrouping took place just before Arras.

On the hill of St Catherine, Edouard Muller and the men from Marseilles,
Raoul Remy and Victor Penac, went away. For a very short time the latter
was on his own after his two companions were delayed with mechanical
problems.

It was back to square one when thirty riders went through Wattignies with
twenty two kilometres to go to the Roubaix velodrome.

This was the moment when Claes, who had been very vigilant the whole day,
felt strong enough to attack. Behind him Le Nizerhy broke clear in company
with Gauthier. However, only the latter had the strength to get onto Claes'
wheel.

At Lesquin at two hundred and twenty nine kilometres, the position had
become clear. Claes and Gauthier preceded Le Nizerhy by several hundred
metres, while the first chasing group comprised: Kint, Bonduel, Devreese,
De Simpelaere, Danguillaume, Vlaemynck. The latter, an old hand at the
event, counter-attacked and after a superb effort managed to rejoin the two
runaways in the streets of Roubaix.

At the entrance onto the track, eight hundred metres from the line, the
superpowerful Gauthier, nicknamed "the breaker of chains", confirmed his
reputation by this time snapping a toe-strap!

The sprint was quickly launched, the spectators saw that nothing could stop Claes, the incomparable winner of the sprint in front of Gauthier and Vlaemynck.

While Claes was riding his lap of honour, Le Nizerhy was inconsolable after having missed the decisive break by so very little. Replying to a journalist who told him that he had ridden a magnificent race and that he would be on top form for the Paris-Tours, he replied: "Yes, of course, but you know there is only one Paris-Roubaix, and it's here that you have to show yourself."

1946

1. Georges CLAES (Belgium)
   GS.Rochet
2. Louis GAUTHIER (France)
3. Lucien VLAEMYNCK (Belgium)
4. Frans BONDUEL (Belgium)
5. Camille DANGUILLAUME (France)
6. Georges BLUM (France)
7. Maurice DE SIMPELAERE (Belgium)
8. Victor PERNAC (France)
9. Joseph SOFFIETTI (France)
10. Marcel KINT (Belgium)

George Claes disposes of Louis Gauthier.

L'ÉQUIPE
Élans

LUNDI
7 AVRIL 1947
13, Fg Montmartre
PARIS (9ᵉ)
PROvence 85-21
QUOTIDIEN
SAUF LE
DIMANCHE
4 fr. · 2ᵉ ANNÉE
N° 297
Afr. du Nord : 5 fr.

• LE QUOTIDIEN • DU SPORT •

Bataille, dans un très grand PARIS-ROUBAIX, à près de 40 kms de moyenne, sous la pluie

BIZZI DOMINE PENDANT 235 Kms, MAIS...

...CLAES BONDIT ET GAGNE !

Seconde victoire consécutive du lévrier belge

et consécration du type rouleur-sprinter

LA VICTOIRE
que nous n'aurions pas voulu rater

(D'un de nos envoyés spéc. Jacques GODDET)

ROUBAIX. — Après Milan-San Remo de tourmente, Paris-Roubaix et. Pluie cinglante, bora lourde, véritable inondations recouvrant les chaussées détrempées chaotiques, mais, pour l'abaissement dramatique d'une course qu'aucun élément ne parvenait à policer, qu'elle est vibrante cette course, si claire en son déroulement, inexorable dans ses conséquences.

Un espoir — celui de remporter consécutivement un deuxième Paris-Roubaix, à une époque où les engagés sont aussi exaspérés que ceux des espérances — est déçu par un autre espoir. Claes est un magnifique vainqueur qu'on ne discute plus. Bizzi, ce petit Italien de trente ans, pédaleur intelligent mais extraordinairement consciencieux, reposant son maître avec une part rigueur nordiques, ne peux battuisante et triompheront.

La victoire qu'il a prise si clairement, mais qu'il a remportée aussi aux cœurs d'hommes de sport, avant qu'elle qu'il aurait failli pour enrichie la légende aux pages du Paris-Roubaix.

Parti à l'aventure dès les premiers kilomètres, malgré le poids de l'ignorance, malgré la montée et l'énigme, pour un Italien du chemin d'enfer qui, aujourd'hui qui fera nos ornements, bordait la rive à l'Athéron, tenait en rapport 235 kilomètres durant, tenait la première à l'heure qu'une chasse aux faiblesse...

La Claes parle

Le lot courante du sport veut que ce gloréification du vainqueur dit à moral à rabattu la valeur du vainqueur acté. L'émouvante performance de Bizzi prime incontestablement tout ce qui a pu être réalisé dans ce petit Paris-Roubaix. On y trouve audace, décision, courage, résistance, brio dans la conception et la réalisation, sinon dans l'allure extérieure de l'individu, mais la surface pas, ce qui donne à la performance de Claes un relief particulier.

(Lire la suite page 2 en rubrique Cyclisme)

Course héroïque des Italiens — Belle tenue des Français qui terminent mal — Thiétard encore premier des nôtres — Rentrée courageuse de Charpentier — Idée malchanceux

1947 : GRAND CRU

(D'un de nos envoyés spéciaux Claude TILLET)

ROUBAIX. — Milan-San Remo : victoire solitaire après échappée, poursuite, nouvelles échappées ; Zurich-Lausanne : autres très longues fugues avec vent défavorable et victoire des meilleurs parmi les fugitifs ; Criterium national : arrivée d'un combatif entre les combattifs. Épreuve longue de début de saison ! Sans doute moins brillante, mais à l'arrivée de Paris-Roubaix deux Belges ! Et ce Paris-Roubaix a été lui-même course extraordinaire.

La saison européenne 1947 s'annonce donc à la manière de ces « grandes années » dont « honorent une crête arbres la jute » comme notre Bourgogne. De tous côtés, des jeunes surgirent, des anciens se dressent la tête, des « revenants » se remontent au premier plan.

Honneur aux anciens

Les anciens ? Ce sont l'italien Olympio Bizzi qui, dès le 8ᵉ kilomètre, a pris la large avec l'idée bien arrêtée d'aller jusqu'à l'arrivée... ou de cette course finie, dont il oubliera tout. — le Brugé Vlaempnck Claes, cet étonnant d'une échappée malheureuse terminée à quelques kilomètres du but la retour de Claes, Gauthier, Bondurt ; cet autre Belge qui a nom Georges Claes et qui, s'inscrire à nouveau son nom au palmarès « Dorslumin » ; cet inusable Français Thiétard et, cet autre Rbry vieux Thiétard, parvenant vainqueur, mais toujours superlatrment classé ... ; Il y aurait d'autres, mais nous y restredrons un peu plus loin.

L'inoubliable poursuite

Ne convient-il pas de parler d'abord de la poursuite en match-pour-suite qui se poursuivit, par un vent froid épouvantablement pluvieux, de l'île-de-France au pays minier, à peine de 40 de moyenne ?

Certes, le vent s'avérait presque continuellement favorable... mais la

(Lire la suite p. 2, rubr. Cyclisme)

PEU AVANT L'EFFONDREMENT Vlaempnck, ce valeureux petit Belge, roule dur depuis que l'échappée initiale a pris corps. Bientôt, hélas ! il devra, après Hénin-Liétard, où on le voit passer en tête devant Fazio et Bizzi, lâcher prise. C'est l'effondrement des espoirs de ces trois hommes qui furent les trois héros de la course pascale.
(Radioreportage de L'ÉQUIPE)

AUX 26ᵉˢ CHAMPIONNATS DE FORCE

Ferrari, le meilleur et Héral s'affirme...

...égalant les seniors

Quatre nouveaux champions : Moulens (coq) Baril, 42 ans (plume) — Bouladou (léger) Firmin (moyen) — Thévenet (coq) établit le record mondial du développé sur 85 kgs

Il n'y avait guère qu'un millier de spectateurs hier après-midi sous le marquise de la gymnase Japy qui dispensait une fraîcheur aigre et froide. Mais c'était là un public de connaisseurs, d'amateurs au bon sens du terme qui se réchauffa bien vite dès la confrontation des « coqs » alors que Walter et Thévenet battirent et rétablirent le record de France du développé.

Épreuve de force, mais aussi de volonté où l'athlète concentre, ac- selle la barre saisissant de mouvements qui ont quelque chose d'impression...

Maurice MAUREL
(Lire la suite p. 3, rub. Haltérès)

A CLEVELAND LE 1ᵉʳ JUIN

RAY ROBINSON
défendra son titre
contre Jimmy Doyle

(De notre env. spéc. perm. R. BRE...)

NEW-YORK. — Deux semaines après le championnat du monde hors Abrams, le champion du monde des « welters » Ray Robinson mettra son titre en jeu, le 1ᵉʳ juin à Cleveland, contre le Californien Jimmy Doyle. C'est un des plus dangereux adversaires du mi-moyen.

Rappelons que R. Robinson avait annoncé son retour en France pour la fin du mois de mai.

EN SECOND COMBAT

CHARRON-AMANINI
le 4 mai
à la Croix de Berny

AU GRAND PRIX DE PAU, SOUS LE PATRONAGE DE L'ÉQUIPE

CHABOUD
un peu moins vite
mais Sommer devra se ravitailler
ET J.-P. WIMILLE NE SERA PAS LOIN !

En moto, le Belge Laurent et l'Anglais Anderson se partagent les victoires

(D'un de nos envoyés spéciaux Maurice HENRY)

PAU. — Le résultat des deux séances d'entraînement qui ont eu lieu hier et aujourd'hui n'a apporté au rentablton que bien minces aliens après l'intérêt de ce premier Grand Prix de Pau d'après guerre organisé par l'Automobile-Club Basco-Béarnais, sous l'intérêt en présence de L'ÉQUIPE.

Déception aux Championnats des États-Unis

Jany, désuni, battu sur 220 yards
puis écrasé sur 100 yards !

Il fut éliminé en série par Morgan, qui ne fut pas qualifié pour la finale. - Vedettes à Columbus : W. Ris, B. Smith, J. Verdeur

(De notre cor. spéc. par Jean NAU)

Jany second, vendredi, du 220 yards des Championnats d'Amérique. Bravo !...
...Mais à 3" 7/10 du vainqueur, hélas !...
...Et enfin éliminé en série du 100 yards, samedi.

Le bilan surprendra les lecteurs de L'ÉQUIPE. Dès vendredi, nous avions clairement laissé entrevoir ces éventualités. Pour trois raisons :

Les lutteurs russes
déjà en route
pour Prague !

(De notre cor. spéc. par Jean NAU)

MOSCOU. — L'équipe d'haltérophilie de l'URSS pour les Championnats d'Europe (11 avril) à Prague, a quitté Moscou, hier dimanche, sous la direction de M. Dukanoster, vice-président du Commissariat aux Sports. Les lutteurs sont : Novak, G. Koteralova, A. Sokolov, A. Karapetian et L. Egorov.

BATTUE PAR Mᵐᵉ RURAK

Pauline Betz
ne vaut pas
Alice Marble...
...et Bergelin a battu sans gloire
l'Américain Falkenburg

(Lire en rubrique Tennis, page 3, l'article de notre envoyé spécial Jean GAMAZEUILH)

La journée s'annonçait calme elle fut dramatique...

Grâce à la fougue de Montpellier

REIMS, BATTU, EST REJOINT PAR ROUBAIX

Lille en échec ; Strasbourg vaincu et Le Havre seul vainqueur hors de chez lui. -- Stade et Racing ne peuvent vaincre sur leur terrain

Pour désigner l'événement principal de la journée d'hier, nous n'avons certes pas l'embarras du choix. Raisons : dimanche de Championnat nous aura apporté autant de surprises, ou, pour mieux dire, autant de résultats contraires à la logique de l'épreuve.

Il nous semble cependant que celui qu'il convient de mettre en évidence, et qui n'y met d'ailleurs pas bien tout seul, c'est la défaite de Reims à Montpellier.

Maurice PEFFERKORN
(Lire la suite page 4)

DIVISION NATIONALE
31ᵉ JOURNÉE

Classement

	P	J	G	N	P	P.
1 REIMS (1)						
2 Lille (3)						
3 Sochaux (2)						
4 Marseille (4)						
5 St-Étienne						
6 Roubaix (8)						
7 Rennes (7)						
8 Red Star (9)						
9 CANNES (5)						
10 Metz (10)						
11 St-Étienne						
12 Nice						
13 Strasbourg						
14 Toulouse						
15 Lens (16)						
16 Montpellier						
17 Rouen (13)						
18 Le Havre						

EN HOCKEY SUR GAZON A FOLKESTONE

La France
battue (2-1)
fait grosse impression

(Lire en rubrique Hockey, l'article de Marcel FURGEOT)

NOTRE TREIZE AMATEURS A JOUÉ EN ÉQUIPE

45 à 5 !

La mariée
est trop belle !

L'AMATEURISME EN FRANCE EST PLUS FLORISSANT QU'EN ANGLETERRE ON LE SAVAIT...

(De notre envoyé spécial Louis FERDINAND)

CARCASSONNE. — Une marge de 45 à 5 en match international suffit l'événement et les seules excuses que l'on puisse inscrire à la décharge de la défaite britannique sont une mauvaise condition physique, la fatigue d'un long voyage et une température printanière ! A vrai dire...

À L'ÉCOLE LES JUNIORS !

BIEN QUE VAINQUEUR
le "XV" de France
fut aussi décevant que son aîné

Un seul joueur : le Tarbais Vaslin

Le match France-Galles à Colombes, le 23 mars, avait été tristement médiocre. Samedi, au Parc des Princes, nos juniors ne l'ont pas été suffisamment à leurs aînés.

En réplique que l'équipe de France l'a tout de même emporté, on s'attendait par 8 à 5, ne peut être qu'une bien faible compensation.

Marcel de LABORDERIE
(Lire la suite p. 3, rubr. Rugby XV)

POUR LA FINALE

Le marché noir
des billets est ouvert

(De notre envoyé spécial Louis FERDINAND)

TOULOUSE. —

Georges Claes
confirms with a double

The year was 1947 and the real resumption of international cycling was under way. The Tour de France - after a rehearsal the previous year (Monaco-Paris 1946 won by Apo Lazarides) - was going to be finally reborn in July after being interrupted for eight years.

Paris-Roubaix still remained the number one Spring classic. Beating a peloton of the stars of the road, Georges Claes was going to confirm his first victory. This time however the hero of the day - who would nevertheless not figure in the final result - was an Italian called Olimpio Bizzi.

In fact he very nearly won it, for this Tuscan, a former Italian champion, was clear for two hundred and twelve kilometres!

From the start of this forty fifth edition, the race went off like a rocket in spite of the Dantesque weather conditions.

Scarcely twenty kilometres were covered when three riders went clear, Macorig, Desmoulins and Vlaemynck. A few minutes later another four men rejoined them: Robert Charpentier, the Olympic champion at Berlin eleven years before, who was using the occasion to make his big comeback, Edouard Muller and the only two Italians in the bunch Olimpio Bizzi and Mario Fazio. The numbers in this front group were rapidly reduced as Macorig and Desmoulins were eliminated with punctures, then on the road to Amiens, Charpentier and Muller crashed.

The bunch which had not yet picked up the pace considered this break to be nothing more than minor episode as by now there were only three runaways to struggle against the wind.

But Bizzi decided not to give in without a fight. On the cobblestones he first of all dropped Fazio and then surprisingly, Vlaemynck.

Among the cottages of the mining sector, in front of thousands of supporters, it was a unique spectacle as for the first time ever an Italian was "leading the dance" all alone under the rain and in the mud, on the home ground of the robust Flemings!

With a rare virtuosity he held off the "lords" Claes, Schotte, Impanis, Verschueren, Thiétard and their consorts.

As the kilometres went by, Bizzi was becoming convinced that he was going to win as he had a comfortable lead of two minutes but then he broke his back wheel in a gutter.

The Tuscan was quickly given a new wheel and restarted with a lead of forty seconds over his nearest challengers, but the excited crowd could see that "the spring was broken". Behind, Georges Claes had been made aware of what had happened, so he accelerated. The little Verschueren jumped onto his wheel and Thiétard, always attentive in the final stages of a classic, followed them.

In a few minutes and just two kilometres from the velodrome, the trio caught Bizzi whose eyes were filled with tears.

At the appearance on the flooded track of Claes, Verschueren and Thiétard, the spectators rose to their feet. Thiétard, the eternal second placed, on this accursed velodrome wanted to add this prestigious classic to his record at least once.

The Frenchman started the sprint from a long way out with Verschueren and Claes on his wheel. Verschueren counter-attacked but Claes pounced like a cat and easily passed his two rivals in the final straight.

Claes was delighted. The Roubaix track had become his kingdom. After the traditional flowers, he explained his success to the journalists in a few simple words before adding: "During the race I eat very little, today I needed only three hundred grams of sugar lumps

1947

and seven bananas in order to win" not without adding maliciously and thinking of the performance of Bizzi "and also a little luck!"

The Belgians who at the start had hoped for something from Van Steenbergen greeted this new victory with pleasure.

On the other hand the great Rik once again failed in this event which had so far brought him very little luck. A crash at the start had ruined all his plans.

Destiny made him wait for this race which he wanted so much to win. The champion who had been unable to finish a single Paris-Roubaix had nevertheless promised to return the following year when he believed he would be stronger.

At the finish André Leducq and Georges Speicher, two former winners and connoisseurs of the event were unanimous in proclaiming it was the finest Paris-Roubaix they had ever seen.

1947

1. Georges CLAES (Belgium)
   GS.Rochet
2. Adolf VERSCHUEREN (Belgium)
3. Louis THIETARD (France)
4. Raymond IMPANIS (Belgium)
5. Albéric SCHOTTE (Belgium)
6. Olimpio BIZZI (Italy)
7. Edouard FACHLEITNER (France)
8. Maurice DE MUER (France)
9. Lucien TEISSEIRE (France)
10. Lucien VLAEMYNCK (Belgium)

SPORTS ECLAIR

LUNDI
7 AVRIL 1947
5 Frs

DANS CE NUMÉRO : 26
HARNES, club sympathique d'Artois
La boxe au R.C. Roubaix
Paris-Roubaix, course pascale
Paris-Nord de basket-ball
Le match C.O.R.T.-Toulouse
Au service de l'athlétisme
Notre grand concours de la coupe

REDACTION ET ADMINISTRATION
27, Rue Faidherbe, LILLE (Nord)

Le 45e Paris-Roubaix s'est déroulé sous la pluie et dans la boue. Après avoir rejoint, puis lâché l'Italien BIZZI le Belge CLAES a renouvelé son succès de l'an dernier. Voici le vainqueur porté en triomphe par ses admirateurs après avoir franchi la ligne d'arrivée.

Cliché SPORTS-ECLAIR
Robert VILAIN

LE 46e PARIS-ROUBAIX

VAN STEENBERGEN est l'homme à battre

...MAIS 60 CHAMPIONS sont des vainqueurs possibles

ILS ONT GAGNÉ

REINE des classiques, Paris-Roubaix pose au peloton cycliste le plus difficile de l'année.

On en connaît les données, elles restent immuables. Pour la 46e fois, les routiers se précipitent vers le légendaire vélodrome du Nord, dont la porte étroite s'ouvre au flanc d'un talus de chemin de fer, à la sortie de Wattignies, au 236e kilomètre.

[column of biographical text]

Il s'en est passé des choses dans Paris-Roubaix depuis... 1896

[text]

L'attaque à l'italienne peut-elle réussir ?

[text]

Ils doivent tous capituler... sauf un !

[text]

R.I.K. VAN STEENBERGEN

SPEICHER

CLAES

SYLVÈRE MAES

VAN SIMPELAERE

KINT

P. MAYE

MASSON

Paris-Roubaix la course des Belges

PARIS-ROUBAIX ! C'est l'aventure de la bonne internationale, la grande aventure. Cette course est l'épreuve des Belges.

[text]

par Georges SPEICHER

Composition de CELLO

[Map labels along route, from top to bottom:]

ROUBAIX 246 Km — 15 h 44
HEM 240 Km — 15 h 34
WATTIGNIES 224,4 Km — 15 h 04
CARVIN 211 Km — 14 h 41
HENIN LIETARD 203 Km — 14 h 25
ARRAS 182 Km — 13 h 50
DOULLENS 147 Km — 12 h 54
BEAUVAL 141 Km — 12 h 44
AMIENS 116 Km — 12 h 02
DURY 110 Km — 11 h 54
BRETEUIL 84 Km — 11 h 13
St JUST en CHAUSSÉE 66 Km — 10 h 44
CLERMONT 50 Km — 10 h 19
CREIL 35 Km — 9 h 52
CHANTILLY 27 Km — 9 h 42
LUZARCHES 17 Km — 9 h 26
St DENIS CONTROLE
DÉPART DE PIERREFITTE 9 h.

231 routiers internationaux à la conquête de la gloire

ILS PEUVENT GAGNER

ROCHET-DUNLOP
1. CLAES, vainqueur en 1946 et 1947.
2. BOURLON
3. FAMULLIAK
4. ABEILLARD
5. DELULE
6. BLUM
7. LOWERS
8. DUBUISSON
9. GEUS
10. MATHIEU G.
11. DUPONT N.
12. GHYSSELYNCK
13. BRIER
14. GRYVOELLES
15. PIMREZ
16. CHAPALAIN
17. ERMACORA

FRANCE-SPORT-DUNLOP
18. VIETTO
19. LAZARIDES Apo.
20. LAZARIDES Lucien
21. MAGAS
22. FAUTREL
23. GALLIUSSI

METROPOLE-DUNLOP
24. TEISSEIRE Lucien
25. GUEGAN
26. HUGUET
27. MAGORA
28. BLANC
29. DEMINIANI
30. LAUCK Lucien
31. LAUCK Rene
32. BEVERS
33. DECORTE
34. CAMELLINI
35. BRAMBILLA

ALCYON-DUNLOP
36. GAFF
37. MULLER
38. BARRET
39. IMPANIS
40. DE SIMPELAERE
41. MASSON
42. SCHOTZ
43. STERCKX
44. VLAEMYNCK
45. HENDRYCKX M.
46. REMUE
47. NETERMEN
48. LEBAGE
49. LEONI

LA FRANCAISE-DIAMANT-DUNLOP
50. LUCAS
51. ROSSEL
52. RONDELEZ

ARLIGUIE-HUTCHINSON
53. GEMPELAERE
54. DELACOTTE
55. LAMBLIN
56. THOBOIS
57. RAMON
58. ANGUTTON
59. COUVREUR
60. DAENEKINDT
61. THOMAS Roi
62. STAEDDLER

BENOIT-FAURE-HUTCHINSON
63. CLERMONT J.
64. VAN DIJK I.

CARRARA-DUNLOP
65. CARRARA
66. GOUTIER
67. VAN WORLD
68. BAUWENS H.
69. BUYL G.
70. DE HOOG

CIMATTI
71. ZANAZZI A.
72. MONCASSINI
73. CASOLA
74. MONALDI
75. CECHI

STELLA-DUNLOP
76. ROBIC
77. MAHE
78. GAUDIN
79. POITEY
80. AUDAIRE
81. ADRIAN
82. DANIELOU
83. BARBOTIN
84. LAMBRECHT

DILECTA
85. MAYS
86. PREVOTAL
87. LEVEQUE
88. BLANKAERT
89. REMY
90. LE SPRAY
91. BONNAVENTURE
92. ROLDABARI
93. BERTON
94. GRAZZO
95. VERT

LA PERLE-HUTCHINSON
96. PACHLEYNER
97. GUEURDET
98. CLAR
99. GOYTHAL
100. REMY
101. RENAUDIN
102. PELLAROUT
103. MARTIN
104. KETELEER
105. DEPREDHOMME
106. REGNARRY
107. MALBHDHOT
108. DILL
109. LEYSEN

MERCIER-HUTCHINSON
110. AUBRY
111. CARPENTIER
112. GAUTHIER R.
113. GAUTHIER L.
114. GUEBELEN
115. ROLLAND
116. KINT
117. VAN STEENBERGEN
118. BRUSSELMANS

[right column continued:]
119. CALLENS
120. DE BARRE
121. DESPLENTER
122. MAES Syh.
123. MOLLIN
124. RYCKAERT M.
125. VERSCHUEREN A
126. MOMMORENS A.V.
127. RITSEVELD
128. TAICA
129. KLAKNSAV
130. CHAPATTE
131. COLSEN
132. PERNAC
133. MOLUGA
134. MAERFAIT
135. REDOLF
136. GLARDON
137. DESPREZ
138. MACKLAK
139. LAFRAXE Guy
140. DESRATE

GENIAL-LUCIFER-HUTCHINSON
141. NOEL
142. QUENTIN
143. THIVARRE
144. BERNELLE
145. GUILLIER G.

GABIN-WOLBER
146. FIEL
147. BERNARDONI
148. RANDONS
149. ROGIERS
150. VAN DRIX H.
151. VAN VERHOVE
152. DEPOORTER Rich.
153. BOGAERT
154. NOORKLAMP Th.
155. JANSSEN Joe
156. KIRCHEN

BERTIN-DUNLOP
157. BERG
158. OLLIVIER
159. OMEL
160. DEBREF Roger
161. DE SWEDT Maym.
162. BOLLINKS
163. DE WACHTER A.

PEUGEOT-DUNLOP
164. IDEE
165. DANGUILLAUME C.
166. DE HILKS
167. DEVESSE
168. DOGGEBRAY
169. DE GRABALDY
170. PIOLET
171. LONG
172. SALEN
173. VERSCHUEREN M.
174. MEULENBERG
175. LEENEN
176. JOMAUX

OLYMPIA-DUNLOP
177. CAPUT
178. GREGOIRE
179. CHARPENTIER
180. MIGNAT
181. KERGOET
182. HYZ
183. JOLY VICT.
184. ORTELLI

BARDENNE-DUNLOP
185. TAICA
186. TAGLIU
187. ENDALL
188. DEPORTER John.
189. HAMELNVICA

RHONSON-DUNLOP
190. BARBANOVA
191. ROLLAND AM.
192. BARATIN G.
193. BOOA

STAKNORD-WOLBER
194. WITTEKE
195. DELVALLEE
196. PINAFFKENS
197. MAGNAT
198. DIDDEN Ant.

FOLLIS-DUNLOP
199. MARTIN Georges
200. QUELPA
201. AUDER

FRRA-DUNLOP
202. NEFFNEL
203. VIERVIN
204. BONVARLEZ
205. JANSSENS Julien
206. VERBOVEN

THOMAS-ROSSET-DUNLOP
207. POLLAND Andre
208. PRICEN

RIVA-SPORT-DUNLOP
209. BORY V.
210. BUCHAMET

RICCI
211. BIZZI
212. FAU
213. BERTOGNI

WILLIER-TRIESTINA
214. MAGNI
215. MARTINI

INDIVIDUELS
216. TROVILL
217. GOUTORBE
218. BAFFERT
219. LOMME
220. BUYSSE Achille
221. NEUVILLE
222. RAGU
223. FRELVOGEL
224. KERR Willie
225. MORETTI
226. ALVAREZ
227. DERANDZERRE
228. HENDRYCKX Albert
229. KUBLER

TEISSEIRE

BIZZI

SERCU

IDÉE

IMPANIS

PERNAC

VAN STEENBERGEN

The Blue Riband
for Van Steenbergen

On the 4th April 1948 on the Legion d'Honneur Square at St Denis, there were heated discussions between the journalists. In fact the forty sixth edition of Paris-Roubaix looked like being very open. The same questions kept coming back: who would be good enough to beat Georges Claes who was by now the number one specialist? Would the French champions at last be able to stand up to the Belgian pressure? How would the "Van Steenbergen phenomenon" perform, he had never proved himself over these Northern roads so was it still conceivable that he could win?

A few hours later at the Roubaix velodrome Rik's reply was scathing: the man from Flanders had just picked up his first Paris-Roubaix at the record average speed of 43.612 kph, a new blue riband of the road. It was the distinction given to the race run at the highest average speed (previously held by Jules Ross since the 1937 Paris-Tours with 42.092 kph).

The French showed themselves near the front of the race especially in the first part of the event, and finally Claes, by once again being on the podium, confirmed he was effectively the "new Rebry".

Right from the gun a violent tailwind was pushing the two hundred and seventeen competitors along. The Parisian Robert Chapatte broke away from the imposing peloton. Rapidly the Italian ace Fiorenzo Magni, Piot, Danielou, Caput, Kergoet and a strong man with the shoulders of a furniture remover, dressed in an orange and green check jersey, who was totally unknown but went by the name of Monari, joined him.

The carefree bunch had no desire to engage in a pursuit too early. The gap grew progressively: to a minute and a half at Chantilly where Kergoet and Piot were dropped after puncturing, two minutes at Clermont, a little more at Breteuil at the nineteenth kilometre.

At Amiens, the half way point, another flat tyre eliminated Danielou but the lead of Chapatte, Caput, Magni and Monari was not really diminishing. The runaways crossed the town at more than forty kilometres an hour preceding the bunch by two and a half minutes.

This demonstration of strength reminded the followers of the desperate attempt of Bizzi the year before which had not succeeded.

Had the bunch been trapped this time?

The question was asked again at Doullens, where Magni went through in the lead and the bunch had not pulled a single second back on the leaders. But on the famous hill the young Chapatte, who had been particularly frisky up to that point, broke two spokes. Forced to put his foot to the ground the Parisian would not see his companions again..

In the circumstances the three men could not hold off the mounting pressure from the peloton. The solid André Mahé

Rik VAN STEENBERGEN
(Belgium, 1924)

Known universally as 'Rik 1' by virtue of his 270 road race victories, he was also a great track rider with 40 victories in the six-day races.

1943 : Belgian Champion
1944 : Tour of Flanders
1945 : Belgian Champion
1946 : Tour of Flanders
1948 : Paris-Roubaix
1949 : World Champion, Flèche Wallonne
1950 : Paris-Brussels
1952 : Paris-Roubaix
1954 : Belgian Champion,
        Milan-San Remo
1956 : World Champion
1957 : World Champion
1958 : Flèche Wallonne

1948

was the first to open hostilities. The Breton attacked as Arras came into sight and went through a minute behind on the fugitives.

The rest of the bunch raced through the town one minute and twenty seconds down. Mahé rejoined, the attack of Carrara and sounded the knell for the hopes of the trio Caput, Magni, Monari. The popular "Milo" was the first to catch them at Carvin after two hundred and eleven kilometres of racing. The Belgians who had not for one moment played any other role than that of observers came to the front at the end of the mining sector. Their tactics proved to be excellent as from now on they were the masters of the event. Among the leading twenty at the big bend at Wattignies were Sercu, Claes, Hendrickx, Schotte and......Van Steenbergen.

The final showdown started with a "festival" of punctures between Wattignies and Ascq. Successively Sercu, Schotte, Remue and Danguillaume were left behind and then Muller, Keteleer, Jomaux, Caput, Carrara, Gyselinck, Ryckaert, Léoni and Mahé were dropped one after the other.

At Hem, six kilometres from the finish there was no more jostling at the front. Emile Idée the worthy champion of France was away in company with Fiorenzo Magni and the Belgian Adolf Verschueren.

Just down the road Van Steenbergen decided that it was now or never and

Rik Van Steenbergen congratulated
by Antonin Magne

PARIS - ROUBAIX
à 44 kms 350 de moyenne !...

chased with three men on his wheel: Marcel Hendrickx, soon to be eliminated with a puncture, Georges Claes and the astonishing Monari.

The Fleming achieved his ends when he joined the leading group as they hit the streets of Roubaix.

Emile Idée knew all about Van Steenbergen's fantastic sprinting ability. He decided to throw everything into one final attack. When he turned round he saw with despair Van Steenbergen behind him. The others were dropped.

The Frenchman was certainly beaten but not resigned. He entered the track in the lead with the Belgian two lengths down, before gallantly launching the sprint and naturally being overcome.

Powerless when faced with the Belgian's speed, he dropped off before the finishing line.

A few moments after the finish, on the grass of the track centre, the "King of the Chevreuse" was downcast: "I did not have the strength to get away from Van Steenbergen and what can anyone do against him in the sprint?" he asked those around him and continued "There's always a 'Flahute' to steal the victory from under my nose, Schotte at Tours (referring to the previous years Paris-Tours when Schotte had beaten him), Van Steenbergen here," and left for the showers totally disillusioned.

For Van Steenbergen, on the other hand it was his big day of glory.

Completely surrounded he affirmed: "This will be my best and my worst souvenir. The best because my return to the road has allowed me to win one of the greatest races. The worst because I have never suffered so much. I was going well in Milan-San Remo and was only stopped by punctures. I was very motivated because I knew that a victory in Paris-Roubaix would give a lot of pleasure to Antonin Magne my team manager, and to Mercier, whose colours I am defending."

Among those less fortunate was the Belgian Albert Sercu. He was "riding like thunder", maintained the witnesses and according to him without his puncture he would have attacked and he would have won.

Although the Belgians won the race as they usually did, at least the French featured well. Among them were two young men who were both very poorly rewarded: Louison Bobet and Bernard Gauthier. The first picked himself up from an accident with a broken collar bone, the second was knocked down by a car six kilometres from the finish and arrived at Roubaix in an ambulance.

Nevertheless the succession was perhaps assured.

1948

1. Rik VAN STEENBERGEN (Belgium) GS.Mercier
2. Emile IDEE (France)
3. Georges CLAES (Belgium)
4. Adolf VERSCHUEREN (Belgium)
5. Fiorenzo MAGNI (Italy)
6. Egidio MONARI (Italy)
7. Marcel RYCKAERT (Belgium)
8. Adolfo LEONI (Italy)
9. André MAHE (France)
10. Roger GYSELYNCK (Belgium)

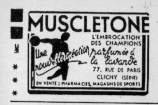
LUNDI 18 AVRIL 1949
10, Fg Montmartre
PARIS (9e)
L'Altbrul 70-80
Petites Annonces
TAI 73-40, 41, 42
Vente : PRO 97-18
Cpe Postal 4 237-93
9 fr. 4e ANNÉE
Afr. du Nord : 10 fr. N° 941

L'ÉQUIPE
LE QUOTIDIEN 6 pages DU SPORT

SCANDALE A L'ARRIVEE D'UN DECEVANT PARIS-ROUBAIX, TROPHEE RIZ-LA-CRO...

MAHE, PREMIER après avoir parcouru 200 m. de plus
EST DÉCLASSÉ
au bénéfice de... Serse Coppi

Les leaders avaient été mal aiguillés par la police. MOUJICA et le Belge LEENEN - les 2 autres meilleurs hommes de la course - sont également victimes de cette faute

Loupée... la "Course du siècle" !
(De notre directeur général Jacques GODDET)

ROUBAIX. — Dans fois raté ce grandissime Paris-Roubaix ! Raté dans son développement général, par la neutralisation réciproque des vedettes, loupé lamentablement dans sa conclusion. On trouvera, dans une autre colonne, le récit détaillé de la gaffe monumentale commise par la police roubaisienne, renvoyant sur le parcours réservé aux voitures officielles, et non sur l'itinéraire destiné aux coureurs, les trois hommes de tête, Moujica, Mahé et Leenen, juste au abords où le vélodrome, alors qu'ils possédaient assurait la voiture à l'avance [...]

L'application de la réglementation qui, se refusant à toute interprétation arbitraire, prévoit le déclassement automatique des coureurs n'ayant pas accompli le parcours [...]

Les organisateurs que nous sommes devons supporter la responsabilité de cette faute grave. Nous n'imaginions pas, en effet, que plusieurs policiers, commandés à cette dérivation par un commissaire spécial, allaient s'amuser à jeter sur la fausse piste les coureurs qu'ils étaient chargés de ce et de protéger. Le service d'ordre, en France, manquant déjà l'organisateur sur ses tarifs exorbitants. [...]

Nous savons que, trop souvent, l'indiscipline des voitures suiveuses, et particulièrement celles des rondeurs d'actualité, [...]

(Lire la suite p. 1, rubr. Cyclisme)

L'ITALIE champion du monde à l'épée

Défaite complète des Français, qui terminent quatrièmes derrière la Suède et l'Egypte

(Lire page 4 en rubr. Escrime l'article de notre envoyé spécial Armand LAFITTE)

Classement

1. Serse COPPI, les 244 km., 6 h. 11' 59" (sur bic. Bicnett, pneus Pirelli)
2. Deciercs, 1. Hatrieu, 4. Ghyssinck, 5. Anciaux, 6. Verhaert, 7. Georges Martin, 3. Callens, 9. Impanis, 6 h. 12' 20"
10. Le même, à un peloton comprenant Coppi, Klabinski, Breyer, Magni, Van Steenbergen, Logli, Pieters, Sterckx, Gaminiani, Schotte, Stadelder, Geffi, Remon, Capet, Thietard, Maeseig, Thomas, Wuschaht, Anderson, Verscbueren, Chupin, Babet, Idée, 5. Janssens, Clons, Buhl, Ronald, Desbats, Grux, Goudin, Leoni, Maegremon, Ricci, Kettelesr, Mulson, De Hog, Fernel, Fragneart, Rémy, Decay, Bonhoeff, Conte, Lucas.
51. Bessert, 6 h. 13' 42"; 54. Jeausseau, 6 h. 13'45"; 55. Grementi, 6 h. 13' 55"; 56. Olivier, 57. Plattner, 6 h. 13' 44"; [...]

LES TROIS PREMIERS "HORS CONCOURS" !

DANS L'ENFER. — Entre Hem et Roubaix, phase décisive ; dans l'ordre, Mahé, Leenen, Moujica, foncent vers le but, tout proche. Voyez position de Mahé : elle dénote l'intensité de l'effort victorieux — ou présumé tel !

Pour compenser le tort causé aux vainqueurs moraux, L'EQUIPE partagera entre Mahé, Moujica et Leenen une prime équivalant au total des trois premiers prix de la course.

Les vedettes se sont marquées, ont oublié d'attaquer mais Fausto Coppi n'était qu'en petite forme
(D'un de nos envoyés spéciaux Claude TILLET)

ROUBAIX. — La mariée était trop belle... Trop de monde au départ ; trop de grandes vedettes internationales parmi les 216 compétiteurs ; et, surtout, trop beau Paris-Roubaix... Sous le chaud soleil, dans une tiédeur de juin, les éliminations se faisaient rares, le peloton ne fondait pas... Le passé Arras, on le chaud regrettera amèrement, sinon les neiges d'antan, du moins la bise et le crachin traditionnels, qui nous préservent habituellement de tels mécomptes. [...]

ÉDITION SPÉCIALE GRATUITE
Dimanche 17 Avril 1949
LA COURSE LA PLUS RAPIDE DU MONDE
L'ÉQUIPE
LE QUOTIDIEN Elans DU SPORT

Le 47e PARIS-ROUBAIX
Organisé par L'ÉQUIPE
TROPHEE PAPIERS A CIGARETTES
RIZ LA +

LE TRIPLE HORAIRE POSSIBLE DU 47e PARIS-ROUBAIX

LE RUBAN JAUNE (43 km. 612) EST-IL EN DANGER ?

Deux difficultés majeures : DOULLENS et L'ENFER DU NORD

...MARQUÉ LE RENOUVEAU DU L.O.S.C.

...a « étrillé » NANCY
...RVE DES CHANCES INTACTES...

...a peiné pour prendre ...AUX, pourtant affaibli ...essure de Lorius

...ims aura tiré meilleur parti que Lille ...n'aura pas pour cela éliminé définitive...

...points jeudi grâce au fameux but de ...oute devant Nancy. Hier il a perdu un ...avance. Alors que le LOSC écrasait ...rait, malgré une quasi constante domi... ...acher le match il y a une heure, Lorius, ...lus d'une heure, le portier de... [...]

DIVISION I (31e journée)

REIMS (1) et Sochaux (16) 3-2
LILLE (2) b. Nancy (17) 4-1
TOUL... (5) b. Saint... 3-0
St-Etie... (7) et RENNES (9) 1-1
STRADE... (11) b. RCP (3) 2-1
METZ (12) b. Nice (13) 1-1
CANNES (13) b. Mont... (14) 1-0
ANNEC... (10) b. Colom... 2-1
METZ (17) b. Roubaix (18) 2-2

Classement
P G N P p c
1. REIMS (1) ...
2. LILLE (2) ...
3. Mars... (3) ...
4. Sochs (5) ...
5. St-Et... (7) ...
6. RCP (3) ...
7. St-Etien. (7) ...
8. TOUL... (5) ...
9. RENNES (9) ...
10. ANNEC. (10) ...
11. STRADE. (11) ...
12. METZ (12) ...
13. CANNES (13) ...
14. Mont. (14) ...
15. Nice (13) ...
16. Sochaux (16) ...
17. Nancy (17) ...
18. Roubaix (18) ...

LA FUGUE DU STADE FRANÇAIS NE DURE QUE 7 KM., PU...

LE RACING S'ENVOL... et résiste victorieusem... au retour offensif du Stad...

dans le XIe Relais à Travers Paris organisé le Stade Français, sous le patronage de L'EQUI...

Nous avions demandé au soleil d'accorder son concours pour XIe édition du Relais à Travers Paris ; il fut fidèle au rendez-vous, sans nulle pitié pour les rayons incendiaires dignes d'un 15 août ou des athl... regaillardis par une telle offensive estivale.
Le Racing a enlevé, comme prévu, sa cinquième victoire, mais sans avoir donné chaud (et le soleil n'y était pour rien !) à ses diri... et fidèles supporters, tandis qu'un public nombreux et profane applaudi...

Paul DUPONT
(Lire la suite p. 4, rubr. Athlétisme)

MOTOCYCLISTE DE PAU
...renzetti-Pagani ...urse des 500 cm3
...ood domine nettement ses adversaires
...yé spécial Maurice HENRY)

...que comprenait le Grand Prix de Pau, ...-Béarnais, l'une, celle des 350 cmc, ne laissa ...aus d'un Anglais Ander... ...victime d'un accident au cours de ... ...un complique, il releva avec une ... ...lui permettra de prendre ... ...ne de reparaître en course. ...Belge Griffin ...et club plus ... ...position en course ... ...iera... ...Franta...
(Lire l'article page...)

FANGIO FAIT le meilleur temps à l'entraînement des voitures

Les Catalans ONT ÉTOUFFÉ ALBI

...prolongations, ils en étaient au même point qu'au début de la rencontre, mais ils bouleversèrent en... ...l'ordonnancement du calendrier.
L'infortune turbinaise
...sur les 20 mare un seul club était qualifié pour les quarts de fi...
Parfaitement ! Et ce club part ... le vieux Stadoceste Tarbais qui ...attendu le renouveau en courage...

Louis FERDINAND

(Lire p. 5 en rubr. Rugby XIII l'article de Roger BASTIDE)

Two winners
for one bouquet

Never had Paris-Roubaix known such an outcome. The 1949 edition was a burlesque worthy of Charlie Chaplin himself. It would have been laughable if it had not taken place at the finish of the greatest of the classics.

This being the case, it was distressing, and the despair of Henri Boudard, the judge at the finish was painful to see.

As the riders came onto the track the spectators understood nothing of the race. So what had happened on the road leading to the velodrome?

A banal mistake over the route due simply to panic. By wanting to make the cars turn one way an official made an unclear gesture and sent the three leading riders the wrong way!

These three men were the Frenchmen André Mahe and Jacques Moujica and the Belgian Frans Leenen. By the time they had realised the blunder they had covered a few hundred extra metres before getting lost behind the velodrome! In the confusion Moujica fell and broke a pedal. Leenen and Mahé came onto the track through the little door in the press stand!

While Mahé the fastest of the two was first over the line the peloton arrived in its turn on the right side of the track.

The bunch sprint was won by Serse Coppi, the brother of the "Campionissimo". In total confusion Boudard first of all rewarded the victor's bouquet to André Mahé, who rapidly completed his lap of honour.

However the Coppi brothers would not accept this result. Fausto incited his brother to lodge an official complaint. According to him Mahé had simply not covered the proper route!

The protest was upheld. As he came out of the showers André Mahé learned that he was no longer the official winner. The Coppi family had won.

Poor Boudard, totally overwhelmed by events justified himself by claiming to those who were prepared to listen that he had only applied the rules.

"The Affair" lasted six months.

Five days after the finish and after two hours of discussion, the Sporting Commission of the French Cycling Federation classified Mahé first and Frans Leenen second.

President Joinard even confirmed: "André Mahé remains the sole winner. It could not be otherwise."

On the other side of the Alps the Italians did not want to know anything about this - nobody jested with the name of Coppi!

So the Italian Federation appealed against the decision. In the month of August the Union Cycliste Internationale decided to cancel the result of the race and meet again in November at Zurich!

The Belgians and naturally the Italians were in agreement over placing Serse Coppi first. Moreover, Joinard, who was applying for the job of president of the UCI became a little more flexible. At the time of the vote it was the Belgians and Italians who were to swing it.

On the 13th November 1949, just before the congress of Zurich, Fausto Coppi who was racing at the Vel d'Hiv told several journalists when talking about the 1950 season: "I could not ask for more than to come back to ride Paris-Roubaix again, as much as this magnificent race is missing from my record, I want before everything else that Serse is given his 1949 victory. If this does not happen it is likely that you will not see me at the start next year." It was a clear threat.

In order that nobody suffered, and especially, it must be said, to keep Coppi happy, those present at the UCI congress

1949

André MAHE
(France, 1919)

An aggressive and brave Breton, who brimmed over with energy. One of the better French riders of the 1950's.

1946 : Tour of Finistère,
3rd Grand Prix des Nations
1948 : Grand Prix de l'Equipe
1949 : Paris-Roubaix, Grand Prix de l'Equipe
1950 : Paris-Tours
1951 : Grand Prix de l'Echo d'Alger
1952 : 3rd Paris-Roubaix

Serse COPPI
(Italy, 1923-1951)

Brother and faithful team-mate of Fausto, to whom he devoted his career.

1945 : Milan-Varzi
1947 : 2nd Grand Prix de l'Equipe
1949 : Paris-Roubaix

The Northerner Louis Déprez is already watching Fausto Coppi.

decided to classify André Mahé and Serse Coppi equal first.
At the conclusion of the congress Mahé was torn between two sentiments. He was at the same time happy but asked himself questions: "I received the bouquet, I was the winner, my joy was enormous. Then I felt that someone had punched me right in the face when Boudard announced that I was disqualified. Was it my fault that I was directed the wrong way? Was it my fault that we found ourselves at the back of the velodrome? I am disgusted and swear as a Breton that I will get my revenge."
Right up to the present day so many years later, André Mahé does not understand exactly what happened: "Everything took place so quickly. There were a lot of cars surrounding us. With Leenen we followed them and became lost behind the velodrome.
I owe my victory to a journalist Albert De Wetter who jumped off his motorbike and showed me the entrance to the press stand. Without him I would never have been able to find my way into the track."
For Serse Coppi, this victory was the first big break in his career. At the finish not being used to being honoured, he merely said to the Italian journalists who were there only for the "Campionissimo": "I won Paris-Roubaix and I am not coming back again. What upsets me most is not having ridden a lap of honour with the bouquet. Fausto said to me three kilometres from the finish: Do not wear yourself out, save it for the sprint."
Serse lived in the shadow of his elder brother. He was not gifted like Fausto but played a simple role as team man for the person he admired so much. A little more than two years after the race, in June 1951, Serse Coppi came to

André Mahé with his bouquet alongside Paul Le Drogo and Jacques Goddet.

a tragic end. After a crash in the last kilometre of the Tour of Piedmont, he finished the event and went back to the hotel on his bike.

The same evening he suddenly felt very ill and was rushed to hospital where he was pronounced dead, due to severe head injuries.

When Paris-Roubaix 1949 is talked about only the controversial finish is remembered. However at the start, the race promised to be a good one.

The stars formed the front rank of the favourites: Idée, Schotte, van Steenbergen, Claes, Coppi, Bobet, Mahé, Kubler.

Everyone was waiting for the match between Coppi and Van Steenbergen. The Belgian as the holder of the title was merely polite to his Italian challenger who was new to this Northern event.

Several different skirmishes enlivened the first few hours. The only real thing to report was a few incidents even if they were important ones, crashes which delayed or eliminated Kubler, Hendrickx, Idée, Van Steenbergen, Marcelak. Two men got away as Doullens came into sight, Bernard Gauthier and the Northerner Louis Deprez. The small lead they gained was quickly neutralised. At Seclin, just twenty six kilometres from Roubaix, the "right" break went. Jacques Moujica went away by himself. He was rejoined by the Belgians Florent Mathieu and then Frans Leenen. The peloton was at 1min 45secs when André Mahé escaped alone. At Forest there were four of them, then three when Mathieu slipped and fell at Hem.

Mahé then decided to attack in order to arrive alone at the velodrome. He had a lead of a few metres before he got to the track, where everything was to be turned upside down.

1949

1. André MAHE (France)
   GS.Stella
   &
   Serse COPPI (Italy)
   GS.Bianchi-Ursus
3. Frans LEENEN (Belgium)
4. Jacques MOUJICA (France)
5. Georges MARTIN (France)
6. André DECLERCQ (Belgium)
7. Florent MATHIEU (Belgium)
8. Roger GYSELINCK (Belgium)
9. Albert ANCIAUX (Belgium)
10. Josef VERHAERT (Belgium)

And Fausto decided to go it alone

"A monument to international cycling, Paris-Roubaix crushes the riders as much by its legend as it does by its diabolical difficulties. To he alone, seeming to ignore the hullabaloo of the cobblestones, a pure stylist on the chaos of the awful surface he looked as if he was riding on a home trainer, Fausto Coppi the totally prodigious has himself crushed Paris-Roubaix.

It was well worth while to assemble the bigwigs of road cycling. Be it Magni the terror of Flanders, Van Steenbergen the hero of Milan-San Remo, Bobet, Coste, Diot, Mahe, our men on form. And all these Belgians formerly the masters of bad roads and Schulte too who reigned on the tracks, all, all suddenly appeared, when the machine got going, as poor little worms grovelling submissively to their master's move, like the ocean, in spite of its power submits to the movement of the tide."

This editorial by Jacques Goddet appeared in L'Equipe on Monday 10th April 1950. The day before, Fausto Coppi had carried off one of his finest victories, one of those that will always stand out in a career: Paris-Roubaix.

However, at the start at St Denis under torrential rain, there was a question mark over the form of the Campionissimo. Certainly glorified with a superb victory in the 1949 Tour de France, he appeared more invincible than ever, but the previous edition of the Northern event had left him with a taste of incompleteness. He had only been able to play the minor role of an extra, and

Fiorenzo Magni and Rik Van Steenbergen after the Campionissimo.

Coppi one lap from his great exploit.

did not hide it from the journalists at the start. They had perhaps as well sown doubt in the mind of the Campionissimo who had been able to read, here and there that he would be unable to stand up to the Flemish attacks on the cobbles. From the start the pace was rather relaxed. Attacks by Frans Gielen and Edouard Fachleitner hardly troubled the tranquillity of the peloton led most often by Van Steenbergen, Maurice Diot and André Mahé.

Jacques Moujica, one of the unfortunate ones in 1949, unleashed the battle and attacked on the hill of Doullens. Fausto Coppi took advantage of it to ask a few questions of his own. He wanted to make a first selection and then above all test the form of his principle rivals. The Italian passed Moujica and was first over the top of the hill. Only six men were able to stay on his wheel, among whom were; Moujica, Fiorenzo, Magni and Mahé. The big surprise was that Van Steenbergen was not there. Of course he got up a few kilometres later in company with fifteen other riders but this did rather comfort Coppi's aggressive mind.

Straight away on the road to Arras, Gino Sciardis and Maurice Diot departed. Coppi stuck to his plan: he decided to "burn" the feeding zone at Arras in order to gain the maximum surprise on his rivals.

At the entrance to the town he was one of a group of twenty eight men, then shrewdly, in view of the feeding station, Fausto placed himself at the head of the bunch, and abandoning his

Diot's and Coppi's lap of honour.

1950

food he attacked.

By the time the others were able to get their food musettes on their backs, they were trapped Coppi was away he could not be brought back. Rapidly the Campionissimo caught Diot and Sciardis. He was pushing an enormous gear of 52x15 and being launched on the road to success. Sciardis was quickly discouraged and dropped back.

Only the little Diot was able to maintain the incredible pace set by the leader of the Bianchi team. Sometimes the Frenchman even did his turn at the front but he was part of the Mercier team of which the established leader was Van Steenbergen. Suddenly Antonin Magne, his team manager, drew alongside and ordered him to stop working for the Italians. Magne hoped that Coppi would wear himself out and that perhaps Van Steenbergen would be able to get up to him.

Under these conditions Coppi decided to forget all about the poor Diot. He accelerated a little more and forty five kilometres from the finish the flying Fausto found himself alone in the lead.

Behind it was total disarray. The riders were spread out over several kilometres. Van Steenbergen, the Italian's main rival kept struggling but his efforts were in vain. At the big bend at Wattignies, twenty two kilometres from Roubaix, the situation was clear. Diot, who was still resisting his pursuers, was two minutes down, Fiorenzo Magni and Charles Coste at five minutes, Sciardis at seven minutes and the rest even further back.

"The Mass was over". Nobody would see Fausto again, not even in the showers. For as soon as he finished Coppi took the road to Como, where the next day he had to race ...and win, a track event!

As he reached his car, Coppi just had time to give a few impressions: "...at no

FAUSTO COPPI A REUSSI DANS PARIS-ROUBAIX
l'exploit le plus sensationnel de sa carrière de super-champion

Bâtissant sa victoire à l'occasion d'une échappée Diot-Sciardis, après Arras, il s'enfuit avec le premier nommé, puis le lâche irrésistiblement

Magni et Coste, remarquables finalistes aux troisième et quatrième places, à près de trois minutes d'un Diot très courageux Lâché et victime d'une crevaison, Van Steenbergen finit néanmoins très près de Sciardis et Molinéris, excellents

Le jeune Français Meunier s'affirme rouleur d'avenir, tandis que Schotte, l'un des grands favoris, abandonne après une chute

(D'un de nos envoyés spéciaux Claude TILLET)

COPPI LE COUREUR H
(De notre directeur général Jacques GODDET)

L'ESTOCADE... DU GRAND COPPI

Fausto at work.

...un uomo solo è al comando della corsa...

Fausto COPPI
(Italy, 1919-1960)

The legendary "Campionissimo" is remembered for his innumerable exploits on road and track and for the misfortunes that dogged his career.

1940 : Tour of Italy
1942 : Italian Champion
        The Hour Record (45,871 km)
1946 : Milan-San Remo, Tour of Lombardy,
        Grand Prix des Nations
1947 : World Pursuit Champion
        Italian Champion, Tour of Lombardy
1948 : Milan-San Remo, Tour of Lombardy
1949 : World Pursuit Champion
        Italian Champion, Tour de France,
        Tour of Italy, Milan-San Remo,
        Tour of Lombardy
1950 : Paris-Roubaix, Flèche Wallonne
1952 : Tour de France, Tour of Italy
1953 : World Champion, Tour of Italy
1954 : Tour of Lombardy
1955 : Italian Champion

time was I really suffering. My race was simple, up until Doullens I was happy to just watch my adversaries. I took advantage of the hill to attack. There were still too many of us and the feeding station at Arras gave me the opportunity to go clear. Then I tried to keep Diot with me as long as possible but Antonin Magne forbade him to work with me so I took off. I covered the last forty kilometres without going flat out and the applause at Roubaix encouraged me as well as permitting me to enjoy my victory."

Diot was second at the finish 2mins 41secs behind the champion. Delighted with this, he made a remark which was to enter the annals of cycle sport: " I won Paris-Roubaix. Coppi was supernatural.."

Further back at 5mins 24secs was Fiorenzo Magni, the Frenchman Charles Coste, then Sciardis at 7mins 7secs, Molineris at 7-40, and the first Belgian, Declerck, seventh at nearly eight minutes.

Everyone was unanimous -Coppi had achieved one of the most sensational exploits of his career.

Charles Pélissier was staggered: "During my career, I have mixed with a lot of champions. Up until now none of them has made an impression on me like Coppi has done in this Paris-Roubaix. He controlled the race with an authority which was never challenged. He did what he wanted to and dropped his adversaries when he desired to .."

Even Van Steenbergen agreed: "Coppi was the strongest, there's no question about it. I have no regrets for today, one way or another, he would have dropped me."

1950

1. Fausto COPPI (Italy)
   GS.Bianchi
2. Maurice DIOT (France)
3. Fiorenzo MAGNI (Italy)
4. Charles COSTE (France)
5. Gino SCIARDIS (Italy)
6. Pierre MOLINIERS (France)
7. André DECLERCQ (Belgium)
8. Georges MEUNIER (France)
9. Georges CLAES (Belgium)
10. Marcel KINT (Belgium)

Ses avants faisant bloc, le XV de France a arraché une grande victoire sur Gall...

(LIRE LES DÉTAILS PAGE 8)

L'ÉQUIPE

LE QUOTIDIEN — 8 pages — **DU SPORT**

15 FRANCE

LUNDI 9 AVRIL 1951
6e ANNÉE — N° 1557

10, Fg MONTMARTRE, PARIS (9e)
TAITBOUT 70-80 ET LA SUITE

PETITES ANNONCES : TAITBOUT 73-40, 41, 42 — SERVICE VENTE : PROVENCE 97-18 — COMPTE POSTAL : 4.237-91

Vainqueur de haute classe d'un empoignant PARIS-ROUBAIX - Coupe Source Communale d'Alet

"TONIO" BEVILACQUA, surpuissant, ARRACHE LA VICTOIR...

A NEUF CHAMPIONS

toute l'élite sauf Fausto Coppi !

L'ENFER 51 dominé par une élégante bande de démons

(De notre directeur gén. Jacques GODDET)

ROUBAIX. — Paris-Roubaix typique qui se décompose selon les normes habituelles : rupture par le côté de Doullens ; se sectionnements plus rigoureux dans la morne plaine entre Arras et Hénin-Liétard où les pavés...

(Lire la suite p. 4, rub. Cyclisme)

Mais le stupéfiant retour de BOBET et son sprint victorieux devant Van STEENBERGEN furent le sommet de l'épreuve

BARBOTIN avait lui aussi fait un retour fantastique mais faiblit...

(D'un de nos envoyés spéciaux Claude TILLET)

ROUBAIX. — Pouvait-on croire en la victoire d'Antonio Bevilacqua dans ce Paris-Roubaix ? Oui, bien sûr, mais, par contre, on eût plutôt imaginé un succès acquis qu'une finale solitaire...

Le classement

1. Antoine BEVILACQUA (It.), les 247 km. 331, km. à 6 h 7' 16"...
2. Bobet, à 6", 4"-46"...
3. Van Steenbergen (B.)...
...

BOBET FAIT SOUFFRIR « RIK »

ROUBAIX. — Nous sommes ici les cyclables de « l'enfer » et la course se joue...

...se poursuit : NIMES et NIC... LENS et SÈTE...

L'événement attendu de tous les spor...

RESULTATS PREVUS DANS LA COUPE LORD-DERBY

L'A.S Carcassonne ÉLIMINE Marseille XIII

Lyon, les Catalans et Libourne qualifiés pour les dem!-finales

(Lire p. 3, un article de Louis FERDINAND)

The Exploit of 'Poor Tonio'

The start of the 1951 season was remarkable for the supremacy of a French "tandem". In fact Louison Bobet, the French champion, dominated everything in company with his faithful team-mate Pierre Barbotin. Successively they monopolised the first two places in Milan-San Remo, National Criterium, then a little later the French championship. At twenty-six, Bobet, "The Baker of St Meen" had reached maturity. If he had not yet succeeded in his attempt at winning the Tour de France, he was slowly completing his range of classics. In October he would also be the only one to surprise Giuseppe Minardi and Fausto Coppi in the Tour of Lombardy.

Two other French champions had agreeably surprised the fans in the Tour of Flanders. Dominated for the third consecutive time by Fiorenzo Magni since nicknamed " the Tuscan (Lion) of Flanders", Bernard Gauthier and Attilio Redolfi surrounded him on the podium.

To these few names must be added those of Camille Danguillaume and Jacques Moujica, two who riders prominent in several editions of Paris-Roubaix. Theirs was a cruel end. Danguillaume the winner of the Liège-Bastogne-Liège in 1949, was mown down by a motorbike the following year in the French championship. Victim of a fracture of the petrosal, he died eight days later. Moujica for his part was a young hope of twenty four but already the winner of the 1949 Bordeaux-Paris, sadly lost his life along with Jean Rey, a former champion of France, in a car accident in November 1950.

Thankfully, in spite of these cruel losses French cycling was flourishing. So at the start of the Paris-Roubaix the French were in the unusual position of having several potential winners in their ranks.

Under the rain the international elite was present. Only Fausto Coppi, victim of a broken collar bone following a crash at the end of the Milan-San Remo, was absent. On the road to Roubaix, Raymond Impanis decided to show himself. Since 1947, the year he turned professional, he had shown tremendous promise but he had not lived up to his potential and remained in the antechamber of stardom.

From the start the Belgian attacked several times. Finally he escaped with his compatriot Lionel Van Brabant and the Algerian Molines. The gap over the peloton, which was quite used to such suicidal moves, grew regularly: 1min 25secs at Chantilly, 2-15 at Breteuil and then 2-50 at Flers at the one hundred kilometre point.

At the exit to Amiens, Molines was completely exhausted and had to let his two companions go. The remaining pair climbed the hill of Doullens with a lead of two and a half minutes.

However, the counter-offensive had begun. Towards Arras, Impanis and Van Brabant were still holding them off, but weariness was overcoming them. At a moment when Bobet was delayed by a puncture, the Italian Antonio Bevilacqua, Attilio Redolfi and Bernard Gauthier, the two stars from the Tour of Flanders had closed the gap to less than a minute. The inevitable junction was effected forty six kilometres from the finish. On the first cobbles of Hénin-Liétard the five men had a lead of thirty seconds over a group where Louison Bobet was doing most of the work. His efforts were rewarded three kilometres from Seclin when

1951

Antonio BEVILACQUA
(Italy, 1918-1972)

A World track pursuit champion who switched to road racing at the highest level, winning 11 stages of the Giro d'Italia.

1942 : 2nd Milan-San Remo
1950 : World Pursuit Champion
　　　　Italian Champion, Baracchi Trophy
　　　　2nd Tour of Lombardy
1951 : Paris-Roubaix,
　　　　World Pursuit Champion
　　　　3rd World Championships
　　　　3rd Italian Championship

the French champion joined the head of the race in company with Fiorenzo Magni, the ever present Rik Van Steenbergen, Ferdi Kubler and the colossal Belgian André Declerck.

At the turning at Wattignies these ten men had a lead of only two hundred metres on another bunch of ten. In spite of the combined efforts of Diot, Kint and Schotte, nobody managed to join them.

In front, Gauthier, at the top of his form, tried his luck several times but Magni never allowed a proper gap to open and always brought the eight others up to him. At Faches there were only seven after Redolfi's puncture. Roubaix was getting close. The escapees all had the one idea which was quickly becoming an obsession: to get rid of Van Steenbergen as quickly as possible for if the Belgian arrived with them the result of the sprint was beyond doubt. The powerful Italian Bevilacqua whose torso was moulded into his superb "Benotto" jersey knew this as well as anyone and gave everything he had as he went away by himself. As the current World pursuit champion he was well used to this type of effort.

Behind, Bobet once again organised the chase of the now broken group and caught Van Steenbergen, Magni and the Declerck. A little later at Lesquin, Magni took one risk too many and crashed heavily jumping up a pavement. He wrecked a wheel and his race towards victory was finished. Bevilacqua was asking no questions and as he smoothly turned his very big gear of 52x15 he was thinking about neither punctures nor accidents. Only a goose crossing the road hotly pursued by its owner nearly robbed him of a well deserved victory!

The Italian crossed the finishing line with a lead of one minute and thirty seconds over Bobet who was strong enough to beat Van Steenbergen for second place. Surrounded by journalists who were getting used to Italian successes, Tonio was radiant: "I congratulate myself for attacking, for in a sprint against Van Steenbergen and Bobet my chances were very slim. Paris-Roubaix is one of those races which look very good on your record and with me it will take pride of place."

The escape led by Bernard Gauthier followed by Redolfi, Impanis and Bevilacqua.

The bunch in the midst of which is Rik Van Steenbergen and Roger Decock.

For his part Bobet was satisfied to continue his series of good performances, but nevertheless noted with a suspicion of regret: "I think I can say that without my puncture, I would have been able to win Paris-Roubaix. It was a hard blow to me in the middle of the battle and I lost a lot of time repairing it. Moreover I am not saying that I am faster than Van Steenbergen, but I finished stronger than he did." The day before the race Bevilacqua, ignored in the forecasts, had said : "They are not talking very much about me. It is not important but on Sunday evening things will be different."

The observers' doubt was understandable for this was only the Italian's second road race of the season and he had covered less than five hundred kilometres in training! The "Poor Tonio", according to his own terms, who had begged to be pushed on the big climbs of the Tour de France, confirmed that he was a superb champion. A few months later he was to put on his second rainbow jersey by beating in the world pursuit a certain Hugo Koblet who was at the height of his glory.

Always enamoured with the bicycle, he died at the age of fifty four when out training with a group of young riders. It is said that the corneas of his big black eyes were transplanted, one onto a blind man, the other onto a young girl. Poor Tonio...

1951

1. Antonio BEVILACQUA (Italy)
   GS.Benotto
2. Louison BOBET (France)
3. Rik VAN STEENBERGEN (Belgium)
4. André DECLERCQ (Belgium)
5. Jean GUEGUEN (France)
6. Raymond IMPANIS (Belgium)
7. Bernard GAUTHIER (France)
8. Lionel VAN BRABANT (Belgium)
9. Maurice DIOT (France)
10. Ferdi KUBLER (Switzerland)

Van Steenbergen
for a second time

At the appearance of the two champions on the track the stands crowded with Belgians started to shake.

The result was already known to them: Coppi, the great Coppi would not be able to do anything in the home straight when faced with Van Steenbergen, "their" Rik. And that was the way it happened.

Unfortunately for the Campionissimo, the Rik in question was seeking revenge. In fact the day after a disastrous Tour of Flanders, Van Steenbergen was criticised in Belgium as never before. His photo on the front pages of the newspapers showing him walking up the Mur De Grammont, still haunted his memory. He was criticised for being too much of a trackman and treating road events too casually!

Rik wanted to use the rendezvous at Roubaix to straighten things out. On this April day it was clearly Fausto who paid the price.

This fiftieth Paris-Roubaix, ran under a Spring sun, brought together most of the international stars. Coppi was on the way back and accompanying him from the other side of the Alps were Bevilacqua, Magni and Petrucci, winner of Milan-San Remo.

The irremovable Belgians were there, from Van Steenbergen to Claes by way of Impanis and Schotte and the others. Ferdi Kubler had come to show off his rainbow jersey while his compatriot Koblet was still trying to find his wonderful form of 1951.

This left the French. Louison Bobet wanted to climb still higher in the international hierarchy. The classic specialist André Mahé had come back to the roads of his greatest exploit. Idée, Diot, Robic, Caput and Géminiani were also there. Finally, for some time people had been speaking well of a young man from South West France as fast as lighting, a certain André Darrigade.

Faced with all this talent the Northerners nevertheless remained very motivated with riders such as Louis Deprez, César Marcelak, Edouard Klabinski and Gilbert Scodeller. From the start the race proved to be very fast. The first to enter into the action was Ménéghetti. Six men joined him on the hill of Chantilly: Jarrige, Lambrecht, Blomme, Gaudot, Quentin and Bonnaventure.

Only the latter four continued their fugue towards Doullens where they were joined by Lajoie and Cieleska. Blomme led over the top of the climb but their adventure was over.

In sight of his home town of Arras, Gilbert Scodeller "lit" the touch paper. He provoked the first decision. Raphaël Géminiani, Loretto Petrucci, Renzo Soldani, Bernard Gauthier and Jean Baldassari escaped.

While Baldassari found himself alone in front, with Kubler and Dupont in pursuit, Fausto Coppi went into action at Courrières. Before Carvin, the Campionissimo was on the heels of the Swiss, Jacques Dupont and Baldassari.

It then seemed that nobody would be strong enough to join the leaders who were flying across the cobblestones. A determined Van Steenbergen thought otherwise. At Wattignies where he had a deficit of nearly fifty seconds he was part of a small group containing, among others, Gauthier, Blomme and Petrucci. He counter attacked by himself behind the three runaways who had lost Baldassari with a puncture.

On the cobbles of Lesquin, after a staggering sprint of five kilometres, the great Rik made everyone admire him when he got up to Coppi, Kubler and Dupont. Dupont punctured, then Kubler cracked under the pressure of the Campionissimo. There were now just two of them, two exceptional champions both seeking a second prestigious

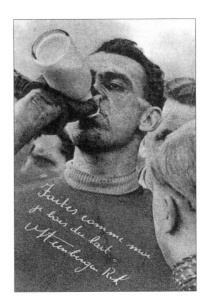

1952

OOTBALL : tout est à refaire... Nice, Bordeaux, Metz battus. Lille grand triomphateur

(LIRE EN PAGES HUIT ET SEPT)

L'EQUIPE
Elans
LE QUOTIDIEN · DU SPORT

18 FRANCS

LUNDI 14 AVRIL 1952
7e ANNÉE · N° 1872

10, Fg MONTMARTRE PARIS (9e)
TAITBOUT 70-80 ET LA SUITE

PETITES ANNONCES : TAITBOUT 73-40, 41, 42 — SERVICE VENTE : PROVENCE 37-18 — COMPTE POSTAL : 4.237-93

PARIS-ROUBAIX,
ENCORE LA PLUS SEVERE et toujours la plus belle

Pour triompher du grand FAUSTO COPPI, il fallait...
... UN ÉBLOUISSANT VAN STEENBERGEN

Fin de course infernale, marquée par de sensationnels retours...

L'ENFER D'OU JAILLIRENT LES DIEUX
par Jacques GODDET

Et le sort qui s'acharna sur les Français : tout d'abord GEMINIANI (qui lança la bataille générale), puis BALDASSARI et DUPONT (longtemps en tête), enfin André MAHÉ (freiné près du but)...

Tandis que BOBET « plafonnait » KUBLER flanchait dans les derniers kilomètres

(D'un de nos envoyés spéciaux Claude TILLET)

Ruban Jaune imbattu malgré l'excellente moyenne réalisée

VOYANT TRES LOIN...

JONCTION

VAN STEENBERGEN VOULAIT GAGNER ce 50e Paris-Roubaix
pour assurer l'avenir de ses 5 enfants

(D'un de nos envoyés spéciaux Albert de WETTER)

VAN STEENBERGEN SONGE (sérieusement) AU TOUR DE FRANCE

TRIOMPHE DE LA LOGIQUE DANS LE XIVe « A TRAVERS PARIS » PATRONNÉ PAR « L'ÉQUIPE »

LE STADE FRANÇAIS
rejoint le Racing à mi-parcours
se détache irrésistiblement
et rate le record de 13"

Les « bleu et rouge » remportent un confortable succès dans l'épreuve organisé avec le concours de la Suze

Le classement

Paul DUPONT

POUR LE PREMIER DES HUIT « GRANDS PRIX DE FRANCE » organisé par l'A.C. Basco-Béarnais, patronné par « L'Equipe » et l' « Action Automobile »

A PAU LES ÉCARTS DE TEMPS
ne seront pas importants
EN RAISON
du parcours accidenté...

(D'un de nos envoyés spéciaux Charles FAROUX)

LE STADE VA S'ENVOLER

victory at Roubaix. Fausto knew that the Belgian was much faster than him in the sprint and tried everything he could do to drop him. Rik knew the route very well indeed and was sure that if he got past the last major difficulty at Hem in the company of the Italian, then the bouquet was his.

Coppi multiplied his attacks on the hill at Hem. Van Steenbergen went through hell to stay with him but he did not crack. Perhaps nobody has ever suffered so much but on the day this was the price of victory. When the two men came onto the track together, there were no more surprises.

In third place, André Mahé was a mere eleven seconds down on the winner. The Breton was unhappy. As he showed his flat tyre to the journalists he complained: "I rode the last twenty kilometres like that, my tyre was going down slowly. You know its very hard to push a gear of 52x14 like that. Without this handicap I would have got up to Rik and Coppi."

Van Steenbergen had won his second Paris-Roubaix four years after his first: "From the moment that I knew Coppi and Kubler were at the front," he said, "I gave everything that I had. On the hill at Hem after Kubler was dropped, Coppi was riding so quickly that I did not think it would be possible to stay with him and I was happy when he eased off a little." Rik later swore that if Coppi had attacked just one more time, he would have cracked.

For his part the Campionissimo did not know that his rival was at the end of his tether: "Bearing in mind that Van Steenbergen stayed on my wheel in spite of my repeated attacks, I thought that he was much fresher and still had something left. If I had known that he was close to giving in. I also made another mistake for when I came up to Kubler, Baldassari and Dupont, I should have gone away myself but I lacked the courage to do it. I was beaten in the sprint by Van Steenbergen but today it would have been difficult for me to change the result."

Years later, the Campionissimo still spoke about his two blunders in Paris-Roubaix 1952 and bitterly regretted not having escaped alone twenty kilometres from Roubaix. For his part, Bobet the great French star, said simply that he was not on a good day. A puncture before Doullens had certainly held him back, but objectively it must be said that this did not explain everything.

1952

1. Rik VAN STEENBERGEN (Belgium)
   GS. Mercier-Hutchinson
2. Fausto COPPI (Italy)
3. André MAHE (France)
4. Ferdi KUBLER (Switzerland)
5. Jacques DUPONT (France)
6. Désiré KETELEER (Belgium)
7. Louison BOBET (France)
8. Robert VARNAJO (France)
9. Loretto PETRUCCI (Italy)
10. Antonin ROLLAND (France)

A jubilant Van Steenbergen wins his second Paris-Roubaix.

L'EQUIPE
LE QUOTIDIEN DU SPORT
'ET DE l'Automobile

LUNDI 13 AVRIL 1953
8e ANNÉE — N° 2182

10, Fg MONTMARTRE PARIS (9e)
TAITBOUT 70-80

PETITES ANNONCES : TAITBOUT 73-40, 41, 42 — COMPTE POSTAL : 4.237-95

18 FRANCS

TRIOMPHE DE L'OFFENSIVE : UN PARIS-ROUBAIX, ORGANISÉ PAR *L'ÉQUIPE*, SENSATIONNEL, GAGNÉ A 43 KM. 322 DE MOYENNE (RUBAN JAUNE 43 KM. 700)

Une chute de Van Steenbergen, à 36 km. du but, casse l'échappée décisive et condamne Géminiani, Grosso et Pardoen

GERMAIN DERYCK BAT LE PELOTON PAR K.O.

TROPHÉE DURALUMIN

puis ajuste au sprint Piazza et Wagtmans

autres beaux contre-attaquants

LE GRIS TOURNE AU BLEU

(D'un de nos envoyés spéciaux Pierre ABOUT)

BOBET bon quatrième devant le reliquat des poursuivants. — PERTRY et PARDOEN remarquables

de notre Directeur
JACQUES GODDET

GALLAY, réalis...

ARTISANS ... SUR FOUG...

SPECKER, le meilleur...

MATCH INTERNATIONAL DE BOXE AMATEUR A MONTARGIS

LA FRANCE (battue 6-4) méritait le nul contre la FINLANDE

Hamalainen (Finl.) et Candau (Fr.) les meilleurs

(Lire page 3, en rubrique Boxe l'article de Georges PEETERS)

...NTS DE PUIG-AUBERT ...r de CRESPO

Classement de la Coupe Jean-Galia

CHAMPIONNATS DE FOR... HIER AU GYMNASE JA...

FIRMIN... meilleur haltérophile français

Marcombes bat le reco... de France du jeté (co...)

(Lire page 7, en rubrique Haltérophilie, l'article de René MOYSET)

LE PACK DE MIAS ET VANNIER ont battu l'Armée Britannique

STADE BUFFALO...

Marcel de LABORDERIE

Germain Derycke comes to power

1953 marked the accession of a champion of class, a good "rouleur", rapid in the sprint and possessing, when he was on form, an irresistible "punch": Germain Derycke. Although he turned professional in 1950, he only reached the top level in 1953. Coming back disappointed from a Milan-San Remo once again won by Loretto Petrucci, he promised himself that he would finally win a great classic. Bad luck prevented him from playing a major role in the Tour of Flanders so he put all his hopes on the Northern classic.

At the start of Paris-Roubaix the Belgian was among the favourites; along with his compatriots Van Steenbergen, Impanis and Ockers, the Frenchman Bobet and Gauthier, the Italians Magni and Petrucci and a few "individuals" such as Koblet and Poblet. Flu had struck down a Coppi, always susceptible to such things, but the Campionissimo had delegated several team-mates such as the athletic Donato Piazza, who was to prove the revelation of the race.

One hundred and sixty eight riders were there under a cloudy sky to cover the two hundred and forty five kilometres. As in every other year, several aspiring young riders wanted to bring attention to themselves, at first seven reckless ones, then eleven and then sixteen. Nothing serious among them, even if the illustrious Fiorenzo Magni and Roger Hassenforder were among them.

The streets of Amiens apparently stimulated Raphaël Géminiani who escaped just after the general regrouping. However nobody dared to sit on his rather dangerous wheel as just after the start his frame gave way under his weight and the top tube of his frame came unsoldered!

The reaction of Van Steenbergen turned out to be more surprising. There remained almost one hundred and thirty kilometres to cover before the velodrome was reached, but after a moment's hesitation he got up to the "big gun" in company with Isidore De Ryck, Hassenforder and Grosso. These five men rejoined the three leaders Pardoen, Bertaz and Canavèse.

On Doullens hill, the stars raised the pace so as to effect the traditional selection. An attentive Germain Derycke found himself at the head of the bunch thirty five seconds behind the leaders.

Just before Arras where the gap had hardly changed, there were only four men at the front: Geminiani, Van Steenbergen, Grosso and Pardoen. Crossing the town Koblet lost all chance when a tyre went flat. His team manager Francis Pélissier was not there to help him.

As they reached Hénin-Liétard Derycke finally made his move. The promising young athlete from the Alcyon team escaped and in eight kilometres he caught Geminiani, Van Steenbergen and Grosso. Unfortunately for Rik, a crash on the bridge at Courrières removed all hope of his repeating his exploit of 1952. Between Carvin and Seclin, Donato Piazza and the Dutchman Wout Wagtmans in their turn shook off the peloton. They managed to rejoin Derycke, Geminiani and Grosso. Twenty kilometres from the velodrome, five men were at the head of the race, then three as Grosso and Geminiani, victims of mechanical problems dropped back.

At the back only Emile Baffert tried to extricate himself from the peloton which was going to sleep three hundred metres from the trio.

Derycke was proving to be the most positive. On the other hand Wagtmans did not lead for a single metre. This provoked the anger of the Belgian who also demanded that

Germain DERYCKE
(Belgium, 1929-1978)

Germain Derycke's class and strength ensured his reputation as one of the outstanding riders of the last fifty years.

1951 : 2nd Liège-Bastogne-Liège
1953 : Paris-Roubaix, 2nd World Championships,
     3rd Ghent-Wevelgem
1954 : Flèche Wallonne, 2nd Paris-Brussels
1955 : Milan-San Remo,
     2nd Belgian Championship,
     3rd World Championships,
     3rd Paris-Brussels
1957 : Liège-Bastogne-Liège
1958 : Tour of Flanders, 3rd Paris-Nice

1953

Germain Derycke's lap of honour.

PARIS-ROUBAIX
TOUJOURS EN TÊTE !

18 FOIS VAINQUEUR

1953 : 1er DERYCK

ALCYON

AFFICHE D'INTÉRIEUR

LE QUOTIDIEN DU SPORT
ET DE
l'Automobile

51e PARIS-ROUBAIX

12 AVRIL 1953

TROPHEE **DURALUMIN**

COUREURS. — Samedi, à « L'Equipe », de 10 à 12 heures et de 15 à 18 heures, remise des dossards et plaques de contrôle.

DIMANCHE. — Stade municipal de Saint-Denis, contrôle de signature de 8 heures à 9 h. 30. Appel à 9 h. 40. Départ : 10 heures précises.

SUIVEURS — PRESSE — MARQUES. — Samedi, à « L'Equipe », de 10 à 12 heures et de 15 à 18 heures, distribution des macarons des véhicules et laissez-passer.

HORAIRE

	Km. parcourus	Km. à parcourir	PASSAGES PREVUS		
			à 43.700 km.	à 40 km.	à 66 km.
			h. m.	h. m.	h. m.
SAINT-DENIS (départ)	0	245	10	10	10
Pierrefitte	3	242	10 05	10 05	10 05
Sarcelles	6	239	10 09	10 09	10 09
Ecouen	9	236	10 13	10 13	10 14
Le Mesnil-Aubry	13	232	10 18	10 19	10 20
Luzarches	20	225	10 28	10 29	10 31
La Morlaye	25	220	10 35	10 36	10 39
Chantilly	30	215	10 41	10 43	10 47
Creil	38	207	10 52	10 55	11
Nogent-sur-Oise	40	205	10 55	10 58	11 03
Laigneville	43	202	10 59	11 02	11 08
Rantigny	46	199	11 02	11 06	11 13
Clermont (C.V.)	53	192	11 13	11 17	11 24
Saint-Just-en-Chaussée	69	176	11 35	11 40	11 49
Wavignies	76	169	11 44	11 50	12
Breteuil-sur-Noye	87	158	12	12 07	12 18
Esquennoy	90	156	12 03	12 11	12 23
Folie-de-Bonneuil	93	152	12 07	12 15	12 28
Flers	100	145	12 16	12 25	12 38
Essertaux	102	143	12 19	12 28	12 41
Saint-Saufflieu	107	138	12 26	12 36	12 49
Hebecourt	110	135	12 30	12 40	12 54
Dury	113	132	12 35	12 45	12 58
Amiens (C.V.)	119	126	12 43	12 54	13 07
Villers-Bocage	131	114	12 59	13 12	13 27
Talmes	135	110	13 05	13 18	13 34
La Vicogne	137	108	13 08	13 22	13 39
Beauval	143	102	13 15	13 31	13 49
Doullens (C.V.)	149	96	13 21	13 40	13 59
Pomméra	156	89	13 33	13 50	14 10
Larbret	166	79	13 48	14 05	14 26
Beaumetz-les-Loges	174	71	13 59	14 17	14 39
Arras (C.R.)	184	61	14 10	14 31	14 55
Bailleul	193	52	14 24	14 44	15 11
Arleux	196	49	14 28	14 48	15 15
Bois-Bernard	200	45	14 33	14 53	15 25
Drocourt	201	44	14 34	14 55	15 27
Hénin-Liétard (C.V.)	205	40	14 40	15 01	15 33
Courrières	209	35	14 45	15 07	15 39
Carvin	213	32	14 50	15 13	15 46
Seclin (C.V.)	221	24	15	15 25	16 02
Wattignies	225	20	15 06	15 32	16 09
Faches	227	18	15 10	15 36	16 13
Lesquin	230	15	15 16	15 42	16 19
Ascq	236	9	15 23	15 53	16 29
Forest	239	6	15 27	15 58	16 35
Hem	241	4	15 30	16 01	16 39
ROUBAIX (vélodrome)	245	0	15 37	16 07	16 45

Piazza worked. It seemed however that the Italian did not totally understand. Derycke was not prepared to be made a fool of especially with so much at stake. He tried to go clear on the hill at Hem, the last difficulty on the route. Not only was he unable to do so but had the impertinence to counter-attack and escape under his nose.

This time the cup was full. Unchained Derycke rejoined him after a few hundred metres. A sprint at the velodrome was inevitable.

On the penultimate banking Piazza attacked on the inside but as they came into the home straight nobody could get past Derycke.

Piazza was second, Wagtmans third. Bobet won the sprint for fourth place. A poor consolation for the men who had nourished other ambitions at the

Derycke leaves Piazza no chance.

start.

The Belgian had won his first great classic. As he came out of the showers he still had not come round: "It has not sunk in that I have just won one of the finest classics on the calendar. You are only a true rider when one of these competitions figure on your record."

A few months later at Lugano, he would be the only one able to resist Coppi for a little while at the world championships. In the following years his successes included Flèche Wallone 1954, Milan-San Remo 1955, Liège-Bastogne-Liège 1957 and the Tour of Flanders 1958. But this Paris-Roubaix, the real trigger to his career, would always remain special in his memory as the Queen of the Classics.

1953

1. Germain DERYCKE (Belgium)
   GS. Alcyon
2. Donato PIAZZA (Italy)
3. Wont WAGTMANS (Holland)
4. Louison BOBET (France)
5. Emile BAFFERT (France)
6. Roger DECOCK (Belgium)
7. Raymond IMPANIS (Belgium)
8. Désiré KETELEER (Belgium)

Impanis in company with Koblet.

When Impanis joined Rebry

April 1954. Since the beginning of the season the Mercier team had been dominating the racing. At the start of Paris-Roubaix, Antonin Magne's young hopefuls were more than ever the favourites after picking up thirteen important victories. Raymond Impanis who had only just started to wear the purple jersey already found himself transformed.

After seven years as a professional the popular Belgian champion had certainly won numerous victories, but on the threshold of 1954 he was still looking for a major success. Then in just a few months he had first been triumphant in Paris-Nice then in the Tour of Flanders. At the start at St Denis he found himself pushed into the front ranks of the favourites.

The peloton, as was often the case, played no part in the development before Arras. Up until then twelve men had retained the attention of the followers. The first of them to enter into action was called Buchaille. He vainly escaped for a first time, then made a second attempt. This time eleven riders came up to him: Voorting, Gauthier, Dacquay, Varnajo, Decuax, Poblet, Meunier, Leullier, Dolhats, Canavèse and Tonello. The inevitable Merciers were already in a majority.

The gap between the leaders and the bunch was unstable, two and a half minutes at Clermont (63 kms), then three minutes at Flers (100 kms) before

Alone at the Roubaix track...

falling again to more than a minute at Amiens.

At the top of the hill of Doullens the bunch nevertheless went through almost two and a half minutes down on the leading group from which Dolhats and Voorting had just been dropped.

A little later, the ten leaders obtained a little respite when the chasing peloton became disorganised following a collective crash at Villers-Boccage.

The pitiless selection really began at Hénin-Liétard, when the ten escapees were caught first of all by Desbats, Demulder, Matthys, then Rémy, Gismondi, Petrucci, Renaud and Blusson. The partial regrouping was inevitable.

At the start of the cobbles the spectators were as usual waiting for a Belgian attack, but surprisingly, it was Pasquale Fornara who was the first to take action. Surprisingly, the new Italian professional Ricardo Filippi then pursued his elder. However, Fausto Coppi's protege and former amateur champion did not have the necessary strength to keep up the pace. Not only was he unable to rejoin Fornara but he was caught and dropped by two Frenchmen; Hassenforder and the tiny Papazian.

At Carvin, these two men managed to rejoin Fornara who was still parading himself in the lead!

With three of them together their chances seemed more realistic especially as the Alsatian Hassenforder was obviously in excellent form as was proved by his recent success in the National Criterium. But once again the "witch with green teeth" was to decide otherwise: Fornara, victim of a blowout, left the two Frenchmen alone at the front.

1954

When Papazian weakened the capricious "Hassen" was isolated and with little hope in the face of a peloton determined to bring about his downfall.

At Wattignies the Alsatian was joined first of all by Bartalini, then by Derycke who at Faces, eighteen kilometres from the velodrome attacked hard. He wanted to repeat his performance of the previous year. his action however provoked the regrouping of about twenty men, most of the favourites from which only Bobet and Van Steenbergen were missing, both beaten by bad luck.

Redolfi, Marinelli, Blusson, Hassenforder, Piazza, Filippi, Koblet, Kubler, Impanis, Derycke, Ockers, De Bruyne and a few others were getting ready for the final battle.

At Hem, De Bruyne punctured, then a crash eliminated Koblet, Albani, Filippi, Piazza, Hassenforder, Storms and Mertens.

On the long straight boulevard leading to the Roubaix track the crowds were lit up with excitement. Raymond Impanis attacked but Demulder brought the group up to him. The Belgian intelligently went back to the back of the group but fifteen hundred metres from the line, prodded by Antonin Magne who was following him, he went again in one last mad attack.

This time nobody managed to follow him. Impanis came onto the track with a lead of one hundred metres to be greeted by thunderous applause.

From then on Ockers was obliged to be content with second place on front of Ryckaert, Kubler and nine others.

Impanis joined the illustrious Rebry in the annals of cycling, both winners in the same year of Paris-Nice, Tour of Flanders and Paris-Roubaix, with the second triple coming twenty years after the first one.

A few moments after the finish in the centre of the track, while Impanis was doing his lap of honour, the truculent Kubler surrounded as always, summed up the situation in a few simple words: "Raymond Impanis? He's an aeroplane you know. We could do nothing when he took off..."

1954

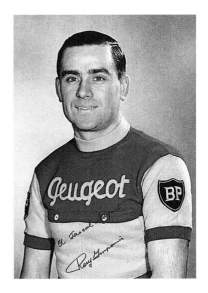

Raymond IMPANIS
(Belgium, 1925)

One of the biggest names in Belgian cycling in the post war period.

1947 : 2nd Liège-Bastogne-Liège
1948 : 2nd Liège-Bastogne-Liège
1949 : 2nd Belgian Championship,
       2nd Tour of Belgium
1950 : 2nd Flèche Wallonne
1952 : Ghent-Wevelgem, 2nd Het Volk,
       3rd Paris-Nice
1953 : Ghent-Wevelgem
1954 : Paris-Roubaix, Tour of Flanders,
       Paris-Nice
1955 : 2nd Liège-Bastogne-Liège
1956 : 3rd Tour of Spain
1957 : Flèche Wallonne,
       2nd Paris-Brussels
1960 : Paris-Nice
1961 : 2nd Ghent-Wevelgem

1. Raymond IMPANIS (Belgium)
   GS. Mercier-Hutchinson
2. Stan OCKERS (Belgium)
3. Marcel RYCKAERT (Belgium)
4. Ferdi KUBLER (Switzerland)
5. Serge BLUSSON (France)
6. Raoul REMY (France)
7. Marcel DEMULDER (Belgium)
8. Germain DERYCKE (Belgium)
9. Henri SURBATIS (France)
10. Roger DECOCK (Belgium)

Victoires sans gloire des XV de FRANCE sur l'ITALIE et l'ALLEMAGNE

(LIRE NOS ARTICLES, EN DERNIÈRE PAGE)

L'ÉQUIPE
LE QUOTIDIEN DU SPORT
ET DE l'Automobile

LUNDI 11 AVRIL 1955
10e ANNÉE — N° 2803

10, Fg MONTMARTRE, PARIS (9e)
TAITBOUT 70-80

PETITES ANNONCES : TAITBOUT 73-40, 41, 42 — COMPTE POSTAL : 9-287-93

Après s'être débarrassé de Dupont, Scodeller (accidenté) et B. Gauthier au cœur de l'«Enfer»

PARIS-ROUBAIX est une organisation **L'ÉQUIPE** dotée du **TROPHÉE DU SUCRE**

J. FORESTIER, le "matraqueur" de Mons-en-Pévèle
résiste durant 30 km. à la contre-attaque d'un groupe prestigieux dont

COPPI (2e), BOBET (3e), SCODELLER (4e) et KOBLET (7e)

... et enlève avec 15 secondes d'avance une course d'Apocalypse

La course pascale courue dans des conditions atmosphériques rigoureuses et sur une fin de parcours dantesque offrit une succession ininterrompue d'échappées généralement provoquées par les favoris

(D'un de nos envoyés spéciaux Pierre CHANY)

ROUBAIX. — Jean Forestier, qui s'était acquis une solide réputation de coureur par étapes en remportant, l'an passé, le Tour de Romandie et l'étape lyonnaise du Tour de France, vient de compléter son registre d'une manière absolument sensationnelle. En terminant détaché devant les plus nobles champions de la route un Paris-Roubaix d'Apocalypse, le jeune Lyonnais a réalisé une sorte de gageure. Livré à lui-même dans une équipe régionale très sympathique, certes, mais numériquement inférieure à ses grandes rivales, engagé dans une aventure inédite dont le souvenir hantera longtemps ceux qui la vécurent, Forestier a gagné l'un des plus beaux Paris-Roubaix de l'histoire. Il pourra désormais s'enorgueillir d'une victoire remportée à la force du jarret, aux dépens de MM. Fausto Coppi et Louison Bobet, classés dans l'ordre aux seconde et troisième places : une victoire que les conditions atmosphériques exécrables (froid, vent, pluie) et qu'une fin de parcours dantes...

LE MAGNIFIQUE EFFORT SOLITAIRE DE JEAN FORESTIER

ROUBAIX. — Après avoir décramponné Dupont et Bernard Gauthier dans la côte de Mons-en-Pévèle, voici Jean Forestier qui poursuit son magnifique effort dans la seconde côte pavée et meurtrière de «l'enfer» : Mons-en-Pévèle. Le Lyonnais grimpe en puissance, sans se lever de sa selle.

(Reportage de notre envoyé spécial Philippe ABDUT)

CHÉRUBIN
condu...

de notre Direc...
JACQUES G...

et mais comme de l'émo... tions qui nous avons d... la plaine, sans autre fi... Et tant de méchancet... me fut pas Balzac qui, s... tendre si doux, aux yeux... était remplacée par une... se dépister toutes les... Forestier, à travers la... ans même temps que la... les qualités qu'on lui sou...

Le cyclisme sur rou... pour trouver sa véritabl... milieur de nos organisa... tout en prestige. Le... peut pas tromper. Le... que le tout un grand... rumeur, Sordeaux Paris... suprême : celle des ho... poussés par la nécessit... raison l'expression du Gi... d'avoue que, après a... la fameux nouvi, mira... praçement d'une part a... et les 20 dernière kilo... bien, vituperant les sp... en une lutessa de Flan... champion du monde un... tant formidablement [...]

LA MÉCANIC...
Pierre Constant, qui... ler plus qu'un met... électricité, le La Rivier... très pratique et... et en vente partout... Riviera France.

...LISATION DE BLIARD SUR COUP FRANC) ET...

...N POINT A SES RIVAUX
...r le titre de champion

...a subi un désastre à MARSEILLE
...RG est tombé devant le RACING

...YES et le C.O.R.T. (4 et 5 points de retard sur le 16e) sont virtuellement en Division II

...UVELLE DÉFAITE DE SEDAN ...AU HAVRE CETTE FOIS !

...vent ces quatre ...répondre au titre. ...nous vous don... ...le programme que ...veut ser trois par ...au fait, il serait ...que Strasbourg ou ...campions il serait ...dants? Comme outsiders : oui. Qui ...pourrait préjuger l'avenir? Mais ...ils possèdent tout de même cinq ...points de retard, et doivent jouer...

Jean CORNU.

...a coup. Il s'est détenté. Biojaspai ...la grande vedette, a tombé tout ...comme l'a jeunes Muller et Wend... ...ling. Cette équipe a peu extrê... ...mement émotive. Elle non plus ...n'est pas mûre pour faire un cham... ...pion.

L'étonnante troisième place ...des Lensois

Ces deux défaillances ont permis ...aux LENSOIS, qui recontraient les ...TROYENS, de revenir au niveau ...des Strasbourgeois. Faut-il com... ...ter les mineurs parmi les préten...

(Lire la suite page 8, rub. Football)

...Coupe du Championnat ...des États-Unis, records se ...condaires il est vrai.

• A Francfort, pour la Coupe ...d'Europe, de gymnastique, ...Chakhline (U.R.S.S.) est en ...tête, mais Dot et Mathiot ...(France) occupent de très ...honorables 5e et 8e places.

• A Varsovie, en volley-ball ...la Pologne a battu la ...France, 3 sets à 1.

(Lire les détails dans nos différentes ...rubriques)

LES TROIS DERNIERS MATCHES DES QUATRE LEADERS

	24 AVRIL	1er MAI	22 MAI
REIMS : 39 pts	reçoit SOCHAUX	va à BORDEAUX	reçoit NICE
TOULOUSE : 37 p.	reçoit NICE	reçoit TROYES	va à LENS
STRAS. : 35 pts	va à LENS	reçoit ROUBAIX	reçoit METZ
LENS : 35 pts	va à STRASBOURG	reçoit R.C. PARIS	va à TOULOUSE

Forestier
overcomes the Lords

When Louison Bobet and Fausto Coppi met each other at the start of the fifty third Paris-Roubaix they were simply polite with each other. There was no warmth between them and there never would be either. In 1955 the two champions no longer felt, as they used to, the pleasure of meeting each other.

The distant period when Louison admired his elder was past. As far as the Campionissimo was concerned he appreciated the panache of the Breton...providing he was not a direct rival! But time had done its work. Up until 1953, the Italian had for the most part dominated his rivals. Then he had reached his peak. Moreover the Campionissimo had had to hand his rainbow jersey over to Louison, a perfect example of the handing over of power.

At the top there was no room for two stars. From that time on their friendly relations inevitably got worse. This Paris-Roubaix was going to widen the breach a little more. Coppi had returned to the Northern roads. His success in the event went back five years already, but his prestige remained intact. His presence at the start of aroused considerable interest in Italy. Fausto had just won the first event of the season there, the Circuit of Cagliari then, as in his finest days the Tour of Campania with a lead of almost five minutes over Fiorenzo Magni.

For his part, Bobet arrived crowned with success of a prestigious win in the Tour of Flanders acquired in front of Koblet and Van Steenbergen.

As well as the two stars a number of other champions jostled together to sign the start sheet. Among them were Derycke, Koblet, Gauthier, Darrigade, Dupont, Geminiani, Anquetil, Van Steenbergen, Poblet, Kubler, Schotte, Impanis and Ockers.

The riders also had to battle over a new route. The towns of Courrières, Carvin, Seclin, and Wattignies were abandoned. From Hénin-Liétard the race now went towards Courcelles, Evin, Leforest, the hills of Moncheaux and Mons-en-Pévèle, the new strategic points, Mérignies, Pont-à-Marcq, Fretin, Péronne before returning to the old route at Ascq.

From the start the one hundred and fifty nine riders were faced with cold and rainy conditions. Quickly ten men were detached. Among them were several of the top riders: Caput, Darrigade, Privat and Koblet. The handsome Hugo was certainly no more than a shadow of the "Pedaller of Charm" of the 1951 Tour de France, but he was far from finished.

A first group rejoined them at Breteuil then the whole peloton came up to neutralise the attempt.

At the foot of the hill of Doullens, as often, the real race began. Under the rain, which was now pouring down, the spectators could hardly make out the riders. Bobet's world champion's jersey was already covered in mud.

The regional Scodeller powerfully went clear at Courcelles. There remained forty one kilometres to Roubaix. Straight away Bernard Gauthier and Jean Forestier jumped on to his wheel. Scodeller was recompensed for his boldness by a puncture, the French champion Jacques Dupont replaced him at the front.

The hill of Mons-en-Pévèle, a few kilometres later decided the issue. Jean Forestier from Lyons accelerated.

JEAN **FORESTIER**
TOUR DE FRANCE 1953

Jean FORESTIER
(France, 1930)

A pillar of the French national Tour de France team - four stage victories, green jersey) his honours also include the toughest classics, Paris-Roubaix and the Tour of Flanders.

1954 : Tour of Romandy
1955 : Paris-Roubaix
1956 : Tour of Flanders,
3rd Paris-Roubaix,
3rd Tour of Luxembourg,
3rd Criterium National
1957 : Criterium National,
Tour of Romandy,
3rd French Championship
1959 : 2nd French Championship
1960 : 4th Paris-Roubaix
1964 : 3rd Paris-Nice

1955

Successively Dupont and Gauthier were dropped.
In the group of ten behind in a position to come back on his heels, there were the "Lords": Bobet, Coppi, Koblet, Impanis, Scodeller, Sterckx and Planckaert.

Forestier appeared to be an excellent prey for the stars who estimated that the runaway would inevitably soon weaken.

But the man from Lyons covered the kilometres at the same speed, without weakening. Inspired by leading the race and the hope of carrying it off he jumped from one pavement to another like a Flemish virtuoso. Behind there was no "entente cordiale".

There were quickly only three of them just a few hundred metres behind the leader: Louison Bobet, Fausto Coppi and..Gilbert Scodeller. However only the last of them was riding with any sense of conviction for Coppi knew that if he made too much of an effort he would risk losing the sprint on the Roubaix track. In any case he did not want to give Bobet this type of present, the one who was pushing him off his pedestal.

For his part Bobet did not want to make too many unnecessary efforts. The Breton believed he had the measure of the Italian but was worried about Scodeller, the winner of the last Paris-Tours in front of.....Bobet himself!

Fausto Coppi at the finish.

Forestier's only worry was to keep his speed up over the cobblestones. In the event nobody managed to rejoin him and he crossed the finishing line with a lead of fifteen seconds over the trio.

Never, perhaps, had the Roubaix spectators seen such a furious sprint for second place as they did in 1955, for there was much more at stake than the minor placings. Fausto attacked from the third position and Bobet gave in immediately, with Scodeller fourth.

As he got off his machine the normally polite and restrained Bobet was furious: "This traitor, this coward. If Coppi had been prepared to work then we would certainly have caught Forestier as Scodeller was still quite strong. Unfortunately Coppi was playing to lose and wanted to be sure of being second. In his place I would not have dared to have sprinted. I was riding to win but Coppi was riding with sole intention of beating me."

Coppi defended himself by explaining that he was still not at the top of his form. He was in fact surprised to still be in the main group before Doullens. However one thing was sure, for his return into French racing the Campionissimo was determined to beat the world champion. If he managed to do that he would return to Italy satisfied. But on the evening after the race was he really?

The two men left without saying a word to each other.

As for Forestier, he was exhausted. Streaming with sweat he sat in the centre of the track getting his breath back. In the morning he was just one of the many hopefuls, by the evening he had become a champion!

To the journalists surrounding him he confirmed: "Certainly I knew that I was in excellent form since the Grand Prix of Cannes which I won fifteen days ago, but I was not thinking of winning Paris-Roubaix in front of all the aces." Forestier was not forecast to win. He even did not know the final part of the route as the previous year he had retired at the beginning of the race!

A very quiet champion, he never complained about not being well known and up until that time had, at international level, only won the Tour of Romandy and one stage of the Tour de France...at Lyons!

This Paris-Roubaix allowed him to show himself. The following year in 1956 he sacrilegiously beat the Flemish on their home ground in the Tour of Flanders. By escaping in sight of the finish he strung out Ockers, the world champion, Léon Van Daele, of whom we will talk of later, Van Steenbergen, Matthys, Derycke, Vlayen, Schotte. Then he accumulated victories like the Tour of Romandy 1957, National Criterium 1957 and four stages of the Tour de France. But Paris-Roubaix remained his favourite: "It was a race which I always liked, not only because I won it but also because it is very hard and there, on the cobblestones, it is every man for himself."

1955

1. Jean FORESTIER (France)
   GS.Follis
2. Fausto COPPI (Italy)
3. Louison BOBET (France)
4. Gilbert SCODELLER (France)
5. Raymond IMPANIS (Belgium)
6. Ernest STERCKX (Belgium)
7. Hugo KOBLET (Switzerland)
8. Bernard GAUTHIER (France)
9. Jacques DUPONT (France)
10. Joseph PLANCKAERT (Belgium)

L'ÉQUIPE

LE QUOTIDIEN DU SPORT ET DE l'Automobile

10, Fg MONTMARTRE, PARIS (9°)
TAITBOUT 70-80

LUNDI 9 AVRIL 1956
11° ANNÉE — N° 3114

20 FRANCS

PETITES ANNONCES : TAITBOUT 73-40, 41, 42 — COMPTE POSTAL : 4.237-95

avec ma Vespa 1956
tous les jours... je vais au bureau !

club méditerranée
4, Rue de la Bourse, Paris-2 - RIC. 78-00

écoles de ski nautique et d'exploration sous-marine

TROPHÉE DU SUCRE

Six champions émergent dans "l'Enfer" de Paris-Roubaix

LOUISON BOBET, ÉPAULÉ PAR BERNARD GAUTHIER

ATTAQUANT DE CHOC

AJOUTE A SA COURONNE
l'une de ses
plus belles perles

Il devance au sprint DE BRUYNE et l'ennemi n° 1 VAN STEENBERGEN • FORESTIER, qui avait répondu aux attaques des Mercier-BP, était aussi avec LAURÉDI, de l'échappée victorieuse

(D'un de nos envoyés spéciaux Pierre CHANY)

C'est une organisation L'ÉQUIPE

Sachez aussi que...

FRANCE
René
ne

ROUBAIX. — Il est des hommes dont on ne devrait jamais douter. Louison Bobet est de ceux-là. Il y a quatre mois, ce champion hors série souffrait sur un lit de clinique d'un mal qui devait, selon toute logique, le tenir éloigné des compétitions pour un long moment. Un de ces derniers jours, il terminait second de... Paris-Camembert, une course de renommée bien modeste pour un routier de grands chemins ! Et, hier, il remportait Paris-Roubaix, un Paris-Roubaix du meilleur cru, couru contre le vent à 41 km. 531 de moyenne ho...

Ockers anxiously awaits a new tyre.

Alfred De Bruyne ahead at Hem, in front of Derycke, Gauthier and Bobet

Bobet at last

At the beginning of 1956, international cycling was in the middle of a transformation. The first "extra-sportive" or "sponsored" teams appeared in the pelotons. The Italians and particularly Magni had jumped on the bandwagon. However, in France for example it was still forbidden to wear jerseys in the colours of those teams which were considered to be "hybrid". In this way Magni, who could not bring himself to abandon his "Nivea" jersey, had to strike Paris-Roubaix from his programme!

In France the sporting world seemed to be mainly concerned over the medical bulletins of Louison Bobet.

The first worries of the Breton in fact had started in July of the previous year. Louison, then World champion, realised his dream of winning a third Tour de France. This victory was nevertheless painfully achieved for during the event an old injury reappeared. Bobet suffered like a martyr.

At the start of the winter he had an operation in the clinic at Dinan. The surgeon extracted from him a big ball of dead flesh and left a scar twenty centimetres long. The doctor, dubious about Louison ever being able to ride a bike again, explained that the surgery was urgent and if delayed could have put Louison's life at risk. Many said that it was the end of Bobet's career and placed their hopes in the rising generation led by the young prodigy Jacques Anquetil.

However, Bobet did not give up. He spent several days holiday in the Canary Islands and then started to prepare for the 1956 season. The French champion returned to the bicycle under the sun at Les Issambres. The return proved to be difficult. Much later he even swore that he was on the point of retiring from the sport on the evening following a disastrous National Criterium.

By the force of courage he came back little by little. The Sunday which preceded Paris-Roubaix, he won at Frejus and then finished second in Paris-Vimoutiers. In spite of this, his participation remained uncertain for the Queen of the Classics. According to his surgeon, he could only start if the weather was fine.

It was not raining at the start but the forecast was not good. Bobet signed the sheet but his chances were thought to be slim. Not a single journalist tipped him to win. Most of them thought that Louison had missed the boat in 1952, Bevilacqua's year, then in 1955.

Jean Forestier, the previous winner had on the other hand just won the Tour of Flanders from under the noses of the Flemish. These hard proud men wanted to wash away the affront at all costs. It was clear that the main task would be to beat them on the Roubaix track.

At their head, Fred De Bruyne looked thin as a scarecrow. The team-mate of Bobet at Mercier had just successively won Paris-Nice and Milan-San Remo. His sense of the race and his sprint must sooner or later pay off over these Northern roads.

For his part, Van Steenbergen, upset at having been outmanoeuvred like a debutante at the finish of the Tour of Flanders, was seeking revenge. Among the other fancied riders: Ockers, Impanis and several Frenchmen such as Bernard Gauthier, Jacques Dupont and Jean Stablinski who was slowly climbing in the hierarchy.

The young Belgian generation was waiting for the race with

1956

Louison BOBET
(France, 1925-1983)

Adored by the French fans for his style, courage and perseverance, Bobet became the first man to win the Tour de France three times.

1950 : French Champion
1951 : French Champion
Milan-San Remo, Tour of Lombardy,
Criterium National
1952 : Paris Cote d'Azur,
Grand Prix des Nations,
Criterium National
1953 : Tour de France
1954 : Tour de France, World Champion
1955 : Tour de France, Tour of Flanders
Tour of Luxembourg,
Dauphiné-Liberé
1956 : Paris-Roubaix
1959 : Bordeaux-Paris

equal impatience. Van Looy, winner of Ghent-Wevelgem, Vannitsen, Planckaert and Janssens and others would be without question the targets of the old guard.

Just after the start five men went to the front: Max Cohen, Fanuel, Petinatti, Bovay and Grosso. After Creil another seven men including Schils, Coterno and Minardi joined them. Their maximum lead was five and a half minutes at the one hundred and thirtieth kilometre.

At Arras the escapees had no more than 3mins 15secs. A closed level

crossing at Evin-Malmaison sounded the death knell for their last hopes.

The real race began at Moncheaux and then on the hill at Mons-en-Pévèle where suddenly the rhythm increased. Three men were just clear at the top: Bernard Gauthier, Bruno Monti and confident Fred De Bruyne.

A few metres behind them the stars crowded together, Van Steenbergen, Lauredi, Forestier, Ockers and Derycke, then a handful of seconds behind were Bobet, Bauvin, the Belgian champion, Van Cauter, Cérami, Van Looy, Janssens, Schotte, Vlaeyen, Hassenforder and Van Kerkhove.

The evidence was that the Belgians were more than ever present. However, the joyful Hassenforder was the first one to try to go clear. On the day "Hassen", recent winner of the National Criterium, was not laughing, he was working. But the Alsatian could do nothing against "the express" which swallowed him up. It was composed of De Bruyne and Gauthier. Van Steenbergen on the other hand found himself totally isolated after Stan Ockers punctured at Pont-à-Marcq. But Rik with his incredible sprint was certainly not yet beaten. Bobet therefore successively launched his team mates De Bruyne and Gauthier into the attack. Harassed from every side Van Steenbergen stuck like a leech each time. But the last pursuit behind Gauthier, just before the entrance to the velodrome had its effect.

The man from Grenoble, followed by Van Steenbergen, was first onto the track. Bobet was only in fifth position. Quickly De Bruyne took over the lead and Van Steenbergen felt his strength leaving him. He understood that a third success at Roubaix today was going to be impossible.

The convalescent Louison Bobet went past him at a faster speed. The Breton was turning his gear of 52x14 to perfection. Nobody could get in the way of his irresistible will to win.

An indescribable ovation shook the stadium. Bobet, the idol of the French had triumphed in the finest of all classics.

Scarcely had he time to savour his victory then he found himself on the hard cement of the track for when De Bruyne the second place man drew alongside to congratulate him his tyre rolled off the rim and he brought the winner down in a crash.

Bobet picked himself up and laughed off the incident as the reporters crowed round him: "You did not tip me as a possible winner at the start and I have to say that I too was very sceptical at being able to win. It has been five months since my operation and only two since I got back on my bike."

As he came out of the showers, Van Steenbergen showed himself to be particularly disappointed with his fourth place: "I have never before been so strong but what could I do alone against the three Merciers? If Ockers had been with me, we would have shared the work and things would have happened differently."

Ockers, the unfortunate, like Stablinski, was in the leading group on the hill of Moncheaux then irremediably dropped after a broken wheel and a puncture.

The rest of the season did not go so well for Louison Bobet. His injury first of all caused him to abandon the Tour of Spain, then not to start the Tour de France. A few months later, Van Steenbergen put on a second world champion's jersey at Copenhagen, finishing in front of a certain Rik Van Looy.

The "battle of the Riks" had only just begun, to the great good fortune of Belgian cycling.

The lap of honour of Bobet, De Bruyne and Forestier.

1956

1. Louison BOBET (France)
   GS. L.Bobet-Hutchinson
2. Fred DE BRUYNE (Belgium)
3. Jean FORESTIER (France)
4. Rik VAN STEENBERGEN (Belgium)
5. Bernard GAUTHIER (France)
6. Nello LAUREDI (France)
7. Germain DERYCKE (France)
8. André VLAYEN (Belgium)
9. Jean ROBIC (France)
10. Gilbert BAUVIN (France)

A 'Puncher' named De Bruyne

In Belgium, several days after the 1956 Paris-Roubaix, the critics did not spare De Bruyne. The Flemish did not understand his actions. One question made the front pages of the dailies: "Why did De Bruyne help Bobet win on the track at Roubaix?"

De Bruyne, who won Liège-Bastogne-Liège a few weeks later, did not reply but did seem to express regret in not winning at Roubaix. During the winter he decided to emigrate, with his faithful friend Désiré Keteleer, to the Italian team Carpano-Coppi.

Even if he came up against Miguel Poblet in the Milan-San Remo, the beginning of the season was excellent for him, notably with a superb success in the Tour of Flanders. The popular Fred was now even more the man to beat on the Northern roads when on the 7th April, the day of the event, he celebrated his ten years of competition.

As well as the Belgians, always confident and usually dominating, several Frenchmen inspired by the efforts of Forestier and Bobet, were getting ready for the great battle. In this way Géminiani was proclaiming loudly to all and sundry for some time: "Sunday, they will not drop me easily on the cobbles or on the bumps. I am on form and this week I have ridden five hundred training kilometres."

On the other hand, Jean Robic, was only following the race as a spectator. Paul Wiegant, his team manager, though that his form was not good enough for such a difficult race. Poor Biquet.

"La Pascale" had a rendezvous with cold grey weather. The one hundred and forty six starters left wrapped up in their woollen jerseys.

From the start the race unfolded in the traditonal way. Riding into a powerful headwind the bunch formed into the inevitable echelons. The weakest were pushed to the back and for most of

1957

Alfred DE BRUYNE
(Belgium, 1930-1994)

The puncher of the peloton he enjoyed a brief but intense career.

1955 : 2nd Paris-Tours
2nd Tour of Lombardy
1956 : Milan-San Remo
Liege-Bastogne-Liege
Paris-Nice, 2nd Paris-Roubaix
1957 : Paris-Roubaix, Tour of Flanders
Paris-Tours, 2nd Milan-San Remo
1958 : Liège-Bastogne-Liège, Paris-Nice
2nd Paris-Tours,
3rd Ghent-Wevelgem
1959 : Liège-Bastogne-Liège, 2nd Het Volk

left: Fred De Bruyne finishes.

bottom: Van Steenbergen second in front of Van Daele and the peloton.

them found themselves forced to retire.

A partial regrouping took place as they left Hénin-Liétard. The flight of Roger Rosselle and the Portuguese Barbosa really launched the race. A Portuguese in the lead on the cobbles, that was unheard of, but he was unable to follow the pace very long that was imposed by his companion who was much more used to the cobblestones.

However, the Belgian in spite of his efforts could do nothing when caught by two men, top rank competitors: Nicholas Barone and the Italian Coletto, a team-mate of De Bruyne in the Carpano-Coppi squad.

This supercharged tandem led the race for twenty six kilometres with a lead of around about thirty seconds. The first man to come up to them was none other than Fred De Bruyne. At Sainghin-en-Mélantois, twenty kilometres from Roubaix, he had shrewdly broken clear of a group of forty men. The Belgian understood that the aces were watching each other. Up to that point none of them had made the least suggestion of an attack. At his third attempt De Bruyne had opened a gap and in just a few minutes had caught the leading pair.

Straight away Coletto gave up, then at Ascq, eleven kilometres from the velodrome, Barone did the same, for the pace of the Belgian was much too fast. He was riding with such ease that only a puncture at the kilometre to go point slowed him up. His team manager, Ettore Milano, changed his wheel in less than twenty seconds.

From then on the others could only fight for second place. Van Steenbergen showed himself to be the best of them in front of Léon Van Daele, a name to remember, and a group of twenty men 1min 11secs behind the winner.

De Bruyne was naturally radiant. However as he got off his machine he said that he had trembled after his puncture, adding: "I am so much more happy with my victory as Paris-Roubaix was missing from my collection. Last year I failed by a whisker behind my team-mate Louison Bobet. This time I decided to take a striking revenge, by finishing, if possible, by myself. There is no way that I could better celebrate my tenth year in competition, for my career as a rider started precisely on the 7th April 1947 at Berlare. When I saw that the two riders in the lead were no more than one hundred metres in front, I said to myself: this is the right moment to attack. I went away and then caught Coletto and Barone. Only the Frenchman was able to stay on my wheel but on the cobbles at Ascq, I went even faster and Barone fell back."

A few days after the Belgian's victory, the press was asking another question: "Can De Bruyne win the Tour de France?"

Opinions were divided. Bobet thought that he was the most dangerous of the Belgians. But where Ockers and Brankart had failed, De Bruyne would not be able to do any better. However he consoled himself by winning Liège-Bastogne-Liège again in 1958 and 1959.

As for the Tour de France, which the Belgians had not won since 1939, they still had to wait a little longer, for in 1957 a certain Eddy Merckx was only twelve years old and was thinking mainly about football!

1957

1. Alfred DE BRUYNE (Belgium)
   GS.Carpano-Coppi
2. Rik VAN STEENBERGEN (Belgium)
3. Léon VAN DAELE (Belgium)
4. André DARRIGADE (France)
5. Maurice MOLLIN (Belgium)
6. Raymond IMPANIS (Belgium)
7. Serge BLUSSON (France)
8. Norbet KERCKHOVE (Belgium)
9. Joseph GROUSSARD (France)
10. Jacques DUPONT (France)

Van Daele's takeover by force

At the announcement of the imminent arrival of the riders, the public rose to its feet, the Belgians shouted. The French, warned of Darrigade's puncture, were much calmer and frankly, no longer had any great hopes.

Suddenly, down at the entrance to the velodrome the first motorbikes appeared. The tension mounted. In a flash behind the vehicles, two men, two anonymous riders came into sight. They were the Irishman Shay Elliott and the astonishing Belgian Verplaetse. Twenty little metres behind, the pack of road men- sprinters were ready to devour them.

For the first time for ages, the victory was going to be judged by a royal sprint. The very best were there, tightly bunched. Van Looy was most people's favourite, however he had to get past a superb string of champions, all wonderful sprinters: the world champion Van Steenbergen, the worrying Miguel Poblet, the subtle Fred De Bruyne, the giant Léon van Daele and several others.

A few kilometres from the finish Barone leads in front of Truye, Verplaetse and Anquetil.

There remained less than a thousand metres to cover and there would only be one victor at the end of the home straight.

Elliott and Verplaetse could not long resist the pressure of a peloton which was riding at more than sixty kilometres an hour. As the bell rang the two unfortunate escapees were reeled in and the sprint was launched.

Suddenly, three hundred metres from the white line, a man powerfully shot out of the front of the group. In a second the rider gained a lead of five or six lengths. It was a perfect demonstration of force. The others could do no more than get up to his back wheel. Poblet was second, Van Looy third, Van Steenbergen fourth! The winner was called Léon Van Daele and he had just beaten the very best sprinters in the world in the most sought after classic on the calendar.

After his lap of honour, surrounded by a mob of journalists, Van Daele expressed his joy: " Six hundred metres from the velodrome, I was sure that I would triumph. Since the Paris Six-day, I have thought only about Paris-Roubaix. I also said to my friends that I was going to win it. This year up until now I had no luck at all; a crash close to the finish in Milan-San Remo robbed me of any chance in the sprint, then I broke my bike in the Tour of Flanders. Before Paris-Roubaix I admit that I was pessimistic, nevertheless I went out to inspect the last sixty kilometres on Friday. When Jacques Anquetil was caught three kilometres from the finish, I felt transformed. I was certain of winning in spite of the presence of Van Looy, Van Steenbergen, Poblet and De Bruyne. I attacked in the back straight and nobody could get past me."

At the start, however, one name was on the lips of the one hundred and fifty competitors, Rik Van Looy. He was the unanimous favourite. The winner of Milan-San Remo was riding with astonishing ease. As the older ones said since the "great days of Coppi nobody had ever flitted around like this".

Even Antonin Magne, who always thought a long time before expressing himself laconically, replied immediately: "Van Looy is the one to beat." Coming from him it was indeed a compliment. The official odds were three to one. After that was De Bruyne and Poblet at five to one and then Anquetil, Bobet, Forestier, Van Steenbergen and Derycke at six to one, then the sprinters Van Daele and Darrigade at seven to one.

Jacques Anquetil found himself in the front line and made no secret of the fact that for the first time in his career he had the firm intention, not only of showing himself but also of winning his first classic.

The Norman rapidly confirmed this wish when at St Just-en-Chaussee, two hundred kilometres from Roubaix, he already figured in an initial escape composed of twenty men.

After Arras, sixteen riders were still in command at t he front with a lead of four and a half minutes. Success seemed very much to be on the cards because in the break, apart from Anquetil, were several other pretenders such as Antonin Rolland, François Mahé, Jean Bobet, Noël Foré, Jean Stablinski, Joseph Groussard, Nicholas Barone and an astonishing Belgian, yes, yet another one, by the name of Verplaetse.

On the hill of Moncheaux, Noël Foré, the recent victor of Ghent-Wevelgem, attacked hard. Nicholas Barone and François Mahé reacted immediately. For several kilometres they had a lead of one hundred metres over the rest of the group. Anquetil came up to them, then at twenty five kilometres from the track he decided to stake everything and escaped, jumping from one pavement to another like a veteran!

The effort was certainly necessary, for the pack of pursuers had considerably reduced its deficit. Van Looy, Van Steenbergen, Van Daele and others were closing fast.

Suddenly, thirteen kilometres from Roubaix, a puncture immobilised "Master Jacques, so Verplaetse took command in company with Willy Truye and Nicholas Barone. However an

Léon VAN DAELE
(Belgium, 1933)

Fast and classy, his career hit a peak when he won the 1958 Paris-Roubaix.

1954 : Kuurne-Brussels-Kuurne
1956 : 3rd Tour of Flanders
1957 : Paris-Brussels,
      Three Days of d'Anvers,
      Milan-Mantoue,
      3rd Paris-Roubaix
1958 : Paris-Roubaix
1959 : Ghent-Wevelgem,
      3rd Milan-San Remo
1961 : Kuurne-Brussels-Kuurne

A disappointed Anquetil at the velodrome.

1958

unleashed Anquetil did not throw in the towel. As motivated as he always was in the Grand Prix des Nations, the classic time trial that he had made his own, stroking the pedals harmoniously round, the Norman came back to the trio in less than three kilometres.

The effort was in vain for at Hem, at the gates of Roubaix and to the great despair of the French, the four were swallowed up by the flying bunch. It was a poor recompense for such a magnificent effort.

Out of the big bunch came Forestier and ...Van Looy.!

Léon Van Daele wins the sprint.

Forestier was only riding for first place and this being the case Van Looy was certainly not the ideal companion. The last try by Verplaetse and Elliott dominated the final few minutes before the entrance to the track.

Under the showers Anquetil admitted to being disillusioned: "When I saw the peloton rejoin us three kilometres from the end, I did not believe it. Frankly, in spite of my puncture, I thought that we could hold to the end as we had more than a minute's lead with ten kilometres to go. It would have been difficult to have got away alone but I was convinced that I could win the sprint."

This failure, even if it was panache, was to enter into the mind of the Norman and increase his aversion to the classics. He won Ghent-Wevelgem and Liège-Bastogne-Liège much later, after having run off with an impressive number of stage races.

Léon Van Daele for his part, after Paris-Brussels 1957, completed his record in an outstanding way when Ghent-Wevelgem fell to him the following year at the expense of Hoevenaers and a decidedly persecuted Jacques Anquetil!

Today, many years later, Van Daele has an emotional memory of this April day in 1958. For him as for Forestier, there is little doubt, that Paris-Roubaix remains the finest race of them all, leading to undying fame for the winner.

1958

1. Léon VAN DAELE (Belgium)
   GS.Faema
2. Miguel POBLET (Spain)
3. Rik VAN LOOY (Belgium)
4. Rik VAN STEENBERGEN (Belgium)
5. Jean FORESTIER (France)
6. Alfred DE BRUYNE (Belgium)
7. Marcel JANSSENS (Belgium)
8. Roger HASSENFORDER (France)
9. Raymond IMPANIS (Belgium)
10. Jan ZAGERS (Belgium)

The Confirmation of a Champion

The 1959 edition of Paris-Roubaix seemed without any doubt to be very open. The older generation were slowly laying down their arms. Van Steenbergen, in spite of his second place in Milan-San Remo, gave more importance to the lucrative contracts offered by the directors of the velodromes. Louison Bobet was approaching retirement age and Jean Robic who certainly started but the bunch left him to his sad fate after eighty kilometres of racing.

Fausto Coppi for his part, signed the start sheet for this his last Paris-Roubaix. The Campionissimo was in his fortieth year. Everybody wanted him to retire from competition, but unfortunately nobody dared to talk to him about it.

The event at the beginning of the season was none other than the war of communiques between the two national stars Jacques Anquetil and Roger Rivière. In the early part of March the latter was laughing at Anquetil's poor form. The Norman remained impassive and simply said he would meet up with the man from St Etienne on the Northern roads.

Anquetil was beginning to get to know the cobbles, he estimated that if one

As the end approaches Noël Foré leads in front of Gilbert Desmet.

day he should win a classic, that it would be Paris-Roubaix. "Master Jacques" prepared very carefully and went for several long training rides after the Tour of Flanders. He wanted to wipe the disappointment of 1958 from his memory which at that time he thought to be the most unfortunate day of his career.

On the other hand the "Pascale" was unknown to Rivière. The elegant pursuiter had, according to certain rumours, enjoyed his recent preparation over the cobbled sectors. Would he nevertheless be able to overcome them in the race when the conditions were totally different?

The opposing pair were going to come up against the foreign stars with Van Looy at their head. Rik had just majestically won the Tour of Flanders. Miguel Poblet was the winner on the Via Roma in the Milan-San Remo and remained that much more motivated after his second place at the Roubaix Velodrome in 1958.

The observers also put forward the named of Vannitsen, Elliott the surprising winner of Het Volk, Van Daele, Van Steenbergen, De Bruyne, Derycke, Demulder, Nencini, Defilippis, Ronchini. As for the French they also hoped for something from Darrigade, Graczyk and a few others.

Under the rain one hundred and forty four men answered the call in the stadium at St Denis. Right from the start Germain Derycke, the former winner, surprisingly chose the role of hare.

The Belgian was away by himself for forty kilometres. At Creil, the Italian Fini joined up with him. The gap grew regularly up until St Just-en Chaussée but the "Tandem" was swallowed up at Breteuil.

The first selection took place before Amiens. The bunch had just exploded. About fifteen men climbed the Doullens hill together. The climb had long since ceased to be a strategic point in the race but the atmosphere there was still the same. The spectators only left a narrow passage for the champions.

Under the rain there was only eleven of them left at Hénin-Liétard. The group contained a few favourites such as Miguel Poblet, Joseph Groussard, Noël Foré and Angelo Conterno. Two other Frenchmen were also there, Gilbert Scodeller and the young Henri Anglade. After incidents to Groussard, Anglade, Poblet and Falaschi there were only seven of them left to attack the hill at Mons-en-Pévèle.

At this point there was a reaction from the peloton. Twelve men were pushing their big gears: Darrigade, De Bruyne, Van Looy, Elliott, Impanis, Aerenhouts, Rivière, Demulder, Sabbadini, Vannitsen, Keteleer and Molenaers. Only Anquetil had missed the right move, he had just crashed. The junction seemed to be inevitable but the men at the front resisted better than expected. At twenty five kilometres from Roubaix, the seven leaders still almost fifty seconds in hand.

Everyone was shaken at Louvil, just before Cysoing when Riviere "blew up" in a big way. The double holder of the World Hour Record and also the double world pursuit champion was simply not hardened enough to win Paris-Roubaix. He was unable to stand up to the infernal pace and the constant attacks of De Bruyne, Darrigade and especially an unleashed Van Looy who seemed to be the strongest of them all.

At Baisieux, the leaders were no more than two hundred metres in front. Suddenly on the cobblestones a motorbike skidded. Darrigade could not miss it and went over the top of the machine. An equally surprised Van Looy did the same. The two men restarted a minute later but they had left their hopes behind them on the cobbles.

At the front in the meantime three riders had taken things into there own hands: Marcel Janssens, Noël Foré and Gilbert Desmet. They had just dropped their four

Noël FORE
(Belgium, 1932-1994)

A specialist in the harsh and fiercely contested Flandrian events, he achieved one victory in Paris-Roubaix.

1958 : Tour of Belgium, Ghent-Wevelgem
1959 : Paris-Roubaix,
          2nd Criterium des As,
          3rd World Championships
1960 : Flèche-Flamande
1962 : Tour of Belgium,
          2nd Paris-Brussels
1963 : Tour of Flanders,
          Kuurne-Brussels-Kuurne
1967 : 2nd Tour of Flanders,
          3rd Bordeaux-Paris

1959

companions and were now a minute in front. The victory was going to be played out among them.

The three riders normally rode in the shadow of Van Looy or De Bruyne but they had all known successes of their own in the past. Janssens knew the Roubaix Velodrome very well, he had won a stage there in the 1957 Tour de France, Gilbert Desmet was the last winner of Paris-Tours and Noël Foré had picked up the Tour of Belgium and Ghent-Wevelgem in 1958.

The trio were riding flat out without any let-up and it was Foré who strung out his two breakaway companions at the velodrome.

Foré's success was also a triumph for Belgian cycling. In fact ten men from Flanders were among the first eleven finishers! Only Tino Sabbadini was able to infiltrate himself in to fifth place.

The superiority of the "Vans" had turned into a tornado.

At the finish the Belgians were jubilant and Foré took pleasure in explaining: "When the gap opened I hardly thought that this was to be the decisive moment, For many kilometres we were barely two hundred metres in front then suddenly the gap opened and we were told that we had two minutes at the start of the cobbles. however it was only fifteen kilometres from the finish that I really believed that we could succeed."

Desmet sportingly said that the winner deserved the bouquet. Even Darrigade hardly seemed surprised for after the Het Volk run the week before, he had tipped Foré for Roubaix.

The best, with Foré, was without any argument Van Looy. His fourth place did not satisfy him at all: "There is no doubt about it, Paris-Roubaix always lets me down. Without my crash and my puncture we would have got up to the leaders and I think I could have beaten Darrigade at the finish."

Finally Van Steenbergen said when he was under the showers that this Paris-Roubaix, his fifteenth, run in the rain was the hardest of his career.

Seven minutes and thirty nine seconds after Foré, in forty fourth place, an anonymous rider with a jersey covered in mud crossed the line: Fausto Coppi.

Since 1955, the Campionissimo had had very little success. Worse he always finished with the unknowns, those who he had played with a few years before. From then on he trailed his sadness at the back of the pelotons.

Broken, as much physically, because of the efforts he had made without counting the cost, as he was morally, he none the less was unable to leave the profession which had brought him everything. Tormented by the demon of competition, even if he did not win anymore, Coppi kept putting off his farewell. He promised to stop for good in 1960 after one last tour to Africa. Destiny stopped him from doing so. In December 1959, in company with Géminiani, Anquetil, Rivière, Anglade and Hassenforder he went to Upper Volta, to ride a criterium and join in several hunting parties.

On the 13th December, he finished second in the criterium of Ouagadougou behind Anquetil. For the rest of his stay he seemed very tired. On the 18th he took the plane back together with Géminiani.

After he had returned to Italy his illness rapidly got worse a short time after Christmas. Fausto had a fit of vomiting on the 27th December. Treated at home he was then taken to hospital on the 1st January 1960.

It was the end. The undetected malaria had done its work on his worn out body: the Campionissimo died on the 2nd January at 8.45am.

He remained in the memory of his contemporaries, and many others, as the greatest of all time. Unique and unforgettable, the incomparable and mythical Campionissimo.

1. Noël FORE (Belgium)
   GS.Groene Leeuw
2. Gilbert DESMET (Belgium)
3. Marcel JANSSENS (Belgium)
4. Rik VAN LOOY (Belgium)
5. Tino SABBADINI (France)
6. Fred DE BRUYNE (Belgium)
7. Frans DEMULDER (Belgium)
8. Léon VAN DAELE (Belgium)
9. Frans AERENHOUTS (Belgium)
10. Raymond IMPANIS (Belgium)

L'ÉQUIPE

LE QUOTIDIEN DU SPORT ET DE l'Automobile

10, Fg MONTMARTRE, PARIS (9ᵉ)
TAITBOUT 70-80

LUNDI 11 AVRIL 1960
15ᵉ ANNÉE — N° 4.360

NF 0,35 (35 FR.)

M

PETITES ANNONCES : REGIE-PRESSE, 85 bis, RUE REAUMUR — GUT. 99-30

L'humidité ambiante et les pavés glissants de Paris-Roubaix n'ont pas ralenti les coureurs favorisés par le vent : 45 km. 538 de moyenne

TROPHÉE D SUCRE

CERAMI LE RUGUEUX (38 ANS) TRIOMPHE A L'USUR

d'un SIMPSON étourdissant mais témérair

L'Anglais à mené seul train d'enfer pendant 40 k

- En tête depuis Montchaux, le Britannique s'est incliné à kilomètres de Roubaix, sur une contre-attaque de Cera Sabbadini. Ce dernier, distancé à l'instant décisif, co la seconde place

- Poblet (3ᵉ) a battu cinq coureurs au sprint, dont Fo (4ᵉ), Dewolf (5ᵉ), G. Desmet (7ᵉ), Anquetil (8ᵉ)

- Échappés dès le 23ᵉ kilomètre, Louison Bobet et Rivière avaient traversé Arras avec... 50 mètres d'ava

- Nombreuses chutes et accidents mécaniques. Principal times : Anglade, Darrigade, Graczyk, Impanis, Forestier, Van Steenbergen

- Molenaers, sur le point de rejoindre Simpson à 15 kilomètres de Roubaix, fut retardé par une creva

(Lire les artic   teur   )

CERAMI ET SABBADINI A LA POURSUITE ... APSON

...suite de Simpson, Cerami et Sabbadini von... peut apprécier sur ce document la p... ...aussi) à se débarrasser de Sab... ...spéciaux Robert LF...

Pino's big performance

Certainly, it was known for ages that the "Queen of the Classics" was only available to talented and experienced champions. It was very rare for a "néophyte" to carry it off at Roubaix. The example of Rivière, presented as one of the favourites of the 1959 edition, finally finishing in a modest forty eighth position was proof, if needed, of this tradition.

From there from believing in the triumph of an almost forty year old, was a step that nobody was prepared to take in the fifty eighth Paris-Roubaix. However it was certainly a man of thirty eight years, or almost, who was going to finish alone on the Roubaix track.

At the start, once again, Van Looy seemed to be the man to beat. His successive failures in a Milan-San Remo won by René Privat, then in the Tour of Flanders, only sharpened his thirst to win.

Once again his compatriots were the principal favourites. In order to win he obviously had to overcome de Cabooter, Demulder, Schoubben, Desmet, De Bruyne and naturally Noël Foré.

A fine line-up to which could be added several Frenchmen, all very active over the two previous months: Jean Graczyk, second in the Milan-San Remo and the Tour of Flanders, an always motivated Anquetil, Darrigade moulded into his superb rainbow jersey, Rivière, Anglade, Privat, then the Northerners Everaert, Annaert, Stablinski and Scodeller, all wanting to show themselves on the roads they so often used for training.

Finally Tino Sabbadini, the only "non-Flemish" rider to be in at the kill twelve months earlier, said that he felt even stronger than in 1959.

On the other hand Van Steenbergen for his sixteenth participation was not really too confident. The man from Antwerp had only seven hundred kilometres of training behind him and knew by experience that there was no substitute for this type of exercise.

Finally the observers waited with interest the debuts of three young gifted riders of whom everybody was speaking so well - Rudi Altig, Tom Simpson and Raymond Poulidor.

At the Municipal Stadium at St Denis the one hundred and fifty six starters observed a minute's silence in memory of the great hope Gérard Saint killed in a car crash three weeks before. The older ones also spared a thought for Fausto Coppi whose tragic death had turned the sporting world upside down.

The first to go into action, in sight of Lamorlay, at the twenty third kilometre was none other than Louison Bobet!

Three kilometres farther on, a single rider came up to the wheel of the Breton: Roger Rivière!

This strange "tandem", worthy of the Baracchi trophy, rapidly developed into a real escape - forty seconds at Chantilly, 2mins 25 secs at Laigneville to grow to more than four minutes at about the fiftieth kilometre.

Van Looy decided to stop the haemorrhage and sounded the charge. Straight away the peloton exploded. The lead fell to two minutes at Breteuil when eighty five kilometres had been covered.

However when the bunch reformed the gap started to grow again: three minutes at Amiens, and another thirty seconds at the foot of the hill of Doullens.

On the traditional climb the leaders started to show signs of weakness. The regular rhythm of Rivière, the "pedalling machine" was transformed. Bobet too was grimacing more and it was certainly much more than a sign of willpower. At the top of the slope the gap had fallen to 2mins 50secs.

In the streets of Arras, they had a lead of no more than fifty metres.
An exhausted Rivière capitulated when the Italian Michele Gismondi and René Van Menen joined them. The determined

1960

Pino CERAMI
(Belgium, 1922)

He crowned a long and distinguished career with a victory in the most coveted classic when approaching his fortieth year.

1953 : 2nd Tour of Lombardy,
3rd Tour of Belgium
1957 : Tour of Belgium, 2nd Het Volk
1958 : 2nd Paris-Brussels,
2nd Bordeaux-Paris,
2nd Tour of Romandy
1959 : 3rd Tour of Luxembourg
1960 : Paris-Roubaix, Flèche Wallonne,
3rd World Championships
1961 : Paris-Brussels, Flèche-Brabancone
1962 : 2nd Flèche Wallonne
1963 : 2nd Liège-Bastogne-Liège

Tom Simpson on the attack.

Bobet settled in with his two new companions. But this time the attempt was nullified at Courcelles a few kilometres later.

The strategic sector of the "cobbled hills" was approaching. This aroused the bellicose sentiments of the master Van Looy. At Leforest the Belgian attacked but his hopes were dashed when he was unable to go clear.

A little later on the hill of Moncheaux, René Privat in his turn attacked before being passed and dumped by a phenomenon by the name of Tom Simpson. It was the beginning of a fabulous one man show by "Major Tom".

Progressively the Briton augmented his advance: thirty seconds at Mons-en-Pévèle, thirty five at Pont-à-Marcq on two men, the Belgians Zagers and Molenaers and fifty seconds on the bunch.

At Cysoing, eighteen kilometres from the end he was still flying in the lead with forty seconds on Molenaers, alone after Zagers had had a problem and 1mins 25secs on the first peloton where Van Looy was doing an enormous amount of work. For a while it seemed as if Molenaers was going to catch the Englishman but a puncture prevented him from doing so. It was at Baisieux, just thirteen kilometres from the velodrome that, against all expectations Pino Cérami and Tino Sabbadini escaped from the peloton. Crossing through Willems the pair were no more than forty five seconds down on the runaway who could no longer manage to hide his fatigue.

At Hem the fugitives was swallowed up by Cérami and Sabbadini. The latter went wide on two successive corners, so Cérami took a lead of a few metres.

At a venerable age for a cyclist, the brave Pino understood that this was the chance of a lifetime. Since he started racing in 1937, he had always ridden at the service of others. Today luck was smiling on him, these few metres, these few seconds would be impossible to take away from him. Sabbadini was only to play a secondary role.

At Hem-Bifur, Cérami and Sabbadini have passed Tom Simpson.

Pino Cérami's second place in Antwerp-Ougrée, the previous Thursday had been a demonstration of his good form but at the start his principle worry was to look after, as usual, his leader Van Steenbergen. The latter's retirement after two crashes and as many punctures, freed him to ride for his own account. For once Pino would ride his own race.

At the velodrome his success was welcomed with joy. The public, the journalists and even his adversaries recognised that it was a fine and just recompense.

On the other hand Sabbadini's face was full of disappointment: "I really believed it. I was at the front for the whole of the race. It's really terrible to come so close to winning this great event."

Legend had it, and he was certainly no exception, that the winner did not succeed in closing an eye all night. He was later to swear that the following day was the most difficult one of his career because of the many people who wanted to interview him. This Paris-Roubaix marked for him the start of a new career for another success in the Flèche Wallonne and a third place in the World championships were to class him among the top riders in 1960.

Then he went on to lift Paris-Brussels and then at forty one years old, in 1963, for his farewell, a stage in the Tour de France in front of Darrigade!

Once again Van Looy figured among the big losers of the day. His most ardent supporters were beginning to ask themselves if there was not a curse on him to stop him winning Paris-Roubaix. "The Emperor of Herentals" was prevented from finishing because of broken forks at Hem.

Everyone was forced to admire two other men who did not finish off much better than Van Looy. Bobet and Rivière had left their mark on Paris-Roubaix. Neither of them would be able to return to these Northern roads. Bobet ended his career eighteen months later. As for Rivière, his life would be turned upside down after his crash on the descent of the Col du Perjuret in July during the Tour de France. He was never able to ride a bicycle again.

1960

1. Pino CERAMI (Belgium)
   GS.Peugeot-BP
2. Tino SABBADINI (France)
3. Miguel POBLET (Spain)
4. Jean FORESTIER (France)
5. Henri DEWOLF (Belgium)
6. Frans AERENHOUTS (Belgium)
7. Gilbert DESMET (Belgium)
8. Jacques ANQUETIL (France)
9. Tom SIMPSON (Great Britain)
10. Raymond IMPANIS (Belgium)

FOOTBALL : NICE-MONACO

RACING-STADE EN VEDETTE

(Lire les détails en pages 8 et 9)

L'ÉQUIPE
LE QUOTIDIEN DU SPORT ET DE l'Automobile

NF 0.35 (35 FR.)

10, Fg MONTMARTRE, PARIS (9e)
TÉL. 70-80 - C.C.P. Paris 4.237-93

SAM. 8, DIM. 9 AVRIL 1961
16e ANNÉE N° 4.671

MAROC 45 Fr. M
BELGIQUE 5 Fr. B

PETITES ANNONCES : REGIE-PRESSE, 85 bis, RUE REAUMUR - GUT. 99-30

RUGBY XV : MONTFERRAND-VICH

BRIVE-LIMOGES

GRENOBLE-VIEN

(Lire les détails en dernière page)

Paris-Roubaix (Trophée du Sucre) : rendez-vous international des hommes en for...

GRACZYK LANCÉ CONTRE VAN LOOY ET DE CABOOTE
mais, s'il échoue, F. ANASTASI
GROUSSARD ET... ANQUETIL SERONT LA !

Autres "diables" qui peuvent sortir victorieux de l'Enfer : Van Geneugden, Poblet, Ronchini, Baldini et surtout Rudy Altig, Simpson, Geldermans, A. Darrigade, Everaert, Annaert, Poulidor, Stolker et Mahé

On attend de mieux juger Jean Forestier, Edouard Delberghe, Gilbert Scodeller, Henry Anglade sur un parcours encore renforcé

● **EN MARGE DE PARIS-ROU- BAIX :** Rostollan et R. Pavard contre les Suisses Strehler et ...

● **AMATEURS :** Paris-Troyes (aujourd'hui), encore A. Ramsbottom favori. — Paris-Pacy-sur-Eure (demain), Suter contre Arze et ...

LA JOURNÉE
EN QUELQUES PHRASES

BASKET : P.U.C. OU LYON SACRÉ DÈS DIMANCHE ?

La deuxième journée de la poule finale peut livrer le secret du Championnat. Le P.U.C. ou Lyon, peut être sacré dès dimanche. Le résultat de Bagnolet-Caen risque de donner la clé de l'énigme.
(Page 11)

● **Automobile**
UNE EXCLUSIVITÉ :
le nouveau moteur Porsche de formule 1

COMPETITIONS :
Grand Prix de Bruxelles Le duel Brabham-Moss sera arbitré par la « nouvelle vague » de jeunes pilotes britanniques. Essais pour les 24 heures. On s'attend, au Mans, aujourd'hui et demain, à des vitesses record pour les Ferrari 1961.
(Page 2)

● **NATATION : NOS ONDINES A NAMUR**
Les ondines belges et françaises de moins de 18 ans se rencontreront ce soir à Namur.
(Page 7)

● **FOOTBALL :**
KENTISH à ORAN

● **TENNIS : P. DARMON FAVORI DU TOURNOI DE NICE**
Battu en double, hier, avec Piles, Pierre Darmon sera opposé, aujourd'hui, à l'Australien Philips-Moore pour les demi-finales du simple du Tournoi de Nice. Il devrait confirmer sa performance de Monaco sur le vainqueur de l'autre demi-finale, Woodcock-Alvares.
(Page 6)

● **BOXE : SCHOLZ ET PAPP A VIENNE**
A Vienne, ce soir, Scholz, champion d'Europe des moyens, et Papp, son challenger, seront, dans le même ring, opposés respectivement à l'Allemand Wohlers et au Français Sangaré.

SURPRISE A WAGRAM ! PONCY BATTU PAR LAMINE !
Envoyé à terre à la deuxième reprise, Louis Poncy a été encore malmené durant les derniers rounds par l'ex-champion de France amateurs Ahmed Lamine.
(Page 7)

1961 : ...yards

GRACZYK ÉTAIT ENCORE, H... SUR LE PARCOURS, MAIS...

ROUBAIX. — Jean Graczyk a voulu répéter encore, le final de Paris - Roubaix... Il s'est sur la route de l'Enfer, mais a dû renoncer projet et battre en retraite devant la pluie transformait les bas-côtés de la route en bour...
(Photo Jacques BOISLEMEL)

Pas de fu... sans feu... par Fernand ALB...

L'exemple de l'enfant de ch... AMÉDÉE DOMENECH

Lors de son sermon pascal, qui traitait temps à consacrer au travail et au rui... Saint-Martin, situe dans le petit village ... a été, pour frapper son auditoire, l'... de chœur de la localité. Il ... cet contraste d'inspirer.
Yves Noé, qui nous conte cette anecdote, ... « Ce ne sont pas les Britanniques qui croira... Duc » est un ange de douceur.
(Lire la suite page ...)

SAN JOSE (Californie). — Le Jamaïquain De Johnson s'est imposé comme le meilleur spr... actuellement aux Etats-Unis. Deux fois de suite 11 mars (notre photo) et le 1er avril, il a cour... 100 yards (91 m. 44) en 9" 3, ce qui équiva... 10" au 100 mètres, égalant un record du m...

Le C.I.O. en fumée !
Les 60.000 fr. suisses dus par le C.O.N.I. n'ont pas été ...

Van Looy, At last !

World champion, Belgian champion, Milan-San Remo, Tour of Flanders, Paris-Tours, Tour of Lombardy, two Ghent-Wevelgems, two Paris-Brussels. Such was the roll of honour of the great Rik Van Looy at the start of the 1961 season. However there was one event that was cruelly missing - Paris-Roubaix.

In Belgium, and elsewhere, "The Emperor" drew a large number of supporters who were all looking forward to see him winning at Roubaix. Certain of them were even asking how it was possible for Rik to have ridden six times without winning it once.

The Northern race was effectively right up his street. Rik was the perfect master of the classics where he dominated everyone with his power and strength and when this was not enough his devastating sprint put the finishing touches to his work.

Bearing this in mind, it was hardly astonishing that Paris-Roubaix tormented him. Moreover he never hesitated to say: "To win it, just once, but above all to win it."

As the Easter race approached, the question tirelessly returned each year: How, but how could you beat the Belgians at Roubaix?

This time again, Van Looy dressed in his rainbow jersey, presented himself as their uncontested leader. However his compatriots Cérami, Impanis, Foré, Van Daele and even perhaps Van Steenbergen, all former winners, then the others like De Cabooter, Van Geneugden, Molenaers would all be hard to follow on the hill at Mons-en-Pévèle.

The Belgian supporters were waiting all the more for a good performance as the two classics at the start of the season had astonishingly escaped them. Milan-San Remo was taken by Raymond Poulidor in front of Van Looy and the Tour of Flanders fell to Tom Simpson. The snub was too much!

This Simpson was worrying. Van Steenbergen named him as the number one favourite: "At the moment Simpson is just stroking the pedals round" he said, "In the Tour of Flanders he left us all standing when he thought the right moment had come." The images of the Briton alone in the lead close to Roubaix in 1960 were engraved in everybody's memories. This time he had more experience of the race, something very valuable over these Northern roads.

The French were especially counting on Jean Graczyk who was on form. In the second rank they put Anquetil, naturally, then Poulidor who openly regretted the absence of a "Poggio" at the entrance to Roubaix. The hill at Hem, the final difficulty on the route was, unfortunately for him, not a first-category climb!

Forestier, Darrigade, Everaert, Annaert, Mahé, Groussard then formed the peloton of the "possible".

Finally a few "foreigners" such as Baldini, Ronchini, Altig or Poblet did nothing to hide their ambitions.

This Paris-Roubaix was certainly promised to the Belgians but two Italians Bailetti and Domenicali and the Frenchman Anatole Novak launched the race. These three men left from the eighth kilometre at Ecouen. The trio were to lead the event for one hundred and fifty kilometres and to gain a lead of almost four minutes before capitulating at Larbret, just after Doullens.

From the moment that the regrouping took place, the battle was relaunched when Cazala and Anastasi attacked at Arleux. The serious things really started when Joseph Planckaert, Molenaers, Derboven and Borra came up to them before Hénin-Liétard.

However under the pressure of the strong men the peloton reformed at the exit to Mons-en-Pévèle. Up to this point the elimination was essentially from the back.

Rik VAN LOOY
(Belgium, 1932)

A great specialist in the classics - the only one up to the present day to have won all them at least once - he was also World road race champion in successive years. Rik "II's" record is superb, with no fewer than 482 victories on the road.

1956 : Ghent-Wevelgem, Paris-Brussels, Tour of Holland
1957 : Ghent-Wevelgem
1958 : Belgian Champion, Milan-San Remo, Paris-Brussels
1959 : Tour of Flanders, Paris-Tours, Tour of Lombardy
1960 : World Champion
1961 : Paris-Roubaix, World Champion, Liège-Bastogne-Liège, Tour of Belgium, Criterium des As
1962 : Paris-Roubaix, Tour of Flanders, Ghent-Wevelgem
1963 : Belgian Champion
1965 : Paris-Roubaix
1967 : Paris-Tours
1968 : Flèche Wallonne

1961

At Hem, Van Looy and Geldermand lead the group of escapees.

At Pont-à-Marcq Henry Anglade and Vanderveken decided to get involved. Without really knowing it they had just started the right break for only Marcel Janssens, Molenaers, Kerckhove, Daems, Geldermans and Van Looy were strong enough to join them.

The race was over, nobody would see them again before the changing rooms! The instigator of the initiative, Henri Anglade received poor recompense in the form of a puncture which eliminated him from the contest at Baisieux, then Molenaers was dropped by the leaders.

So it was six men who entered the Roubaix track together: Marcel Janssens, René Vanderveken, Norbert Kerckhove, Emile Daems, Rik Van Looy and Albertus Geldermans. Five Belgians against one Dutchman!

There were no surprises in the sprint which took place in front of the stands crowded with Flemings. Emile Daems, the only one who had any real chance against Van Looy, took the initiative in the back straight but even he could do nothing in the face of the devastating speed of the "Emperor" who was a clear winner on the line.

Van Looy easily...

Rik had ridden an intelligent race. With his team-mates he had first of all controlled the race marvellously then chosen to move to the front at Hénin-Liétard, sixty kilometres from Roubaix, in order to watch everyone closely.

So he was not surprised by Anglade's attack on a smooth section of the road and he got up to him with stupefying ease. From then things went as expected. As he got off his bike, the robust Van Looy had his eyes misted over. He had been trying to win Paris-Roubaix for such a long time. According to his friends he dreamed of it all the time, the Northern classic was the principal objective of the season.

To the journalists who surrounded him he kept repeating: "I've won Paris-Roubaix. I've won Paris-Roubaix. I am the happiest of men. Tomorrow, perhaps it will be different but today I can say that this success has given me more joy than my triumph last year in the world championship. I was very afraid because with one kilometre to go I could feel my back tyre going soft. That's why I waited for the exit from the last bend before attacking. I was afraid to go up the banking. If my tyre had come off, it would have been a catastrophe."

A little later, when a journalist asked him if the World championship was going to be his next objective, he replied straight away with a large smile: "The World championship? But I've just won it."

Perhaps now liberated from all his complexes, Van Looy went on to finish his 1961 season with thirty one victories. After Paris-Roubaix, he won again, between others, Liège-Bastogne-Liège and the World championship disputed at Berne.

1961

1. Rik VAN LOOY (Belgium)
   GS. Faema
2. Marcel JANSSENS (Belgium)
3. René VANDERVEKEN (Belgium)
4. Norbet KERCKHOVE (Belgium)
5. Albertus GELDERMANS (Holland)
6. Emile DAEMS (Belgium)
7. Bas MALIEPAARD (Holland)
8. Armand DESMET (Belgium)
9. Arthur DE CABOOTER (Belgium)
10. Gilbert DESMET (Belgium)

L'ÉQUIPE
LE QUOTIDIEN DU SPORT
et de l'Automobile

NF 0.35 (35 Fr.)

MARDI 10 AVRIL 1962
17e ANNÉE — No 4.983

10, Fg MONTMARTRE, PARIS (9e)
TAI. 70-80 - C.C.P. Paris 4.233-93

PETITES ANNONCES : REGIE-PRESSE, 85 bis, RUE REAUMUR — GUT. 99-30

service quotidien
• PARIS-AMSTERDAM 1 h 05
• PARIS-HELSINKI 5 h 10
3 fois par semaine
• PARIS-HAMBOURG 2 h 30 par Caravelle

FINNAIR
LA LIGNE DE L'HOSPITALITÉ FINLANDAISE
11, RUE AUBER - RESERVATIONS RIC. 35-11

SOIXANTIÈME PARIS-ROUBAIX (TROPHÉE DU SUCRE) :
une magnifique course par élimination à partir de Doullens

VAN LOOY HORS CONCOURS

Il a liquidé la dernière opposition (Poulidor-Daems-Schoubben) avec la complicité de son garde du corps Planckaert, à 1 km. de l'arrivée

Le champion du monde seul à Roubaix

● Il avait déclenché la bataille dans la côte de Doullens avec... Raymond Poulidor.

● Wouters, Simpson, Everaert, De Cabooter et François Mahé, compagnons de Van Looy après Mons-en-Pévèle, éliminés par des incidents.

● Everaert radiographié à l'hôpital de Roubaix : pas de fracture, quelques hématomes à la cuisse.

(Lire les articles de nos envoyés spéciaux pp. 5, 6 et 7)

Pas de fumée sans feu...
par Jacques MARCHAND

VAN LOOY CONDAMNÉ... AU TOUR

ROUBAIX. — Guillaume Driessens, le directeur sportif de Flandria-Faema, considère maintenant la participation de Van Looy au Tour, non plus comme un fait acquis, mais comme une obligation.

Car lui-même se lasse de victoires dorénavant « classiques » du champion du monde. « Que pourrait-il gagner qui l'asse encore estimation... sinon le Tour », répète-t-il à ses amis. Et comme on lui faisait remarquer que Van Looy avait récemment déclaré qu'il souhaiterait dans le Tour s'il gagnait auparavant le Giro, Driessens, qui a réponse à tout, précise : « Oui, mais il est ainsi possible qu'il s'abstienne dans le Giro pour être plus sûr de gagner le Tour ! »

(Suite page 7.)

RIK VAN LOOY PRÉPARE SON COUP DE FORCE

ROUBAIX. — Plus que quinze kilomètres, la [...] Van Looy, que suivent Schoubb[...] et le petit Daems. Le champ[...] n'est pas le moins du monde trou[...]. Il roule, les mains en haut [...] partir le grand jeu pour terminer s[...]

Les équipes de France et de Pologne à pied d'œuvre depuis hier

POULIDO[...]
ROUBAIX. — Le[...]
vigueur, mais V[...]

[...]RES DE SPORT

[...]OLUTION
[...]ESSAIRES

effet, a adopté un projet proche des thèses que nous [...]

ment des ligaments du genou

(Lire nos articles en pages 8 et 9)

Van Looy's repeat performance

April 1962. Rik Van Looy entered his twenty ninth year. Arriving at physical maturity and being a fine strategist he had never before been so dominating. From the start of the season he had been lining up the successes: the Tour of Sardinia with two stage wins, also two stages in Paris-Nice, then above all Ghent-Wevelgem and the Tour of Flanders where he massacred his rivals.

At the start of the sixtieth Paris-Roubaix, his rainbow jersey was the unique focal point of his one hundred and sixty four adversaries. The opposition remained invariably the same led by, Vannitsen, Altig, Anquetil, Elliott, Everaert, Graczyk, Cérami, Groussard, Daems, Hoevenaers, Poulidor, Anglade, Darrigade, Forestier and Simpson.

Also to them must be added several young ones: Jos Wouters, the Belgian prodigy, the last winner of Paris-Tours when he was still only an 'independent', Benoni Beheyt, the former terror of the Flemish amateurs, something that was a real compliment, Germany's Rolf Wolfshohl who was only slowly consenting to ride outside his home country where he remained the master and finally several Italians who were still looking for a real leader. The blessed period of Coppi, Bartali and Magni had been completely transformed. From now on the fans had to place their faith in Balmamion, Adorni and Carlesi. From the start, the peloton rapidly entered into the spirit of things. In fact at the eighth kilometre, a collective crash dislocated everything. Noël Foré had to retire and several aces such as Cérami, Schoubben and Marcel Janssens were forced to chase for thirty five kilometres, something not exactly on the programme, to catch the peloton!

As often, it was the Italians who dominated the first hours of the race. The protagonists were this time Bailetti, Miele and Cestari. They were trying to justify their presence at the start and wanted to grab a little bit of history, but when the serious things started their hopes rapidly disappeared.

For today, Van Looy's Faema-Flandria team decided to close the race down. The leader's harmless crash at the half way point was the only alert for "The Red Guard" but the incident was quickly forgotten when the hill at Doullens appeared. There, Van Looy shook the peloton and crossed over the top in front before Groussard and Poulidor. The World champion not only wanted to eliminate the weak ones, but also, and especially to physiologically impress his adversaries.

As Arras came into view, the front bunch now consisted of only forty men. The inevitable incidents and punctures reduced this figure to twenty nine at the entrance to the cobbled sector at Hénin-Liétard.

The Breton Camille Le Menn went through slightly clear at Courcelles, the start of the strategic sectors, but the omnipresent Van Looy decided to rapidly call things to order. He first of all caught the Frenchman, then attacked three kilometres from Moncheaux hill which he climbed alone in the lead.

Behind several favourites such as Carlesi, Groussard, Simpson, and Altig had been the victims of accidents. "The Emperor of Herentals" did not force the pace. He sat up for a while and allowed a group of fourteen to catch him: Poulidor, Joseph Planckaert, Daems, Schoubben, Defilippis, Van Tongerloo, Aerenhouts, Simpson, Wouters, De Cabooter, Impanis, Cérami, Everaert and François Mahé.

The hazards of Paris-Roubaix were brought home to the Northerner Pierre Everaert the victim of a crash and quickly taken to hospital. Then Mahé, De Cabooter, Wouters and Simpson could

1962

not follow the infernal pace and laid down their arms.

At the exit to Fretin, nineteen kilometres from the velodrome, five men managed to go clear: Poulidor, Schoubben, Daems, Joseph Planckaert and naturally Rik Van Looy.

The goal was agreed. Their lead did not stop growing. At Sainghin-en-Mélantois they had fifty seconds on Forestier and a minute on a group of nine including Cérami, Wouters, Impanis and Carlesi.

In the suburbs of Roubaix, Poulidor demonstrated his form by making the suggestion of an attack but Van Looy seemed to have the answer. A simple acceleration at the kilometre point took him into the lead alone.

This time "The Emperor in the rainbow jersey" decided to arrive alone.

Twenty four seconds later, Emile Daems won the sprint for second place in front of Schoubben, Planckaert and Poulidor.

"The greatest rider at the same level as the greatest race" was the way that Jacques Goddet summed up in a few apt and striking words Van Looy's second victory, before going on to say: "Paris-Roubaix with its outstanding route, remarkably restructured, was obviously created for an exceptional being as Rik Van Looy is. They were in marvellous harmony, on this day that was made so hard by the biting cold."

At the velodrome Van Looy simply explained: "I went clear without attacking. I would have been quite happy in a sprint. After Poulidor's attack I simply found myself alone in the lead, I didn't jump away I just continued turning my 54x 4."

Van Looy would have naturally been able to win in a sprint but in the eyes of the public nothing can replace a solitary finish.

1962

Left:
Emile Daems in front of Van Looy and Cérami.

1. Rik VAN LOOY (Belgium)
   GS. Faema-Flandria
2. Emile DAEMS (Belgium)
3. Frans SCHOUBBEN (Belgium)
4. Joseph PLANCKAERT (Belgium)
5. Raymond POULIDOR (France)
6. Jos WOUTERS (Belgium)
7. Frans AERENHOUTS (Belgium)
8. Jean FORESTIER (France)
9. Raymond IMPANIS (Belgium)
10. Guido CARLESI (Italy)

BELGIQUE

MARDI 9 AVRIL 1963.
20ᵉ ANNÉE. — 2 fr. 50

NORD ECLAIR

LE GRAND QUOTIDIEN FRANCO-BELGE

MOUSCRON 32 Grand.
Place - Tél. 31001

TOURNAI 9 rue de la
Tête-d'Argent . Tél. 256.88

LILLE 27 rue Faidherbe
Téléphone 55.08.72

PARIS-IX° 28 Bd Poisson-
nière. Tél. Prov. 7784

ATTAQUÉES PAR LES PRO-COMMUNISTES
Les forces neutralistes en difficulté au Laos

APPUYÉS, éléments
du Nord, t...
du Pathet Lao...
ont violé le c...
attaquant les...
stationnées da...
Jarres. Celles-c...
dement du co...
dû évacuer X...
raient repliées...
d'aviation, pres...
La route des...
presque ouver...
Le prince Sour...
tiplie les appe...
ragé par les A...
en présidence ...
Genève. Mais...
le prince Souph...
du Pathet Lao...
rager ses trou...
Washington...
cette violation ...
les accords de...
la conférence ...
nie à Paris, s'...
côté.

Voir en av...

En marge de la conférence de l'O.T.A.S.E.
DE GAULLE A REÇU M. DEAN RUSK
PREMIER ENTRETIEN HOMME-COUVE DE MURVILLE DEPUIS LA RUPTURE

DAEMS GAGNE PARIS-ROUBAIX
battant Van Looy au sprint

L'HEURE DU CHOI... POUR LES VACANC...
« NORD ECLAIR » présente aujourd'...
à ses lecteurs : VACANCES A LA M...
(Voir en dernière page)

★

Action unie des travailleurs
pour la rénovation de l'Univers...
demande à Dijon le congrès de l'U.N.E.F.
(Voir en page 2)

Daems seizes his chance

Never were there so many reversals of fortune in the outskirts of Roubaix as there were in the 1963 edition of the race. Two kilometres from the finish, victory seemed to be assured once again to Noël Foré who had been alone in the lead for twenty kilometres. A few hundred metres further on, Germany's Rolf Wolfshohl suddenly came up to his wheel and passed him like a whirlwind! It looked like Wolfshohl was going to join Fischer in the record books, but in a few seconds he found himself in turn absorbed at the entrance to the velodrome by a thin peloton led by the inevitable Rik Van Looy.

In this select group were Marcel Janssens, De Cabooter, Simpson, Daems, Looy, Jan Janssen, Poulidor and a few others. Van Looy presented himself as the logical favourite as Vannitsen and Wouters were relegated to the rear. De Cabooter started the charge from a long way out. He took a lead of three lengths. The huge Peter Post went after him with Van Looy on his wheel. The red carpet was being unrolled for the "Emperor of Herentals". The plan was working marvellously. In the last bend the young Janssen attacked while Van Looy went up to the top of the banking. And it was there that Van Looy made his unforgivable mistake: he opened the door for Emile Daems who could never have asked for so much. The latter swooped to the inside of the track and took two length's lead on Van Looy who would never be able to get them back. It was not easy to regain a single metre on the man from Brussels who was already the winner of Milan-San Remo and the Tour of Lombardy! A few moments later, as he dismounted from his machine, it still had not sunk in: "The sprint went better than I ever dared to hope. At the beginning of the last bend Janssen attacked and Van Looy went up to the barriers. Like a flash of lighting I saw the hole and I plunged into it without hesitating."

It was not surprising that at the start of this Paris-Roubaix, the Belgians were the favourites as they had not been defeated since 1957, and there was least twenty Flemish riders who could reasonably hope to carry it off. As well as Van Looy who wanted to join to Lapize and Rebry as three times winners, logic designated Noël Foré, a former winner at Roubaix but above all recently victorious in the Tour of Flanders, then Jos Wouters, Melckenbeeck, Vannitsen and...Emile Daems.

Van Looy nevertheless found himself in a delicate position. He had changed teams at the start of the season and from now on wore the GBC jersey. In fact Rik wanted to have Guillaume Driessens as team manager but the Flandria bosses would not hear of it. Divorce remained the only possible solution.

In spite of several stage wins picked up in the Tour of Sardinia and Paris-Nice, rumour had it that he was less invulnerable that he used to be. But the impassive Rik, had simply told his detractors to be present on the grass of the track centre at about five in the afternoon at the end of the race!

One hundred and thirty two riders lined up at the start at St Denis. The morning escape this time comprised three Frenchmen: Leborgne, Foucher, and Battais. Their maximum lead halfway through the race was four minutes. At Doullens they still had three but on the plateau of Arras the fugue came to an end.
The peloton exploded and eighteen men went clear on the

Emile DAEMS
(Belgium, 1938)

Small in stature but a giant of the road. Daems was one of the best roadman sprinters of the 1960's.

1960 : Tour of Lombardy
　　　　Tour of Appenins
　　　　Grand Prix Longines,
　　　　Putte-Kapellen
1961 : Tour of Sardinia,
　　　　Week End Wallonne
　　　　Tour du Tessin
1962 : Milan-San Remo,
　　　　Tour du Tessin
　　　　2nd Paris-Roubaix,
　　　　3rd Belgian Championship
1963 : Paris-Roubaix

1963

hill at Caouin. The elite who had managed to get to the front were: Poulidor, Wolfshohl, Gilbert Desmet, Van Looy, Joseph Planckaert, Janssens, Simpson, Foré, Vannitsen, Aerenhouts, Daems, Altig, Post, Maliepaard, De Cabooter, Armand Desmet, Bocklant and a new boy by the name of Jan Janssen.

Paris-Roubaix was only just beginning. Some of the pretenders such as Vannitsen, Aerenhouts, Bocklant, then Desmet, Maliepaard and Rudi Altig disappeared with mechanical problems.

Then at Ennevelin, twenty four kilometres from the velodrome, Noël Foré and Rolf Wolfshohl took flight. At Fretin the pair were twenty seconds up on a group of ten. At Sainghin-en-Mélantois, Wolfshohl was the victim of a puncture, and as Foré could not wait for him, he took a lead of two hundred metres.

At Annappes, ten kilometres from Roubaix, the fate of the race was in the balance. An obstinate Foré refused to obey his team manager the wily Brik Schotte, who ordered him to wait for Wolfshohl.

With two of them, the leaders would have had much more chance of resisting the pressure of the peloton. Schotte found it difficult to understand his protégé's attitude as he was clearly a much better sprinter than the German!

So the two men rode flat out using up all their energy just a few hundred metres apart....to the great good fortune of the pursuers who soon absorbed them in the streets of Roubaix.

It was not to be Foré's day for no sooner had he been rejoined by Wolfshohl than he punctured and crashed, before falling a second time in the velodrome itself. For his part Wolfshohl was extremely disappointed in the way the race unfolded. He had sworn to inscribe his name in the record books so as to overcome his fate in the Milan-San Remo where Joseph Groussard had beaten him by the width of a tyre! In the showers the other

bottom left:
Gilbert Desmet awaits his supportcar.

bottom right:
Noël Foré still in the lead at Lys-les-Lannoy.

Poulidor counter-attacking with Gilbert Desnet.

frustrated man was Jean Stablinski. The hopes of the Northerner in the rainbow jersey, often at the front of the field, were ruined by two crashes.

Among the eleven men who dispute the final sprint, all experienced road men, the presence of Jan Janssen was rather intriguing. In fact, the bespectacled Dutchman was taking part in his first Paris-Roubaix and only three stage wins in the Tour de l'Avenir had drawn anyone's attention to him. Surrounded like the winner at the finish, he was nevertheless modest when he said: "Certainly I am happy with my third place, but perhaps we shouldn't exaggerate. I will continue to persevere and work hard."

The apprentice champion stuck to his words, to confirm, in future years the potential seen in this edition of Paris-Roubaix.

1963

1. Emile DAEMS (Belgium)
   GS.Peugeot-BP
2. Rik VAN LOOY (Belgium)
3. Jan JANSSEN (Holland)
4. Marcel JANSSENS (Belgium)
5. Armand DESNET (Belgium)
6. Raymond POULIDOR (France)
7. Peter POST (Holland)
8. Tom SIMPSON (Great Britain)
9. Arthur DE CABOOTER (Belgium)
10. Joseph PLANCKAERT (Belgium)

Close to the finish, Post leads in front of
Molenaers, Beheyt and Bocklant.

The First Dutchman

"The Renaix Affair" inevitably poisoned the start of the 1964 season. It went back to the previous world championship. The Belgian team was at the service of Rik Van Looy who wanted to put on another rainbow jersey. Everything went perfectly...until the final sprint when his compatriot Benoni Beheyt pipped him on the line!

There was a scandal at the finish, as it was thought that nobody would mess with the name of Van Looy, who moreover, was on his home ground. There was almost a riot! A few months later, the rancour between the two men remained as strong as ever. Since the opening of hostilities, Belgian cycling was accumulating defeats. Britain's Tom Simpson lifted Milan-San Remo, while Germany's Rudi Altig the Tour of Flanders. The Belgian press denounced the Van Looy-Beheyt rivalry and held the two Flemish riders partly responsible for the lack of early season success. Exceptionally, the victory of a "non-Belgian" was even being predicted for Paris-Roubaix.

Several names stood out from the rest, among whose were those of the enemies Van Looy and Beheyt, naturally, but also others such as Rudi Altig, Jan Janssen, Tom Simpson, Peter Post and Raymond Poulidor all with their arguments for doing well.

Van Looy announced for example that Paris-Roubaix was his principal objective for the season. Jan Janssen had the back-up of the powerful

Van Looy further back in company with Foré and Verbeeck.

Pelforth team. As for Beheyt, who according to the expression was "tickling the pedals", he had just won the Tour of Belgium and had finished second in the Tour of Flanders. Finally Poulidor, often isolated on the cobbles among the Flemish riders, was starting to get used to the situation and a rare thing, he even stated his case: "Two years ago I was flirting with victory. I was fifth in 1962 and sixth last year, always in the leading group. This time I believe myself capable of finishing very much better.!"

The organisers also noted with satisfaction the progressive return of the Italian teams and their riders: Zilioli, Adorni, Baldini, Cribori, Baffi, Dancelli and Motta, in other words the country's elite were there to rub shoulders with the Northern pack.

From the start, under the rain, the race went off at top speed. Nedellec, Beaumont and Fornoni escaped at Creil. At Wavignies, at kilometre twenty four, seventeen men among who were several favourites like Beheyt, Stablinski, Altig and Foré came up to the front. The peloton, which had already suffered a lot in the weather conditions, exploded. At the approach of the hill of Doullens, Poulidor lit up the touch paper. He easily gained a lead of fifty metres, but then, satisfied with his efforts, he sat up, and then missed the key breakaway! On the plateau of Arras about thirty riders went clear. Among those were Simpson, Janssen, Foré, Zilioli, Post, Darrigade, Beheyt, Delberghe and Stablinski. As they passed the town of Pas-de-Calais the first pursuers passed through forty seconds down and the peloton which included Van Looy, Altig and Poulidor

1964

followed at 1min 45secs.

The serious business had started. Nijdam, Bocklant and Gilbert Desmet rapidly spotted the danger. After a fierce chase they managed to rejoin the group at the head of the race. All the others gave up at Hénin-Liétard where the gap was two minutes.

The fate of the race was sealed, the elimination in the leading group was about to start. At Thumeries, Janssen was the first to be stopped, by a puncture, then it was the turn of Bocklant, Stablinski, Melckenbeeck, Joseph Planckaert and then again, in a crash on a corner of Foré, Zilioli, Hoban and Haast. In the "trench" leading to Attiches, thirty three kilometres from Roubaix, five riders went away. There were two "Flandrias", Post and Bocklant who had just joined up with the group after his puncture, and three "Wiels-Groene-Leeuw", Beheyt, Molenaers and Desmet.

The entente was perfect, the gap rapidly opened. Then Desmet was betrayed by a flat tyre. At Ennevin there were no more than four of them. Behind, Tom Simpson tried to react but could not rejoin the quartet. At Annappes everything became orderly again.

The way was open for the leaders. Molenears had no other ambition than to help Beheyt. Bocklant for his part was sacrificing his chances for his leader Peter Post. In the last few kilometres, Willy Bocklant kept the speed high and was first on to the velodrome and on his wheel were Beheyt, Post and Molenaers. In the back straight Beheyt attacked but as they came off the last bend Post surged up from behind to win.

"The Blue Riband", otherwise known as the record of the fastest average speed, was beaten. Post had completed the 265 kilometres of the course, at an average speed of 45,131 kph.

The feelings of the four leading men were naturally very dissimilar. Peter Post happy to have last won a great classic was quickly assured that he would be able to augment the value of his contracts for the winter season on the European tracks. Beheyt was very distressed at the finish, having already finished second in the Tour of Flanders. He was particularly piqued as this was the first time that Post had ever beaten him in a sprint!

Molenaers and Bocklant the two model team men had no other alternative than to help their leaders. Bocklant had ridden an excellent race made difficult by two punctures. His fourth place nevertheless left a taste of incompleteness. The decision of this Paris-Roubaix was taken more than one hundred kilometres from the end. The peloton containing many of the bigger names went to sleep little by little. So Van Looy, for example, finished only sixteenth.

Nevertheless Post was a fine winner. A specialist on the track, he quite happily made many forays on the road. Before this success, he had notably already won the 1963 Dutch Championship, and the Tours of Holland 1960, Germany 1962 and of Belgium 1963.

However, the race did not placate Jean Garnault, the man responsible for the organisation and the route. For some while he had been hearing the alarm bells ringing and was aware of the forthcoming disaster, that of the disappearance of the cobbled sections.

According to the highways department, in four years time there would not be a single stretch of cobbles between Courcelles and Roubaix!

The future of Paris-Roubaix, the Queen of the Classics, the one by which the others were judged, was precarious. Jean Garnault criss-crossed the region in vain in order to find these tracks in the process of disappearing.

In spite of much pleading with the department in charge of the roads, the situation was only getting worse. The dialogue which always fell on deaf ears was punctuated by an unequal battle. That of the cobblestones versus the asphalt..

1964

Peter POST
(Holland, 1933)

A remarkable athlete who was outstanding on the track and the road. Winner of 65 Six-day races, Post was the first Dutch winner at Roubaix.

1958 : 2nd Tour of Holland
1960 : Tour of Holland
1962 : Tour of Germany.
       2nd Tour of Belgium
1963 : Dutch Champion
       Tour of Belgium,
       2nd World Pursuit Championships,
       3rd Flèche Wallonne,
       3rd Paris-Brussels
1964 : Paris-Roubaix,
       Criterium des As,
       2nd Tour of Belgium,
       3rd Flèche Wallonne
1967 : 2nd Flèche Wallonne

1. Peter POST (Holland)
   GS.Flandria-Romeo
2. Benoni BEHEYT (Belgium)
3. Yvo MOLENAERS (Belgium)
4. Willy BOCKLANT (Belgium)
5. Louis PROOST (Belgium)
6. Frans MELCKENBEECK (Belgium)
7. Jean STABLINSKI (France)
8. Jan JANSSEN (Holland)
9. Gilbert DESMET (Belgium)
10. Tom SIMPSON (Great Britain)

L'ÉQUIPE
LE QUOTIDIEN DU SPORT ET DE l'Automobile

10, Fg MONTMARTRE, PARIS (9°)
Tél. 70-80 - C.C.P. Paris 4.237-93

LUNDI 12 AVRIL 1965
20° ANNÉE — N° 5.920

0,40

PETITES ANNONCES : RÉGIE-PRESSE, 95 bis, RUE RÉAUMUR — GUT. 99-30

TROIS VAINQUEURS D'UN PARIS-ROUBAIX — TROPHÉE DU SUCRE BEGHIN — AU COBALT :

VAN LOOY SUPERCHAMPION RETROUVÉ...
SELS ET LA BELGIQUE !

Rik, prodigieux maître à courir, s'est envolé à 10 kilomètres de l'arrivée et a terminé seul

Sels s'est détaché à son tour après avoir facilité la tâche de son coéquipier

● Cinq autres Belges parmi ces sept coureurs classés ensuite : Vannitsen (3°), Van Schil (4°), Huysmans (5°), Adorni (6°), Simpson (7°), Kerkhove (8°) et Foré (9°), le plus combatif.

● Stablinski, Janssen et Wolfshohl, l'instigateur de l'offensive, accablés par la malchance, accompagnaient Van Looy dans l'« Enfer ».

● Stablinski (11°) et Anquetil (16°) meilleurs Français.

(Pages 6 et 7)

LA JOURNÉE EN QUELQUES PHRASES

BASKET. — Villeurbanne, Bagnolet, Nantes et Le Mans en demi-finales de la Coupe
(Page 11)

● **AUTO.** — Surtees (Ferrari) : 225 km.-h. au tour aux essais du Mans.
(Page 3)

● **TENNIS.** — Barthès face à Lundqvist, Drysdale et Fletcher dans le tournoi de Monte-Carlo, qui commence aujourd'hui.
(Page 4)

● **BOXE.** — Victoire des amateurs français à Innsbruck devant l'Autriche (4-2).
— Yves Desmarets a conservé son titre national des plume.
(Page 4)

● **KARATÉ.** — Sauvin conserve le titre de champion de France.
(Page 11)

● **HALTÉROPHILIE.** — Le Hongrois Foeldy améliore le record mondial du développé (plume).
(Page 11)

● **RUGBY.** — Sensation : les Springboks battus à Dublin (9-6).
(Page 14)

ULTIMATUM DES FÉDÉRATIONS INTERNATIONALES AU C.I.O.
(Lire l'article de Gaston Meyer en rubrique J.O.)

VAN LOOY A REJOINT... OCTAVE LAPIZE

ROUBAIX. — Rik Van Looy vient de se détacher du groupe d'avant-garde et file vers son troisième succès dans Paris-Roubaix (Trophée du Sucre Béghin). Après ses victoires de 1961 et 1962, Van Looy a égalé, sans le savoir, Octave Lapize, victorieux en 1909, 1910 et 1911. Du même coup, le champion belge a dépassé à jamais son ancien rival Rik Van Steenbergen qui figure deux fois au palmarès (1948 et 1952).
(Téléphoto de l'un de nos envoyés spéciaux)

FOOTBALL : UN FORMIDABLE SPRINT SE PRÉPARE

BORDEAUX REVIENT NANTES CRAQUE

3 leaders : Nantes, Strasbourg et Bordeaux
mais Lyon, V.A. et Rennes ne sont pas loin

● Cinq buts de Lens contre le Stade. Angers (1-1 devant Lille) n'a pu rejoindre Toulon.

● **DIVISION II.** — Cannes a rejoint le Red Star (2-2 devant Nice). Montpellier candidat aux barrages.

(Pages 8, 9 et 10)

ÉQUIPE DE FRANCE
Bonnel, Sauvage, Lech, Loncle en forme à sept jours de Belgrade

RANDY MATSON RAVIT LE RECORD MONDIAL DU POIDS A LONG
(20 m. 70 contre 20 m. 68)
(Page 3)

Rik in Paradise

"It's the finest victory of my career. They said that I was finished as I had not won any classics since my Paris-Roubaix of 1962." The first words of Rik Van Looy at the end of his third victorious Paris-Roubaix were clear. When a champion dominates his rivals a little less, rumours of his decline are inevitably peddled around. No great rider was ever spared, from Maurice Garin to Fausto Coppi passing by Louison Bobet and all the others.

At the beginning of 1965, Van Looy, in his thirty second year did not escape this rule. He had just however lined up eleven successes! The champion knew that his credibility was at stake on these Northern cobbles. The rest of his career depended on the result.

Rik decided to win with style. He flew away ten kilometres from Roubaix and finished alone with a lead of more than a minute over his team-mate Edouard Sels.

In 1965, Paris-Roubaix remained more than ever the most coveted classics event to win. Thus it was an exceptional starting list, with the stars, quite literally, falling over themselves to sign the start sheet: Janssen, Van Looy, Altig, Bocklant, Sels, Beheyt, Elliott, De Roo, Dancelli, Wolfshohl, Den Hartog, to only mention some of the more illustrious ones, to which should be added a few Frenchmen such as Poulidor, Anquetil and Stablinski. The latter, recent winner of the Tour of Belgium, was in excellent condition. He did not overtly announce his desire for victory but simply hoped to be up with the rest of them.

Vittorio Adorni sensibly stuck to the same line: "Second in Milan-San Remo, second in the world championship...and why not second in Paris-Roubaix. That would gratify me for to win Paris-Roubaix seems a sort of miracle." The Italian champion was this time backed up by a new professional who was very well spoken of, a certain Felice Gimondi. However one man stood out from the rest of them. He wore the world champion's jersey. In fact nobody could forget that Jan Janssen was very difficult to outmanoeuvre not only on the cobbles but also in the case of a sprint.

The one hundred and thirty five starters hesitated to enter into battle too soon. Several skirmishes dominated the first hours. The name of the Italian Stefanoni had scarcely been written down in the journalists notebooks, than everything came together again at Clermont.

A crash at Flers, just before the one hundred- metre point was first event of any importance, and riders such as the quality of Graczyk and Anglade were forced to retire.

At the approach to the hill of Doullens, Raymond Poulidor decided to show himself. The Limousin attacked and took a thirty-metre lead from Tom Simpson, crossed over the top in the lead, then, as was his habit, sat up! At Hénin-Liétard the strategic passages were in sight. The pace accelerated for it was essential for those hoping to win to be at the front for the next cobbles sectors. Van Looy as an old hand, with the aid of his faithful team mate Sorgeloos, raised the tempo as they crossed Leforest. In less than five kilometres the peloton broke up. In the confusion, several crashes held up the progress of the first group. Among the victims were Durante, Elliott, Groussard and Stablinski.

Rolf Wolfshohl really wanted revenge on the Northern roads. Driven on by an exceptional will to win he attacked in sight of the terrible hill of Mons-en-Pévèle. After several kilometres of 1965

a solitary "fugue", six men came up to his wheel: Noël Foré Edouard Sels, Hermans, Van Schil and ...Jan Janssen accompanied by Van Looy.

At Attiches, thirty kilometres from Roubaix, four other riders latched on to the leading group: Huysmans, Vannitsen, Adorni and Simpson. A small bunch, with notably Anquetil and Stablinski in followed less than a minute behind. A very restless Wolfshohl went again but he was unable to open a decisive gap. Sels and Simpson caught him. His obstinacy was rewarded a little later by a first puncture.

Twenty five kilometres from the finish the position was clear. The ten men at the front could no longer be caught. The winner was going to be decided between them. The elimination started by a puncture to Jan Janssen, but he managed to get up in company of ...Rolf Wolfshohl! But the German's problems were not over. For him there was another puncture and a crash. Janssen was hardly any luckier. The world champion was to have a second flat tyre, and then a third, before crashing and retiring.

At Annappes, ten kilometres from the velodrome, Van Looy, backed up by his team-mate Sels decide to give it everything. "The Emperor of Herentals" attacked strongly. Only Noël Foré seemed able to go with him but another puncture broke his will.

From then on Van Looy flew away to a new triumph. At the announcement of his solitary arrival, the velodrome bursting with five thousand spectators broke out into wild applause.

All of the privileged witnesses there were happy with his triumph. Rarely had even his supporters given him such a warm welcome. As he appeared on the track his name was chanted as if with one voice. According to Jacques Goddet, Rik was placed on a level with only the most exceptional champions and had caught up with his prestigious past again.

Legend had it that Van Looy was in tears as he crossed the finishing line. In fact Rik who has a very clear memory of his third success at Roubaix, denies the claim. But certainly his eyes misted over as he came onto the track which under the circumstances was quite understandable.

His team-mate, Edouard Sels completed the success by taking second place. After the finish, Vannitsen, placed third, sowed doubts in several minds when he said that he had not really chased Van Looy very hard and claimed: "With Foré, I was too isolated to reverse the situation. If we had caught Van Looy, Sels who was by far the best of us would have won it." The next day, several newspapers, spoke not only about Van Looy's victory but also about Vannitsen's neutrality...

In order to put a stop to a growing controversy, Vannitsen quickly declared that: "I was riding only to win. You do not make sacrifices in a race like Paris-Roubaix.." As for Van Looy, he today asks no questions about it and confirms that Vannitsen was certainly a prisoner of Sels behind. If he had been caught, Sels would have won so Vannitsen would still have been empty handed.

The Van Looy-Vannitsen rivalry filled many pages of the Belgian newspapers. Van Looy's memories on the subject go back to the days when they were still both amateurs. On the last day of the Tour of Limbourg 1953, where Rik won three stages and was wearing the leader's jersey, Vannitsen sat on his wheel and said that he would not get his fourth win. Van Looy said that he had already won his share of the spoils and decided to stop. His rival did the same and without a word they both got into the ....broom wagon! Several years later, when Vannitsen boasted that he was much faster than Van Looy at the finish, the later retorted with a big smile that it was naturally because Vannitsen never did any work in a break, and anyway nobody could ever make any comparison between their two records.

1965

Van Looy and Sels at the velodrome.

Left:
Van Looy on the attack in company with Vannitsen and Adorni.

1. Rick VAN LOOY (Belgium)
   GS.Solo-Supéria
2. Edward SELS (Belgium)
3. Willy VANNITSEN (Belgium)
4. Victor VAN SCHIL (Belgium)
5. Joseph HUYSMANS (Belgium)
6. Vittorio ADORNI (Italy)
7. Tom SIMPSON (Great Britain)
8. Alfons HERMANS (Belgium)
9. Noël FORE (Belgium)
10. Georges VAN CONINGSLOO
    (Belgium)

Gimondi - Coppi's worthy heir

The route of the 1966 Paris-Roubaix was, according to the press "diabolically renewed". In fact, several sectors of the cobbles, at that time totally unknown at Hornaing, Ferrain, Rieulay and Flines-les-Raches were this time added to the traditional difficulties at Moncheaux and Mons-en-Pévèle.

On Sunday 17th April the forty kilometres of cobbles were much more dreaded than reported adverse weather conditions.

Paris-Roubaix looked like being the theatre of a new confrontation between the generations. Since the start of the season the older ones, led by Van Looy had

ROUBAIX. Sorti de l'Enfer du Nord avec une avance de quatre minutes sur le peloton de ses poursuivants, Felice Gimondi fonce vers le vélodrome où il va signer l'une des victoires les plus sensationnelles de l'histoire de Paris-Roubaix. Le vainqueur du Tour de France 1965 rejoint par cet exploit le panache de Fausto Coppi.

been having rather a rough time from the new wave. Certain of these green champions were going to become masters of the cobbles for some time to come.

The most promising of them was Eddy Merckx, a professional since the 29th April 1965, and who had just collected his first Milan-San Remo at the age of twenty. The other potential new Paris-Roubaix star was Felice Gimondi. For his debut in the Tour de France in 1965, the Italian had won it with plenty of style in front of..Raymond Poulidor.

Added to these two were other riders on the way up; Walter Godefroot, Belgian champion in his first year among the elite, Gerben Karstens, already winner of the Paris-Tours, and Willy Planckaert, oldest of the group, with his devastating sprint. According to the journalists victory in this sixty fourth Paris-Roubaix would be contested between Belgians, for never perhaps had they been so strong. Nearly twenty of them appeared capable of taking it on the Roubaix track: Van Looy, of course, Sels who had just carried off the Tour of Flanders, Van Schil, Huysmans, Foré, Van Coningsloo, Godefroot, Gustave and Armand Desmet, Willy Planckaert, Bocklant and this Merckx who all of the country was waiting to see for the first time on the cobbles.

The Dutch also had men capable of shining: Jan Janssen, De Roo, Post and Karstens. Among the "foreigners", the organisers were pleased to see the presence of Vittorio Adorni, recent winner of the Tour of Belgium. Seventh in 1965, the Italian returned with unconcealed ambition and a team of strong riders including Dancelli, De Rosso, Durante and......this devil, Gimondi.

Others signing the start sheet included Rudi Altig, Rolf Wolfshohl and again Shay Elliott. Finally the French who again had hopes for Raymond Poulidor. However, if he wanted to win it he would have to finish alone and faced with such opposition, this really would be an amazing feat.

At the start at Chantilly, the one hundred and thirty four riders were already coming up against the rain which would be with them as far as Denain. The first alert was a massive double crash at the sixtieth kilometre. The peloton, up until then grouped together for protection from the elements, was totally dislocated. Stablinski, Everaert, Melckenbeeck and Hugens retired straight away. Willy Planckaert, Bocklant, Janssen and Van Coningsloo embarked on a unplanned pursuit. But in Paris-Roubaix, history has shown that such efforts were paid for sooner or later.

The young Belgian Theo Mertens took off a little later. The bunch, in a position of force when faced with a single man away were late to react. At Chauny, at eighty eight kilometres, Mertens' lead was a minute and a half, then three times more at St Quentin.

But the peloton decided to bring Mertens' adventure to a close and he was reeled in at Busigny after an escape of sixty seven kilometres. At Solesmes, the Frenchman Salmon then tried his luck. He "opened the road" for twenty kilometres before everything came back to order again at Saulzoir. So it was one big bunch which arrived at the first section of cobbles at Hornaing. Three thousand metres further on, De Boever in his turn escaped. At Flines-les-Raches, the Belgian had a fifty five seconds lead on a thin peloton where the list of accidents were getting longer. Wolfshohl broke his bike, Merckx punctured twice, Aimar, Gustave, Desmet, Beheyt, Van Coningsloo were also delayed. At the spot where everyone was expecting a Belgian attack, it was surprising to see two Italians shoot out from the bunch. They rejoined De Boever before tackling the hill at Mons-en-Pévèle.

1966

Felice GIMONDI
(Italy, 1942)

An outstanding champion and gentleman cyclist. There is no doubt he would have won even more great titles had his career not coincided with a certain Eddy Merckx.

1965 : Tour de France
1966 : Paris-Roubaix, Paris-Brussels, Tour of Lombardy
1967 : Tour of Italy, Grand Prix des Nations
1968 : Italian Champion, Tour of Spain, Grand Prix des Nations
1969 : Tour of Italy, Tour of Romandy
1972 : Italian Champion
1973 : World Champion, Tour of Lombardy
1974 : Milan-San Remo
1975 : Tour of Italy, Paris-Brussels

A little after in the famous "Pas Rolland", at forty one kilometres from Roubaix, Felice Gimondi shook off his last two rivals and flew away in a manner worthy of the heroic times. After the obstacle of the Pas Rolland, Dancelli and De Boever followed ten seconds down, while seven men were already nearly a minute behind: Poulidor, Janssen, Van Looy, Bocklant, Huysmans, Gustave Desmet and De Cabooter.

After the descent of Mons-en-Pévèle, a small group composed notably of Delberghe, Sels, Willy Planckaert, Merckx and Godefroot came up to the aforementioned group. In spite of these precious reinforcements, the protagonists were powerless in the face of Felice Gimondi whose ride was turning into a demonstration.

Under an icy rain which accentuated the difficulties of the route even more, the gap kept getting wider. At Fretin, it was more than two minutes, then 3mins 45secs with sixteen kilometres to go. Gimondi rode round the velodrome with four minutes and eight seconds in hand on Jan Janssen who took second place on the podium. After his victory in the Tour de France, Gimondi became a god in the hearts of his fans. This Paris-Roubaix brought him closer still to the venerable Coppi whose era he was starting to relive.

As he got off his bike, Felice Gimondi, a simple and approachable champion, immediately paid tribute to his team mates: "I finished strongly, but I was lucky. Not a puncture, not a crash and then my comrades helped me a lot".

The name Fausto Coppi was mentioned to him, but Felice was quick to play down the enthusiasm: "No, No. I am not yet "Mr Coppi", he said, but I very much hope that one day I will be worthy enough to succeed him."

A few hours after the finish, Gimondi received the journalists at the Grand Hotel at Roubaix. Pressed with questions, he simply related his day: "The harder the

race was, the better it was for me. I was obliged to open an important gap in order to counter the menace of the sprinters.

I am not a very fast finisher so in order to win I had no other choice. When I went over the route with Adorni, I came to the conclusion that I had to attack at Pas Rolland to spoil anyone else's plans. Everything, thankfully, went as expected."

It seemed the bunch had not believed in the young Italian's final success but he had built a lead so quickly that his chasers were only able to contest the minor placings. Janssen finished second, in front of Gustave Desmet, Willy Planckaert and Jos Huysmans.

As expected it was a battle between the Belgians and the Dutch but behind an Italian, Gimondi! Eddy Merckx remained one of the most unfortunate of the race. On the second cobbled section his chain became stuck between his two chain rings. He changed his bike and chased by himself for fifteen kilometres on a bike which was not his size. He nevertheless finished in fourteenth position.

Van Looy, who was classified ninth, remembered very well the debut of the future "Cannibal", for Merckx, no doubt a little nervous rode the first cobble sections at a hellish pace. Jean Stablinski rode up to Van Looy to ask him the name of this young hothead. Rik replied in the following terms: "Don't worry, Jean, you'll soon get to know him, he's called Eddy Merckx..."

1966

1. Felice GIMONDI (Italy)
   GS.Salvarani
2. Jan JANSSEN (Holland)
3. Gilbert DESMET (Belgium)
4. Willy PLANCKAET (Belgium)
5. Joseph HUYSMANS (Belgium)
6. Rudi ALTIG (Germany)
7. Willy BOCKLANT (Belgium)
8. Arthur DE CABOOTER (Belgium)
9. Rik VAN LOOY (Belgium)
10. Gerben KARTENS (Holland)

Felice Gimondi forces the pace with Dancelli and De Boever on his wheel

The Sprint of Master Jan

In a few moments ten men are going to contest the victory of the sixty fifth Paris-Roubaix. Never has the term royal escape been so appropriate. In fact, since Mons-en-Pévèle where they went away, ten names were inscribed in the journalists' notebooks. As so often happened on the Northern roads, at the finish it was going to be a battle of the greats.

The inventory of the break required no comment as there were four world Champions riding together: Van Looy, Janssen, Altig and Merckx (a winner of the amateur worlds in 1964), the former national champions, Edouard Sels and Raymond Poulidor, Gianni Motta, last winner of the Tour of Italy, Arthur De Cabooter and Willy Planckaert, the green jersey in the last Tour de France.

The Belgian Vandenberghe, the tenth man, a top class rider, presented a visiting card that was not quite as full as the others, but who nevertheless could list a stage win in the last Tour de France. His main job today was to help Willy Planckaert.

As the champions came onto the track, any forecast was difficult, for Van Looy, already a three-time winner wanted to surpass Lapize and Rebry in the records books. Janssen had already been twice on the podium but not on the top step. Willy Planckaert knew that he would probably never have such a good chance as this again. Merckx wanted to accomplish the rare double of Milan-San Remo and Paris-Roubaix, and Altig wanted to honour his rainbow jersey, while Motta dreamt of becoming a legend like Coppi and Gimondi. In short, each of them had an especially good reason for winning it.

At the appearance of the riders led by De Cabooter, the Roubaix fans rose to their feet as one man, Edouard Sels had the eight others on his wheel already with elbows touching. The Belgians went wild with delight for who could reasonably hope to match up to their champions.

Just after the first passage across the line there remained just five hundred metres to cover. Janssen accelerated and went to the front. His usual tactic was simple, he rode flat out to suffocate the sprinters. All that remained was for him to have the strength to do it.!

In spite of a head wind on the back straight, he seemed to have made the right move, for in the last few metres nobody was able to make up any ground on him. So the Dutchman took his Paris-Roubaix. Van Looy failed by a quarter of a length, Altig by a wheel, then in the width of a handkerchief was Vandenberghe, Sels, Planckaert, Poulidor, Merckx, De Cabooter and Motta.

Janssen, clearly the freshest of them all, had done much more than his share of the work in the break. His triumph was fully deserved. Since his third place in 1963 behind Daems and Van Looy, his compatriots had been waiting for him to win. On the grass of the velodrome, the former world champion enjoyed replying to the numerous questions of the journalists:

"As we approached Roubaix, I thought about my previous results when I had finished third and second. This time I decided I was going for broke for I had the feeling that the sprinters were a bit tired. I went at the bell and put everything into it that I had and

Jan JANSSEN
(Holland, 1940)

A complete bike rider. He won a World road title, single-day classics and was the first Dutch winner of the Tour de France.

1962 : Zurich Championships
1963 : 2nd Flèche Wallonne,
        3rd Paris-Roubaix
1964 : World Champion, Paris-Nice
        2nd Flèche Wallonne
1965 : Tour of Holland
1966 : Bordeaux-Paris, Flèche-Brabanconnr
        2nd Paris-Roubaix
        2nd Tour de France
1967 : Paris-Roubaix, Tour of Spain
        2nd World Championships
        2nd Ghent-Wevelgem
1968 : Tour de France
        3rd Flèche Wallonne
1969 : 2nd Bordeaux-Paris

1967

thought about nothing else. However never before had the final straight seemed so long."

Van Looy, astonishingly seemed well satisfied with his second place: "It's hard to be beaten by so little, but I prefer that it was Jan. He is a great champion and he knows how to take risks." The truth was rather different, as Rik was especially afraid of Merckx winning, his national rival, whose star was in the ascendant.

Altig had no complaints either: "Yes, of course, like all of us, I believed that I could win. But I have no regrets, quite the opposite. My crash in Ghent Wevelgem delayed my preparation and here I simply resurfaced."

As for Poulidor, he was content with his seventh place, the best of the French: "This was my best Paris-Roubaix. All that was missing was a hill on which I could have tried my luck. How rare the hills are in Paris-Roubaix..."

On the other hand Vandenberghe bitterly regretted having ridden for

Van Looy, always so powerful on the cobbles, in front of Motta and Merckx.

Master Jan at the end of a magnificent sprint.

Planckaert who made a complete mess of the sprint. In spite of his work for his team-mate he finished fourth in the sprint, so close to the winner.

The only other rider to express disappointment was Merckx. In this, only his twenty second year, he had just picked up a second Milan-San Remo, and then Ghent Wevelgem before finishing third in the Tour of Flanders. His eighth place here, one of his worst of the season, seemed in his eyes to be a poor performance:

"Since Denain, I never stopped working to try and break up the group. I paid for my efforts in the end but then unlike the first few I did not ride the Tour of Belgium." At the start at Chantilly, under the rain, opinion was divided on this Tour of Belgium question. Was Merckx right in not riding it?

Jan Janssen, who finished third in the event, was quite adamant. He claimed that if you wanted to win at Roubaix then you just could not miss it. Even if Janssen and Merckx along with Gimondi formed a major trio at the start, there were others who could not be forgotten. The hard-wearing Van Looy, always so motivated as "La Pascale" approached, Foré, Planckaert, Altig, Post Bocklant, Motta, Van Coningsloo, Godefroot, Poulidor, Simpson, Sels and even Anquetil, were all there.

The stars were in the thick of it right from the start as the first attacker was Zilioli, one of the leaders for the Italians. However his adventure only lasted a little longer than Anquetil's appearance in the race. Jacques was sick and preferring not to risk the rest of the season, retired at the twenty sixth kilometre, but not before predicting the success of - Jan Janssen!

Then the Dutchman Braspenning launched himself off the front, with more success, in a solitary break. Rapidly he was caught by Schepers and two Frenchmen, Bouton and Benet. At the hundred-kilometre point the peloton was 1min 20secs down, then three minutes and forty seconds thirty five kilometres later. But the efforts began to tell and after one hundred and fifty kilometres had been covered it was only Bouton who was still making a fight of it, but not for long.

The first important selection was decided by an initiative from Merckx. After Denain, thirty two men formed the front group, then Rudi Altig launched the decisive attack. At Mons-en-Pévèle, the German took off. Janssen, Sels, Merckx and Poulidor came up to him, then Van Looy, De Cabooter, Planckaert, Vandenberghe and Motta did the same a little later. The group was now not going to change and the deficit of the peloton was three minutes.

Sadly, the 1967 season brought the sport onto the front pages, as during the Tour de France, which was won by Roger Pingeon, there was a fatality. The 13th July, on the thirteenth stage, on side of a heated Mont Ventoux, the British rider Tom Simpson, victim of a cardiac arrest, collapsed on the road. Evacuated by helicopter, he died an hour later at the St Marthe hospital at Avignon.

As for Eddy Merckx, after what he considered to be the failure of Paris-Roubaix, he redeemed himself by winning Flèche Wallonne and more notably the World championships at Heerlen in front of none other than ..Jan Janssen. As for the next Paris-Roubaix, the young Cannibal was preparing his revenge. He had already given notice that victory at the Roubaix Velodrome, especially with the rainbow jersey on his shoulders would not displease him.

1967

1. Jan JANSSEN (Holland)
   GS.Pelforth-Sauvage-Lejeune
2. Rik VAN LOOY Belgium)
3. Rudi ALTIG (Germany)
4. Georges VANDENBERGHE
   (Belgium)
5. Edward SELS (Belgium)
6. Willy PLANCKAERT (Belgium)
7. Raymond POULIDOR (France)
8. Eddy MERCKX (Belgium)
9. Arthur DE CABOOTER (Belgium)
10. Gianni MOTTA (Italy)

LES POINTS NÉVRALGIQUES DE LA COURSE

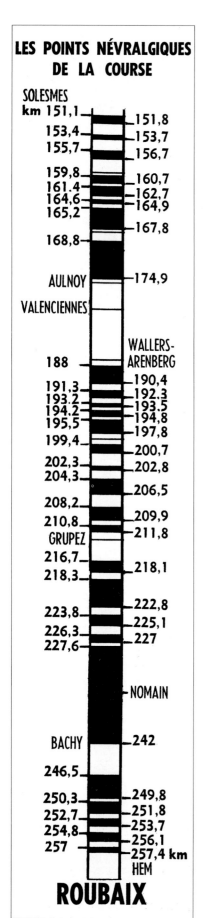

SOLESMES
km 151,1 — 151,8
153,4 — 153,7
155,7 — 156,7
159,8 — 160,7
161,4 — 162,7
164,6 — 164,9
165,2 — 167,8
168,8 — 174,9
AULNOY
VALENCIENNES
WALLERS-ARENBERG
188 — 190,4
191,3 — 192,3
193,2 — 193,5
194,2 — 194,8
195,5 — 197,8
199,4 — 200,7
202,3 — 202,8
204,3 — 206,5
208,2 — 209,9
210,8 — 211,8
GRUPEZ
216,7 — 218,1
218,3 — 222,8
223,8 — 225,1
226,3 — 227
227,6 — NOMAIN
BACHY — 242
246,5 — 249,8
250,3 — 251,8
252,7 — 253,7
254,8 — 256,1
257 — 257,4 km
HEM

ROUBAIX

An Extraordinary Paris-Roubaix

Jean Garnault, several years previously, was right to pull the communication cord and embark on a crusade to save the cobbles. His obstinacy had held up the concrete mixers a little but by now the situation was becoming critical. Each year complete sections of cobbles disappeared. Certain parts used twelve months earlier in the race such as Moncheaux and Mons-en-Pévèle now looked more like a motorway than part of the route of Paris-Roubaix.

The event had changed its countenance in 1966. It's point of departure was pushed forward to Chantilly fifty kilometres from the capital. Research was undertaken on the final part of the route and some new "cobbled villages" like Escaudain, Hornaing, Vred and Flines-les-Râches were included.

Since the start of the 1968 season, Jean Stablinski, who was beginning his last year as a professional, had been acting as a guide over the Northern bye-ways for his friend Albert Bouvet, the successor to Jean Garnault at the head of the Paris-Roubaix organisation. Nobody had to wait very long for the result. Following the first inspection of the new route the press announced that the 1968 edition would be, without doubt the most difficult and the most extraordinary in history and the Queen of the Classics would see a legendary winner in the manner of the heroic times.

The cobbled sections started at Solesmes, one hundred and twelve kilometres from Roubaix. From then on the itinerary quit Denain to head for Valenciennes. The riders were going to then discover eight kilometres later the most formidable portion situated in the commune of Wallers-Arenberg: a straight road with the most terrible cobbles which lasted for a little more than two kilometres.

The total distance over the cobbles went up to 56.6 kms. The longest section was between Templeuve and Bachy with almost fifteen kilometres without a single metre of asphalt.

The wearer of the rainbow jersey, Eddy Merckx, had not really started the season very well. A pain in his knee forced him to retire on the Col de la Republique during Paris-Nice, but everyone was waiting for Milan-San Remo

which the Belgian had won on the two previous occasions.
The result however was disappointing, Altig won, while Merckx was not even in the winning break. Rik Van Looy, aware of the generation gap was jubilant: "If Merckx is the boss, let him show it."
The Van Looy-Merckx battle had reached its peak in the Grand Prix E3 at Harelbeke. Having escaped together, Merckx rode fast, very fast with Van Looy on his wheel, who swore that he was unable to go through to do his turn in front of the world champion, and so the race saw victory go to Jacques De Boever.
The success of Walter Godefroot in the Tour of Flanders only rubbed salt in the wounds, and while Van Looy regained his popularity, Merckx found himself being criticised from all sides and whose popularity was being called in question. At Chantilly though, in spite of everything, the Belgian champion was the man to beat .
He was opposed above all by Van Looy.
This remarkable man, now thirty five years old, claimed that although he was not as strong as he used to be, he was starting the race in order to win it, as always. He emphasised that he was far from unhappy with the new route: "So much the better, it will make the legs of the young hurt."
Joining Merckx and Van Looy at the start were others

1968

Eddy MERCKX
(Belgium, 1945)

Acknowledged to be the greatest bike rider of all time. With no fewer than 525 victories on the road, the tall and very powerful Merckx was known as 'The Cannibal'.

1964 : World Amateur Champion
1966 : Milan-San Remo
1967 : World Champion,
       Milan-San Remo, Ghent-Wevelgem
       Flèche Wallonne
1968 : Paris-Roubaix, Tour of Italy
1969 : Milan-San Remo, Tour of Flanders,
       Liège-Bastogne-Liège,
       Tour de France, Paris-Nice
1970 : Paris-Roubaix, Ghent-Wevelgem,
       Flèche Wallonne, Tour de France,
       Tour of Italy, Tour of Belgium,
       Paris-Nice, Belgian Champion
1971 : World Champion,
       Milan-San Remo,
       Liège-Bastogne-Liège,
       Tour of Lombardy, Het Volk,
       Tour de France, Tour of Belgium,
       Paris-Nice
1972 : Milan-San Remo,
       Liège-Bastogne-Liège,
       Tour of Lombardy, Flèche Wallonne,
       Tour de France, Tour of Italy
       The Hour Record (49,431 km)
1973 : Paris-Roubaix, Liège-Bastogne-Liège,
       Amstel Gold Race, Het Volk,
       Ghent-Wevelgem, Paris-Brussels
       Grand Prix des Nations, Tour of Italy
       Tour of Spain
1974 : World Champion, Tour de France,
       Tour of Italy, Tour of Switzerland
1975 : Milan-San Remo, Tour of Flanders,
       Liège-Bastogne-Liège,
       Amstel Gold Race
1976 : Milan-San Remo

including: Altig, Godefroot, Sels, Janssen, Van Springel, Gimondi, Post, Bocklant, and the two Frenchmen Jourden and ...Poulidor.

The first serious attempt at a break-away started at Fresnoy-le-Grand at seventeen kilometres. Van der Linde, Casalini, Leblanc, Haeseldonck and Néri attacked. Five thousand metres later Roger Pingeon joined them. As they entered the Region du Nord the gap was more than a minute. At Cateau, it had grown to two minutes and thirty five seconds and more than four minutes at Solesmes.

The formidable sight of the first cobbles woke the peloton and the gap started to diminish. Pingeon could see that his companions were starting to tire and decided to go away by himself. After punctures to Jean-Marie Leblanc, Néri, Casalini and Van der Linde, the situation became much clearer. At the feeding station of Valenciennes, Pingeon was 2mins 40secs in front of the bunch.

However, as he reached the Wallers-Arenberg gap alone in the lead, his strength left him and a puncture he hardly needed, meant the end of his hopes. At Warlaing, Cooreman attacked. Sels joined him, then Merckx left the peloton at Marchiennes. This bubbling up provoked the escape of fourteen men. All the favourites were there except Van Looy who in his turn had a flat tyre.

After a brief look round, Merckx thought that his rivals were too numerous for his taste. At Coutiches he forced the pace and broke up the group. Only Sels was strong enough to follow him. A little later Van Springel and Bocklant got up to the two attackers. Behind them fifteen men were working perfectly together, but all to no avail, as from now on they would play only secondary roles.

At Templeuve, in spite of two counter-attacks by Godefroot, who would not accept defeat, the gap remained about one minute and forty seconds. At the point known as "Le Quimberge", twenty six kilometres from the velodrome, Bocklant reached his limits and had to let his three companions disappear slowly into the distance.

Then Sels, let down by a puncture, left Van Springel isolated on the back wheel of the unleashed "Cannibal". At the exit to each corner the poor Herman was forced to sprint hard just to regain his wheel.

Victory was going to be decided between Van Springel and Merckx. Nobody was under the least illusion.

It was Van Springel who was first onto the track but Merckx quickly took command, going up to the barriers on the penultimate bend and then plunging down on the inside.

Van Springel had only willpower to oppose an imperial Merckx, fresher, used to the track and a better sprinter. Too many trumps which made him an indisputable winner. Eddy Merckx won his first Paris-Roubaix in a magisterial fashion. The world champion was beaming at the finish:. "I had two punctures on the cobbles, but got back without too much trouble. It was then that I swore to myself that I would win this Paris-Roubaix. When I attacked, I understood that there were quite a few who were thinking more about recovering, and so it was then that I gave it everything I had while I was still fresh.."

Van Looy was terribly disappointed. First and above all, it must be said, because of the victory of his young rival, but also because of the bad luck with three punctures. Yet in spite of this, he figured among a group sprinting for ninth place eight minutes behind the winner, but a place of honour was of no interest to him, he did not go on to the track at the finish, heading straight for the showers. Yet the Emperor's reign finished on a high, as a short time later he won Flèche Wallonne, the only classic still missing from his collection.

1968

Eddy MERCKX
& PARIS-ROUBAIX :

1966 : 15th
1967 : 8th
1968 : 1st
1969 : 2nd
1970 : 1st
1971 : 5th
1972 : 7th
1973 : 1st
1974 : 4th
1975 : 2nd
1976 : 6th
1977 : 11th

1. Eddy MERCKX (Belgium)
   GS.Faema
2. Herman VAN SPRINGEL (Belgium)
3. Walter GODEFROOT (Belgium)
4. Edward SELS (Belgium)
5. Victor VAN SCHIL (Belgium)
6. Raymond POULIDOR (France)
7. Henk NIJDAM (Holland)
8. Jan JANSSEN (Holland)
9. Guido REYBROUCK (Belgium)
10. Frans MELCKENBEECK (Belgium)

Survêtements *Trévois International...*
GROUPE KOPA

M

L'EQUIPE
LE QUOTIDIEN DU SPORT
ET DE l'Automobile

0,70

10, Fg MONTMARTRE, PARIS (9°)
Tél. 824-70-80, CCP Paris 4.237-93
24° ANNÉE — N° 7.151
LUNDI 14 AVRIL 1969

Algérie, 0,60 dinar ; Allemagne, 0,70 D.M. ; Belgique - Luxembourg, 7,00 F.B. ; Espagne, 10 pesetas ; Grande-Bretagne, 1/6 ;
Hollande, 0,90 florin ; Italie, 120 lires ; Maroc, 0,70 dirham ; Suisse, 0,85 F.S. ; Tunisie, 70 millimes.
SERVICE DE VENTE : 124, RUE RÉAUMUR, PARIS (2°) — TÉLÉPHONE : 488-75-20

Chaussures de sport RESISTEX - NOEL FRERE
Culottes de sport J.B. SOLEILLANT
GROUPE KOPA

GODEFROOT A FAIT PLIER MERCKX

Ce Paris-Roubaix rendu très pénible par les conditions atmosphériques a provoqué une sélection impitoyable (35 arrivants !)

Godefroot, couvert par les De Vlaeminck, assomme ses derniers adversaires, Merckx, Gimondi, Vekemans Zoontjens, en attaquant de nouveau à 34 km du but

L'épreuve était dotée du Trophée des Fabricants de tissus pour habillement de Roubaix-Tourcoing.

(Pages 2, 3, 4 et 5)

UN NOUVEAU NALLET VOUS ATTEND DANS

ATHLÉTISME-MAGAZINE

Exigez le ...

Merckx second in the sprint before Vekemans and Gimondi

...'envole ...ne titre

...affi à Strasbourg

...laissent ...Monaco

PLUS DE CONSEIL FÉDÉRAL
(sauf pour les affaires courantes)
C'est peut-être un bien pour un mal

(Pages 8, 9 et 10)

Un télégramme des organisateurs de Paris-Roubaix au directeur général de l'O.R.T.F.

« Les organisateurs de Paris-Roubaix, « Le Parisien libéré » et « L'Equipe », protestent contre l'ostracisme dont ils sont victimes de la part de la T.V. Stop. Ils déplorent l'absence de mentions des noms des organisateurs de la course. « Le Parisien libéré » et « L'Equipe », dans les images du départ de 12 h. et 13 h. de Chantilly et sur celles de fin d'épreuve. Stop. Récemment encore à l'occasion des cross (ici figuraient les noms des organisateurs), course cycliste Paris-Nice (ici figure le nom de l'organisateur), les noms de ces journaux ont figuré en bonne place sur l'écran et fait l'objet de citations verbales. Stop. Paris-Roubaix, cependant, est avec le Tour de France la plus importante des compétitions cyclistes internationales. Stop. Toutes les nations cyclistes en renom y participent généralement et cela était plus particulièrement le cas cette année. Stop. Les organisateurs de Paris-Roubaix ne peuvent admettre pareil traitement discriminatoire. Stop. Considérations distinguées. »

Par le télégramme ci-dessus, les organisateurs de Paris-Roubaix, notre journal et « Le Parisien libéré » dénoncent nettement le caractère tendancieux de ce omissions répétées. L'ORTF, étant un service public à l'usage du public, se doit de donner toutes les informations aux téléspectateurs ; la mention du nom de organisateurs est une de ces informations. L'auto plus, comme on a pu le lire dans le télégramme, qu s'agit d'un usage établi, utilisé largement par le pass

GALA... au P...

EN V... CONTRE DE LIMA

LE RETO...

EXCLUS...

(Page 6)

Automobile	14 à 16	Football	8 à 10	Rugby XV	11, 12
Aviron	13	Hippisme	13	Rugby XIII	13
Basket	7	Indiscrétions	6	Scolaires	13
Boxe	6	Lutte	13	Télévision	2
Cyclisme	2 à 5	Natation	7	Tennis	6

Merckx in the face of "Flandria" ...or the success of a Tourist!

Since the beginning to the 1969 season, Merckx felt more than ever that he was the target of them all. So in all the classics the powerful Flandria team faced up to him with top quality riders such as Walter Godefroot, his long-time enemy, Eric Leman, Jean-Pierre Monseré and the De Vlaeminck brothers.

Up until that time everyone knew Eric De Vlaeminck. Roger his younger brother had just used his first professional licence for a victory in the coveted Circuit Het Volk!

The recent Tour of Belgium had also been dominated by the riders from the Eeklo region who had each managed a stage win embellished for Eric with a prestigious victory in the final classification.

In spite of this bitter rivalry Eddy Merckx had, as so often, been piling up the wins: Paris-Nice, Milan-San Remo in front of Roger De Vlaeminck, and the Tour of Flanders after a solitary escape of seventy kilometres. However, several times he had suffered with a pain in his right knee and it was this which caused his retirement in the Flèche Brabanconne.

General opinion had it that Paris-Roubaix would be played out between Merckx, if he curbed slightly his enthusiasm that he showed in the Tour of Flanders, the De Vlaemincks and Godefroot. The day before the race, Walter, not really in a mood to sacrifice his own chances, tried to clarify the situation: "Tomorrow I am playing my own card. I will stay at the front and watch things very closely..."

The Belgians wanted moreover to improve on their 1968 score when they had taken the first five places.

Without question they had the means to fulfil their ambition for pressing through from the second rank were riders such as: Verbeeck, Van Coningsloo, Van Springel, Reybroeck, Bocklant and others such as Van Ryckeghem and Sels. Each one of them, without exception had the calibre to figure in the records of "La Pascale". For his part, Rik Van Looy was taking part in his fourteenth Paris-Roubaix in order to officially help his team. However he told some friends that he had ridden the Tour of Flanders not to win it but to put in some kilometres for Paris-Roubaix.

Facing the powerful Flemish riders were other nationalities: Italians, Gimondi, Adorni, Basso and Dancelli, the Dutchman Post and Frenchmen, Poulidor, Guimard, Riotte, Anquetil with several young Northerners such as Leblanc, Samyn, Guiot, Crépel and the brothers Sylvain and Alain Vasseur. The appearance of the latter was welcomed as he had won the previous year's amateur event in a most convincing way.

The one hundred and fifty four competitors left Chantilly at a fast

1969

Walter GODEFROOT
(Belgium, 1943)

A feared finisher with a rapid sprint he was a fierce opponent of Eddy Merckx.

1965 : Belgian Champion
1966 : 2nd Het Volk
1967 : Liège-Bastogne-Liège
1968 : Tour of Flanders,
       Ghent-Wevelgem,
       2nd Liège-Bastogne-Liège,
       2nd Paris-Tours,
       3rd Paris-Roubaix
1969 : Paris-Roubaix, Bordeaux-Paris,
       2nd Belgian Championship
1970 : Zurich Championship
       2nd Tour of Flanders,
       2nd Tour of Belgium
1971 : Belgian Champion
1973 : 2nd Paris-Roubaix,
       3rd Liège-Bastogne-Liège
1974 : Zurich Champion,
       3rd Amstel Gold Race
1975 : 3rd Liège-Bastogne-Liège
1976 : Bordeaux-Paris
1978 : Tour of Flanders

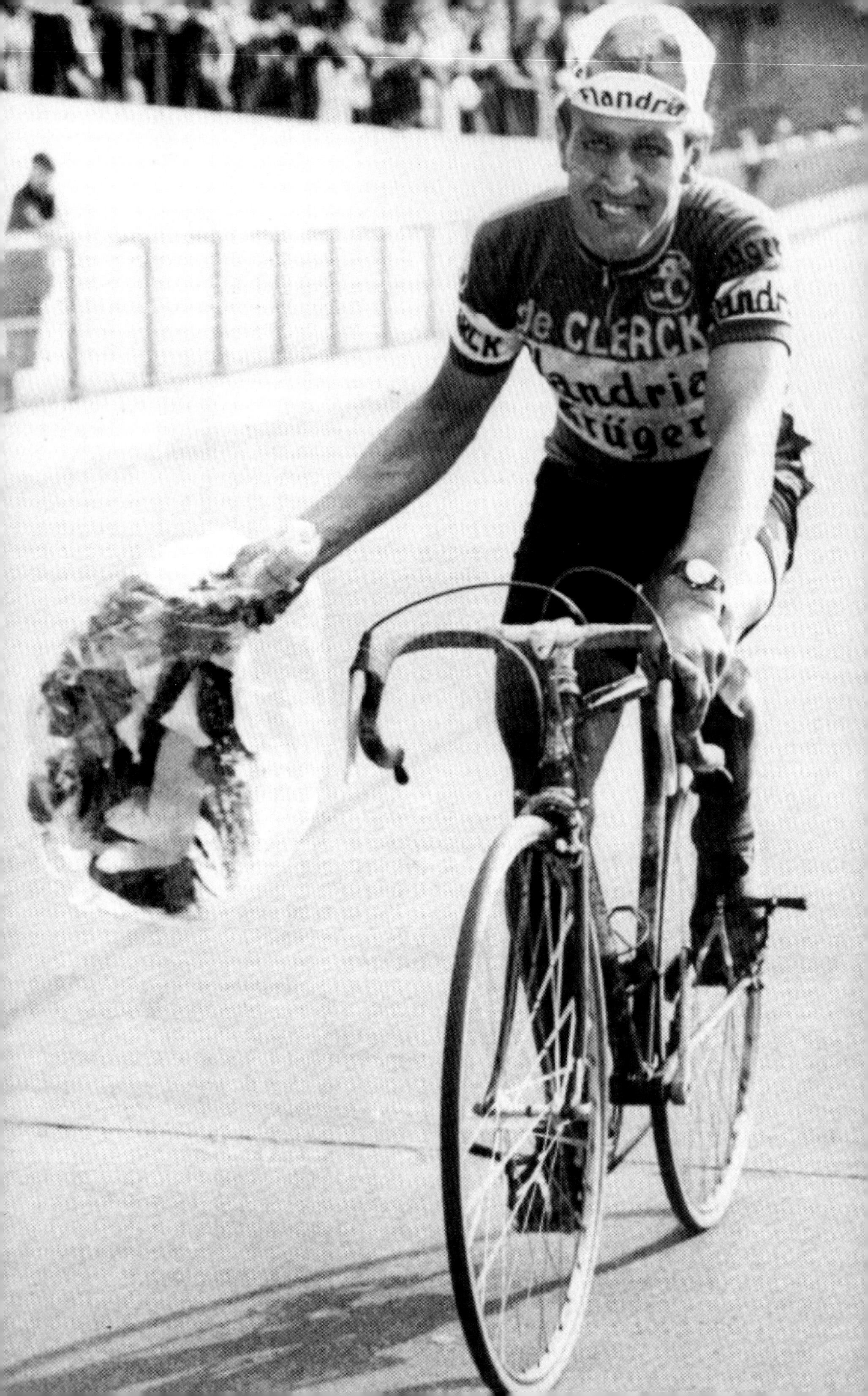

Flandria
de CLERCK

pace. At the exit to Noyon, after sixty four kilometres, the peloton broke up into several groups. As they went through St Quentin at the hundred kilometre point, forty men, more or less, still had a realistic chance of winning.

As they passed through the scenic forest of Arenberg, the new important and strategic area of the route, five men went clear: Godefroot, Roger De Vlaeminck, Schroeders, Huysmans and... Merckx. While Schroeders found himself eliminated with a puncture, Gimondi, frustrated at having missed the right move, counter-attacked. Under his impulsion several riders latched onto the leading group which now counted twenty eight men.

At sixty kilometres from the finish, Godefroot escaped. Straight away Zootjens, Gimondi and Merckx got on his wheel, then Eric De Vlaeminck, his brother Roger and Vekemans managed to do the same a little later. Walter Godefroot, without knowing it had just launched the right break, for these men were going to seize, two hours later the first seven places.

At Coutiches the first bunch found itself fifty seconds down. Godefroot, despite a puncture, was able to regain his place at the front in less than three kilometres. Just after that Eric Leman achieved the extraordinary feat of catching the leaders after a long lone chase. Thanks to this reinforcement the Flandria team now had four riders in the leading group and were now masters of the race. Walter Godefroot, as expected, took off just before Templeuve. Merckx and Gimondi started a few counter-attacks, but always in vain because the De Vlaemincks and Leman were watching them too closely.

Right up until Roubaix, the gap between Godefroot and his pursuers did not stop growing: one hundred and fifty metres at Ouvignies, forty seconds at La Posterie, fifty seconds at Bachy, a minute and a half at Chereng, two minutes at Hem and precisely two minutes and forty nine seconds at the velodrome.

Walter Godefroot who fully deserved his victory had quite simply won in the style of...Merckx!

The former Belgian champion had launched his first attack seventy five kilometres from Roubaix. Driven by an absolute will to win he had remained calm and confident: "Even if I had been caught," he said, "I was sure of winning the sprint."

This triumph was also that of Pol Claeys, the boss of Flandria. Just before the event he had flayed Godefroot, calling him a "tourist". It is hardly necessary to say that the champion from Ghent did not appreciate the remark and was looking for an opportunity to put the record straight.

Merckx finished second in front of Vekemans, Gimondi and the De Vlaeminck brothers. Poulidor retired with forty kilometres to go but at the beginning of the race observing Roger De Vlaeminck, he could see the man's potential. The Limousin said: "I had heard people speaking about this young Belgian, although I hardly knew him myself. I can confirm though that he has the makings of a great champion."

Unfortunately, he was not French, as for them Paris-Roubaix was turning into a real nightmare. Only Guimard, eighth, Catieau, twenty first and Jourden twenty third finished the race!

Anquetil had handed in his race number at Valenciennes. On the other hand the thirty six year old Van Looy on his last appearance on these Northern roads finished twenty second, far in front of many young ones.

1969

1. Walter GODEFROOT (Belgium)
   GS.Flandria-De Clerck-Kruger
2. Eddy MERCKX (Belgium)
3. Willy VEKEMANS (Belgium)
4. Felice GIMONDI (Italy)
5. Roger DE VLAEMINCK (Belgium)
6. Eric DE VLAEMINCK (Belgium)
7. Cees ZOONTJENS (Holland)
8. Cyrille GUIMARD (France)
9. Patrick SERCU (Belgium)
10. Willy BOCKLANT (Belgium)

Merckx -
An Extra Terrestrial

At less than twenty five years old, Eddy Merckx had an incomparable record. An outstanding world champion at Heerlen he had steadily been building up the trophies on his sideboard. A Tour de France in which he had outclassed all his rivals, a Tour of Italy, three Milan-San Remos, Paris-Roubaix, Liège-Bastogne-Liège, Tour of Flanders and two Ghent Wevelgems.

Since his victory in the amateur world championship in 1964, at the age of nineteen, the superlatives had not stopped coming his way. However there was perhaps never such a consensus of opinion in the press as there was on Monday 13th April 1970.

The day before, Eddy Merckx had crushed Paris-Roubaix with his class. For the others, all of the others, it was a humiliation. Roger De Vlaeminck, the runner-up, came onto the track five minutes and twenty seconds adrift!

Everyone was unanimous and several of the older followers who generally avoided the trap of comparing generations estimated that the "Cannibal" had surpassed all of the illustrious names of the past. For his part Patrick Sercu, under the showers said: "Today Merckx was Formula One ...the others were simply touring cars.."

At the start at Chantilly, Merckx was the uncontested number one favourite. The Belgian had dominated the beginning of the season as never before. Two stages in the Tour of Sardinia, three

1970

On the cobbles ... behind Merckx:
Eric De Vlaeminck, Monséré, Verbeeck,
Van Sweevelt, Sels, Roger De Vlaeminck
and De Boever.

stages and overall winner in the Paris-Nice, Ghent Wevelgem, the criteriums of Sanary and of the Col San Martino and forty eight hours before Paris-Roubaix, the Tour of Belgium won by three minutes from Walter Godefroot and eight from Eric De Vlaeminck. However at the end of this event, run in deplorable weather conditions, it was said that the champion had caught flu. Guillaume Driessens, his team manager, did nothing to stop the rumour circulating that Merckx intended to retire after about fifty kilometres!

Behind Merckx in the list of potential winners, was Godefroot, and then to a lesser degree, Van Springel, Verbeeck, Leman, Eric and Roger De Vlaeminck, Vekemans and Rosiers. The ambition of the French, if one can call it that, was just to follow these big names for as long as possible.

For his part, Albert Bouvet was afraid of the lighting that was forecast. He went so far as to say the day before that if the bad weather continued there was a risk of counting the finishers on the fingers of two hands.

The first important incident was a crash at Hem, after eighty nine kilometres of racing. Already the peloton had split into four parts and numerous men had disappeared. For the favourites it was though, just the beginning.

Much later, under the deluge, the meagre peloton arrived at the Wallers-Arenberg "trench". Punctures and crashes multiplied, forcing the best to make a decision. Merckx was at the front of the group and was going flat out while his main rivals were huddled on his wheel. There now remained only Karstens, Janssen and four Flandrias: Leman, Dierickx, Roger and Eric De Vlaeminck.

At Bouvignies, fifty six kilometres from Roubaix, Eddy Merckx suffered a second puncture. In order to confirm his supremacy he was back in a few kilometres and going straight to the front, he continued his war of attrition.

One by one his rivals dropped off. Soon there were only two riders on his wheel: Roger De Vlaeminck and Eric Leman. As they crossed through Hucquinville, forty kilometres from the Roubaix velodrome, the situation became a little clearer when it was Roger De Vlaeminck's turn to suffer a puncture. By this time Eric Leman appeared to be weakening more and more.

An imperial Eddy Merckx decided it was time to take flight. He increased the pace even more and went clear. The Belgian

1970

champion wanted not only to distance De Vlaeminck and Leman, but also, and perhaps above all, to put Godefroot, Verbeeck and Janssen in their place.

In spite of three more punctures and a change of bike, Merckx arrived at the velodrome with more than five minutes in hand. The margin was even bigger than that of Gimondi in 1966, who with more than four minutes had realised, according to the statisticians, the best post-war performance.

At the finish while the winner was exhibiting a remarkable state of freshness, Roger De Vlaeminck cursed his luck and claimed: "If I had not punctured, Merckx would never have been able to drop me."

The winner had taken the race apart. Nevertheless several of the younger riders put up noticeable performances. Roger Rosiers finished eighth, Jean-Pierre Monseré, still only twenty one was an excellent tenth in spite of his three punctures, in what was sadly to be his only appearance in the event.

This Paris-Roubaix was, a veritable disaster for the French. The best of them, Raymond Poulidor, was thirteenth at nearly eleven minutes.

Some of them, such as Jean-Marie Leblanc who broke his frame or Alain Vasseur who crashed, punctured as well as having mechanical problems and could justly say that this was bad luck...but the others?

During the course of the following months, Eddy continued to dominate the international pelotons. During 1970, the Belgian grabbed a total of fifty two victories including a second Tour of Italy, a second Tour de France with eight stage wins, Flèche Wallonne and the Belgium Championship after a break of fifty kilometres...

1. Eddy MERCKX (Belgium)
   GS.Faemino
2. Roger DE VLAEMINCK (Belgium)
3. Eric LEMAN (Belgium)
4. André DIERICKX (Belgium)
5. Walter GODEFROOT (Belgium)
6. Frans VERBEECK (Belgium)
7. Jan JANSSEN (Holland)
8. Roger ROSIERS (Belgium)
9. Gerben KARSTENS (Holland)
10. Jean-Pierre MONSERE (Belgium)

Roger De Vlaeminck... the Dolphin.

Rosiers has just caught Eric De Vlaeminck.

Roger Rosiers
unapproachable

The 1971 season had hardly started, but the whole of cycling was in a state of shock. On the 15th March Jean-Pierre Monseré, who proudly wore the world champion's jersey died on a Belgian road close to Retie. Hit by a car going in the opposite direction, Monseré was killed instantly. Just before the accident, he had won the Tour of Andalucia, and his future looked bright. Sadly fate decided otherwise.

It was with this painful memory that Merckx, as soon as he started to turn the

The peloton led by Van Springel in front of
Janssen, Leman, Roger De Vlaeminck,
Merckx and Gimondi

pedals, began to crush the peloton again. The "Cannibal" successively won the
Tour of Sardinia, Paris-Nice, his fourth Milan-San Remo, the Het Volk in front of
Roger Rosiers and the Tour of Belgium. Only two setbacks, in the Tour of
Flanders and Ghent Wevelgem cooled his ardour a little.

As often, the Belgian champion arrived at Paris-Roubaix in confident mood in
spite of the long list of his habitual rivals led by the formidable De Vlaeminck
brothers, than Verbeeck, Godefroot, Janssen, Gimondi, Motta and Cyrille
Guimard, an excellent third in the Tour of Flanders.

For the one hundred and thirty nine starters, this sixty ninth edition of Paris-
Roubaix was, unlike the previous year, dusty. Six kilometres from Senlis the
Belgian Coulon decided to take flight. The first serious attempt
was started at Fresnoy-le-Grand when twelve men including
Gimondi and Godefroot rocketed off the front. Merckx could not

1971

tolerate this situation, he rounded up his troops and the movement was nullified nine kilometres later.

Immediately the Italian Crepaldi left in company with Catieau and Schepers. Soon after Alain Vasseur managed to make up the difference after a superb solitary effort. At Neuvilly the four leaders had a minute's lead over an already scattered bunch.

Twenty four men came up to them before the feeding zone at Valenciennes. At the exit to the town Gimondi tried an escape but a closed level crossing at the entrance to the Wallers-Arenberg section held up his progress which was then stopped completely by a first puncture.

At Hasnon, just before the two hundred kilometre mark, Jean Jourden escaped. Amazingly the first to come up to his wheel was none other than Gimondi! At Warlaing, six thousand metres further on, the "tandem" had an advantage of twenty five seconds, but this came to nothing as Jourden punctured twice and Gimondi once.

On the road to Nomain, twelve men dominated: Merckx, Spruyt, Van Springel, the De Vlaemincks, Leman, Gimondi, Motta, Janssens, Pintens, Jourden and Poulidor. Eric De Vlaeminck decided to take advantage of the help of his team-mates and went away by himself. Roger Rosiers, who had been slightly delayed by an incident, came through from the back and set off in the pursuit of the eldest of the De Vlaemincks. Nobody was able to take his wheel!

In just a few minutes Rosiers came up to De Vlaeminck and promptly dropped him. The man was ambitious for there were still twenty eight kilometres to cover before the stadium at Roubaix.

At Cysoing, Rosiers had increased his advantage to forty five seconds, then, ten kilometres from Roubaix, it went to over a minute. On this April day Rosiers was unapproachable. Finally he was victorious with a lead of one minute and twenty six seconds over a group of seven men composed of Van Springel, Basso, Janssen, Merckx, Leman, Roger De Vlaeminck and Gimondi, classed in that order.

Rosiers' attack was unstoppable and his victory did not astonish his followers as for two years he had been flirting with success in a major event. He had won this time in spite of two punctures and a crash. At the finish he said to the journalists surrounding him: "It was only at the velodrome that I believed in victory. I was thinking that Merckx or someone else would come up. After my puncture I could see that the pedals were going round easily and that I was feeling strong. In coming back to them I was using my big gear and kept it going in order to catch Eric De Vlaeminck. When he weakened I gave it everything I had."

Just before the start, Rosiers was confident because of his fifth place in the Tour of Belgium and assured some of his compatriots that he had never ridden so well and that apart from the eternal Merckx, he feared no one. Confidence was instilled into him even more since the beginning of the season as he had already received eight winner's bouquets.

Back in the bunch several riders had more than their share of bad luck. Godefroot lost all hope when following a puncture there was a delay in changing his wheel. As for Janssen, an excellent fourth, he could not give the best of himself over the cobbles. In fact the Dutchman with glasses was the victim of a crash before the start of the event. He finished in spite of an injection in the hand just before the start!

Finally Eddy Merckx, who suffered five punctures, was the first to sportingly recognise the superiority of Roger Rosiers who really on this day of April 18th 1971, flew over the cobblestones.

1971

Roger ROSIERS
(Belgium, 1946)

A durable competitor with a fast sprint who specialised in Paris-Roubaix and Bordeaux-Paris.

1967 : Flèche-Brabanconne
1968 : 2nd Amstel Gold Race
1970 : 2nd Het Volk, 3rd Bordeaux-Paris
1971 : Paris-Roubaix, 2nd Het Volk,
       3rd Amstel Gold Race
1972 : Tour of Luxembourg
1973 : Paris-Roubaix
1974 : 3rd Paris-Brussels
1977 : Three Days de La Panne
1978 : 2nd Bordeaux-Paris

1. Roger ROSIERS (Belgium)
   GS.Bic
2. Herman VAN SPRINGEL (Belgium)
3. Marino BASSO (Italy)
4. Jan JANSSEN (Holland)
5. Eddy MERCKX (Belgium)
6. Eric LEMAN (Belgium)
7. Roger DE VLAEMINCK (Belgium)
8. Felice GIMONDI (Italy)
9. Eric DE VLAEMINCK (Belgium)
10. Georges PINTENS (Belgium)

Roger Rosiers charges towards Roubaix.

M **L'ÉQUIPE**

LE QUOTIDIEN DU SPORT ET DE L'AUTOMOBILE

LUNDI 17 AVRIL 1972   27ᵉ ANNÉE — Nº 8086

Spécial lundi 1,20

Algérie, 0,90 dinar ; Allemagne, 1,20 D.M. ; Belgique-Luxembourg, 12 F.B. ; Espagne, 15 pesetas ; Grande-Bretagne, 10 pence Hollande, 1,30 florin ; Italie, 200 lires ; Maroc, 1,20 dirham ; Suisse, 1 F.S. ; Tunisie, 80 millimes.

Succès de la fusée De Vlaeminck

Roger De Vlaeminck a remporté un Paris-Roubaix de tradition, et même de tradition d'un lointain passé.

Le Belge a non seulement triomphé de tous ses adversaires, qu'il a franchement et irrésistiblement attaqués dans la traversée de l'« Enfer » mais il a résisté à des éléments défavorables qui ont constamment contrarié le déroulement de la course : le vent, d'abord, en plaine, puis ensuite le froid et les ondées qui ont rendu les routes et leurs accotements particulièrement dangereux.

La course fut lancée, dès la portion défoncée de la forêt d'Arenberg, par une échappée de Willy Van Malderghem et d'Alain Santy, qui devaient être rejoints et dépassés l'un après l'autre par Roger De Vlaeminck.

Si ce dernier a trouvé une consécration à la mesure de sa classe, Eddy Merckx, qui fut victime d'une chute, conserve pourtant son prestige intact.

Bien sûr, comme il fallait s'y attendre, les Belges ont envahi les premières places du classement ; et Raymond Poulidor est le seul Français intercalé dans les treize premiers.

Mais on doit aussi souligner la place honorable de Cyrille Guimard (14ᵉ) et le panache d'Alain Santy.   (Pages 2 à

PARIS - ROUBAIX

(Trophée CONFORAMA)

EST UNE ORGANISATION

L'ÉQUIPE et **Le Parisien**

The Gypsy's first one

Since his entry into the professional ranks in 1969, the observers were unanimous: if a Mr Paris-Roubaix existed, as he did in the heroic times under the name of Gaston Rebry, the only one in modern times it could possibly be was Roger De Vlaeminck.

In fact, on these Northern roads, the one who was already nicknamed "the Gypsy" perfectly combined his sharp sense of reading a race with his exceptional physical qualities. Moreover his low centre of gravity and his participation in top level cyclo-cross events greatly helped him ride the cobbles. Finally his thirst for victory and his eternal worry about bringing himself up to the level of the great Merckx in the classics, were all to work in his favour.

Van Springel leads the bunch from which Roger De Vlaeminck will shortly escape.

From that moment on, the 1972 edition, at the end of a difficult day, would fall into his pocket without anybody being able to prevent it. The riders struggled all day long against an adverse wind before finishing the event under an icy rain. Real cyclo-cross weather which De Vlaeminck liked so much.

The beginning of the race was marked by several crashes. In this way Frans Verbeeck, recent winner of the Het Volk, saw the end of his campaign, when on one of the first cobbled sections, a fall led to a broken collar bone. Eddy Merckx launched his big offensive at the feeding station at Valenciennes and went off in company with Peelman and Opdebeeck.

Jan Janssen was the first to understand the danger. The Dutchman caught the trio with ..the peloton on wheel. This trial run, even if it came to nothing, nevertheless permitted the "Cannibal" to get rid of some of the weaker men at the back. The leading **1972**

group were approaching the terrible Wallers-Arenberg section. From the entrance to the track, made slippery by the never ceasing rain, a monumental crash muddied the peloton. About forty men, including Eddy Merckx found themselves on the ground.

At the exit of the Arenberg forest, Roger De Vlaeminck tested his rivals. The rider from Eeklo escaped for a few moments but realised that the time was not really opportune and relaxed.

There remained seventy two kilometres to cover. Seventeen men, all the favourites except Eddy Merckx who although delayed, did not take too long in getting back, now formed the front group. A little later Willy Van Malderghem tried to profit from the rivalry of the stars. Alain Santy also seized the occasion and jumped on his wheel. At Marchiennes the two leaders were forty five seconds up and then two minutes at the exit to Coutiches, fifty kilometres from Roubaix.

The break was interesting as the Northern roads stimulated not only Van Malderghem, who had almost won the Four Days of Dunkirk the previous year, but also because Alain Santy was the local boy. Unfortunately for him, Santy, a little too fragile for this type of exercise was dropped thirty five kilometres from the velodrome.

Behind, Van Malderghem, Peelman, Rosiers, De Vlaeminck, Merckx and Poulidor organised the pursuit. After they crossed through Templeuve, Dierickx, Swerts, Van Springel, Hoban, Karstens, Ritter and Teirlinck joined them.

At Nomain, Van Malderghem was still resisting and still had one forty in hand. Just after, at Bachy, with only twenty three kilometres to go, Roger De Vlaeminck found his strength. The Gypsy had realised that his companions were not strong enough to being back Van Malderghem. The leader was only finally caught at the entrance to Cysoing after an adventure lasting fifty six kilometres!

From then on De Vlaeminck proved to be untouchable. Almost two minutes separated him from his first pursers at the Roubaix velodrome. Dierickx, in spite of five punctures, was second in front of Barry Hoban, Teirlinck, the astonishing Van Malderghem, Van Roosbroeck and Eddy Merckx.

The latter was especially disappointed with his seventh place, his worst in the event since 1967!

His crash at Arenberg, when he hit a tree, did not explain everything. The champion had only an ordinary day and did not succeed in dominating the bunch like he normally did.

Roger De Vlaeminck for his part added a new dimension to his career. Normally not very talkative at the finish, he this time spoke of his race at great length to anybody who wanted to listen, claiming that it was a big advantage to be among the principle favourites at the start.

Once again the French performance had verged on disaster, the only light being Poulidor who on his thirty sixth birthday finished a commendable tenth.

Gilbert Bellone from Southern France, who experienced an avalanche of punctures went home to the mild climate of his home town of Grasse unhappy. The harsh weather of the North was certainly not to his liking.

Finally Van Malderghem, in spite of being away for nearly sixty kilometres and an excellent fifth place had the greatest difficulty in getting to sleep that evening. The man was one of those classy riders who had quite simply decided to devote himself to the cause of his leaders.

For them opportunities were rare and occasions to win Paris-Roubaix unique.

1972

Roger DE VLAEMINCK
(Belgium, 1947)

Will always be known as "Mr Paris-Roubaix". A record four victories and nine podiums ... he was also one of the very few great cyclists to win cyclo-cross championships.

1968 : World Amateur Cyclo-Cross Champion
1969 : Belgian Champion, Het Volk
1970 : Liège-Bastogne-Liège
1971 : Flèche Wallonne
1972 : Paris-Roubaix, Tirreno-Adriatico
1973 : Milan-San Remo, Tirreno-Adriatico
1974 : Paris-Roubaix, Tour of Lombardy, Tirreno-Adriatrico
1975 : World Cyclo-Cross Champion, Paris-Roubaix, Zurich Championship, Tour of Switzerland, Tirreno-Adriatico, Criterium des As
1976 : Tour of Lombardy, Tirreno-Adriatico
1977 : Paris-Roubaix, Tour of Flanders, Tirreno-Adriatico
1978 : Milan-San Remo
1979 : Milan-San Remo, Het Volk
1981 : Belgian Champion, Paris-Brussels

1. Roger DE VLAEMINCK (Belgium) GS.Dreher
2. André DIERICKX (Belgium)
3. Barry HOBAN (Great Britain)
4. Willy TEIRLINCK (Belgium)
5. Willy VAN MALDERGHEM (Belgium)
6. Gustave VAN ROOSBROECK (Belgium)
7. Eddy MERCKX (Belgium)
8. Eddy PEELMAN (Belgium)
9. Ole RITTER (Denmark)
10. Raymond POULIDOR (France)

Eddy Merckx flies over the cobbles.

"Merckx above even Merckx"

"Merckx above even Merckx". The headline was spread across the front page of L'Equipe on Monday 16 April 1973. The day before, the Belgian champion had massacred his adversaries on the Northern cobbles. The verdict was without any appeal, for at the velodrome his immediate pursuers; the valiant Walter Godefroot and Roger Rosiers finished two minutes and twenty seconds down. As for Walter Planckaert, the fourth man home, the deficit went right up to more than seven minutes!

However, fifteen days before this seventy first edition of Paris-Roubaix, Merckx was said, as was so often the case, to be "finished".

In fact the champion, worried not to compromise his chances for Paris-Roubaix had retired on the fourth stage of the Tour of Belgium in a snow storm.

The man appeared to be a little annoyed by this persistent bad weather: "I held on to the limit of my strength. I have lived through some very trying moments but I have been so ground down that I cannot put up with such weather conditions..."

Since the start of the season, the Belgians had been dominating the main events. Ironically, only the Tour of Belgium fell to the Dane Lief Mortensen. Roger De Vlaeminck took his first Milan-San Remo and Eric Leman his third Tour of Flanders, in front of a new rider by the name of Freddy Maertens. Up until then, apart from what

1973

MERCKX AU-DESSUS DE MERCKX

Merckx a encore surpassé Merckx pour remporter son troisième Paris-Roubaix en solitaire. Il a forcé la décision à 45 kilomètres de l'arrivée, dans une traversée de l'Enfer hallucinante, avec des pavés gluants qui défiaient constamment l'équilibre et exigeaient une parfaite lucidité pour maîtriser tous les éléments de la course. Merckx, qui avait auparavant rejoint et dépassé Rosiers, resta

d'abord en tête en compagnie de Roger De Vlaeminck, le vainqueur de l'an dernier, mais sur une accélération en puissance il décrocha et écœura son dernier compagnon et augmenta implacablement son avance sur ses poursuivants : Godefroot et Rosiers, eux aussi spécialistes et anciens vainqueurs de l'épreuve. Malgré une chute, sans gravité, dans sa chevauchée majes-

tueuse, Eddy Merckx a terminé avec d'avance sur Godefroot et Rosiers, 7' Plankaert (4°) et Maertens, le jeune Belge, sur Verbeeck, Roger De Vlaeminck Springel et 11' 53" sur les trois premier çais, Delépine (9°), Poulidor (10°) et Pér

(Pages 14 à 16)

L'ÉQUIPE
Spécial lundi 1,20
LE QUOTIDIEN DU SPORT ET DE L'AUTOMOBILE
LUNDI 16 AVRIL 1973   28° ANNÉE — N° 8.196
Algérie, 0,90 dinar ; Allemagne, 1,40 D.M ; Belgique-Luxembourg, 12 F.B. ; Espagne, 15 pesetas ; Grande-Bretagne, 12 pence ; Hollande, 1,50 florin ; Italie, 250 lires ; Maroc, 1,20 dirham ; Suisse, 1,10 F.S. ; Tunisie, 90 millimes.

ILS ONT SEULEMENT OUBLIÉ DE GAGNER.

MERCKX, DÉCIDÉMENT INSATIABLE, REJOINT DANS LES ANNALES, LAPIZE, REBRY ET VAN LOOY EN EMPOCHANT UN TROISIÈME ET DERNIER SUCCÈS ROUBAISIEN EN 1973. ON LE DIT ALORS SUR LE DÉCLIN MAIS EN CE JOUR D'AVRIL IL PARAPHE EN SOLITAIRE UNE PRESTIGIEUSE TROISCENTIÈME VICTOIRE.

33

Roger Rosiers and Walter Godefroot try to resist.

for him were minor successes in the Tour of Sardinia and the Het Volk, Merckx made a mess of the classics after withdrawing from Milan-San Remo because of tonsillitis and a third place in the Tour of Flanders.

Aggravated by what he considered to be an average start to the season, the "Cannibal" reacted just before Paris-Roubaix by successfully rounding up Ghent-Wevelgem then, four days later, the Amstel Gold Race, finishing alone three minutes before the durable Frans Verbeeck.

At Chantilly, four men stood out in the forecasts: Merckx, of course, Van Springel, Godefroot and Verbeeck. This time Roger de Vlaeminck was not among the favourites, for a crash in Ghent-Wevelgem left him with twenty five stitches in his arm.

On the list of one hundred and twenty eight starters, the presence of Luis Ocana seemed strange. Following the advice of Maurice de Muer, the Spaniard, recent winner of the Tour of the Basque Country, had only come here to take several points of reference in view of the Tour de France that he was going to win after a first outing on the cobbles!

Finally, in the town of Nieuwpoort, everyone was attentively following the progress of Freddy Maertens. The twenty one year old Belgian, in his first season with the upper ranks, had been accumulating good performances: second in Kuurne-Brussels-Kuurne and the Tour of Flanders, then a brilliant eighth in the Amstel Gold Race.

The first man to go clear was called Vermeulen. He stayed in the lead until the ninety fifth kilometre. The second, more serious attempt got off the ground about twenty kilometres from the first cobbled sectors of Neuvilly.

Raymond Riotte attacked soon followed by another Frenchman, Charley Rouxel.

At Neuvilly the pair had a lead of twenty seconds on the first bunch where LeMond, Godefroot and Gimondi had just been delayed by a crash. At one hundred and sixty eight kilometres, Rouxel punctured a tyre. Riotte, now alone, soon realised that it was useless to brave the wrath of the peloton and gave up!

The crossing of Wallers-Arenberg provoked a selection accentuated by several crashes which broke the group up. In this way Zoetemelk went over the top of his bike to land head first in a pool of mud.

Van Maldergham, who remembered his trip the year before, came out of the "trench" with a lead of ten seconds over a group of sixteen.

On the cobbles of Bouvignies, Roger Rosiers relaunched the movement. This time a vigilant Merckx could not allow another "coup" as happened in 1971. He quickly got on to his wheel in company with Roger De Vlaeminck. On the cobblestones of Coutiches, Rosiers dropped off.

The situation seemed clear. Merckx and De Vlaeminck "led the dance" from then on and were followed at two hundred metres by Godefroot, Van Springel and Leman, then further back were Guimard, Verbeeck and Maertens, held up by a crash.

Forty four kilometres from Roubaix and Merckx decided to rid himself of the Gypsy. Roger's injured arm was causing him to suffer on the difficult cobbled sectors and he found himself obliged to lift off a little. De Vlaeminck would only finish seventh, nearly eight minutes down on the winner.

In spite of a crash Merckx never stopped increasing his lead. Behind him, Godefroot and Rosiers were putting up a fight. The two former victors were going to contest second place.

The Belgians were monopolising, once again, the first few places. The first "non Belgian" according to the expression in vogue, Regis Delepine finished ninth, just before Raymond Poulidor!

At the velodrome De Vlaeminck spoke about his injury: "I had no illusions. In a normal race I would have been able to hold on much longer, but in Paris-Roubaix you have to be in perfect form and above all intact, which in my case I wasn't. From the first cobbles I suffered with my arm, with the stitches and as the wound had not healed over, you can't expect miracles..."

Merckx, on the other hand, was enjoying his triumph: "This Paris-Roubaix was harder than those that I had won in 1968 and 1970. When I went away with De Vlaeminck fifty six kilometres from Roubaix I had to do all the work. He was complaining about his injured arm. I left him without accelerating. There remained forty four kilometres for me to cover alone."

The world hour record holder inscribed his name in the record books alongside the other triple winners: Lapize, Rebry and Van Looy.

All of the observers had been impressed by the demonstration of Merckx. Jacques Goddet was best placed in his race director's car: "I found him sublime, the Merckx of his third Paris-Roubaix," he wrote the next day in L'Equipe. "He decided everything, led everything and succeeded in everything. He detached himself from his last opponent, Roger De Vlaeminck, smoothly and without violence. Like that, by asphyxiation, by disillusionment. Everything seemed so simple."

Merckx celebrated his third victory. What followed was just as good, for a week later he carried off Liège-Bastogne-Liège, then the Tour of Spain, the Tour of Italy, Paris-Brussels and the Grand Prix des Nations.

The correct sort of balance sheet for a Merckx, according to some, "on the decline."

1973

1. Eddy MERCKX (Belgium)
   GS.Molteni
2. Walter GODEFROOT (Belgium)
3. Roger ROSIERS (Belgium)
4. Walter PLANCKAERT (Belgium)
5. Freddy MAERTENS (Belgium)
6. Frans VERBEECK (Belgium)
7. Roger DE VLAEMINCK (Belgium)
8. Herman VAN SPRINGEL (Belgium)
9. Régis DELEPINE (France)
10. Raymond POULIDOR (France)

1974 : Roger De Vlaeminck confirms...

For once, it is rather rare to have to underline it, the laurels changed sides, for the Belgians did not dominate the early part of the 1974 season.

The top team was French, the Merciers swept all before them: Paris-Nice with Zoetemelk in front of Alain Santy, the Tour of Flanders mastered by the elegant Cees Bal, Ghent-Wevelgem won in a sprint by Barry Hoban, the Amstel Gold Race which revealed Gerry Knetemann and again Zoetemelk dominator of the Catalan week.

Louis Caput's team wanted to continue in the same way on the Northern roads in spite of the opposition of the robust specialists.

Among them, in the first rank, Eddy Merckx appeared to be a little irritated. Since the beginning of the season, the Belgian champion had only managed four wins, hardly worthy of his standing: the Laigueglia Trophy and three stages in Paris-Nice. So suspicion was in the air when Merckx said that he would be in at the kill at Roubaix.

As well as "the Cannibal", the older riders monopolised the front pages of the dailies. It was true that on the cobbles those like Godefroot, Verbeeck, De

De Vlaeminck in company with Merckx before taking off alone.

Vlaeminck, Leman or Van Springel would always be difficult to out-manoeuvre. Several young ones were also "pointing their noses to the horizon". In this way the notoriety of Freddy Maertens was beginning to spread beyond the frontiers of the kingdom, especially since the "Montjuich Affair", when during the 1973 World Championships he was accused of the sacrilege of betraying Merckx.

Other notables were: Marc Demeyer, Hennie Kuiper and above all Francesco Moser who were all climbing quickly in the cycling hierarchy. The Italian was the youngest of the "Moser clan" with Aldo, the eldest of the family, who was the notable winner of the Grand Prix des Nations in 1959 in front of Roger Rivière!

Twenty three years old, Francesco was for the first time competing in the Queen of the Classics. For several years already Italy had eyes only for him. However, the world champion, Felice Gimondi was not in the race. After his victory in Milan-San Remo, he planned to take part in the other spring classics but a dispute with the organisers of the Tour of Flanders caused him to strike it from his initial programme. Without this necessary curtain-raiser his chances in "La Pascale" were greatly reduced.

The one hundred and seventy six competitors were going to encounter forty nine kilometres of cobbles in spite of cutting out the famous section through the Arenberg forest.

From the start, the Frenchman Michel Demore showed himself to be the most active. After several attempts he went clear at the eighty seventh kilometre and was only to capitulate at the exit to St Quentin.

1974

As the first cobbled sections of Neuvilly came into sight, the tension mounted in the first ranks of the bunch. The pace went up and this provoked several crashes. So at Busigny, Walter Godefroot found himself on the ground along with Cael and Misac. The first section left just forty men in the lead. Moser had already tried his luck on the cobbles at Solesmes. But everything came rapidly together again before a new attempt by his compatriot Ercole Gualazzini who got away in company with Joseph Spruyt, a team-mate of Merckx.

The pair possessed a lead of twenty seconds when, a little farther, a closed level crossing ended the attempt.

At Bouvignies, an unruly Moser tried again. Merckx did not appreciate the gesture and immediately brought him to heel.

These various exchanges were fatal to the hopes of several dozen riders - Van Linden, Sibille, Zoetemelk and Fussien all said good-bye to the front of the race. At the entrance to Coutiches, Merckx changed a wheel but quickly got back to the front in company with Verbeeck, a previous puncture victim.

Just before Templeuve, twenty nine kilometres from the velodrome, Moser went on the offensive again along with Walter Godefroot. Merckx found himself a prisoner in the chasing group of twenty who seemed reluctant to help the world hour record holder to chase.

The leading pair started to build up their lead up until Godefroot's flat tyre. So Moser was by himself twenty five kilometres from Roubaix with fifty five seconds in hand on the chasing group which Roger De Vlaeminck had managed to get clear.

The Gypsy, being the fine strategist that he was, could see that he would have to very quickly catch the young runaway who seemed to have the bit between his teeth. His decision was certainly the wisest as behind the group had broken up completely and after a puncture to Maertens there were no more than four of them chasing: Merckx, Leman, Dierickx and Demeyer.

At the front the pursuit match was reaching its climax. De Vlaeminck was slowly closing the gap until Moser's puncture at Bachy. In spite of a very quick change of wheel the Italian only managed to keep one hundred metres of his lead. It was not enough to prevent the return of the champion from Eeklo, who latched on to his wheel with eleven kilometres to go. The final showdown seemed uncertain as several days previously the young Francesco had beaten Roger De Vlaeminck at the finish of the Tout of Calabria. The man from the other side of the Alps still seemed fresh but the Belgian who was "playing at home" really wanted to achieve his double two years after his first win!

Suddenly, on a corner, Moser slipped and fell. De Vlaeminck couldn't have asked for more and went away alone. Francesco's "spring was broken". He was now in the position of outsider and his fluid pedalling style was now broken.

In front of a record crowd, Roger De Vlaeminck penetrated the stadium with fifty seven seconds in hand on Moser and nearly a minute and a half on the quartet composed of Marc Demeyer, Eddy Merckx, Eric Leman and André Dierickx.

The Flemish spectators who had come to see one of their countrymen win exulted even more than the Italians who had discovered an exciting new talent. According to them, the young "Checco" would certainly have won if it had not been for his puncture. The old hand De Vlaeminck insisted that he would have no trouble dropping his rival long before the velodrome.

Directly after the finish Merckx said that he was not too disappointed at the way things had turned out. He simply regretted the fact that once again he had to bear the weight of the race on his shoulders. However, after a little reflection he admitted that he was really incapable of going any faster.

Memories of his fourth place were softened with a new double of the Tour de France and the Tour of Italy, augmented by a Tour of Switzerland and a World championship!

1974

1. Roger DE VLAEMINCK (Belgium)
   GS.Brooklyn
2. Francesco MOSER (Italy)
3. Marc DEMEYER (Belgium)
4. Eddy MERCKX (Belgium)
5. Eric LEMAN (Belgium)
6. André DIERICKX (Belgium)
7. Freddy MAERTENS (Belgium)
8. Herman VAN SPRINGEL (Belgium)
9. Herman VRIJDERS (Belgium)
10. Michel PERIN (France)

Jean-Pierre Danguillaume resists
in company with Hermans,
an 'off balance' Perin and ... Francesco
Moser !

Roger Swerts in trouble.

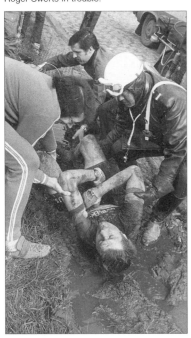

Paris-Roubaix
in the middle of the
De Vlaeminck years ...

Since the beginning of the 1975 season Eddy Merckx's had dominated the scene. The previous year he had not been able to snatch a single classic, this time the Belgian had managed a full house, by first of all beating Moser on the via Roma in the Milan - San Remo, then Maertens in the Amstel Gold Race and above all the brave Frans Verbeeck, the only one able to stay with him over the last one hundred kilometres of the Tour of Flanders.

In fact, only Ghent-Wevelgem escaped him, to the great joy of Freddy Maertens.

Naturally, the world champion was more than ever the great favourite of Paris-Roubaix. Facing him was first of all Francesco Moser who had been recently demonstrating his good form. The Italian wanted not only to win a fine victory which would promote him from the ranks of the hopefuls to the level of a confirmed champion but also to make people forget about the performances of his "enemy" Baronchelli.

The Belgians had, as was their custom, monopolised the first places in the Tour of Flanders. The same men would do the same over the Northern cobbles, riders such as the ambitious Maertens, Dierickx, Walter Planckaert, Demeyer and the older Rosiers, Godefroot and Van Springel.

Merckx at the head of things on the cobbles
in front of De Vlaeminck, Dierickx
and Demeyer

As for Roger De Vlaeminck who had acquired the art of preparing in secret and being present on D-Day, it was said that he was suffering from bronchitis. In the Tour of Flanders and Ghent-Wevelgem he certainly did not shine. However, these were not really "his" races.

In the French camp their hopes remained more than ever limited. Poulidor for his sixteenth participation seemed to be ready but the hope was for that of Cyrille Guimard. The joker in the French pack was called Bernard Hinault, another Breton, newly arrived on the scene but apparently very ambitious and who had aroused much interest with some of his performances.

One hundred and fifty riders started from Chantilly under a covered sky. The bunch dawdled and the first few kilometres served only to warm up riders. Only a crash at Noyon got the crowd going a bit, Maertens, Pollentier and Baronchelli were the principal victims. The Italian suffered injuries to his chin and retired. This hardly gave him the taste to come back very often to these roads which were nothing like the Dolomites.

As his home town of St Quentin came into sight, José Catieau decided to drop the peloton. Rapidly, a few men joined him. The movement failed. It was no doubt too early to embark on such adventures.

On this 13 April 1975, if a few rays of sunshine had poked through the clouds, the rain over the previous few days had flooded the first cobbled sector at Neuvilly. Trying to get through there was a disaster, the motorbikes fell, the cars became stuck, the peloton exploded and already the number of retirements started to build up.

At the exit to Neuvilly, six men had managed to avoid all the

1975

After his puncture, Eddy Merckx comes up to the wheels of his last adversaries ...before attacking...

traps: Dierickx, Van Sweevelt, Maertens, Karstens, Delepine and Godefroot. A few moments later Merckx, De Vlaeminck, Van Sweevelt and Demeyer came up to the front. Further on at the entrance to Valenciennes, Swerts, Catieau, Moser, De Cauwer, Rosiers and Dewitte also latched on. At ninety kilometres to the finish, the others, all the others five minutes down, were already beaten. Just after Valenciennes, Marc Demeyer, the faithful team-mate of Freddy Maertens, started his usual work of wearing down the others in favour of his leader and went clear alone. In the Arenberg section, where Demeyer had a lead of fifty seconds, Merckx tried in vain to escape the vigilance of his companions.

The leading group was still substantial but the progressive elimination started at Wandignies, Guimard crashed and provoked the loss of Rosiers, Catieau, De Cauwer, Dewitte and Karstens.

Just before Coutiches, Demeyer after a "fugue" of forty kilometres, was caught. The Belgian was certainly tired but he would not lay down and attacked again several times.

This obstinacy saw the end of Bach, Demeyer, he again, went off the front. This time against all expectations Maertens and Moser were dropped.

From then on, there were only four of them in with a chance: Roger De Vlaeminck, who had been a little forgotten about, André Dierickx, Eddy Merckx and this devil of a man....... Marc Demeyer.

Merckx seemed to be the freshest when only eight kilometres to go to the velodrome a flat tyre stopped him. At the end of a brief but intensive pursuit he rejoined his former companions on the hill at Hem. Straight away he tried to

surprise them but the wily De Vlaeminck was watching him closely.

A sprint was inevitable. The Belgian public, always numerous at the stadium were over the moon when it became apparent that the decision was to be contested by four of their countrymen. The Merckx supporters were the noisiest. It seemed that his success was wished for by all. It would make him the first man to win four times. It was an historic moment.

The world champion launched the sprint on the back straight. On his wheel Roger De Vlaeminck buckled but did not crack, and in the very last few metres drew level and then finally passed him.

The Gypsy picked up his third Paris-Roubaix in four years and joined Lapize, Rebry, Van Looy...and Merckx who in an instant had lost everything!

The champion from Eeklo was voluble: "This morning I took the start in order to win...as I always do in Paris-Roubaix and the race turned out as expected. Merckx led out the sprint with three hundred metres to go. I was on his wheel and I jumped in the home straight. It's nice to win...especially when Merckx is second!"

For his part the world hour record holder was just as disappointed as he had been the previous year. He simply said that he had made no mistakes and cursed his puncture so close to the finish.

Finally, the performance of Marc Demeyer made a great impression on the followers who simply regretted that the man slipped to easily into the role of "domestique". They hoped that this Paris-Roubaix would make him think..

1975

1. Roger DE VLAEMINCK (Belgium)
   GS.Brooklyn
2. Eddy MERCKX (Belgium)
3. André DIERICKX (Belgium)
4. Marc DEMEYER (Belgium)
5. Francesco MOSER (Italy)
6. Freddy MAERTENS (Belgium)
7. Roger SWERTS (Belgium)
8. Walter GODEFROOT (Belgium)
9. Guido VAN SWEEVELT (Belgium)
10. Gerben KARSTENS (Holland)

...and failing by a few centimetres at the velodrome !

L'ÉQUIPE

LE QUOTIDIEN DU SPORT ET DE L'AUTOMOBILE   2 F

LUNDI 12 AVRIL 1976   31ᵉ ANNÉE - N° 9.313

pas été sans ce
que Narbonne n'a élimin.
par un drop de Maso. Romans a dû son
salut devant Aurillac (18-15) à un essai de Servien
(auteur des 18 points romanais) dans les dernières

mais Romeu, qui fut son meilleur
joueur, souffre d'une fracture de la mâchoire.
(Pages 12 et 13)

DEMEYER N'A PAS VOLÉ SA RÉUSSITE

Libéré par la chute de son leader, Freddy Maertens, Marc Demeyer a relevé le défi, alors que son équipe Flandria avait exercé une pression permanente durant 120 kilomètres. Le Belge appartenait au commando de pointe qui avait pris d'assaut la piste du vélodrome de Roubaix. Roger De Vlaeminck était entré en tête, suivi de Demeyer, de Francesco Moser et du champion du monde Kuiper. Roger De Vlaeminck, très décidé à s'attribuer le record des victoires, manœuvrait à la manière d'un pistard accompli, mais avait sous-estimé la violence du vent qui soufflait dans la dernière ligne droite. C'est alors que Francesco Moser, plongeant en haut du dernier virage, s'élançait vers une victoire italienne, mais Demeyer surgissait entre les deux vainqueurs présumés, passant De Vlaeminck désemparé et repoussant l'assaut du champion d'Italie (notre photo). Marc Demeyer n'avait pas volé sa réussite, à l'issue d'une longue randonnée de 280 kilomètres dans la grande tradition de Paris-Roubaix. Bien que le Trophée BNP, retardé par des incidents hors parcours, ait bénéficié du soleil, les traîtrises de la route n'ont pas épargné les concurrents : Maertens ne fut pas la seule victime de marque, Godefroot, très fort, eut aussi sa part de malchance et Poulidor a battu pour son 17ᵉ Paris-Roubaix le record des crevaisons. Les Français ont fait la course, d'abord Talbourdet, Boulas, Martinez, puis Sibille et enfin Jean-Pierre Danguillaume (8ᵉ), qui... les meilleurs avec... Poulidor ... le destin.

(... 4)
... et Chr. ROCHARD)

● ATHLÉTISME

La troisième du P.U.C.

Troisième victoire du P.U.C. depuis la renaissance du relais A travers Paris en 1973. Deuxième place à l'A.S. P.T.T. de Bordeaux.
(Page 11)

● AUTOMOBILE

Stuck en F. 2, Hunt en F. 1

Hans Stuck vainqueur de la première course de F. 2 de la saison, à Hockenheim ; mais c'est René Arnoux (2ᵉ) qui marque les points du Championnat d'Europe ; Tambay 3ᵉ. Débuts prometteurs du moteur Renault. A Silverstone, en F. 1, c'est James Hunt qui s'est imposé avec facilité.
(Pages 15 et 16)

● ESCRIME

La Suisse à la pointe de l'épée

The devilish performance of Marc Demeyer

Tuesday 19 January 1982. At about ten o'clock a brief communiqué appeared on the teleprinters: 'The Belgian Champion Marc Demeyer has just died of a heart attack.'

The message was laconic, the news terrible. Who would really have been able to believe in the premature death of this colossus of thirty one?

In the morning he had ridden one hundred kilometres in company with Luc De Smet, then went to collect his new material from the team manager Albert De Kimpe.

After two thin years in 1980 and 1981, when fate had already struck him down (appendicitis just before the 1980 Tour de France and an injury to the achilles tendon at the start of the following season), he seemed happy to begin again in the Splendor team. Thanks to his immense build, Marc Demeyer had this time to lead out the Planckaert brothers in the sprint.

Demeyer was instrumental in numerous victories of his friend Freddy Maertens and, in spite of his obvious qualities, he was quite happy to adopt the role of the model team man.

Sometimes when his team captain was no longer in a position to win, he had the talent to stand in for him. In this way he won Paris-Brussels in 1974 in front of Roger De Vlaeminck and Roger Rosiers, two stages in the Tour de France, and above all this famous Paris-Roubaix in 1976.

Already in 1975 his skill on the cobblestones had not passed unnoticed. The great Marc had been away for fifty kilometres before finishing fourth. This performance perhaps decided him to at last ride for his own account on the Northern roads. The success of Maertens in Ghent-Wevelgem just a few days before, and especially his crash on one of the cobbled sectors after Neuvilly finally convinced him.

At the start of 1976, Eddy Merckx had just picked up his seventh Milan-San Remo, his last classic, but the war between Freddy Maertens and Roger De Vlaeminck was even more in everyone's minds.

The Flemish pair neutralised each other in the Tour of Flanders and offered the victory to Walter Planckaert on a plate who out sprinted Francesco Moser and Marc Demeyer.

The start of this seventy fourth Paris-Roubaix was more lively than expected. A demonstration held up the start for an hour, only the negotiating talent of Jacques Goddet avoided the worst and the four flat tyres of Felix Levitan's car was the only noticeable incident. This would be a day of protests for the workers of Rhône-Poulenc at St Quentin and at Trith-St-Léger those of Usinor in their turn protested. The beginning of the race was favourable to the French. Three of them; Talbourdet, Boulas and Martinez, paraded themselves at the front of the race with notably ten minutes lead at Noyon. But this proved to be insufficient as they were brought back at Neuvilly.

In this area, as usual, the race really started. About forty riders were still together. Just after, Merckx and Maertens suffered accidents. The latter was in despair for once success escaped him on these very inhospitable roads. From then on Marc Demeyer had carte blanche. However, his task was not very easy for Roger De Vlaeminck really wanted to put the mark of his supremacy on the race so as to confirm his title of "Mr Paris-Roubaix". He launched two of his team mates into the attack: Johan Demuynck and Marcello Osler. These two passed through Valenciennes and then Wallers-Arenberg in the lead before being caught at Marchiennes where Guy Sibille tried his chance. For thirty five kilometres the man from Marseilles was alone in **1976**

Marc DEMEYER
(Belgium, 1950-1982)

A good rider who was mainly content to play a team worker's role for Freddy Maertens, but he was also capable of seizing the chance for an occasional victory.

1972 : Grand Prix d'Isbergues
1974 : Paris-Brussels, Grand Prix Cerami, 3rd Paris-Roubaix
1975 : Tour of Flanders
1976 : Paris-Roubaix, 3rd Tour of Flanders
1977 : 2nd Paris-Brussels
1979 : 2nd Tour of Flanders, 3rd Zurich Championship
1980 : 2nd Paris-Brussels

Left:
De Vlaeminck leads in front of Walter Planckaert, Dierickx, Maertens, Catieau, Godefroot, Swerts, Van Sweevelt.

Marc Demeyer still playing the team mate after Freddy Maerten's crash.

the lead. Just after Templeuve, the frisky Jean-Pierre Danguillaume, took over from his team mate, but De Vlaeminck was literally unleashed.

Thirty one kilometres from the velodrome he launched the offensive, only four men managed to stay on his wheel: Marc Demeyer, Francesco Moser, Hennie Kuiper and Walter Godefroot.

Eddy Merckx, tired after changing bikes five times and as many pursuits, was not there. After the race, he confessed that on this Sunday he simply was not strong enough to go with the best.

On the hill at Bachy, Walter Godefroot, who according to his own words, 'flitted over the cobbles' found himself eliminated by a puncture. For De Vlaeminck the plan was working marvellously.

In theory, he was the strongest in the sprint, and apparently the freshest. The Gypsy had no trouble in suppressing the impulses of Kuiper and Moser and confidently waited for the ultimate rush for victory. As well as preventing any attacks and to physiologically impress the others he led over the last few kilometres at a very hot pace. Naturally he was the first on the track and visibly too sure of himself, he led out the sprint like a debutante.

Francesco Moser was the first to try to get past him, but finally Marc Demeyer emerged very quickly and won it in front of Moser, De Vlaeminck and Kuiper!

At the velodrome before this unexpected result the spectators were dumbfounded. However, the Roubaix public rapidly recovered and fervently welcomed the success of this Demeyer whose bravery and self-denial were well

It is close to the final act. De Vlaeminck in front of Demeyer and further back, Moser.

known.

Marc was happy: "As much as if Freddy had won", he said as he got off his bike. That says everything!

On the other hand, the unexpected outcome of the race was very difficult for De Vlaeminck to follow. The man, often impassive, this time mumbled a few words before going off alone to the showers: "They stayed on my wheel for twenty kilometres. I sprinted badly because I was nervous, but I was strong."

Godefroot was raging about his bad luck: "I was in a state of grace. It's even more of a pity. I am thirty years old and I am sure I will never find myself in such favourable circumstances again. The tube that I punctured had been drying out in my cellar for ten years..."

Several young riders performed well, in this way, Jan Raas a young Dutchman with glasses, just like Jan Janssen, in only his second Paris-Roubaix managed the luxury of finishing seventh on Eddy Merckx's wheel.

On another tack it was interesting to note that the first seven in this superb edition were, or would be in the near future, winners of the event: Demeyer, Moser, De Vlaeminck, Kuiper, Godefroot, Merckx and Raas.

For Marc Demeyer, the rest of the season must have been excellent, for his friend Freddy was just a few months later to put on his first rainbow jersey at Ostuni, just one of his fifty four wins in the course of the season.

The inseparable trio Maertens-Demeyer-Pollentier lived through some happy days.

1976

1. Marc DEMEYER (Belgium) GS.Flandria-Velda
2. Francesco MOSER (Italy)
3. Roger DE VLAEMINCK (Belgium)
4. Hennie KUIPER (Holland)
5. Walter GODEFROOT (Belgium)
6. Eddy MERCKX (Belgium)
7. Jan RAAS (Holland)
8. Jean-Pierre DANGUILLAUME (France)
9. Willy TEIRLINCK (Belgium)
10. Frans VERBEECK (Belgium)

De Vlaeminck, The Incomparable....

At the beginning of the year 1977, Albert Bouvet was seriously worried. During his traditional reconnaissance of the route in January, the eternal 'last French winner of the Paris-Tours' was astounded that the Roads Department had again laid tarmac on several precious kilometres of cobbles in the Templeuve area.

In order to find several more thousand metres of bad roads at the end of the route, the start of the Paris-Roubaix had to be transferred from Chantilly to Compiègne. This permitted the exploitation of some new and unknown sectors between Orchies, Landas, Saméon, Aix, Mouchin and Bachy.

On the roads, the rivalry between Freddy Maertens and Roger De Vlaeminck attained its climax. Maertens with the rainbow jersey on his back had arrived at his peak. The champion had first of all lifted the Laigueglia Trophy, then the Tour of Sardinia, the Het Volk and Paris-Nice. A real Merckx-type

achievement.

As for the Gypsy, he had won his sixth Tirreno-Adriatico and the Tour of Flanders. This success had caused a lot of ink to flow as with sixty kilometres to go, Merckx was alone in the lead. Two men, the inseparable enemies, Maertens and De Vlaeminck came up to his wheel and dropped him.

Suddenly, at the bottom of the Koppenberg, Freddy's brother gave a new bike to the world champion. It was an illicit move. No matter what happened he would be disqualified but he chose panache and did more than his fair share of the work up until the finish where he did not dispute the Gypsy's victory!

At the finish Roger, with his bouquet in his hand, mundanely said: "I do not care what people might think. When everything is over and forgotten, it is my name and my name alone that will remain engraved on the records of the Tour of Flanders..." and to conclude Roger said that he would meet up with Maertens on "his" Northern roads.

According to the specialists this bitter rivalry could benefit a third person like the Dutch champion, Jan Raas, who was climbing very quickly in the hierarchy. At the beginning of the season the Dutchman took his first classic: Milan-San Remo, then in his stride he added the Amstel Gold Race to it.

Godefroot, Dierickx, Rosiers, Merckx, Demeyer and Moser were the other outsiders. The French such as they were, limited their hopes to Danguillaume, Sibille, excellent in the Tour of Flanders and...to Poulidor!

The legs of the one hundred and forty nine starters only warmed up slowly for nothing serious happened during the first few hours of the race. As always the scramble started as the first cobbles of Neuvilly came into view, where a monumental crash took place. Moneyron slipped and took several favourites down with him: Raas, Moser, Rosiers and Dierickx.

Merckx was certainly not as fresh as he used to be in his best days but his experience saved him from this incident. It allowed him to be the first onto the cobbles at Neuvilly.

A little later at Montrecourt twenty six men formed the front group. A dozen kilometres further on, another twenty joined these leading riders. The winner was obviously going to come from among them as the next pursuers were already three minutes adrift.

At the head of the race the attacks were coming thick and fast. Marc Demeyer was the first to shake the pack. Then Merckx imitated him at Wattines but in vain. Crashes and punctures thinned out the ranks. Sibille, Dierickx, Walter Planckaert, Moser, Thévenet then especially Freddy Maertens (two punctures, one crash) and Rosiers (five punctures!) were the principal victims.

At Mouchin, about thirty kilometres from the end, twenty two riders were at the front. Everyone was on their toes, all the men knew each other and were watching each other. Van Springel attempted an adventure at Nomain before being swept up by Demeyer who was preparing the 'putsch' for Maertens. But the latter did not manage to create the hoped for difference.

At the end of the cobbled sector, Roger De Vlaeminck as a fine strategist, escaped and started his acrobatic number. As usual the Gypsy flew over the hard bits and the twenty five kilometres which separated him from the Roubaix velodrome were no worry to him.

Only Francesco Moser, who had just rejoined after a puncture, reacted. But this devil of a Gypsy, in his usual stretched out position, was inspired. On these roads which he held in the greatest affection, nobody managed to regain a metre from him.

Under the red kite Willy Teirlinck escaped to snatch second place from Freddy Maertens who was third at one minute and thirty nine seconds.

After his failure in 1976, Roger De Vlaeminck had managed to set the record straight: "Yes, a fourth victory in Paris-Roubaix, that is something wonderful. When I attacked I quickly opened

Roger DE VLAEMINCK
& PARIS-ROUBAIX

1969 : 5th
1970 : 2nd
1971 : 7th
1972 : 1st
1973 : 7th
1974 : 1st
1975 : 1st
1976 : 3rd
1977 : 1st
1978 : 2nd
1979 : 2nd
1981 : 2nd
1982 : 6th

1977

Roger at work...

a gap and I did not panic. However, this was not my best Paris-Roubaix, last year when Demeyer beat me, I was even stronger still"

Merckx, eleventh in his last Paris-Roubaix was full of praise for his great rival :"I have never seen that before. Roger slipped over the cobbles as if he knew exactly where each cobblestone was."

However, not all of the followers appreciated the way the race had been run, they thought that behind De Vlaeminck the pursuit was not very lively. So Jacques Goddet declared the next day in L'Equipe that: "I never liked this bunch of defeatists. There was only the vanquished behind the exterminating angel. The victory of De Vlaeminck was worth more than that." But that, as always in such a case, could certainly not have worried the winner.

Poulidor, forty one years and two days old, finished twelfth on the wheel of Merckx and before Moser. His last appearance on these Northern roads had permitted him to finish the best Frenchman. The fact was depressing.

The young Bernard Hinault did not finish but two days later at Wevelgem, the bunch was going to discover its new boss...

1977

1. Roger DE VLAEMINCK (Belgium)
   GS.Brooklyn
2. Willy TEIRLINCK (Belgium)
3. Freddy MAERTENS (Belgium)
4. Ronald DE WITTE (Belgium)
5. Piet VAN KATWIJK (Holland)
6. Jan RAAS (Holland)
7. Willem PEETERS (Belgium)
8. Dietrich THURAU (Germany)
9. Herman VAN SPRINGEL (Belgium)
10. Hennie KUIPER (Holland)

Ramirez sans problèmes

Le Mexicain Raul Ramirez s'est logiquement adjugé le Tournoi de Monte-Carlo en battant en finale le Tchécoslovaque Thomas Smid (6-3, 6-3, 6-4). Une rencontre assez quelconque au cours de laquelle le Mexicain, qui remportait ainsi son premier grand tournoi de la saison, ne connut guère de problèmes pour mettre à la raison la révélation de ce tournoi. Samedi, en demi-finales, Smid s'était imposé à Barazzutti, visiblement hors de forme (6-3, 6-1). De son côté, Ramirez avait éliminé l'Américain Vitas Gerulaitis (8-3, 4-6, 7-6).

(Page 15)

COUPE : ÇA CONTINUE POUR LES BASTIAIS

Après les durs efforts fournis pour se qualifier devant les Grasshoppers de Zurich en Coupe de l'U.E.F.A., on attendait Bastia au virage de la Coupe de France. Devant Monaco, en match aller des quarts de finale, les hommes de Cahuzac ont remporté une victoire méritée (2-1) qui ne les met cependant pas à l'abri d'une éventuelle élimination au terme du match retour, demain soir, à Monaco. Les Corses ont longtemps mené 2-0 avant de concéder au Monégasque Moizan le but qui remet tout en question. Il est de plus en plus probable que le match aller de la finale de la Coupe de l'U.E.F.A. Bastia - P.S.V. aura lieu le 26 avril courant au stade de Furiani. La décision devrait être officialisée aujourd'hui. De leur côté, les dirigeants d'Eindhoven, après accord avec les dirigeants corses, ont décidé de fixer le match retour au 9 mai, alors que la date du 11 mai avait aussi été évoquée.

● En match en retard de Division I, Troyes a battu Saint-Etienne 1-0.

● En Deuxième Division, les deux leaders du groupe A, Angers et Toulon, ont été tenus en échec. Dans le groupe B, Lille et Paris F.C., vainqueurs, ont augmenté leur avance sur le Red Star.

● Johan Cruijff annonce sa retraite définitive à la fin de la saison.

(Pages 5 à 9)

HUCK DANS LE CLUB DES 40

Michel Hidalgo a rendu publique, samedi, la liste des quarante joueurs présélectionnés pour la Coupe du monde, dans laquelle il choisira nécessairement avant le 15 mai, dernier délai, les vingt-deux joueurs qui effectueront le voyage en Argentine. Parmi les surprises, la présence de Huck, de Guesdon et, dans une mesure moindre, de Dominique Baratelli. Du côté des éliminés, Synaeghel, souvent blessé cette saison, est le plus marquant.

L'ÉQUIPE

LE QUOTIDIEN DU SPORT ET DE L'AUTOMOBILE

M

LUNDI 17 AVRIL 1978 — 33e ANNEE — N° 9.929

Algérie, 2,25 dinars ; Allemagne, 1,30 DM ; Belgique, 24 FB ; Canada, $ 0,75 ; Espagne, 35 pesetas ; Grande-Bretagne, 24 pence ; Hollande, 2,25 florins ; Italie, 300 lires ; Luxembourg, 21 FL ; Maroc, 2,90 dirhams ; Suisse, 1,30 FS ; Tunisie, 240 millimes. — COMMISSION PARITAIRE N° 20.385. ISSN 0153-1069.

Spécial lundi 2,60

UN ARC-EN-CIEL SUR ROUBAIX

Enfin ! Après quatre années de vaine obstination, Francesco Moser est parvenu à remporter Paris-Roubaix. Un Paris-Roubaix (Trophée Merlin-Aquitaine) qui côtoya le pire dans les nouvelles et épouvantables portions pavées dénichées par les organisateurs, « L'Equipe » et « Le Parisien libéré », mais un Paris-Roubaix grandiose, dompté par le surpuissant porteur du maillot arc-en-ciel, avec l'aide de son coéquipier de luxe, Roger De Vlaeminck. Francesco Moser (notre photo) a rallié seul le vélodrome de Roubaix, avec 1' 40" d'avance sur De Vlaeminck, qui battit au sprint Raas et Maertens. C'est en prolongeant une attaque de Raas sur les pavés de Bachy que Moser forgea son succès, après que les pavés de Mons-en-Pévèle (km 202) n'eurent laissé que dix-huit hommes en course pour la victoire. Le premier Français est Bernard Hinault, treizième, à 7' 19", mais le jeune professionnel Joël Gallopin se mit en évidence en attaquant dès le départ et en arrivant dans la zone de l'« enfer » avec près d'un quart d'heure d'avance.

(Pages 2 à 4)

(Reportage photographique Marcel GUERARD, Christian ROCHARD, Jean-Claude PICHON.)

● ATHLETISME

A LA RECHERCHE DE Mr. JUANTORENA

Un nouvel Américain sur les traces de Juantorena : Willie Smith (vingt-deux ans) a couru le 400 mètres du meeting de Tuscaloosa en 44" 73. Meilleure performance mondiale de l'année. Dans la même réunion, 8' 14" 7 au 3.000 m steeple pour le Kényen Henry Rono. (Page 8)

● AUTO

LES AVENTURES DE WOLLEK ET DE « PESCA »

L'équipage français Pescarolo - Wollek a remporté à Dijon la troisième épreuve du Championnat du monde des marques. En raison des intempéries, la course avait été ramenée de 1.000 km à quatre heures. C'est la première victoire de la saison pour la paire Wollek - « Pesca » au volant de la Porsche 935. (Page 16)

● BASKET

PROBLEME A UNE INCONNUE

A une journée de la fin du Championnat de France, une seule inconnue subsiste. Qui de Tours, de Challans ou de Berck prendra la dernière place en Coupe Korac ? L'équipe de France juniors, deuxième à Izmir, est qualifiée pour le Championnat d'Europe. (Page 13)

● BOXE

MARTIN : LES POINTS SUR LES « i »

En battant facilement aux points son challenger Joël Bonnetaz, à Saint-Malo, Claude Martin a conservé son titre de champion de France des super-welters. Une formalité. (Page 8)

● HANDBALL

PAS DE TULIPES POUR LES FRANÇAIS

L'équipe de France a complètement raté sa sortie au Tournoi de Hollande remporté par la Suisse. Les Tricolores, qui n'ont gagné qu'un seul match contre la Hollande, ont terminé troisièmes et ont perdu Gilles Meyer (ménisque). (Page 14)

● MOTO

HENNEN : LE LAUREAT

L'Américain Hennen a créé une grosse surprise en enlevant l'épreuve reine des 500 cm3 du Grand Prix d'Espagne, à Jarama. Il a battu tous les favoris, et notamment ses compatriotes Roberts et Sheene. En 125 cm3, deuxième place pour Thierry Espié. (Page 15)

● RUGBY

ILS IRONT TOUS AU PARADIS

Dax a surpris en battant Biarritz, mais les favoris Béziers, Agen et Narbonne ont gagné. Ils se retrouveront tous les quatre en demi-finales du Challenge Yves-du-Manoir où l'on s'achemine vers une finale Béziers - Narbonne. (Page 12)

CETTE SEMAINE DANS "L'ÉQUIPE"

- **FOOTBALL. — Mardi** : Coupe de France (quarts de finale retour), Monaco - Bastia, Nantes - Nice, Marseille - Sochaux, Nancy - Valenciennes. **Mercredi**, matches amicaux : Angleterre - Brésil (à Wembley), Suède - Allemagne de l'Ouest (à Stockholm). **Jeudi** : Lyon - Rouen (match avancé). **Vendredi** : journée de Championnat de France, avec notamment Monaco - Saint-Etienne, O.M. - Metz, V.A. - Nantes, Bastia - Nice, Paris-S.-G. - Lens.
- **CYCLISME. — Jeudi** : Flèche Wallonne ; départ du circuit de la Sarthe.
- **RUGBY. — Samedi**, à Colombes, Biarritz - Aurillac (match avancé) en seizièmes de finale du Championnat de France.
- **AUTO. — Mardi** : départ du Rallye du Portugal.
- **BASKET. — Vendredi**, match avancé : Villeurbanne - Le Mans. **Samedi** : dernière journée de Championnat, avec Caen - Tours, Bagnolet - Nice.
- **BOXE. — Vendredi**, à Toulon, Ruocco - Acariès, Championnat de France des welters. **Samedi**, à San Remo, Valdes - Corro, Championnat du monde des moyens ; à Lille, finale du Tournoi de France amateurs.
- **MOTO. — Samedi** : départ des 24 Heures du Mans ; à Brands Hatch, épreuve de 750.
- **JEUNES. — Mercredi** : notre page des jeunes, avec une enquête sur l'orientation des espoirs.
- **SPORT ET VIE. — Vendredi**, dans nos pages spéciales « Sport et Vie », des reportages, enquêtes, conseils.

Francesco, uno

Since 1974, the year of his first appearance on the Northern cobbles, Francesco Moser had not missed one edition of the Queen of the Classics. In fact, following the example of Roger De Vlaeminck he fawned on it.

The event perfectly suited his physical makeup. Powerful in stature, his talent as a 'rouleur' and above all his taste for panache, meant he was predisposed to shine there. Moreover contrary to certain champions he never stopped giving everything of himself because of the fear of crashing. Indeed he never held himself back in order to prepare for the eternal 'next race'.

In 1978, the Italian wore with pride the World champion's jersey. However even the essence of the success of San Christobal was sometimes criticised. Moreover Roger De Vlaeminck, who had become his team mate at Sanson, had just lifted Milan-San Remo where the 'Checco' had been able to do no better than seventh.

In reality since the beginning of the season, he was always searching for a success that would measure up to his standing. In Italy, where the stars very quickly fell off their pedestals, it was imperative to win frequently. Moser knew it all the more so, since a young man by the name of Saronni, who had finished second in Milan-San Remo, hoped to put him in the shade.

The day before Paris-Roubaix, the favourite of the Italian press, to the great vexation of Moser, was called ....De Vlaeminck!

For the race the two champions had concluded a non-aggression pact. They were to attack alternately, the one behind would protect the flight of the other. On paper everything seemed perfect, it only remained, in fact, to dispute the event.

One hundred and forty one riders signed the start register at Compiègne. The daring man at the start of the race was called Joel Gallopin. Twenty five years old, this young new professional, first of all joined in several escapes before persisting by himself. At seventy kilometres at Lesdins, the runaway possessed a lead of almost fifteen minutes. Several counter-attacks, notably from Gilbert Duclos-Lassalle and Barry Hoban did little to cut into his capital which always bordered on the quarter of an hour.

Under a persistent rain in sight of the first cobbles of Neuvilly, a crash delayed Chalmel, Hinault, Schuiten, Vallet and Le Guilloux. Hinault rejoined the front before the end of the cobbled section where Moser, unquestionably to stamp his authority on his rivals, was first through.

Forty men were at the front, behind Gallopin who still had more than an eight minute lead at Quiévy.

At Viesly, the Italian, feeling that the group was too big, attacked in company with Thurau and Pollentier. Their attempt dislocated the peloton a little more where many where beginning to show their limits.

The fugue of Joël Gallopin, whose advance had been considerably reduced, finished at Aulnoye after three

Parigi · Roubaix
aprile 1986

CICLI Francesco Moser

Francesco MOSER
(Italy, 1951)

An exceptional "rouleur". World Champion and hour record holder. His sensational treble in Roubaix ranks him alongside Octave Lapize in the annals of the race.

1974 : Paris-Tours
1975 : Italian Champion, Tour of Lombardy
1976 : World Pursuit Champion
1977 : World Champion,
       Zurich Championship,
       Flèche Wallonne
1978 : Paris-Roubaix, Tour of Lombardy
1979 : Paris-Roubaix, Italian Champion,
       Ghent-Wevelgem
1980 : Paris-Roubaix, Tirreno-Adriatico
1981 : Italian Champion, Tirreno-Adriatico
1984 : Milan-San Remo, Tour of Italy,
       The Hour Record (51,151 km)

1978

successive punctures. Just after the Dutchman Jan Aling escaped in his turn. The stars watched each others and kept their strength for the difficult sections ahead. In Hasnon, Kuiper, Verschuere and Van Roosbroeck went away. This time it was more serious for at Wandignies the trio possessed a lead of one minute and twenty two seconds, then two minutes fifteen at Bouvigny, eighty three kilometres from Roubaix where an accident to Van Roosbroeck forced him to return to the ranks.

Behind the two escapees the peloton was dwindling. Those riders who had been dropped and who had had accidents could no longer be counted. At Mons-en-Pévèle, on one of the worst stretches of the cobbles, Roger De Vlaeminck took things in hand and counter-attacked. Four men at once came up to his wheel: Ludo Peeters, Thurau, Moser and his friend Ronan De Meyer. Then ten others came up as well: Van Sweevelt, Marc Demeyer, Vandenhaute, Piet Van Katwijk, Zoetemelk, Hézard, Van Springel, Aling, Raas and Van Calster.

These strategic movements caused the gap to close on the leaders to only twenty seconds at Avelin. After a puncture to Verschuere, Kuiper could not stand the pressure for much longer. The former world champion was left behind at Templeuve. Moser and Van Sweevelt, followed by a dozen other men, were first to rejoin him. At Nomain André Dierickx crashed and seriously injured his right knee, Hinault who had just caught this leading group, fell too....

It was at Bachy, twenty three kilometres from the velodrome that Moser increased the pressure. His break provoked a reaction but only De Vlaeminck, Raas, Maertens, Van Springel and Van Sweevelt managed to follow him.

Five kilometres further on the Wannehain section, an incorrigible Moser decided to give the coup de grace to his companions. Three riders seemed as if they were strong enough to follow him: Maertens, Raas and De Vlaeminck who as planned, was protecting his team mate. In spite of the efforts of Maertens and Raas, Moser progressively built up his lead. At ten kilometres from the finish the Italian had a minute.

Motivated by the considerable stakes the 'Checco' entered the track with one minute forty seconds on Roger De Vlaeminck who took second place from Raas and Maertens who were respectively third and fourth.

Twelve years after Gimondi, the Italians renewed a victory at Roubaix. Francesco Moser, moulded into his rainbow jersey, covered in mud, was exultant. He never finished replying to journalists: "First at last. I knew would finish up winning this race one day or another. Basically nothing is simpler than winning Paris-Roubaix. You have to got to be strong and be first on to the cobbles.." He was in agreement here, without knowing it, with Van Looy, nearly thirty years earlier.

For Moser the other great satisfaction was none other than the discomfort of Saronni. As he came out of the showers Giuseppe said it would be a while before he came back.

De Vlaeminck whose individualism and thirst for victory were no longer to be spoken so highly of, seemed almost radiant in the track centre. If Moser had cracked, it was him and certainly him, who would have won it.

The French were once again overwhelmed. Hinault the first of them was thirteenth. Hardly satisfied with his performance the Breton claimed that it was rather like a cyclo cross event but that unlike Saronni, he would certainly return.....

1978

On the cobbles Moser 'leads the dance' in front of....

Francesco, due...

Twelve months after his success the cycling landscape had totally changed. Francesco Moser was still defending the colours of the Sanson team but Roger De Vlaeminck had moved to Gis, their direct opponents. The war of Communiqués between the two champions was declared. The Belgian never hesitated to confirm: "Moser is ungrateful. Last year after Paris-Roubaix, he completely forgot my sacrifice and he tried hard to put sticks in my wheels each time I rode in Italy.."

In spite of the argument, Roger De Vlaeminck, as often, had a very good start to his 1979 season. He won his third Milan-San Remo while Moser was just finishing his fourth.

On the other hand, in sight of Paris-Roubaix, the Italian seemed to have reached peak form. Four days before the Northern confrontation, he won Ghent Wevelgem before .....De Vlaeminck!

The latter was suffering from a chill but nevertheless promised to meet his rivals at Roubaix.

On the first of April, the race was run in sunshine. The first escape developed at Golancourt at thirty eight kilometres. Seventeen men went off the front. Among them the young Duclos-Lassalle, discovered the previous year, then Sherwen, Oosterbosch and the new Northern professional Jean-Philippe Pipart. Up until the one hundred kilometre the lead kept growing until it reached five minutes before

...Hinault, Walter Godefroot and the rest of the bunch.

the first cobbles at Neuvilly. At this spot under the efforts of Duclos-Lassalle, the little group broke up. At Famars, one hundred and forty three kilometres, the situation seemed clear. Serge Périn was just in front of a group of eight. The bunch was a minute and a half down.

In the crossing of Valenciennes, Fraccaro came up from the back, then eight pursuers caught Périn. Following these different movements the gap went up to over two minutes. On the cobbles of Coutiches, Fraccaro, one of Moser's team mates and Duclos-Lassalle went again.

At Attiches, Hinault took things in hand. His action provoked the explosion of the chasing group, the first part of which successively caught the leaders. As they crossed through Templeuve, Fraccaro and Duclos-Lassalle, the last ones to resist were reeled in. At Ouvignies, precisely thirty one kilometres from Roubaix, Marc Demeyer went to the front. A few hundred metres later Hennie Kuiper latched on to his back wheel.

The cobbles were beginning to have their effect, for soon there were no more than eight of them in the pursuit; Moser, De Vlaeminck, Raas, Thurau, Zoetemelk, Van Claster, Planckaert and Ronan De Meyer. Working so well together meant the leaders were quickly brought back.

While Raas and Thurau punctured, Demeyer went again. On the cobbles of Wannehain, Kuiper caught him to reform the inseparable 'tandem of the day. Only two more managed to rejoin them: Moser and De Vlaeminck naturally.

1979

Francesco MOSER
& PARIS-ROUBAIX :

1974 : 2nd
1975 : 5th
1976 : 2nd
1977 : 13th
1978 : 1st
1979 : 1st
1980 : 1st
1981 : 3rd
1982 : 10th
1983 : 3rd
1985 : 12th
1986 : 8th
1987 : 19th

Right:
Moser, in his characteristic style,
completes his last lap of the track.

1. Francesco MOSER (Italy)
   GS.Sanson-TV.Luxor
2. Roger DE VLAEMINCK (Belgium)
3. Hennie KUIPER (Holland)
4. Joop ZOETEMELK (Holland)
5. Jan RAAS (Holland)
6. Willy TEIRLINCK (Belgium)
7. Walter PLANCKAERT (Belgium)
8. Marc DEMEYER (Belgium)
9. Alfons DEWOLF (Belgium)
10. Etienne VAN DER HELST (Belgium)

Behind Moser, who was from now on to remain alone in the lead, Kuiper who had received a very rapid wheel change, was alone in pursuit. Joop Zoetemelk who up until this time had been caught in an ambush, took advantage of this avalanche of punctures to relaunch himself into the race. De Vlaeminck, after a few moments of doubt, did the same.

With eleven kilometres to go, Moser in his turn punctured but still managed to conserve the forty seconds lead which he already possessed. From then on, inspired by thoughts of victory nobody managed to apprehend him, neither Kuiper, nor Zoetemelk, not even De Vlaeminck who took senseless risks, which eventually caused him to crash on a corner.

The gypsy had to content himself with the runner up position which this time no longer had the same flavour as that of twelve months previously. Moser's first words were explicit when he saw the Gypsy arrive: "This time it's clear," he said, "I owe nothing to anyone.."

In the French camp, there was a glimmer of hope on the horizon. Hinault, over and above his place of eleventh, had had an effect on the way the race was run. The Breton regretted that his sixty kilos made him bump about a little to much on the cobbles.

For his part Gilbert Duclos-Lassalle had found a terrain which suited him. He had been at the very front for five hours. His star was in the ascendant, all the more so after the unavoidable Géminiani was reported to have said: "The little ones have no business being there....."

1979

Joop Zoetemelk shows himself on the cobbles ... in front of Ronan De Meyer, André Dierickx, Francesco Moser and Jan Raas

Moser joins Lapize

At the beginning of 1980, Albert Bouvet reluctantly abandoned the sections of race route through Querenaing and Trith-St-Léger. The Arenberg Gap, an outlying part of the course, became the dominant arena.

But the inhabitants of the other villages in the Cambrai region, such as St Vaast, St Aubert, Villers-en-Cauchie, then Douchy-les-Mines and Beuvry-la-Forêt were to see the passage of the Queen of the Classics.

Early season brought a lot of surprises such as the Tour of Flanders where Moser, Raas and Pollentier found themselves clear just before the finish. No Flemish fan would ever have staked his money on the latter. However, Pollentier intelligently attacked within sight of the line. The two others stalled and let the victory slip through their fingers by a few metres!

The French, on the other hand, noticed with satisfaction the blossoming of Gilbert Duclos-Lassalle who had successively won the Tour of Corsica, Paris-

Vandenhaute, Chassang and Willems confront the cobbles.

Nice and finally the Tour of Tarn which finished forty-eight hours before the Paris-Roubaix.

From then on he was logically tipped as one of the favourites for the event which so inspired him. The new episode in the Moser-De Vlaeminck duel excited the crowds. In spite of several victories, rumour had it that Roger was not very motivated. His recent retirement in the Tour of Belgium underlined this impression.

The battle promised to be all the more fierce as facing them were several of their rivals who deserved respect: Raas, Kuiper, Demeyer, Willems, Dewolf, Thurau, Hinault and Sean Kelly who was beginning to discover the extent of his talent.

No doubt the sunny weather sharpened the ambitions of some as from the twenty eighth kilometre, seventeen men escaped including Kuiper, Teirlinck and Ludo Peeters. At Neuvilly the group already had a lead of three minutes. However, at Viesly, the stars woke up. The movement was neutralised just before the one hundred and fiftieth kilometre.

After the feeding station of Valenciennes, about forty riders formed the leading group. Moser and his team-mate Gregor Braun were the principal ones who were driving the group along.

Suddenly, ninety kilometres from the velodrome, there was an attack by the elegant Dietrich Thurau and the race began to come alive.

The German was immediately followed by Bittinger, soon eliminated by a puncture, then Moser, Duclos-Lassalle and De Vlaeminck.

With such riders in the lead, the race for the victory was over. The few counter-attacks by Peeters, Willems, Demeyer, Tackaert, then of Hinault and De Wolf did nothing to reduce the advantage of the leading quartet.

Moser, as so often on these roads which had become so familiar to him, seemed impatient to force a decision. Several times he tried to part company, but Duclos-Lassalle was watching him closely and managed to neutralise all attacks.

Twenty-four kilometres to the finish, Roger De Vlaeminck was the victim of a puncture on a cobbled section crowded with fans. Scarcely back in the saddle a crash was waiting for him just after!

It was definitely too much for the Gypsy who, for the first time in twelve appearances, retired on the road to Roubaix.

Francesco Moser could not have hoped for so much. He continued to impose a furious pace to keep up the pressure. After the elimination of De Vlaeminck, Duclos-Lassalle missed a corner and, in his turn, fell on the cobbles. The man from the South West restarted twenty seconds down on the Moser-Thurau tandem. But the German was starting to lose his superb and harmonious style. His eyes were riveted on the back wheel of the Italian champion, this wheel which fifteen minutes from Roubaix started to get further and further away.

Moser, superb in his tricolour jersey, emerged on to the velodrome as winner for the third consecutive time. He joined Octave Lapize in the illustrious legend thanks to a performance that few people thought would be possible in modern times. As he mounted delightedly on to the podium he said: "I feared Thurau most of all. It was he who made the greatest impression on me during the day. But having said that I felt very strong and if it had come to a sprint I was afraid of no-one.

Once alone in the lead the thing I feared most of all was an accident. In Paris-Roubaix my only tactic is to try to break things up as much and as often as possible in order to get rid of my rivals. This time, I attacked every time I could and if you tell me I was lucky I would say that I went looking for it. That's all."

His team manager quietly said that Francesco liked the race so much because it made his record look so good.

Gilbert Duclos-Lassalle finished second at one minute and

1980

Moser enters the legend.

L'ÉQUIPE
LE QUOTIDIEN DU SPORT ET DE L'AUTOMOBILE

LUNDI 14 AVRIL 1980   35e ANNÉE - N° 10.550

M

Algérie, 2,50 dinars ; Allemagne, 1,82 DM ; Belgique, 30 FB ; Canada, 1,10 dol. can ; Espagne, 50 pesetas ; Grande-Bretagne, 43 pence ; Hollande, 2,50 florins ; Italie, 800 lires ; Luxembourg, 24 FL ; Maroc, 3,70 dirhams ; Suisse, 1,50 FS ; Tunisie, 280 millimes COMMISSION PARITAIRE N° 62 029 — ISSN 0153-1069.

Spécial lundi   **3,00**

SECRETIN - BIROCHEAU CHAMPIONS D'EUROPE

Jacques Secretin a ajouté un nouveau titre à son glorieux palmarès : il a gagné le double des Championnats d'Europe de tennis de table, associé à Patrick Birocheau, les deux hommes disposant en finale des champions du monde Stipancic-Surbek (Yougoslavie). Individuellement, Secretin termine troisième.

(Page 6)

Auxerre bis ?

Auxerre remet ça ! Le finaliste 1979 de la Coupe de France vient, de nouveau, de faire braquer sur lui les projecteurs de l'épreuve 1980 en allant réussir à Metz un 2-2 qui le place en position très favorable avant le match retour, chez lui, demain soir. L'équipe de Guy Roux, bien que privée de son capitaine Serge Mésonès, est bien partie pour un nouveau parcours « héroïque » dans l'épreuve reine du football.

(Pages 10 à 13)

SUPER MOSER, CHAPEAU DUCLOS !

C'est sans doute le plus beau de ses trois Paris-Roubaix que Francesco Moser a remporté hier, à l'issue d'une course qui atteint les sommets. Parvenu seul à Roubaix au terme d'une échappée solitaire de 24 km, le champion italien, qui a rejoint Octave Lapize (vainqueur de 1909 à 1911) s'était dégagé à 90 km du but en compagnie de Thurau, de De Vlaeminck et de Duclos-Lassalle. Ce dernier aura été, avec Moser, le héros de la

classique de L'Équipe et du Parisien libéré. Victime de trois crevaisons et de deux chutes, il a conquis, à la force du jarret, une très belle deuxième place (à 1'48'' de Moser) et confirme ainsi avec éclat qu'il compte désormais parmi les grands. Les Français n'avaient d'ailleurs pas été depuis longtemps à si belle fête, car Bernard Hinault, très opiniâtre, a battu Demeyer au sprint pour finir quatrième, trente-cinq secondes der-

rière un étonnant Thurau. Auparavant, De Vlaeminck avait été éliminé par une chute ainsi que Pollentier, alors que Raas, victime lui aussi d'une cabriole, abandonnait également. Trente et un coureurs seulement ont terminé (sur 164 partants), le vainqueur réalisant, avec l'aide du vent, une moyenne de plus de 43 km dans ce Trophée Merlin-Plage de grande facture.

(Pages 2 à 5)

ROUBAIX. — Image désormais traditionnelle : depuis 1978, Moser a pris la bonne habitude d'entrer seul dans Roubaix. Il donne son récital et, derrière lui, ses adversaires ramassent les miettes...

ROUBAIX. — Ils sont encore quatre derniers compagnons...

● **NATATION**

GAINES : 1'49''16, ECUYER : 51''91

Le sprint en fête, tant aux États-Unis qu'en France aux Championnats d'hiver : Gaines, nouveau recordman du monde du 200 m en 1'49''16, efface le « Soviétique » Kopilakov des tablettes. Deux autres records, pour Ecuyer [...] dixièmes [...] Quatre [...] Frédéric

(Page 14)

Mos[...]

Pour les Américains, [...] samedi à dimanche, [...] Springs, les 275 d[...] américain se sont pro[...] (70 % des voix), [...] compétitions olympi[...] pleinement suivi [...]

La raison d'État, qui ne [...] pose pas avec les senti[...] l'a donc emporté sur [...] sportif. Le Comité olym[...] des États-Unis a rallié la thèse [...] — ou plutôt imposée — par l'a[...] tration de la Maison-Blanche : les [...] cains ne participeront pas aux Jeux [...] Olympiques de Moscou.

Il serait en effet utraliste de [...] crocher à quelque fallacieux espoir [...] genre de celui qui a été formulé [...] liste des délégués des trente-neuf [...] nations nationales réunies à [...] rado Springs : « Si la situation [...] évoluer sensiblement dans les mois [...] qui viennent, en Afghanistan, l'U [...] pourrait revenir sur sa position... » [...]

Il s'agit là d'un additif de [...] forme, destiné à donner bonne [...] cience à ceux qui se sont pronon[...] pour le retrait. Rien ne bougera [...] de l'Afghanistan d'ici au mois de [...] Washington en est tellement con[...] qu'il a bien voulu laisser figurer [...] clause qu'il n'aura pas à respecter [...] plus que le gouvernement n'a[...] qu'une brèche soit ouverte dans le [...] courage total, décidé ainsi à l'e[...] des inscriptions individuelles [...] par certains athlètes qui veulent [...] un procès à la Maison-Blanche [...] atteinte à leurs libertés et abus de [...] Rien n'y fera, car la majorité ob [...] par James Carter au sein de l'[...] est telle que les recours seront n[...] ou souffriront de mesures dilatoire[...] quelque surprise de cette réunion [...] en effet son caractère quasi plébis[...] en faveur du renoncement : 70 [...] voix [...] et admis que la volonté de [...] Jimmy Carter, représenté par le vice-[...]

Robert PARIENTE.

Cette semaine dans « L'ÉQUIPE »

● **FOOTBALL.** — **Mardi** : Coupe de France, huitièmes (retour), notamment Lille-Monaco, Sochaux-Valenciennes, Nice-Saint-Étienne, Auxerre-Metz, P.F.C.-Rennes, Montpellier-Lens. **Vendredi** : journée de Championnat de France, Première Division, avec Metz-Sochaux, Angers-Saint-Étienne, Nice-Nantes, Bastia-Monaco.

● **CYCLISME.** — **Mercredi à samedi** : Circuit de la Sarthe. **Jeudi** : la Flèche Wallonne.

● **BASKET.** — **Lundi et mardi**, suite et fin du Tournoi de Gyor (Hongrie) avec France-Hongrie B et Autriche-France.

● **BATEAUX.** — Toute la semaine : Régates internationales d'Hyères.

● **BOXE.** — **Vendredi**, à Paris (Coubertin) : Tafer-Martin.

● **NATATION.** — **Vendredi**, à Madrid : première journée de la Coupe Latine.

● **MOTO.** — **Samedi** : départ des 24 Heures du Mans.

● **SPORTS ÉQUESTRES.** — **Samedi** : première journée du CSO de Fontainebleau.

● **JUDO.** — **Samedi**, à Paris : première journée des Championnats de France par équipes.

● **ESCRIME.** — **Samedi**, à Carpentras : première journée du Championnat de France de fleuret masculin.

Behind the peloton led by ... De Vlaeminck, Braun, Kuiper, Demeyer

forty eight seconds in spite of another crash and a puncture. He especially gave hope to the unfortunate French who had not been on the podium since 1960! Under the applause of the public who had taken him to their hearts, he said he was sorry that he allowed Moser to get away as he would have liked to have arrived at the track with him. Nevertheless, his cup was full, for on the morning of the race all he had hoped for was a place in the first ten.

But, modestly, he added: "What I did, any French rider should have been able to do a long time ago. You have to make sacrifices, to think about the race and to prepare for it." Behind the two men the gaps opened. Thurau preserved his third place but was three and a half minutes behind Moser.

As for the fourth, a certain Bernard Hinault was six minutes adrift, in front of three Belgians: Marc Demeyer, and two of the younger generation Fons Dewolf and Daniel Willems.

After his arrival, an angry Hinault complained: "It's not a race, it's a cyclo-cross." which was the same thing he had said twelve months previously, but he added: "It's really a load of nonsense". That same evening he swore that he would not come back.

For his part, Jacques Goddet appreciated the third episode of this trilogy and wrote in the editorial of L'Equipe: "The personality of Francesco Moser exactly defines the character of Paris-Roubaix. It needs the excesses of Paris-Roubaix for a champion like Francesco Moser to express himself completely."

From then on the Italian fans were waiting for no more from him than a win in the Giro to make him the equal of Coppi or Bartali.

1980

1. Francesco MOSER (Italy)
   GS.Sanson-Campagnolo
2. Gilbert DUCLOS-LASSALLE
   (France)
3. Dietrich THURAU (Germany)
4. Bernard HINAULT (France)
5. Marc DEMEYER (Belgium)
6. Alfons DEWOLF (Belgium)
7. Daniel WILLEMS (Belgium)
8. William TACKAERT (Belgium)
9. Ludo PEETERS (Belgium)
10. Piet VAN KATWIJK (Holland)

L'ÉQUIPE

LE QUOTIDIEN DU SPORT ET DE L'AUTOMOBILE

SAMEDI 11, DIMANCHE 12 AVRIL 1981. 36ᵉ ANNÉE — N° 10 858

M Algérie, 2,50 dinars; Allemagne, 1,50 DM; Belgique, 35 FB; Canada, 1,10 dol. can.; Espagne, 50 pesetas; Grande-Bretagne, 45 pence; Hollande, 2,50 florins; Italie, 1.000 lires; Luxembourg, 25 FL; Maroc, 4 dirhams; Suisse, 1,50 FS; Tunisie, 230 millimes. COMMISSION PARITAIRE N° 62 029 — ISSN 0153-1069.

4,50

Les plus beaux Paris-Roubaix racontés par Pierre Chany

avec

L'ÉQUIPE MAGAZINE

ET SI LA FLANDRE BRETONNAIT...

(Photos Alain LANDRAIN)

Il y a maintenant un quart de siècle qu'un Français n'a pas remporté Paris-Roubaix, et notre cyclisme cherche toujours un successeur à Louison Bobet qui suivra, d'ailleurs, dimanche, la course de L'Équipe et du Parisien libéré. Cette longue, trop longue période de vaches maigres prendra peut-être fin dimanche, puisque, pour la première fois depuis longtemps, les favoris du Trophée Merlin Méditerranée ne seront pas exclusivement belges, néerlandais ou italiens. Bernard Hinault, surtout si le soleil est de la partie, est en effet de taille à rivaliser avec De Vlaeminck, Moser, De Wolf, Raas, Braun ou Thurau. Et si, dimanche, la Flandre bretonnait, si Hinault succédait à Bobet sur le terrain de chasse préféré des Flamands, cette victoire historique ne serait pas une surprise. Duclos-Lassalle, deuxième l'an passé, qui a fait de la plus fascinante des courses son objectif principal de l'année, et son coéquipier Bossis porteront également les espoirs du cyclisme français. Les personnages centraux de la course devraient être pourtant Roger De Vlaeminck (photo de droite), quatre fois vainqueur, dont la forme étincelante ne se dément pas depuis un mois, Francesco Moser, victorieux en 1978, 79 et 80, mais qui semble légèrement inférieur à ce qu'il était l'an dernier et... Hinault qui a reconnu le parcours hier (avec Bertin dans sa roue à gauche), avant de se reposer dans l'Oise aujourd'hui.

(Pages 2 à 5)

TV En direct sur TF 1, demain, à 16 h 40.

MERCKX JOUE DE VLAEMINCK

Douze participations, trois victoires... Eddy Merckx connaît son sujet, dès lors qu'on aborde Paris-Roubaix. L'ancien champion du monde, qui a mis fin à sa carrière il y a trois ans, avait accepté hier d'enfourcher de nouveau sa bicyclette, à l'invitation d'Eddy Merckx pour sa...

Argen... té FÉLÉE

...TIENNE. — Blessé dans un ... avec Neubert à la fin de Saint-...ienne-Nancy, Michel Platini a passé ...une radio qui a révélé la fêlure d'une côte. Conséquence : il ne pourra jouer mercredi contre Laval, mais il affirme qu'il sera rétabli pour participer à France-Belgique, le 29 avril. Il a encore seize jours devant lui.

...asse six buts à Bor...eaux. L'esprit de Coupe, qui anime Montpellier

Lens, Lille, ne à conserver l'avantage d'un (Pho...

...iquet

MON... Cela a chauffé, sa... soir, devant ...but bastiais. Mais les Corses ont tenu... Malgré les efforts de Barberis, que l'on voit ici cerné par Henry (à gauche) Hiard et Orlanducci et Marcialis (à droite) veillent.

L'ÉQUIPE

LE QUOTIDIEN DU SPORT ET DE L'AUTOMOBILE

LUNDI 13 AVRIL 1981. 36ᵉ ANNÉE — N° 10 859

M Algérie, 2,50 dinars; Allemagne, 1,50 DM; Belgique, 35 FB; Canada, 1,10 dol. can.; Espagne, 50 pesetas; Grande-Bretagne, 45 pence; Hollande, 2,50 florins; Italie, 1.000 lires; Luxembourg, 25 FL; Maroc, 4 dirhams; Suisse, 1,10 FS; Tunisie, 230 millimes. COMMISSION PARITAIRE N° 62 029 — ISSN 0153-1069.

Spécial lundi 3,50

LA VICTOIRE QU'IL LUI FALLAIT

MERLIN

Ce fut un Paris-Roubaix digne de la plus grande légende du vélo, avec ses drames, ses chutes (Raas contraint à l'abandon), et mené à un train d'enfer... du Nord (plus de 45 km dans la première heure après le départ de Compiègne).

Ils sont six à se présenter ensemble au vélodrome de Roubaix : Kuiper, qui pénètre en tête, travaillant pour De Vlaeminck, puis Moser, De Meyer, Van Calster et Bernard Hinault, le champion du monde, se dégage très vite pour ne pas permettre à De Vlaeminck de se placer dans la roue de Kuiper. Il prend la tête à plus de quatre cents mètres de la ligne d'arrivée et conduit son sprint en puissance. Un double démarrage, le premier pour résister à De Meyer qui tente de passer à la corde, et le second pour repousser l'assaut de De Vlaeminck qui n'arrive même pas à la hauteur du pédalier du Français. Irrésistible, Bernard Hinault domine en force les sprinters, et gagne son premier Paris-Roubaix (organisé par L'Équipe et le Parisien libéré), vingt-cinq ans après la dernière victoire française, celle de Louison Bobet en 1956 (après celle de Jean Forestier en 1955).

Pourtant, le Breton avait été victime d'incidents qui eussent pu briser ses ambitions et tomba trois fois, la dernière chute se situant à 15 km du but, à cause d'un chien, mais il revint en moins de 2 km.

(Pages 2 à 6)

ROUBAIX — Bernard Hinault a « survolé » Paris-Roubaix. Dans les fondrières de « l'enfer » du Nord, il est déjà aux avant-postes (notre photo de gauche). Sur la piste du Vélodrome de Roubaix, il s'impose au sprint à De Vlaeminck (à gauche) et à Moser (notre ci-dessus). Au bout de son effort, le visage marqué, Hinault rejoint Louison Bobet dans la légende (ci-dessous).

(Reportage photographique Alain LANDRAIN, Jean-Claude PICHON et Pierre DEGROS)

Hinault by a landslide

"You will never make me take back what I have already said about Paris-Roubaix. It's a big nonsense!" In the traditional post-race showers nobody seemed astonished to hear these unusual lamentations, those of the losers. However, this time the words came from the winner of the seventy ninth edition of the event - none other than Bernard Hinault!

Hinault, as was often the case, was everyone's favourite and this time he did not let them down. In sight of Roubaix, there were five opponents on his wheel: Roger De Vlaeminck, Hennie Kuiper, Francesco Moser, Marc Demeyer and Guido Van Calster. For many long kilometres the Breton had led the group and strictly controlled his companions.

The Gypsy had lost a little of his legendary ease. Moser was content to follow and observe without trying anything, fearing perhaps on this April's day to no longer have the legs to fulfil his ambitions. Hennie thought only of supporting De Vlaeminck who he had helped to win the recent Tour of Flanders. Van Calster seemed quite happy to just stay with these "greats". Only Marc Demeyer, never resigned, showed any signs of his usual power.

As the first motorbikes appeared on the avenue leading to the velodrome the cheering started. Kuiper, the first, surged on to the track with De Vlaeminck on his wheel who had perhaps never been so well looked after.

Rapidly, Hinault decided to move to the front. There were four hundred metres to go - he was preparing for a long powerful sprint.

Hinault was brimming with confidence, all the more so because ten days previously, the Frenchman had already destroyed a very large portion of the peloton at the finish of the Amstel Gold Race. Not a single sprinter had been able to draw level with his bottom bracket and the world champion had won ahead of a certain Roger De Vlaeminck! This time he was turning his 53x13 in the same manner and progressively accelerating. In the back straight he held off a first attack by Marc Demeyer and then in sight of the finishing line, he held off a last desperate assault from De Vlaeminck.

All that under the eyes of Louison Bobet, another great Breton, the last French winner a quarter of a century ago!

After his lap of honour and surrounded by a pack of journalists, the winner declared breathlessly: "I was sure of myself and I felt very strong. I attacked with four hundred metres to go, when Demeyer wanted to pass on the inside, I accelerated at the same time, then when De Vlaeminck tried to go past on the outside, I produced my last effort."

At the start at Compiègne, the rainbow jersey was being watched by everyone. He was on form. This time not only could he win but he also wanted to. Success in this event would permit him to give a scathing reply to opposition who were always saying that he did not like the race simply because he was incapable of

1981

Bernard HINAULT
(France, 1954)

A complete champion, as testified by his win in Paris-Roubaix, a race that he detested.

1977 : Liège-Bastogne-Liège,
        Ghent-Wevelgem,
        Grand Prix des Nations
1978 : French Champion, Tour de France,
        Tour of Spain, Criterium National,
        Grand Prix des Nations
1979 : Tour de France, Tour of Lombardy,
        Flèche Wallonne
1980 : World Champion,
        Liège-Bastogne-Liège, Tour of Italy
1981 : Paris-Roubaix, Tour de France,
        Amstel Gold Race,
        Criterium International
1982 : Tour de France,
        Grand Prix des Nations, Tour of Italy,
        Tour of Luxembourg, Criterium des As
1983 : Flèche Wallonne, Tour of Spain
1984 : Tour of Lombardy,
        Grand Prix des Nations
1985 : Tour de France, Tour of Italy

1
2

3

winning it.

Opposed to him were the "inseparables"; Moser and De Vlaeminck, then Kuiper, Duclos-Lassalle, Demeyer, Raas and the young generation led by Alfons Dewolf, winner of the Milan-San Remo, Greg LeMond, Alain Bondue, Eddy Planckaert, Stephen Roche and Marc Madiot. The last two had shown some potential after their victories in amateur events.

After a relatively calm start to the race, Jan Raas was the victim of the first serious incident. After just one hundred kilometres the Dutchman had to retire after a crash.

It was at Atres after warming up for one hundred and forty kilometres that the race began. Four men went clear, the Frenchmen Bernaudeau and Vichot, the Belgian Verlinden and the Italian Cattaneo. At the feed at Valenciennes the quartet had a minute and a half's lead but found it hard going on the rain-soaked cobbled streets. Behind them the punctures and crashes could no longer be counted.

Sixty three kilometres from Roubaix, De Vlaeminck and Duclos-Lassalle made the junction. Straight away the two stars dropped the original break. They seemed to be in with a chance in spite of the distance which still separated them from the finish.

However, after being away for twenty kilometres, the Gypsy was held up by mechanical problems.

Roubaix in the hands of the Bretons: Hinault 25 years after Bobet.

Duclos-Lassalle had a minute's lead. The Frenchman picked up the challenge and held off his pursuers for about twenty kilometres. But on the cobbles of Wannehain, after a puncture, he was swallowed up. Ten riders caught him. There were only six of them on the outskirts of Roubaix. The valiant Duclos-Lassalle, victim of a crash at Gruson, was not one of them but he was, once again, one of the great men of the day.

Hinault caused a great fright when at the entrance to Gruson, a poodle, no doubt upset by the race, ran under his front wheel. The Breton found himself on the ground but restarted immediately and closed the gap in just a few hundred metres. From then on it was all over.

At the finish Roger De Vlaeminck, after four victories, failed again and for the fourth time ended up in second place. A little fatalistic, he told the Flemish journalists: "I obviously wanted to win a fifth time but today Hinault was really the strongest at the end of the race. I don't know if I'll ever win a fifth Paris-Roubaix, but what I can assure you is that my friend Dewolf will certainly win. Since Merckx retired, no one in Belgium has done better than him."

Effectively, De wolf, in spite of his two crashes, a puncture and as many useless pursuits grabbed tenth place. But, for once, the Gypsy was mistaken, for Dewolf never appeared on the podium at Roubaix. In spite of several important victories, he did not have the great career that everyone hoped for. One of the great disappointments, with Daniel Willems, of Belgian cycling in the 1980's.

On the other hand, the thirteenth, a certain Eddy Planckaert, for his first appearance in the event came back totally won over. That same evening, when he got back home to Nevele, he said to his mother: "One day I'm going to win that race."
How right he was.

1981

1. Bernard HINAULT (France)
   GS.Renault-Elf-Gitane
2. Roger DE VLAEMINCK (Belgium)
3. Francesco MOSER (Italy)
4. Guido VAN CALSTER (Belgium)
5. Marc DEMEYER (Belgium)
6. Hennie KUIPER (Holland)
7. Ferdi VANDENHAUTE (Belgium)
8. René BITTINGER (France)
9. Jean CHASSANG (France)
10. Alfons DEWOLF (Belgium)

1. Roads ... or a bog!

2. An attentive Hinault on the wheel of De Vlaeminck, Duclos-Lassalle and Kuiper.

3. De Vlaeminck followed by Duclos-Lassalle, Ludo Peeters, René Bittinger and Daniel Willems, at work on the cobbles.

e amé-
homme
...naies (12"93
...esister aux siré-
... Il a signé un con-
...u club de San Francisco

la
lars
aux Je
en 1980
100 m, et

L'ÉQUIPE
LE QUOTIDIEN DU SPORT ET DE L'AUTOMOBILE

LUNDI 19 AVRIL 1982 — 37ᵉ ANNÉE - N° 11 176

M

Algérie, 2,50 dinars ; Allemagne, 2 DM ; Belgique, 43 FB ; Canada, 1,10 dol. can ;
Espagne, 80 pesetas ; Grande-Bretagne, 60 pence ; Hollande, 2,75 florins ;
Italie, 1.200 lires ; Luxembourg, 37 FL ; Maroc, 5 dirhams ; Suisse, 2 FS ;
Tunisie, 450 millimes. COMMISSION PARITAIRE N° 62 029 — ISSN 0153-1069.

Spécial lundi
4,50

aller des q...
Coupe, a constitué
déception pour les Giron...
Bordeaux. « Aujourd'hui le ress...
est cassé », reconnaît Bernar...
Lacombe. L'avant-centre international explique que c'est la défaite à
domicile contre Lens, en Championnat, trois jours avant, qui a
rendu fébriles ses coéquipiers et

... du
...pendant
, encore éli-
...s seront privés
... de Gemmrich,
...usso, ... Rohr, suspendu.
De leur côté, les Stéphanois ne
pourront pas utiliser, à Laval,
Johnny Rep, touché à l'œil.

(Pages 7 et 8)

Les Nor...
les Norma...
sion II, mais ave...
gramme de fin de s...
l'emportaient, accepteraie...

Dans le groupe A, Toulouse, ...
Gueugnon (1-0), et Thonon, vainqueur de Marti-
gues par le même score, ont repoussé la
menace représentée par Marseille, défait vendredi soir à Cannes.

(Pages 9 et 10)

HINAULT A CONSACRÉ RAAS

Décidément, les grandes classiques du
cyclisme nous donnent des vainqueurs
inattendus cette année. Bien sûr, Jan
Raas, qui a inscrit son nom au palmarès à
la suite de celui de Bernard Hinault, est un
grand du peloton. Mais peu de personnes
pensaient, au départ à Compiègne, que le
Hollandais, ancien champion du monde,
parviendrait à s'imposer hier, alors que les
courses précédentes ne l'avaient pas montré en pleine possession de ses moyens.
Et pourtant, Jan Raas a remporté une belle
victoire en terminant seul sur le vélodrome
de Roubaix, avec seize secondes d'avance
sur le revenant Yvon Bertin, qui régla au
sprint l'Allemand Braun et le Suisse Mutter, et trente-sept secondes sur un groupe
de cinq hommes dont Bernard Hinault, qui
put longtemps croire à la victoire. Mais
Hinault avait effectué un énorme travail sur
les pavés pour faire avorter une dange-

reuse tentative de Ludo Peeters, l'équipier
de Raas, sans recevoir beaucoup d'aide de
ceux qui formaient le premier groupe de
poursuivants ; Il ne voulut pas tirer,
jusqu'au bout, les marrons du feu pour ses
adversaires, permettant ainsi à Raas, qui
avait démarré à un peu plus de quatre kilomètres de l'arrivée, derrière Mutter, de
déposer le Suisse et de s'imposer en poursuiteur. Dans ce Paris-Roubaix, épargné
par la pluie, mais où la poussière rendit la
respiration difficile, plusieurs coureurs per-
dirent toutes leurs chances sur crevaison.
Ce fut le cas par exemple de Duclos-
Lassalle, de Moser, de Vandenbroucke, de
Kelly, alors qu'une longue échappée de
Patrick Bonnet et de l'Allemand Heine,
relayé ensuite par le Suisse Demierre,
anima toute la première partie de la reine
des classiques.

(Pages 2 à 4)

(Photos Christian ROCHARD et Alain LANDRAIN)

ROUBAIX. — Jan Raas n'a pas beaucoup quitté la roue arrière de Bernard Hinault dans ce quatre-vingtième Paris-Roubaix. Le Hollandais s'était rapidement rendu compte que le / Breton était l'homme fort de la course et le surveilla comme le lait sur le feu (comme sur notre photo de gauche), tandis que De Vlaeminck semble se poser des questions. Raas, / cependant, sut trouver l'ouverture lorsque son équipier Peeters fut rejoint et il s'envola vers la victoire (photo de droite) dans un style de poursuiteur.

Jan Raas
or the victory of a team

The start of the 1982 season was to see everyone just as astonished as they had been the previous year. In fact, on the 20 March, on the via Roma at San Remo, the French took the first two places!

Against all logic, these two men were not called Hinault or Duclos-Lassalle but Marc Gomez and Alain Bondue. If the latter's talent was already recognised due to his world pursuit title, that of Marc Gomez on the other hand still remained to be discovered. The reason for it was quite simply that this Milan-San Remo was the first classic in which he had taken part!

After the Northerner Bondue crashed on the rapid descent of the Poggio, Gomez flew away to his first and resounding professional victory.

Fifteen days later in the Tour of Flanders, not one single punter, not even a Belgian one would have placed a franc on René Martins. Certainly, the qualities of the Flemish rider were not to be called into question, he was of course a "solid" roadman. But from there to lifting a "Ronde" under the noses of the stars. And yet...

Under these circumstances, on the day before Paris-Roubaix, it was difficult to give out any forecast. Francesco Moser and Roger De Vlaeminck were present of course, but they were slowly moving, it was believed at the time, towards well deserved retirement.

Three men stood out a little from the rest of the one hundred and eighty two

Hinault in the pursuit of Peeters
in front of Vandenbroucke, Raas, Dewolf,
Beucherie and Kelly.

riders: Fons Dewolf, Eddy Planckaert, and Bernard Hinault. The first had notably lifted the Het Volk and Three Days of La Panne. The youngest of the Planckaerts had only failed by a whisker in the Tour of Flanders. His desire to get rid of his label of "just a hopeful' was a guarantee. As for Hinault, he was quite simply Hinault! The race looked like being very open and behind this trio, as well as Moser and De Vlaeminck, a dozen men had more or less legitimate pretensions: Braun, Kelly, Roche, Duclos-Lassalle, Kuiper, Willems and Bondue. The man from Roubaix secretly hoped to get mixed up in the struggle and above all to arrive in a good position on the velodrome that was the theatre of the start of his career ten years before. The eightieth Paris-Roubaix was drowned in sunshine and in the dust on the cobbled sectors.

The riders scarcely had the time to warm up when Serge Beucherie, the French champion, tried to escape. At the fortieth kilometre, two men went off the front: Patrick Bonnet and the modest German Gotz Heine. This "tandem" in spite of a strong headwind gained a lead soon to be measured in minutes.

However, this proved to be insufficient and the elegant Swiss Serge Demierre was the first to come up to them before the feeding zone at Valenciennes. About twenty kilometres from there Demierre went off by himself.

On the ninth of the thirty three cobbled sectors, twenty kilometres later, everything was back together again.

1982

Hinault kept the pace high in a peloton thinned out by the various incidents. In this way, Madiot, Lubberding, Bernaudeau, Andersen, Verlinden and Castaing were delayed. Bondue was hardly much luckier. The handicap of the first puncture was rapidly made good thanks to his friend Michel Demeyre who had been assigned to follow him and help in the event of any problems. In a few seconds, the wheel change completed, Bondue restarted to suffer from a second, then a third puncture. Unfortunately, neither Demeyre, nor his team manager were there to help him repair the damage.

It was twenty kilometres from Roubaix when the fate of the race was played out. Nine men remained in the lead: Jan Raas and his faithful team-mate Ludo Peeters, and the others: Marc Sergeant, Eddy Planckaert, Gregor Braun, Stefan Mutter, Bernard Hinault, the unexpected Yvon Bertin and Roger De Vlaeminck. There were no more, no Moser, no Dewolf, no Roche or Duclos-Lassalle - all beaten by bad luck.

The powerful Raleigh team had the race completely under control. Ludo Peeters played the role of hare to perfection. He attacked in order to help the plans of his leader Raas, Hinault found himself in an uncomfortable position. The choice was agonising. If he chased, Peeters was condemned but victory would go to Raas, if he did not then the Belgian would win.

The Breton chose the first solution, with Raas snuggled on his wheel and a malicious look in his eye.

Under his impulsion the junction was effected just before the hill at Hem, at the entrance to Roubaix. Raas, as a fine strategist attacked immediately. Yvon Bertin was the first who managed to join him.

Before the last difficulty at Hem was behind them, Mutter tried to go away. The Swiss gained a lead of fifty metres being still in sight of the others but he was a tempting target for a strong man to get up to. This man, of course, was Raas. The bespectacled Dutchman straightaway caught and dropped the Swiss in a way that he had done so many times before.

In the group behind everyone had a good reason not to react. De Vlaeminck was at the end of his tether. Planckaert, the fastest of them, did not make the least gesture. Bertin was saving himself for the sprint which was to give him second place, while Hinault seemed disillusioned.

Raas won his Paris-Roubaix. His appearance at the velodrome was greeted by a few unjustified whistles. The public seemed to forget all about his tremendous class and remembered the 1979 world championships. He had won there but had got his team-mates to push him several times up the Cauberg, the main climb on the course.

Raas wanted to set the record straight: "Today was my seventh attempt at Paris-Roubaix. Up until now I have had nothing but problems over these roads. I have been furious since the Tour of Flanders. Martens hit the jackpot and my country's press criticised me for it. Today I must say a big thank you to Ludo Peeters."

Peeters, who had devoted himself to Raas found his recompense a little later in the Grand Prix of Frankfurt. However, a few years later, Peeters said about this Paris-Roubaix: "It was the day that my team caused me to lose the race. Even if they later helped me to win others, it never made up for it. To have won Paris-Roubaix would have been worth more than all my other victories put together." Peeters retired at the end of 1990 with apparently a wound which had never healed.

Eddy Merckx, irritated by the behaviour of his successors in the Tour of Flanders where nobody took any risks, was present on these Northern roads and once again was enthusiastic: "On the road to Roubaix, I've seen some real champions."

On the subject of champions, the man knew what he was talking about.

1982

Jan RAAS
(Holland, 1952)

Holland's prolific winner of the classics was a formidable sprinter and a fine tactician.

1976 : Dutch Champion,
2nd Amstel Gold Race
1977 : Milan-San Remo, Amstel Gold Race,
2nd Het Volk
1978 : Amstel Gold Race, Blois-Monthléry,
Paris-Brussels,
2nd Dutch Championship,
3rd Paris-Roubaix
1979 : World Champion,
Tour of Flanders, Amstel Gold Race,
Tour of Holland, 2nd Het Volk
3rd Blois-Chaville
1980 : Amstel Gold, 3rd Milan-San Remo,
3rd Tour of Flanders
1981 : Blois-Chaville, Het Volk,
Ghent-Wevelgem,
2nd Paris-Brussels,
3rd Tour of Flanders
1982 : Paris-Roubaix, Amstel Gold Race,
2nd Tour of Holland
1983 : Dutch Champion,
Tour of Flanders, 2nd Het Volk,
2nd Ghent-Wevelgem,
3rd Milan-San Remo,
3rd Amstel Gold Race.
3rd Blois-Chaville
1984 : Dutch Champion

1. Jan RAAS (Holland)
   GS.TI-Raleigh-Campagnolo
2. Yvon BERTIN (France)
3. Gregor BRAUN (Germany)
4. Stefan MUTTER (Switzerland)
5. Eddy PLANCKAERT (Belgium)
6. Roger DE VLAEMINCK (Belgium)
7. Marc SERGEANT (Belgium)
8. Ludo PEETERS (Belgium)
9. Bernard HINAULT (France)
10. Francesco MOSER (Italy)

NOAH A INQUIÉTÉ WILANDER

Victorieux à Monte-Carlo, le Suédois Mats Wilander s'est imposé une nouvelle fois sur terre battue, à Lisbonne. Mais son succès n'a pas été facile à obtenir. Face à Yannick Noah, il lui a fallu batailler durant trois sets (2-6, 7-6, 6-4), et il dut notamment sauver deux balles de match lors de la deuxième manche. Pour Yannick Noah, cette défaite est, malgré tout, encourageante. Il a démontré un net retour en forme.

● Aujourd'hui, à Aix-en-Provence, commence la Raquette d'Or, avec la participation de Mats Wilander, de Victor Pecci et d'Henri Leconte.

(Page 15)

PROS : «NON AU BLOCAGE»

L'UNFP, le syndicat représentatif des footballeurs professionnels, n'a pas apprécié les mesures de rigueur prises unilatéralement par les dirigeants de la Ligue nationale, concernant notamment les salaires des joueurs. Selon Philippe Piat, leur président, ceux-ci ne sauraient accepter ce plan d'austérité s'il n'est pas accompagné des mesures d'allégement fiscal que les clubs et les joueurs ont demandées aux pouvoirs publics. Or ces derniers ne se sont engagés à rien, et Piat affirme que, en cas de refus, les pros ne voteront pas le plan et sont prêts à aller jusqu'à la grève si les dirigeants tentent de le leur imposer.

(Page 11)

Reims, Rennes à petits pas

Pas à pas, Rennes et Reims semblent s'approcher de la Division I. A cinq journées de la fin, les deux leaders ont accru leur avance d'une longueur. Dans le groupe A, Rennes a battu difficilement le Racing Paris 1 (2-1), mais, dans le même temps, Guingamp a tenu en échec Nîmes sur son terrain (1-1). Rennes a donc maintenant deux points d'avance, et comme Valenciennes a volé en éclats à Angoulême (0-3), Nîmes est quasiment assuré de disputer les barrages. Dans le groupe B, Reims, vainqueur d'Orléans (2-0), a lui aussi, deux points d'avance sur Toulon, tenu en échec (1-1) par Nice. La deuxième place de barragiste se jouera entre ces deux-là.

(Pages 10 et 11)

M **L'ÉQUIPE**
LE QUOTIDIEN DU SPORT ET DE L'AUTOMOBILE

SPÉCIAL LUNDI

4,60

LUNDI 11 AVRIL 1983   38e ANNÉE - N° 11 480

Algérie, 2,50 dinars.
Allemagne, 2 DM.
Belgique, 46 FB.
Canada, 1,10 dol. can.
Espagne, 110 pesetas.
Gde-Bretagne, 60 pence.
Hollande, 2,75 florins.
Italie, 1.200 lires.
Luxembourg, 36 FL.
Maroc, 5,10 dirhams.
Sénégal, 450 C.F.A.
Suisse, 2 FS.
Tunisie, 460 millimes.

Commiss. parit. n° 62 029
ISSN 0153-1069

KUIPER : UN TRAIN D'ENFER !

Cent quatre-vingt-treize au départ de Compiègne, trente-deux classés, sept heures plus tard, à Roubaix. Deux chiffres qui résument assez bien ce que fut le quatre-vingt-unième Paris-Roubaix ; et, au bout de cette route effroyable et implacable, un superbe vainqueur de trente-quatre ans, le Hollandais Hennie Kuiper. Dès la sortie du boyau de Wallers-Arenberg, Kuiper était dans le groupe des hommes qui forçaient la décision ; avec

lui, Moser, Duclos-Lassalle, Ronan De Meyer, Madiot, Bondue, Sherwen et Versluys. Il restait alors dix kilomètres à couvrir, le peloton n'existait plus, et tandis que Roche, Sherwen, Versluys et Bondue étaient tour à tour éliminés sur incidents, Moser accentuait sa pression pour franchir tous les obstacles sans encombre. Mais Kuiper résistait, en dépit de deux chutes et d'une crevaison, celle-ci survenant après son

démarrage sur les pavés de Camphin-en-Pévèle, à dix-sept kilomètres du but. Malgré cette perte de temps, Kuiper repartait de plus belle, menant un train d'enfer pour rallier le vélodrome avec un avantage de 1'15" sur Duclos-Lassalle, Moser, De Meyer et Madiot, démontrant une belle fraîcheur athlétique, en dépit de son âge. Derrière les cinq rescapés de la longue échappée, les écarts étaient considérables : le dixième maintenant à près de neuf

minutes, le vingtième à plus de seize minutes et le dernier repoussé à quarante minutes ! Dans ce naufrage collectif, l'équipe Raleigh tout entière avait sombré, pas un seul de ses coureurs n'étant à l'arrivée. Raas, malade, avait donné le signal de la débandade en renonçant à Valenciennes (km 154), imité, d'ailleurs, par Bernard Hinault, revenu des États-Unis dans la nuit...

(Pages 2 à 6)

HENNIE EN SEIGNEUR

ROUBAIX. — Sur les pavés de Gruson, à moins de douze kilomètres de Roubaix, Hennie Kuiper (photo ci-contre) n'a pas encore course gagnée, mais, déjà, il tient Moser et Duclos-Lassalle à distance. Malgré leur acharnement, l'Italien et le Français (ci-dessus) ne parviendront pas à refaire le terrain perdu, en dépit de la crevaison qui freinera la progression du vainqueur durant le dernier quart d'heure de course.

OOSTERBOSCH COMME PRÉVU

Le premier Tour of America s'est terminé, hier, à Washington, au pied de la Maison-Blanche, par la victoire attendue du Hollandais Bert Oosterbosch, qui avait pris le commandement de l'épreuve lors du contre-la-montre, samedi. Ainsi donc, le rouleur de TI-Raleigh a redoré le blason d'une formation passablement éteinte entre Paris et Roubaix.

(Page 4)

Cette semaine dans « L'ÉQUIPE »

● BASKET. — Lundi : France-Cuba féminin à Tarbes. Vendredi : France-Cuba masculin à Orthez. France-Brésil féminin à Beauvais. Samedi : France-Cuba masculin à Bayonne. France-Brésil féminin à Amiens.

● BOXE. — Jusqu'à samedi : Internationaux de France à Saint-Nazaire.

● CYCLISME. — Jusqu'à samedi : Tour du Maroc. De mardi à samedi : Tour du Vaucluse open. Jeudi : la Flèche Wallonne.

● FOOTBALL. — Mercredi : Coupe Gambardella (huitièmes de finale). Vendredi : Coupe de France (huitièmes de finale retour), avec Monaco-Brest, Nantes-Bordeaux, Toulouse-Rouen, Lyon-Tours, PSG-Strasbourg, Lille-Martigues, Guingamp-Laval, Ajaccio-RCP 1.

● HALTÉROPHILIE. — Mardi à jeudi : Championnats du monde juniors à San Marino.

● HOCKEY SUR GAZON. — Toute la semaine : Coupe du monde féminine.

● KARATÉ. — Vendredi et samedi : Internationaux de France à Coubertin.

● NATATION. — A partir de vendredi : Coupe Latine à Lisbonne.

● SPORTS ÉQUESTRES. — A partir de jeudi : CCI de Badminton.

● TENNIS. — Toute la semaine : Tournois d'Aix-en-Provence, de Los Angeles et d'Amelia Island.

● VOILE. — A partir de jeudi : début de la Semaine olympique d'Hyères.

(Reportage photographique Robert LEGROS et de Patrick BOUTROUX)

● RUGBY

AURILLAC PIÉGÉ PAR BOURG

Une seule véritable surprise dans ces matches de barrage des huitièmes de finale : le succès de Bourg-en-Bresse sur Aurillac (12-10). La rencontre au sommet USAP-Toulon a été marquée par le succès des Catalans (13-9). Le champion de France Agen n'a guère souffert pour éliminer Tyrosse (27-12). Autres qualifiés : Bègles, le Stade Toulousain, Lourdes, Montferrand et Bayonne.

(Pages 13 et 14)

● AUTO

ROSBERG A FERMÉ LA PORTE

Le champion du monde de Formule 1 Keke Rosberg a dû plusieurs fois « fermer la porte », à Brands Hatch, pour empêcher l'impétueux Américain Dany Sullivan de le passer. Dans cette course des champions, Jean-Louis Schlesser (6e) a fait des débuts en F 1 pleins de clairvoyance et de sagesse.

(Pages 18 à 20)

● ATHLÉTISME

SUPER DE CASTELLA

Le Marathon de Rotterdam a tenu ses promesses. Mais, alors que l'on s'attendait à un duel Salazar-De Castella, l'Américain a déçu et n'a terminé que cinquième. Mais l'Australien n'a pas eu la partie facile pour autant. De Castella n'a, en effet, devancé le Portugais Carlos Lopes que de deux petites secondes : 2 h 8'37", contre 2 h 8'39", à vingt-quatre secondes du meilleur temps mondial.

(Page 17)

● BASKET

REVANCHE AMÉRICAINE

Un peu d'homogénéité en plus aura donc suffi aux « Américains » du Championnat pour prendre leur revanche sur la France. Battus vendredi soir à Vichy, les All Stars se sont imposés le lendemain à Tarare (109-84). Les Cubaines, de leur côté, ont, une nouvelle fois, dominé les Françaises (94-68).

(Page 8)

● HANDBALL

BONNE AFFAIRE POUR IVRY

La poule finale du Championnat a fort bien commencé pour Ivry. Déjà leaders au classement provisoire, les joueurs d'Ivry ont singulièrement amélioré leurs positions. D'abord en allant triompher (26-20) à Saint-Martin-d'Hères, ensuite en profitant indirectement du match nul de Gagny, chez lui, contre la Stella Saint-Maur. Enfin, le SMUC a facilement battu le SMEC 24-16.

(Page 15)

● NATATION

KOSTOFF TOUJOURS

Aux Championnats américains, à Indianapolis, quatre meilleures performances mondiales ont été améliorées. Jeff Kostoff, le tombeur de Salnikov, il y a quelques semaines, a réussi 14'46"11 au 1 650 yards, épreuve dans laquelle Frank Iacono a terminé huitième, en 15'15"24. Au 50 yards, Tammy Thomas a réalisé 22"13, tandis que Sue Walsh nageait le 100 yards dos en 54"74 et Tiffany Cohen le 1 650 yards en 15'46"54.

(Page 16)

● TOUS LES SPORTS

XV : POUR OU CONTRE L'INTERDICTION ? A VOUS DE JUGER

A la suite de l'interdiction lancée par le gouvernement à la Fédération française de rugby, lui enjoignant de ne pas envoyer d'équipe en Afrique du Sud, et devant les réactions des premiers intéressés, les joueurs, « L'Équipe » pose la question à ses lecteurs : êtes-vous pour ou contre cette forme d'interdiction ? Le CNOSF réunit la presse aujourd'hui, et cette question sera évoquée, ainsi que la loi sur le sport et les Jeux de l'Avenir.

(Pages 7 et 16)

Kuiper
at his eleventh attempt !

For the first time in years, Roger De Vlaeminck was not present at the start of the Paris-Roubaix. At the age of thirty-six, the Gypsy still had a professional licence but he decided to give the important events a miss in the 1983 season.

His old sparring partner Moser, on the other hand, was still quite active. The champion was now in his thirty second year. Observers thought that his career was coming painfully to an end and that he could no longer have any effect on the outcome of races. However, once again, the Italian was going to play a major role.

On the day before the event, a man who was part of the best team in the world looked like a scarecrow. He was none other than Jan Raas, the winner the previous year. Peter Post's team had grabbed most of the bouquets: Star of Besseges (Ludo Peeters), Three Days of La Panne (Cees Priem), Tour of the Mediterranean and above all Ghent Wevelgem (Leo Van Vliet) and the Tour of Flanders (Raas in front of Ludo Peeters).

Raas, having reached maturity, was reigning over the classics. Opposing him, the country's elite arrived motivated with a few potential winners in its ranks: Eddy Planckaert, Willems, Vandenbroucke, Alfons Dewolf, Hoste and the Dhaenens, Dirk Dewolf and Vanderaerden. The last of them being hailed as the prodigy of the decade. Certainly, it still seemed to soon to be sure, but he had already impressed the world of cycling by, at the very beginning of his career, winning the prologue, and one stage of the Paris-Nice and still at the age of twenty one.

As for the others, Kuiper, Van der Poel, LeMond, Moser, Contini, Prim, Roche, Thurau and Freuler, they could all, given the right conditions pull something off.

The chances of the French essentially rested on the shoulders of Marc Madiot, Alain Bondue and especially Gilbert Duclos-Lassalle. The Frenchman from the South West, was becoming obsessed with the event and always prepared carefully. The Thursday before the race he went to look at the last one hundred kilometres of the route and the next day, he did another one hundred kilometres in the Flemish hills.

No matter what the weather conditions, he remained motivated and never hesitated to say: "Paris-Roubaix is a classic that I love and it doesn't matter what the weather is like on Sunday." Bernard Hinault was finally sure of being at the race. Two days before the race, he had been at the Tour of America and only took possession of his hotel room at Compiègne on Sunday morning at one o'clock.

From the start, the pace was high. Twenty men, among them Freuler, Roche and Vanoverschelde, took charge. At the exit from the first cobbled section of Neuvilly, there was only seven of them left, then at Verchin-Maugré at kilometre one hundred and thirty seven, the move came to an end.

The first cobbled sectors were fatal for Jan Raas and Bernard Hinault. The first, suffering, abandoned the race at Valenciennes and the second, visibly suffering from jet lag,

Hennie KUIPER
(Holland, 1949)

Always reckoned a likely winner of the Tour de France, he never achieved that goal but instead amassed an impressive record in the classics.

1972 : Olympic Champion
1973 : 2nd Zurich Championship,
1975 : World Champion,
       Dutch Champion
1976 : Tour of Switzerland, 2nd Het Volk,
       2nd Paris-Brussels,
       2nd Paris-Nice
1977 : 2nd Tour de France,
       3rd Amstel Gold Race,
       3rd Tours-Versailles
1978 : 3rd Grand Prix des Nations
1979 : 3rd Paris-Roubaix
1980 : 2nd Liège-Bastogne-Liège,
       2nd Tour de France
1981 : Tour of Flanders,
       Tour of Lombardy,
       2nd Tour of Holland
1982 : 2nd Tour of Luxembourg
1983 : Paris-Roubaix
1984 : Milan-San Remo,
       3rd Tour of Flanders

1983

Kuiper crosses over the famous 'hill of Hem'.

followed suit shortly after Neuvilly.

1983 also saw the return of the race to the Wallers-Arenberg Gap. In sight of this obstacle, Moser moved into overdrive. Only four men, Duclos-Lassalle, Versluys, Bondue and Ronan De Meyer managed to hold on to his wheel. A little later Kuiper, Roche, Madiot and Sherwen turned up. Behind them twenty-five men embarked on a pursuit but with little conviction.

In sight of Orchies, the powerful Raleigh team started to break up. After Raas it was the turn of Van der Velde and Ludo Peeters to hand in their numbers! At the front Sherwen and then Roche found themselves eliminated from the leading group by crashes. On one of the cobbled zones in the direction of Bersee, Versluys also found himself on the ground and took with him Madiot, Bondue and De Meyer. Kuiper was off the back at this spot so avoided the worst. Simply balked, he did not take long to get up to the Moser-Duclos tandem, now alone in the lead.

After a very hard pursuit lasting for several kilometres, De Meyer and Madiot, unlike Bondue, caught the leaders. The Northerner alone against five men, in spite of all his determination hovered several hundred metres behind before finally giving up. At the front Moser was certainly going very hard but Kuiper was very impressive. Twice, the former world champion crashed but each time he got back onto the Italian's wheel in less than two kilometres.

Kuiper knew that he would be beaten in a sprint. So he had to finish alone if he wanted to win. This time again, when there remained a mere sixteen kilometres to the Roubaix velodrome, he gallantly launched himself off the front. His former companions hesitated. What should they do? Duclos-Lassalle did not want to be trapped by Moser.

As for Madiot and De Meyer, they started to show signs of weakening.

Launched onto the victorious path, Kuiper knew only one brief alarm when at six kilometres from Roubaix, he broke a wheel in a rut. But his minute and

Duclos-Lassalle takes second place to the detriment of Moser...

...arriving at the velodrome.

a half's lead prevented anyone from catching him.

An excellent Duclos-Lassalle mastered Moser for second place. Ronan De Meyer was fourth in front of Marc Madiot. Kuiper, who had meticulously prepared with very long training rides during the previous week was overjoyed: "This is my eleventh Paris-Roubaix. At thirty four I no longer dared to think of winning. I was Olympic champion, World champion, I won the Tour of Flanders and the Tour of Lombardy but Paris-Roubaix will remain my best souvenir. I remember very well my first Paris-Roubaix in 1973. I finished thirty first on Luis Ocana's wheel. In the showers I learnt that Merckx had won. I could not think that ten years later it would be my turn."

For his part, Duclos-Lassalle had succeeded in "his" Paris-Roubaix but was sorry about his second place: "Second again. They will soon be saying that I am another Poulidor. I am disappointed because I really believed that I could do it. I only had one bad crash, when Kuiper went. I suffered two punctures and two crashes but here it's the same for everyone."

As Bondue appeared on the track a huge ovation broke out from the stands. The man from Roubaix took tenth place in front of Daniel Willems before telling his friends who surrounded him: "I am super-happy even if I fell eight times. I punctured a first time at Neuvilly. My mechanic threw me a wheel which bounced on the pavement before rolling ... under a car. Several hundred metres further, I punctured a second time.

"At Neuvilly I was in last position but one. I was with Willems and we caught various groups before finally rejoining the leaders in sight of Wallers. In spite of a new wheel change I was able to move into second position. After the big crash at Orchies, it was difficult. What I did today made me think that one day I will be there to win it."

1983

1. Hennie KUIPER (Holland)
   GS.Aernoudt-Rossin-Campagnolo
2. Gilbert DUCLOS-LASSALLE (France)
3. Francesco MOSER (Italy)
4. Ronan DEMEYER (Belgium)
5. Marc MADIOT (France)
6. Adri VAN DER POEL (Holland)
7. Patrick VERSLUYS (Belgium)
8. Frank HOSTE (Belgium)
9. Eddy PLANCKAERT (Belgium)
10. Alain BONDUE (France)

GUERRE DES TROIS POUR LE FINAL !

Avec la victoire de Monaco sur Bordeaux (2-1), le Championnat rebondit à quatre journées de la fin. Les Azuréens précèdent désormais les Girondins d'un point et Auxerre, toujours là, de deux. Tout reste à jouer.

(Pages 8 à 11)

LA VOIE DES AIRS

MONACO. — Le sommet du Championnat s'est joué dans les airs puisque les trois buts du match ont été obtenus de la tête. Genghini, auteur du second but monégasque, prend ici le meilleur sur Thierry Tusseau (à gauche).
(Photo André Lecoq)

LUNDI 9 AVRIL 1984

5,20 F

39ᵉ ANNÉE — N° 11 792

L'EQUIPE
LE QUOTIDIEN DU SPORT ET DE L'AUTOMOBILE

« King » Kelly... Superbe Bondue

L'Irlandais, impérial et dominateur, a survolé le 82ᵉ Paris-Roubaix, réglant le Belge Rogiers après avoir rejoint le tandem Bondue-Braun à 21 km de l'arrivée. Le Français, superbe combattant, enfui depuis Wallers-Arenberg avec son coéquipier, a préservé la troisième place.

(Pages 2 à 7)

ROUBAIX. — Kelly, Rogiers, Bondue, c'est l'ordre d'arrivée au vélodrome et l'Irlandais conduit la course avec toute son autorité.
(Photo Alain Landrain)

LAUDA ET PROST SE FONT LA PAIRE

Comme on le pressentait, la hiérarchie des essais a été rapidement balayée par le déroulement du Grand Prix d'Afrique du Sud, où le règne de Piquet et Rosberg fut très éphémère. Le véritable patron, c'était Niki Lauda, et les meilleures, les McLaren-Porsche. A preuve, la fabuleuse remontée d'Alain Prost jusqu'à la deuxième place derrière son équipier. Et au Championnat, les deux (ci-contre) se font la paire...

(Pages 19 et 20)

Kelly
despite Bondue's efforts

19 January 1984. A rumble of thunder arrived from Mexico. Francesco Moser had just beaten the hour record of the prestigious Eddy Merckx. Better still, the Italian had even managed to go through the fifty kilometres barrier. Four days later he went back to the track and this time managed 51.151 kilometres!

It was thought that the triple winner of Paris-Roubaix, in his thirty third year, was at the end of his career. In a single blow, Moser launched and relaunched himself and taking advantage of his preparation, took Milan-San Remo in his stride, then a few months later the Tour of Italy.

However, the Italian, to the great regret of his fans, did not take part in Paris-Roubaix. No more than Jan Raas did who was the victim of a serious crash in Milan-San Remo, which was also going to shorten his career, neither Hinault, nor Duclos-Lassalle who had been injured in a hunting accident and who would not appear until the end of the season. These defections caused new ambitions to be born and many hopes were raised for this eighty second Paris-Roubaix.

Sean Kelly dominated the start of the season. The Irishman successfully lifted Paris-Nice, the Criterium International and the Tour of the Basque Country. His two second places in the Milan-San Remo and the Tour of Flanders had irritated him to the extent that he told his team-mates that he was going to win at Roubaix. The vow deserved to be taken seriously, all the more so because normally Kelly acted first and spoke later.

Facing him were the Panasonic "armada" led by the "brothers" Planckaert and Vanderaerden, then the young wolves Fignon, LeMond, Madiot and Wojtinek, the Belgians Dhaenens, Rogiers, Versluys and Wampers. Moreover, the La Redoute team should not be overlooked, as they had on display Vandenhaute, Vandenbroucke, Roche, Braun and Bondue.

The latter was celebrating his twenty fifth birthday on the day of the race and seemed ready for one of his principal objectives of the season: "I am in better form than I was last year when I finished tenth. I have taken this race to heart and the fact of riding for a Northern team increases my motivation even more." Over the last few days he had been familiarising himself with the final sections of cobbles with Gregor Braun.

On the day of the event the redoubtable pair of pursuiters launched the great battle. Everything began at Wallers-Arenberg. Bondue knew that he had to be one of the first onto the cobbled track. In spite of the traditional scramble, the Northerner managed it and "led the dance" at an infernal pace.

"In fact" he said at the finish "all we had decided to do was to be first into the Arenberg Forest. When I turned round there was only my team-mate Braun on my wheel. The others were already much further back. As we came out of Wallers we had a lead of one minute and twenty seconds. However, there were still one hundred kilometres to the finish. Rapidly we caught two men who had been away since the morning: Lang and Hoffeditz. On the cobbles at Denain the two men could not stay with us for very long. We were not quite sure what to do. Should we lift off a little or keep the pace up and go for broke?"

After Orchies the latter solution was adopted, for since Wallers the gap had stabilised at about one minute and forty seconds."

Further back, Sean Kelly was not worried. According to him the two men, riding into the wind, had little chance of staying away to the finish. While the majority of the work was being carried

Sean KELLY
(Ireland, 1956)

"King Kelly" had to wait until he was in his late twenty's before winning his first classic. He then proceeded to make up for lost time in brilliant style, winning 12 major-one-day classics, more than any other rider since Eddy Merckx.

1982 : Paris-Nice, 3rd World Championships
1983 : Tour of Lombardy,
      Tour of Switzerland,
      Paris-Nice, Criterium International
1984 : Paris-Roubaix,
      Liège-Bastogne-Liège,
      Blois-Chaville, Paris-Nice,
      Criterium International
1985 : Tour of Lombardy, Paris-Nice
1986 : Paris-Roubaix, Milan-San Remo,
      Grand Prix des Nations, Paris-Nice
1987 : Paris-Nice, Criterium International
1988 : Ghent-Wevelgem, Tour of Spain,
      Paris-Nice
1989 : Liège-Bastogne-Liège,
      3rd World Championships
1990 : Tour of Switzerland
1991 : Tour of Lombardy
1992 : Milan-San Remo

1984

Alain Bondue followed by Gregor Braun
encouraged by his public.

out by the Quantum team of Kuiper, Zoetemelk and Dirk Dewolf, then the
Splendor team of Dhaenens and Versluys, Kelly was taking it easy.

Braun, who was beginning to struggle on the cobbled sectors was once again
the victim of a puncture at Mons-en-Pévèle. Bondue decided to wait for him. In
spite of the incident the lead was always more than a minute on a group of eight
men: Kelly, Kuiper, Versluys, Wijnants, Vandenbroucke, Van der Velde,
Hanegraaf and Rogiers. At forty five kilometres from Roubaix, Kelly who had
changed tactics, was the one who was most often to be seen leading the
chasers.

Suddenly, he attacked. Only the young Rudy Rogiers managed to join him. The
Irishman slowly gained ground on the leading pair. They finally joined them at
Wannehain, at the end of a chase lasting twenty five kilometres. Immediately
Braun was dropped.

Bondue continued: "When I saw Kelly come up, I still thought I had a chance. In
spite of my break I still felt fresh. The finish on "my" track could not do me any
harm." But a crash on the last but one cobbled section left him groggy by the
side of the road. He remained on the ground for a full minute and it was even
feared that he had broken his hip. During this time, a Belgian spectator repaired
his bike and he restarted a minute and a half down on Kelly and Rogiers.

The former world pursuit champion rode flat out on these roads he knew so
well. He managed to pull a minute back on the leaders. But this was not enough
to catch Mr Kelly. Bondue saw the sprint from a distance. Rogiers was first on
the track. For Kelly, victory was a mere formality.

For the first time an Irishman had placed his name into the record books of

Paris-Roubaix. One week later he was to do the same thing in Liège-Bastogne-Liège. At the velodrome, Bondue was happy. Not only with his third place but rather the perspectives which opened up before him: "I am only twenty five. I might perhaps need six or seven years but I know that one day I will win Paris-Roubaix." Six years later, Bondue retired from competition without ever having won the Queen of Classics.

Today this Paris-Roubaix has left him with mixed feelings: "For me it remains an excellent memory. The thousands of people who were chanting my name. I climbed on the podium on the day of my birthday. But the other side of the coin is that looking back, I think I missed out on a superb victory. I have often been reproached for going away too soon but if I had waited, the race might have turned out completely different."

He is also convinced that he would never have been able to win on that particular day. In fact his fork blade had broken on the road. His mechanic was surprised to see it after the finish. If he had caught Kelly and embarked on a sprint on the track, his forks would have almost certainly given way before the line. From that moment on destiny took a hand.

1984

1. Sean KELLY (Ireland)
   GS.Skil-Reydel-Sem
2. Rudy ROGIERS (Belgium)
3. Alain BONDUE (France)
4. Johan VAN DER VELDE (Holland)
5. Gregor BRAUN (Germany)
6. Jean-Luc VANDERBROUCKE (Belgium)
7. Jacques HANEGRAAF (Holland)
8. Patrick VERSLUYS (Belgium)
9. Hennie KUIPER (Holland)
10. Rudy MATTHYS (Belgium)

Hennie Kuiper knows that he will not be able to realise the double

L'EQUIPE
IFOP

16% de Français : oui au Loto sportif

Dans un sondage exclusif réalisé par l'IFOP pour L'Equipe, sept millions de Français se déclarent prêts à jouer au Loto sportif. Un sur deux s'intéresse au sport et avoue qu'il jouera justement parce qu'il connaît le sport. Quant au coût du bulletin, il ne paraît pas être un obstacle. En fait, tout le monde attend le premier jeu pour se familiariser avec les grilles. *(Page 7)*

LUNDI 15 AVRIL 1985

5,50 F

40ᵉ ANNÉE – Nº 12 109

★

L'ÉQUIPE
LE QUOTIDIEN DU SPORT ET DE L'AUTOMOBILE

MADIOT ENTRE AU PARADIS

Révélé par une cinquième place dans Paris-Roubaix, il y a deux ans, le Mayennais (notre photo ci-contre) a atteint, hier, la grande consécration, s'adjugeant en solitaire la « reine des classiques ». Il a contre-attaqué à quatorze kilomètres de l'arrivée, après les échecs de Francesco Moser et Eric Vanderaerden. A l'arrivée, il précédait de 1'57'' son jeune coéquipier Bruno Wojtinek (ci-dessous), qui démarra à un kilomètre du vélodrome, pour surprendre Kelly et Eddy Planckaert.

(Pages 1, 3, 4, 5 et 9)

(Reportage photographique Patrick BOUTROUX, Denys CLÉMENT et Alain LANDRAIN)

LES GIRONDINS S'INQUIÈTENT POUR CHALANA

Bordeaux n'a pas chuté à Sochaux. En y faisant match nul (1-1), le leader du Championnat a prouvé qu'il avait bien digéré sa déconvenue européenne de Turin. En revanche, il s'inquiète pour Chalana, blessé au cours de la rencontre et qui souffrirait d'une fracture de côte. En Division II, Mulhouse, battu à Abbeville, a repassé le relais au Havre, vainqueur de Sedan.

(Pages 12, 13 et 14)

BOXE

FAITES VOS JEUX

A 6 heures du matin, la nuit prochaine, aura lieu le nouveau combat du siècle (titre mondial des moyens en jeu) entre Marvin Hagler et Thomas Hearns. Un match qui sent la poudre entre deux hommes très dangereux, Hearns pouvant s'imposer en début de rencontre, Hagler étant favori si le combat dure au-delà de la neuvième reprise. Une affiche, en tout cas, qui enflamme tout Las Vegas.

(Page 19)

TENNIS

REVANCHE POUR LECONTE

En dominant assez nettement le Paraguayen Victor Pecci, Henri Leconte a pris sa revanche sur sa défaite de Coupe Davis. Il s'est surtout réveillé au bon moment après plusieurs mois en demi-teinte. Une bonne nouvelle à six semaines de Roland-Garros.
A Dallas, troisième victoire en trois semaines pour Lendl, vainqueur de Mayotte (7-6, 6-4, 6-1).

(Pages 10 et 11)

RUGBY

NARBONNE DE JUSTESSE

Final à l'arraché. A l'arrivée, après prolongation, un succès d'un tout petit point pour Narbonne qui, ainsi, sauve sa saison avec cette victoire en Coupe de France (28-27) aux dépens du Stade Toulousain. Et ce grâce à un essai d'Estève, inscrit à... la cent quatrième minute.

(Page 6)

BASKET

LIMOGES : TITRE EN VUE

Cette fois, on peut dire que Limoges va sans doute faire le triplé. Le troisième titre de champion de France est au bout de la route et passe, en l'occurrence, par un succès sur Monaco, samedi à Limoges. Chez les dames, le Stade Français, en prenant le meilleur sur le Racing, s'est assuré d'une seconde couronne.

(Page 18)

AUTOMOBILE

MUGELLO SANS SURPRISE

Pas de divine surprise à Mugello, pour la course d'ouverture du Championnat du monde d'endurance. La meilleure Lancia (Wollek-Baldi) s'est contentée de la quatrième place, derrière un trio de Porsche emmené par Ickx-Mass.

(Pages 21 et 23)

UNE PARTIE DE DOMINOS S'ÉTEND SUR 300KM!

Page 24 :
PHILIPS SORT DE LA MÊLÉE

OFFRES D'EMPLOI
Les carrières de « L'Equipe »
(Pages 16 et 17)

UN BÉBÉ BOIT SON BIBERON A 140KM/H!

ET AUSSI...

Athlétisme p. 17
Aviron p. 15
Bateaux p. 20
Equitation p. 17
Escrime p. 20
Glace p. 19
Golf p. 11
Gymnastique p. 15
Handball p. 11
Hippisme p. 20
Hockey p. 20
Jeu à XIII p. 17
Judo p. 15
Moto p. 20
Natation p. 6
Tennis de table p. 19
Volley-ball p. 20

UNE FILLETTE LONGE L'OCÉAN DANS UNE CAGE A POULES!

Marc Madiot's marseillaise

Once again, the 1985 Paris-Roubaix seemed promised to a member of the powerful Panasonic team, the worthy heir to the illustrious Raleigh. Peter Post's major difficulty was not having the means to win the race but rather to create an understanding between the leaders.

Three men of his group had already overtly expressed the wish to win at Roubaix: Eddy Planckaert, Eric Vanderaerden and Phil Anderson. Thanks to his good form Vanderaerden, recent winner of the Tour of Flanders in front of Anderson, was most people's favourite. He was even more so when he won Ghent Wevelgem three days later.

However, on that occasion, victory was promised to Anderson who, unfortunately for him, did not sprint fast enough over the last few metres. So as not to compromise the team's chances Vanderaerden took it on the line!

For his part Eddy Planckaert had been piling up the wins since Het Volk and would not agree to play the role of team-mate on the Northern cobbles.

The big event of the race was the return of Francesco Moser. After his dazzling year of 1984, the Italian was making a return to his roots in this event which had really revealed him to the French public eleven years before.

Certainly, his strength was no longer what it was but his experience enabled him to avoid unnecessary efforts, which, on the road to Roubaix was essential.

This time, the morning escape lasted until the early afternoon. Five men: Yvon Madiot, De Rooy, Castaing, Manders and Frison, counted twelve minutes lead on the first cobbled sector and arrived together at the start of the Arenberg 'trench'. Rapidly, Theo De Rooy went off by himself then Yvon Madiot and Manders got back to his wheel.

The favourites were having mixed luck. Vanderaerden had already been knocked off by a motorbike at Tilloy, Moser found himself in a third peloton as a result of several mechanical mishaps and Duclos-Lassalle had lost all chance in a crash at Arenberg.

Twenty five kilometres from the finish, on the cobbles of Wandignies, Moser, scarcely having joined the leading group, unleashed the battle. In less than eight kilometres he caught De Rooy who had been alone at the front. However, today Moser did not have the means to fulfil his ambition. While he was in the lead for twenty five kilometres, Vanderaerden, accompanied by the young Northerner Lecrocq, counter-attacked on the hill at Mons-en-Pévèle.

At the top he was sixteen seconds from Moser's heels and at Phalempin he joined him. A little later, when Moser punctured a tyre and fell, Vanderaerden found himself alone in the lead. The man wanted to repeat his lone win in the Tour of Flanders. This time, however, he could not make it to the velodrome as, suddenly, his strength left him.

At Wannehain where it was back to square one again, a little peloton comprising of most of the favourites was leading the race. Marc Madiot felt at ease there. Having tested his rivals, he threw everything into it that he had on the famous section of cobbles known as the "l'Abre cross-roads", at fourteen kilometres from Roubaix.

Nobody was able to stop him. Well protected by his team-mate Bruno Wojtinek, the man from Mayenne came onto the Roubaix track with almost two minutes lead over his first pursuers.

In spite of the heralded success of the Panasonic team, Madiot's

1985

Marc MADIOT
(France, 1959)

A specialist on the cobbles, to this day he is the only rider to have won the amateur version as well.

1979 : Amateur Paris-Roubaix
1983 : 2nd Paris-Bourges
1985 : Paris-Roubaix,
      Grand Prix de Wallonne
1986 : 2nd Tour du Haut Var
1987 : French Champion
1988 : 2nd French Championship,
1989 : 3rd Paris-Nice
1991 : Paris-Roubaix

Eric Vanderaerden

Josef Lieckens

Hennie Kuiper with Adri Van der Poel

performance was hardly a surprise. A week beforehand in the Tour of Flanders, he confided to Jean-Marie Leblanc: "This year I have gone out of my way to prepare for the classics. I do not know which one but I hope to win at least one of them."

Since his success in the amateur event in 1979, he had secretly hoped to enter, one way or another, into the court of the great.

At the finish he was covered in mud. It had rained and even snowed for part of the day but the winner was delighted: "Paris-Roubaix is a race which has always pleased me. Not only because of the legend but also because I do like the cobbles.

Thirty kilometres from Roubaix I crossed over the cobblestones at the head of the race and I felt then that I was going to succeed. Fourteen kilometres from the finish was the right moment, The people were crying my name out but I stayed very concentrated. At three thousand metres from the end, I prepared to enter the velodrome. I cleaned myself up a bit and then at the red kite, Cyrille Guimard came alongside and shook my hand. When I came onto the track, the orchestra was playing the Marseillaise. It was a moment of intense joy."

The previous year, Guimard had deplored the lack of success of his young riders, this time, they monopolised the first two places.

The Northerner Bruno Wojtinek, twenty two years old and like an expert, had got rid of Kelly, LeMond, Dhaenens, Planckaert and Lieckens to take the second step on the podium. It was a consecration for him, he confirmed the title of one of the main hopes of national cycling.

Unfortunately, following a training accident, his career was suddenly stopped in 1989. Certainly, he picked had picked up several dozen victories but he had promised so much. The Paris-Roubaix remains for him, as it did for Alain Bondue twelve months before, an unforgettable memory, something that should have led to far greater things.

1985

1. Marc MADIOT (France)
   GS. Renault-Elf-Gitane
2. Bruno WOJTINEK (France)
3. Sean KELLY (Ireland)
4. Greg LEMOND (USA)
5. Rudy DHAENENS (Belgium)
6. Eddy PLANCKAERT (Belgium)
7. Josef LIECKENS (Belgium)
8. Hennie KUIPER (Holland)
9. Adri VAN DER POEL (Holland)
10. Ferdi VANDENHAUTE (Belgium)

Francesco Moser struck by misfortune.

The other side of the north

In February 1986, Mahdjoub Ben Bella, a contemporary artist, thought up something that was just a little mad; to paint a road surface over an area of several hundred square metres. Living in the North of France, scarcely a couple of kilometres from the Roubaix Velodrome, he felt inspired by the Paris-Roubaix cycle race. The idea rapidly matured to the point when the site was selected several days later: Mahdjoub would paint the end of the route of the legendary event!

Thanks mainly to the help from the Conseil General du Nord, Ben Bella found himself faced with the challenge of painting 32,000 square metres in a fortnight!

From the arrival of sixteen tonnes of paint (the pink was ordered from Berlin, the blue from London, the white and the yellow in France) the race against time began regardless of weather conditions.

Nine workmen supervised by the artist realised the impossible and after fifteen days of work the result was a long multicoloured ribbon of twelve kilometres.

In the month of April many of the riders went to see the art. Some of them such as Moser and Kelly, showed a certain reserve. However, nothing had been left to chance for sand was mixed with the paint to make the surface five times less slippery!

Mahdjoub Ben Bella, had in the meantime become passionately involved with the event and for the Centenary of the Paris-Roubaix has produced several works featuring names such as Hippolyte Aucouturier (1904) and Gilbert Duclos-Lassalle.

1986

The mastery of King Kelly

For the first time since 1942, the finish of the Paris-Roubaix would not be at the velodrome. It was to be abandoned for three years from 1986 to 1988 to the profit of the Avenue of the United Nations, a new main road in the centre of town.

The purists and many others said that it was a scandal. They thought that the finish of the Queen of Classics should never be held on a banal and soulless straight line to the detriment of the mythical arena where heroes like Coppi, Bobet and Merckx had arrived in triumph.

As usual, the list of contenders was imposing. However, several favourites were unable to sign the start sheet in the main square at Compiègne.

The first of them was the previous winner. The injured Marc Madiot was obliged to give the race a miss. His compatriots, Hinault, Fignon, Poisson and Gayant were also not to be seen at the start. The same applied to several foreign stars. Kuiper and Roche found themselves on the touch line and Anderson was unable to find the required form. The world number one was Sean Kelly who had dominated the beginning of the 1986 season. Since the start of season the Irishman had already won fourteen events, a sixth consecutive Paris-Nice and then Milan-San Remo. His preparation for Paris-Roubaix had then taken him to the Tour of Basque Country. In spite of the bad weather conditions, Kelly won the final classification and three stages, of which two of them on the Friday were just seventy two hours before the start of the Paris-Roubaix.

Kelly owed his success to his immense physical qualities, naturally, but also to his courage. No matter how hard or painful things were, he never complained, neither about bad weather, his training miles or being so isolated near the finish or being so far from his green land of Ireland.

Having turned professional in 1977, he first of all had to play the role of a team man by preparing the sprint for his leaders. Then with time the results started to come and he started to think of riding for himself.

His team manager, Jean De Gribaldy, often compared him to Louison Bobet: "If he can do all this then it's because ten years ago he led the life of a monk. He is gathering in the fruits the same way as Bobet did previously."

In the second rank of favourites were Eddy Planckaert, Van der Poel, who had won the Tour of Flanders in front of Kelly, LeMond and Moser. The latter swore, as he had done the previous year, that his twelfth Paris-Roubaix would certainly be the last.

The event, at least in the early part, bored the followers. The real race was only really launched forty kilometres from the finish.

Up until this time only the crashes had enlivened the proceedings. The first to be affected were Eric Vanderaerden, Allan Peiper, Bruno Wojtinek and Eric Louvel. The latter two were obliged to retire.

Even the rough crossing through Arenberg did not provoke the usual decision. Certainly the peloton broke up, but a dozen kilometres later they were all back together again.

At Erre, Pascal Jules and Roger De Cnijf took things in hand, they broke clear and led for nearly fifteen kilometres.

Then Francesco Moser, incorrigible, decided to start the selection on the cobbles of Martinsart a good hour from the finish.

About fifty riders found themselves in one long line. Them Rudy Dhaenens decided to escape, Duclos-Lassalle broke his handlebars. LeMond and Bauer both had their ardour cooled

1986

when they punctured.

At Templeuve, behind Dhaenens, a little group went clear notably containing Kelly, Moser and the young Lecrocq.

But at Wannehain, after Dhaenens was caught the regrouping of thirty men was inevitable. On the cobbles of Camphin-en-Pévèle, eighteen kilometres from the velodrome, Sean Kelly decided it was high time to force the pace. Everyone was waiting for a reaction but only Vandenhaute, Van der Poel and Dhaenens managed to stay on his wheel. Behind, Moser was doing the major part of the work. He was helped by Sergeant, Versluys and Eddy Planckaert, who a little later broke his pedal.

Logically, Sean Kelly was the fastest. But he was terribly distrustful of Van der Poel who had just beaten him at the end of an exciting Tour of Flanders. Kelly like a debutante, had led the sprint out from too far and was overtaken just before the line. This time surprise was no longer possible. In spite of a last attack by Vandenhaute four hundred metres from the finishing line, Kelly easily put his three companions in their place.

Dhaenens was second, Van der Poel third and Vandenhaute fourth. King Kelly

Vandenbroucke in front of Leali and Pascal Jules, protects Kelly.

Patrick Versluys on his domain: the cobbles.

seemed happy: "You know Paris-Roubaix is a fine race. If I had to choose between winning here or at San Remo, I would always prefer Paris-Roubaix." On the other hand Moser, only eighth, was terribly disappointed with his race: "I have had a very difficult day. I punctured before the feeding station at Valenciennes and my team car did not see me. I lost at least two minutes and I had to chase for forty kilometres.

I used up a lot of strength. I can't say that Kelly is Merckx but I have to say that he wins in the way he chooses."

The French hardly showed themselves to their best advantage. Alain Bondue, the first of them finished twenty second in front of Dominique Lecrocq. The former world pursuit champion lacked any strength on the final difficult section.

Finally Greg LeMond, perfectly adapted to the European system, said: "There are three races in the season; Paris-Roubaix, the Tour de France and the world championship. If you manage to win just one of these then your career takes off."

1986

1. Sean KELLY (Ireland)
   GS.Kas-Mavic
2. Rudy DHAENENS (Belgium)
3. Adri VAN DER POEL (Holland)
4. Ferdi VANDENHAUTE (Belgium)
5. Ludo PEETERS (Belgium)
6. Johan VAN DER VELDE (Holland)
7. Marc SERGEANT (Belgium)
8. Francesco MOSER (Italy)
9. Patrick VERSLUYS (Belgium)
10. Nico VERHOEVEN (Holland)

Eric VANDERAERDEN
(Belgium, 1962)

A young prodigy who succeeded in living up to his early promise, as his honours list shows.

1984 : Belgian Champion,
Paris-Brussels,
2nd Ghent-Wevelgem,
3rd Milan-San Remo
1985 : Tour of Flanders,
Ghent-Wevelgem,
Tour of Holland
1986 : Three Days de la Panne
1987 : Paris-Roubaix,
Three days de la Panne,
2nd Milan-San Remo,
3rd Tour of Flanders,
3rd Paris-Brussels
1988 : Three Days de la Panne
1989 : Three days de la Panne,
2nd Paris-Tours
1991 : 3rd Milan-San Remo
1992 : 3rd Het Volk
1993 : Three Days de la Panne,
2nd Ghent-Wevelgem,
3rd Het Volk

Vanderaerden rehabilitates himself

"The champion is a very worthy one, he dominated with intelligence, but it must not be forgotten that he should not have ridden Paris-Roubaix." This was Jacques Goddet's first reaction as he got out of his car a few moments after Eric Vanderaerden's win in the 1987 Paris-Roubaix.

The founder of L'Equipe, his point of view perfectly summed up an ambiguous situation created by Eric Vanderaerden's performance in the Tour of the Mediterranean. On the morning of the last day the Belgian had already won a stage, and was going to do the same in the last time trial. However, he was to be disqualified and put out of the race as he had been found hanging on to the door of Peter Post's car!

Vanderaerden was immediately suspended for a fortnight but, for many observers, the penalty was much too lenient.

After his return to racing he wanted to rehabilitate himself as quickly as possible. The man from Limburg only failed by a whisker in Milan-San Remo behind the Swiss Maechler, then finished third in the Tour of Flanders won by Claude Criquielion. A few days before Paris-Roubaix, Peter Post, his team manager, let it be known that Phil Anderson would be the only leader of the team in the Northern event. Vanderaerden from then on had all the more reason for wanting to do well.

The accumulation of classics inevitably provoked a thinning out in the list of starters. How could it be avoided when five classics were run in two weeks: the Tour of Flanders, Ghent Wevelgem, Paris-Roubaix, Flèche Wallonne and Liège-Bastogne-Liège! In this way Fignon, LeMond, Criquielion, Roche, Bernard and most of the Italians watched the race on television.

On the other hand the cobbles specialists were all there in the big square of Compiègne: Kelly, Dhaenens, Kuiper, Planckaert, Vanderaerden, Bondue, Madiot, Duclos-Lasalle, Wojtinek, Van der Poel, Braun and Versluys. Even Moser went back on his word and was participating in his thirteenth Paris-Roubaix.

Several others were among the attractions of the day: the Mexican Alcala, the American Hampsten, and the Californian snake hunter Bob Roll who was particularly taken with this race in which he had finished fifty fifth twelve months previously.

Unlike them, two first-year professionals, great hopes of international cycling, were making their debuts on the Northern roads: Maurizio Fondriest and Edwig Van Hooydonck.

The first of the one hundred and ninety two starters to act was Charly Mottet. He attacked at the twenty second kilometre and took fifteen men with him. In sight of the first cobbled sectors the group still had five minutes lead. The Arenberg Gap provoked a first selection in the peloton where Wojtinek and Planckaert were setting the pace. About thirty men remained together at the exit of Arenberg forest.

At the front tiredness was beginning to have its effect. Only Vanderaerden, Solleveld and De Rooy were able to resist the pressure of the peloton which saw Van der Poel, Lieckens, Dhaenens, Vandenbrande and Versluys go clear off the front. The junction of these five riders and the original escapees was effected at the feeding station of La Rosiere. The group quickly lost Vandenbrouke, Solleveld and Van der Poel, all puncture victims.

At Martinsart, forty kilometres from Roubaix, the situation seemed to be straightforward. Lieckens, Dhaenens, Vandenbrande, Versluys and De Rooy had two and a half minutes on the bunch. In spite of several crashes, notably that of Dhaenens who took down De Rooy and a motorbike, the gap was still stable.

With De Rooy eliminated there were now only four men at the front, then three when Lieckens in his turn was dropped: Dhaenens, Versluys and Vandenbrande. Behind, fourteen riders, most of the favourites, formed the avant-garde of the peloton: Kelly, Vanderaerden, Duclos-Lassalle, Wojtinek, Bontempi, Moser, Marie, Sergeant, Dewilde, Hooydonck, Kuiper and Madiot followed a few hundred metres down.

At Wannehain, twenty five kilometres from the finish things began to take a dramatic turn when Kelly slipped on the cobbles and his handlebars broke.

The incident also held up Moser, Madiot and all the others except Vanderaerden who immediately attacked hard.

The fate of the race was settled in a few seconds. Vanderaerden embarked on a difficult and solitary pursuit match.

Thanks to his "punch"and his courage he managed to augment his advantage by a minute in fifteen kilometres!

He caught the leading trio three thousand metres before the finishing line. Vanderaerden was intrinsically the fastest of the quartet.

Logic would have suggested that the other three would take turns in attacking him but no attempt materialised. A conversation between the protagonists was later to lead to rumours circulating.

For his part Rudy Dhaenens denies all accusations. According to him nobody ever even thinks about "selling" a Paris-Roubaix. Naturally, Vanderaerden proved to be impeccable in the sprint and won in front of Versluys, Dhaenens and Vandenbrande.

The fifth, Edwig Van Hooydonck, completed the Belgian success. At less than twenty one years old he seemed to confirm the enormous potential he had.

The whimsical Bob Roll modestly confirmed the internationalisation of cycling and finished forty eighth at thirty nine minutes. He preceded two of his compatriots, Jonathan Boyer and Andrew Hampsten, who had unquestionably acquired a taste for this cobbled event.

1987

Next page :
Duclos-Lassalle leads Kelly, Vanderaerden and De Wilde

1. Eric VANDERAERDEN (Belgium)
   GS.Panasonic
2. Patrick VERSLUYS (Belgium)
3. Rudy DHAENENS (Belgium)
4. Jean-Philippe VANDENBRANDE
   (Belgium)
5. Edwig VAN HOOYDONCK (Belgium)
6. Bruno WOJTINEK (France)
7. Marc SERGEANT (Belgium)
8. Nico VERHOEVEN (Holland)
9. Bruno LEALI (Italy)
10. Martial GAYANT (France)

Demol after a break of 222 kilometres !

Dirk DEMOL
(Belgium, 1959)

A Belgian "journeyman' professional, he was another rider happiest on the cobbles as he proved, in addition to his 1988 victory, by also finishing second and fourth in the amateur version.

1980 : 2nd Amateur Paris-Roubaix
1983 : Grand Prix de Courtrai
1985 : 3rd Grand Prix de Impanis
1987 : Grand Prix de Grammont,
      3rd Kuurne-Brussels-Kuurne,
      4th Grand Prix Scherens
1988 : Paris-Roubaix
1990 : Circuit des Ardennes Flamandes
1994 : Grand Prix de Courtrai

Certainly, it must be said that Dirk Demol was not a star whose name was like those of Kelly or Fignon which were regularly spread across the front pages of the newspapers. However, this citizen of Bavikhove superbly won the eighty sixth Paris-Roubaix and his victory was certainly not stolen.

This success should not be devalued and Dirk, always so modest, said just after his triumph: "It's true that this was not a great Paris-Roubaix as the stars were all watching each other at the back but I am not responsible for that. I did my job as well as I possibly could and nobody could reproach me for anything."

His victory caused a lot of ink to flow and some tried to minimise the impact of it. This was not the case with Rik Van Looy and Eddy Merckx as for them Dirk Demol absolutely deserved the success and if the stars lost the struggle they should only take it out on themselves.

This 10 April was really a blessed day for Demol, for if the organisers had reduced the number from eight to seven riders for each team as at one time they had been expected to do, Jose De Cauwer, his team manager, would have dropped him from the ADR team! This same De Cauwer who, at the start of the season, had flayed his rider a little in the following terms:

"Dirk, it's time you became a rider. You are twenty eight and you have never really performed at the level of which you are capable."

The first to enter into the action was a Frenchman by the name of Thierry Casas. The Parisian unleashed an attack at the forty fourth kilometre. Twelve riders immediately went with him: Van Rijnen, Boucanville, Le Flohic, Schurer, Demol, Wegmuller, Veldscholten, Peiper, Cornelisse, Van Steenwinkel, Knickman and Joho. At that time there were two hundred and twenty two kilometres to cover and nobody could imagine that two of these men were going to contest the victory at Roubaix!

In less than ten kilometres the group had already opened a gap of four and a half minutes. As was often the case during these morning escapes, the bunch decided not to react immediately. As they crossed the first cobbled sector at Troisvilles situated at one hundred kilometres, the advance of the fugitives had gone up to eight minutes.

The peloton, which was still not riding at any great speed, split up and then reformed just before crossing through Calenciennes. Only a few crashes disturbed the supporters lunch !

In the Arenberg section, misfortune in the form of punctures, hit first of all Knickman, Schurer, Casas and Le Flohic. Then Cornelisse and Van Steenwinkel in their turn were dropped. At the exit to the obstacle there were still seven of them in the lead with five and half minutes in hand.

Several counter-attacks then shook the peloton. The most serious was that of Guido Bontempi. As they left Orchies behind them, seventy four kilometres from Roubaix, the situation seemed clear: Bontempi was 2mins 50secs behind the seven leaders, and the bunch, composed of about forty men passed through twenty five seconds after the Italian At Bersee, while Boucanville and Peiper were dropped from

1988

L'EQUIPE et le Parisien

présentent

La reine des classiques

86e PARIS-ROUBAIX

(Compiègne)

TROPHÉE

Merlin plage

LE PALMARÈS

Lisez Vélo

LE JOURNAL DE LA COMPÉTITION ET DES LOISIRS

the group of leaders, Bontempi got to within 1-27 of them.

However, at the front the pace was increased. At the feeding station of Merignies, sixty kilometres from the finish, Wegmuller, Veldscholten, Demol, Joho and Van Rijnen picked up their musettes 2mins 40secs before Boucanville, 4-40 before Bontempi who was riding at his limit, and with more than five minutes on the bunch who were beginning to question each other. Sean Kelly's crashed, breaking his frame, Mutter, Redant, Vandenbrande and Vanderaerden, among others, were also delayed.

On the hill at Wannehain, there remained just twenty kilometres to go and a deficit of nearly three minutes for the twenty men who had just emerged from the bunch. Laurent Fignon and Bruno Wojtinek tried hard to relaunch the pursuit but most of the stars hesitated to produce an effort that would perhaps be to the advantage of an adversary.

At the Arbre crossroads on one of the last sections of cobbles, Demol and Wegmuller dropped their last companions. Fignon at last went clear of the bunch but the two leaders still had two more minutes in hand. The Parisian certainly caught Sergeant, Joho, Van Rijnen and Veldscholten but there still remained the inaccessible Demol and Wegmuller. A very disappointing third place was waiting for him on the Avenue of the United Nations.

While Demol and Wegmuller were getting ready to dispute the victory in the sprint, the spectators had difficulty in believing that after being away for more than two hundred and twenty kilometres they still appeared to be so fresh.

Roubaix en couleurs (dernière page)

3790105005907 04110

L'EQUIPE

LUNDI 11 AVRIL 1988   LE QUOTIDIEN DU SPORT ET DE L'AUTOMOBILE   ★ 42e ANNÉE — N° 13 040 — 5,90 F

FIGNON LE DAMNÉ DE L'ENFER

Troisième de Paris-Roubaix, le vainqueur de Milan-San Remo était encore l'un des plus forts hier.

Piégé dans une course tactique, il n'a pu revenir sur le Belge Dirk De Mol, étonnant vainqueur, et le Suisse Wegmuller, deuxième.

(Pages 2 à 5)

De Mol, près 222 k...

BASKET

HUFNAGEL S'EN VA

Alors que, conformément à la logique, Mulhouse, Villeurbanne, Nantes et Orthez se sont qualifiés, Hufnagel se prépare à quitter l'Élan Béarnais.

(Page 7)

ÉQUITATION

DURAND TOUT PRÈS

Auteur d'une prodigieuse remontée, Pierre Durand n'a pris cependant que la deuxième place de la Coupe du monde, derrière le Canadien Millar.

(Page 15)

RUGBY

DERNIERS BILLETS

Graulhet, Perpignan, Bayonne, Tyrosse ont arraché les quatre derniers billets qualificatifs pour les huitièmes de finale du Championnat.

(Pages 20 et 21)

Eddy Planckaert in front of Frank Hoste
in the 'trench' of Arenberg

In the final straight, Demol easily disposed of the Swiss Wegmuller and raised his arms to the sky as if in a dream.

The Belgian was drowning in happiness and his first words were for his leader Eddy Planckaert: "I was told by De Cauwer to go with the morning break. I was working for Eddy and waiting for him to come up. But at the back nobody was working. So I said to myself 'stay in front, you're not a bad sprinter, and you never know'. It was Roger De Vlaeminck who built up my morale. Thirty kilometres from Roubaix he came past us in his car and told us that we still had three minutes lead, that the favourites were finished and that I was going to win. When there was only two of us I started to believe it."

If his record, compared with that of his predecessors, seemed a little thin, the observers nevertheless remembered that he was one of the best Belgian amateurs and that he finished second in the amateur Paris-Roubaix behind Stephen Roche. At Bavikhove, the beer was flowing all night long.

The most disappointed on the day was Laurent Fignon. Certainly he was the strongest in the race but he only achieved an insignificant third place. His great mistake was, like everyone else, to have not reacted earlier: "There were too many of us in the chasing group for us to have worked together properly. Everyone was expecting everyone else to do the work and the kilometres went by."

And so the victory went to the least calculating.

1988

1. Dirk DEMOL (Belgium)
   GS.ADR-Anti M-IOC
2. Thomas WEGMULLER (Switzerland)
3. Laurent FIGNON (France)
4. Stephan JOHO (Switzerland)
5. Marc SERGEANT (Belgium)
6. Corné VAN RIJEN (Holland)
7. Gérard VELDSCHOLTEN (Holland)
8. Steve BAUER (Canada)
9. Herman FRISON (Belgium)
10. Johan LAMMERTS (Holland)

Wampers continues the Belgian supremacy

Since the retirement of Eddy Merckx, the Belgians had been looking for a champion of calibre. Bearing this in mind it is hardly surprising to note that the tears of Van Hooydonck at the finish of his victorious Tour of Flanders had moved everyone in the country. At less than twenty three, Edwig was the incarnation of the future of national cycling in the single-day classics. One question, however, was being asked on the front pages of the dailies in the country; will the prodigy have sufficiently recovered from his efforts with the Paris-Roubaix in sight?

If not, the Flemish put forward other major trumps such as Vanderaerden, Planckaert, Dirk Dewolf and also Dhaenens who could all dominate over the cobbled roads.

However, the sensible De Vlaeminck was rather more in the favour of the Dutchman Van der Poel:

"If it rains," he said "I wouldn't hesitate, my favourite would be Van der Poel, then

La surprise des huitièmes aller de la Coupe est venue du Parc, ou Orléans a écrasé le P-SG 4-0 et l'a   (Pages 10 à 13)

L'ÉQUIPE

M 0105 - 0410 0 - 6,00 F

3790105006003   04100

LUNDI 10 AVRIL 1989   LE QUOTIDIEN DU SPORT ET DE L'AUTOMOBILE   ★   44e ANNÉE   — N° 13 352 — 6

EN VENTE DEMAIN MARDI
France Football

UN PAVÉ BELGE DANS LA MARE

Les Belges ont effectué une véritable razzia sur Paris-Roubaix, enlevé par Jean-Marie Wampers devant Dirk De Wolf et Edwig Van Hooydonck, toujours leader de la Coupe du monde.   (Pages 2 à 6)

TENNIS

Les Français sous le joug

Emmenée par un super-McEnroe, qui donn d'entrée le ton en balayant Noah, l'équipe américaine a assuré sa qualification pour les demi-finales dès le deuxième jour (3-0)   (Page 7)

BASKET

Mulhouse la surprise
(Page 15)

HANDBALL

Créteil peut rêver
(Page 15)

MOTO

Podium

A crash for Fignon.

Vanderaerden, providing that the Belgian is on a good day. In the face of them, no Italian has the same gifts as Moser to get over the cobbles. As for Kelly, I think that he is too old to win at Roubaix. Once you're past thirty it is much more difficult to win here. I won, for example, my fourth success at twenty nine and a half. After that I had a lot of punctures and sometimes I even fell. The same thing happened to Moser. I only give a one in five chance to Kelly."

This opinion of an expert, if ever there was one, confirmed that Sean Kelly was not the man he used to be. Numerous observers noted that his last important victory went back to Ghent Wevelgem, a year ago, and that the beginning of his season had hardly been transcendent. However, the Irishman was always on the lookout.

The weather forecast was favourable. After this almost everyone started to tip Laurent Fignon. For the last twelve months the Parisian knew that he had the means to win it. Moreover, he had not yet got over his previous failure.

The rain over the previous few days had flooded certain parts of the route. In the Arenberg Forest, as well as the muddy roadsides, the riders would have to cope with cobbles made even more uneven by recent mining subsidence,

Perhaps in order to avert fate Sean Kelly was the first to make **1989**

Jean-Marie WAMPERS
(Belgium, 1959)

He enjoyed one superb season - 1989 -
highlighted by victory in Paris-Roubaix.

1981 : Tour of Latium
1982 : Grand Prix de Camaiore
1986 : 3rd Ghent-Wevelgem
1987 : 3rd Flèche-Brabanconne
1989 : Paris-Roubaix,
        Grand Prix de l'Escaut
1990 : 5th Paris-Roubaix

his presence felt. During the winter the man had changed teams and from now on wore the colours of the powerful PDM group. This transfer allowed him to have numerous competitive team-mates in this type of race. Thanks to them, he was in the lead on the first cobbled sector after a sprint of several kilometres! In spite of the Irishman being on the ball, the Frenchman Jean-Claude Colotti attacked at the feeding station of Solesmes. On the cobbles of Artres, Sean Yates launched himself into his pursuit and caught him just before the one hundred and fiftieth kilometre. At the back, there was a big regrouping at Valenciennes.

This was not to last for long as the Forest of Arenberg was stretched out on the horizon. A monumental crash took place a thousand metres before the famous cobbled track. Roche, among others, was dropped for good.

In front, Colotti found himself alone after Yates had punctured. The Frenchman was caught by Van der Poel, Verhoeven, Hanegraaf, Freuler and Van Holen. While Colotti, at the end of his strength, was dropped by the group. At the back, Fignon was the victim of a third puncture and put his foot to the ground once again.

Sixty kilometres from the finish the right brake went. To start with Dirk Dewolf, Planckaert, Wampers and Duclos-Lassalle escaped. Two kilometres on, Van Hooydonck and Marc Madiot joined them.

These men were to monopolise the first six places at Roubaix. In fact, their lead never stopped growing and minutes mounted up until there were four and a half of them at the finish!

About twenty men formed the peloton of the vanquished. Among them were Fignon, Vanderaerden, Kelly, Van der Poel and Dhaenens.

The first runaway to attempt the solitary adventure seventeen kilometres from the end was Dirk Dewolf. The final decision seemed to have been made in spite of a pursuit led by Van Hooydonck.

While Planckaert fell, the only one capable of reacting was none other than Jean-Marie Wampers. He managed to rejoin Dewolf nine thousand metres from the velodrome. The pair managed to resist the pressure of the pursuers and

arrived in the streets of Roubaix. Wampers intelligently forced his adversary to enter the track in first position and easily outsprinted him.

The new winner, in spite of his talent, was scarcely known to the public. In this way his 1988 season was totally fruitless. A victim of the blood disease mononucleosis, he had hardly ridden at all and even had difficulty in finding the strength to mow the lawn. Peter Post had kept faith in him and without that he would have quickly hung up his wheels.

After that his name was to appear more and more in the news for he notably won the Grand Prix de l'Escaut and the Grand Prix of Frankfurt, two coveted events in the cycling calendar.

An equally big surprise for the Belgians came from Van Hooydonck, who again confirmed his enormous class, and for the French the always young Duclos-Lassalle.

The South-westerner in his thirty fifth year, had enchanted the Northern public once again. At the finish, Duclos, never short of words, claimed: "I can assure you that at the end of the race I was cooked. I was grovelling in the last ten kilometres. This Paris-Roubaix was physically very hard. My fourth place gave me a lot of satisfaction and I have no regrets. After a training crash in February a cracked sacrum put me on the sidelines for a good month, I am only riding my tenth race of the year here. I came because above all I love the race and I also like to do well here. As long as Paris-Roubaix remains in existence, I will always be here."

As for Sean Kelly, who some were claiming to be finished, a week later he went on to win a second Liège-Bastogne-Liège.

1989

1. Jean-Marie WAMPERS (Belgium)
   GS.Pansonic-Isostar
2. Dirk DEWOLF (Belgium)
3. Edwig VAN HOOYDONCK (Belgium)
4. Gilbert DUCLOS-LASSALLE
   (France)
5. Eddy PLANCKAERT (Belgium)
6. Marc MADIOT (France)
7. Herman FRISON (Belgium)
8. Jacques HANEGRAFF (Holland)
9. Urs FREULER (Switzerland)
10. Johan LAMMERTS (Holland)

Planckaert's millimetres

Never in eighty seven editions of Paris-Roubaix had the victory been as indecisive as it was on the 8 April 1990. However, people thought they had seen everything the previous year when, on the Champs-Elysees at the end of a dazzling Tour de France, eight seconds separated Greg LeMond from the unfortunate Laurent Fignon.

On the track at the Roubaix velodrome, at the end of two hundred and sixty five kilometres, two men threw their bikes at the finishing line.

These two riders, the Canadian Steve Bauer and the Belgian Eddy Planckaert were at the very end of their strength and, side by side, threw their

NDI 9 AVRIL 1990   LE QUOTIDIEN DU SPORT ET DE L'AUTOMOBILE   45ᵉ ANNÉE — Nº 13 662 — 6

DIABLE DE PLANCKAERT

Longtemps seul en tête dans l'Enfer, le Belge Eddy Planckaert a surgi de sa boîte pour devancer ur la ligne le Canadien Bauer et l'autre Belge, Van Hooydonck. Gayant quatrième.   (Pages 2 à 6)

(Photo Didier FÈVRE)

Gilles Dumas dirigea très bien la manœuvre.

JEU À XIII   (Page 17)

Exploit tricolore au bout de 23 ans

BASKET   (Page 14)

Limoges s'assure déjà une Coupe

RUGBY   (Pages 18 et 19)

Brive et Castres dans le bon wagon

HOCKEY SUR GLACE   (Page 22)

Suisses à l'heure Français défaits...

last ounce of weight over the finishing line.

The judge at the finish, Joël Menard, took a long while before he gave his verdict. The thousands of spectators held their breath in the velodrome where not even a whisper came from the bursting terraces. Nobody dared to suggest the name of the winner, neither the public, nor the protagonists themselves!

Four minutes later, an eternity, after the enlargement of the photo-finish, the decision was given: Eddy Planckaert had won Paris-Roubaix by less than a centimetre!

This eighty-eighth Paris-Roubaix entered into history, not only for its ending but also for the quality of the starters.

In fact, in Eastern Europe, in a few months the walls and not only the shameful ones of Berlin, had fallen.

A few years before it would have been unthinkable to see an East German or even a Russian sign the start sheet in the main square at Compiègne.

The liberalisation first of all permitted the creation of a Soviet team in 1989, with notably Andreï Tchmil, then twelve months later the best of the "state amateurs".

So, there were sixteen of them at the start of Paris-Roubaix. Among them were several who were already considered to be potential winners: the Germans Olaf Ludwig, Uwe Ampler, Mario Kummer and Jan Schur, the Poles Joachim Halupczok and Zenon Jaskula, and finally the Russian Dimitri Konyshev, the astonishing world championship silver medallist.

These men who had often dominated amateur cycling started without any complexes. Jaskula, for example, was second in the Tirreno-Adriatico and eleventh in the Tour of Flanders and said without turning a hair: "I very much hope to be in the first ten at Roubaix." Without forgetting to add that the winner would be called Planckaert or Vanderaerden. In two months of being a professional, it must be said that he learned very quickly.

The beginning of the season was marked by two important facts. First of all it seemed that Italian cycling was in good health. Gianni Bugno showed himself to be unbeatable on the hill at San Remo and the talented Moreno Argentin took the Tour of Flanders. It caused Enrico Paolini, the team manager of Maurizio Fondriest to say: "Bugno at San Remo, Argentin in the Tour of Flanders, why not Maurizio on Sunday?" In fact it was no secret, for the former world champion was burning with desire to join the illustrious Francesco Moser in the hearts of the Italian fans.

The other big event was the "war" which had been declared between the Buckler and Panasonic teams. Vanderaerden had left Post in order to join the rivals. The conflict came to a head during the Grand Prix of Harelbeke when at the finish, Vanderaerden had commented: "Planckaert said that he was very strong and I was content to just follow him." Planckaert responded: "If they want me to lose, well they'll lose with me." Victory went to the third man, the Dane Sören Lilholt!

Once again, Fignon was the principal favourite. Fondriest, Planckaert, Van Hooydonck, Dhaenens and Gilbert Duclos-Lassalle had to, it seemed, wait on the events of the day. Only the venerable Sean Kelly, victim of a crash in the Tour of Flanders was unavailable.

One hundred and eighty six riders left Castle Square in Compiègne. From the twentieth kilometre, three men attacked: Pieters, Kleinsman and Joho. The bunch were not really worried about this trio whose lead went right up to sixteen minutes at the entrance

1990

Eddy PLANCKAERT
(Belgium, 1958)

The youngest of the famous Belgian brothers, he achieved the great Flemish double of the Tour of Flanders and Paris-Roubaix.

1982 : 2nd Tour of Flanders,
          5th Paris-Roubaix
1983 : Flèche-Brabanconne
1984 : Het Volk, Tour of Belgium,
          2nd Belgian Championship
1985 : Het Volk
1986 : 2nd Flèche-Brabanconne
1988 : Tour of Flanders
1989 : 2nd Belgian Championship,
          5th Paris-Roubaix
1990 : Paris-Roubaix

With one lap to go Wampers leads the group
with Planckaert and Gayant on his wheel.

to the first cobbled sections at Troisvilles.

While Kleinsman was dropped after a puncture, the selection took place at
the back. Twenty one riders then made up the chasing group.

However, after Wallers, an important regrouping took place ninety five
kilometres from the velodrome and astonishingly, Eddy Planckaert threw
everything into an attack. The Belgian launched himself into the pursuit of
Joho and of Pieters who he caught and then dropped a little later. In his car
Peter Post was furious. He thought that it was too far to the finish and ordered
Planckaert to drop back!

But Eddy did not want to hear anything and quickly said to him: "No, certainly
not, we'll soon see what happens. For me, at thirty two years of age, it's now
or never."

At Orchies, Planckaert preceded the peloton by a minute and fifteen
seconds. On the cobbles at Bersee, two men came up to his wheel: Martial
Gayant and an unknown whose surname was completely beyond all the
French commentators, one by the name of Kurt Van Keirsbulck.

Fifteen kilometres further on, the lead went over two minutes. The chasing
group formed of fifteen riders was most often led by Laurent Fignon. But the
progress of this peloton was upset by Planckaert's team-mates. In fact
Wampers, Freuler, Ludwig and Talen locked up the race perfectly.

At Templeuve, thirty five kilometres from Roubaix, three riders nevertheless
managed to come up to the leaders: Van Hooydonck, then Van den Akker and
Steve Bauer. The six men only had twenty seconds lead on a peloton where
nevertheless nobody dared to engage in a real pursuit.

Fearing a regrouping from the back, Bauer was the first to show. Rapidly
Planckaert and Van Hooydonck realised the danger and got up to his wheel.

The millimetres of victory.
Planckaert (left) and Bauer.

Ten kilometres from the finish, the trio led by forty seconds from Gayant, the astonishing Van Keirsbulck and Van den Akker and by fifty five seconds from the peloton.

The outcome seemed settled but two thousand metres from the velodrome, Gayant in one last desperate effort was getting dangerously close. There was a minor regrouping when he rejoined!

Planckaert, who had led the race for ninety kilometres, was first onto the track in front of Bauer and Van Hooydonck both close on his back wheel, a few metres down were Gayant and Wampers, then in their turn: Duclos-Lassalle, Wegmuller, Van der Poel and Talen. At the beginning of the last lap, Wampers went into the lead. On the final bend Van Hooydonck tried to overtake him before giving way to the Bauer-Planckaert duel. Eddy, the third hero of the Planckaert clan after Willy and Walter, attained his consecration. He added Paris-Roubaix to his 1988 Tour of Flanders.

On this 8 April 1990, he had brought off a fabulous coup on the day of Walter's birthday.

As for Bauer, on the grass in the track centre, he did not seem to be too disappointed. Firstly, he thought it "okay to finish second at Roubaix", but looking back on it he realised that by just a few millimetres he had missed a prestigious victory by which he would have entered into the record books.

Finally the Eastern Europeans were not disappointed. Halupczok was fourteenth and the Olympic champion, Olaf Ludwig was sixteenth. As a team-mate of Planckaert he had protected his escape. Ludwig undeniably had talent and the necessary qualities to rejoin the illustrious Josef Fischer on the record books, who remained the only German winner at Roubaix in...1896!

1990

1. Eddy PLANCKAERT (Belgium)
   GS.Pansonic-Sportlife
2. Steve BAUER (Canada)
3. Edwig VAN HOOYDONCK (Belgium)
4. Martial GAYANT (France)
5. Jean-Marie WAMPERS (Belgium)
6. Gilbert DUCLOS-LASSALLE
   (France)
7. Thomas WEGMULLER (Switzerland)
8. Adri VAN DER POEL (Holland)
9. Rudy DHAENENS (Belgium)
10. John TALEN (Holland)

Redant went alone into the lead. The Flemish rider with a powerful pedalling action seemed to be embarking on an outstanding solitary adventure. He gained twenty, thirty and then forty seconds when a puncture stopped him on a cobbled track twenty kilometres from Roubaix.

He had to wait for assistance and Madiot, Ballerini, Peeters, Talen and De Clercq went past without a second glance. Sergeant was at twenty five seconds, the first group at fifty seconds.

At the crossroads of the Arbre, with sixteen kilometres to go, Marc Madiot decided to launch his attack. He knew the terrain perfectly as it was precisely on this spot that he had forged his first success. Franco Ballerini resisted for a while but then he had to let the man from Mayenne disappear into the distance. Marc was totally fired up with an incredible will to win.

From then on the fate of the race was sealed. Jean-Claude Colotti completed the French success by taking second place in front of Bomans, Bauer and Ballerini.

Surrounded from all parts of the velodrome, Marc Madiot was enjoying his revenge: "I went at the same place as I did six years ago. However, for thirty kilometres I was not flying. I was simply monitoring the events. When there was only five of us left, I was afraid of Ballerini in the sprint and I decided to attack. I really built my victory on experience for I know that in Paris-Roubaix you have to know how to look after yourself; to ride without making many efforts for as long as you can. You must be fresh in order to keep your line and not to lower your rhythm."

On this Sunday 14 April the triumph also gave a taste of revenge for Madiot's "blank" 1986 season and for the fact that he had even found difficulty in finding a place in a team. "I am that much more happier" he said "than I was in the Autumn when no one wanted Madiot."

1991

1. Marc MADIOT (France)
   GS.RMO
2. Jean-Claude COLOTTI (France)
3. Carlo BOMANS (Belgium)
4. Steve BAUER (Canada)
5. Franco BALLERINI (Italy)
6. Wilfried PEETERS (Belgium)
7. Nico VERHOEVEN (Holland)
8. Marc SERGEANT (Belgium)
9. Olaf LUDWIG (Germany)
10. Hendrik REDANT (Belgium)

Duclos at last !

When Gilbert Duclos-Lassalle attacked forty kilometres from Roubaix, on the cobbles of Ennevelin, the thousands of spectators present in the velodrome, their eyes riveted on the giant screen situated near the finishing line, rose in a single block and chanted in one big roar: "Duclos, Duclos, Duclos".

For more than an hour, until the arrival of the champion, the tension remained at its peak and the release all the finer.

The public was waiting for its idol who would soon appear down there at the entrance to the track. In their eyes the sudden acceleration of Olaf Ludwig at the Arbre crossroads could be of no possible danger to Duclos.

His second place behind Moser in 1980 seemed like an eternity away, and the most Northern of the South Westerners was hoping only for this, the success without which he would be considered, albeit unjustly, to have had an unfulfilled career.

Suddenly, behind the cars, his silhouette appeared. It was the perfect communion with these thousands of people who were waiting for the victory of one of their own. From the time that the line was crossed, in the scrum, he embraced Roger Zanier, his sponsor and friend, then Roger Legeay, Michel Laurent and finally Jean-Claude Colotti and Greg LeMond who for many kilometres had protected his flight.

As an old hand, Duclos-Lassalle had laid the foundations for his success when crossing over the Allers-Arenberg track. There, after its two kilometres of cobbles he came out in the lead with only Jean-Paul Van Poppel and Rik Van Slycke on his wheel.

The fifteen cobbled sectors and the one hundred and twelve kilometres which separated him from the velodrome could not dishearten him.

The trio nibbled away the seconds from the leaders who had been clear from the first hour of the race. Successively, Pagnin, Seigneur, Tafi, Joho, Schur, Willems and Wegmuller were swallowed up.

A little later, at Warlaing, ninety kilometres from Roubaix, the only ones still in the lead were Duclos, Van Slycke, Van Poppel and Wegmuller who kept up his resistance until he punctured. The peloton was well controlled by LeMond, Colotti and Casado who were playing the waiting game and were two minutes and twenty seconds down.

The kilometres went past. At the front, each of them played their part in the progress of the break. However, Gilbert knew only too well just how good Van Slycke was in a sprint and above all this devil of a man Van Poppel.

At Ennevelin, precisely where Moser had executed him in company with Thurau and De Vlaeminck twelve years previously, Duclos decided to leave his last companions. The "royal way" was open, the red carpet rolled out with the encouragement of a public lining the roads who had come, you would think, just to honour him.

While behind Van Poppel and Van Slycke were swallowed up by the front of what was left of the bunch, an energetic Duclos flew over the cobbles and increased his lead.

The only alert came in the form of a powerful Olaf Ludwig who was alone behind him at the famous Arbre crossroads. The German was pushing a huge gear and in his turn was eating away at the seconds.

He certainly managed to cut his minute's deficit in half but could not manage the rest.

As he dismounted, Gilbert was wild with joy. It was difficult to make himself heard above the tumult: "Of course," he said "Ludwig's counter-attack worried me but I managed to stabilise the gap. Above all I was afraid of a crash or a puncture. In fact I was not completely sure of

1992

Gilbert DUCLOS-LASSALLE
(France, 1954)

The popular Duclos enlivened many a Paris-Roubaix. He had to wait fifteen long years before an emotional first victory at Roubaix - and then did it again the following year!

1980 : Tour de Corse, Paris-Nice,
       Tour du Tarn, Etoile des Espoirs
1981 : Grand Prix de Plouay
1982 : Tour de l'Oise
1983 : Bordeaux-Paris,
       Tour de Midi-Pyrenees
       Grand Prix de Fourmies
1984 : Etoile des Espoirs
1985 : Tour de l'Oise, Tour of Sweden
1987 : Grand Prix de Plouay
1989 : Route du Sud
1991 : Midi Libre
1992 : Paris-Roubaix
1993 : Paris-Roubaix

my success until I reached the red kite. From then on I could take everything in; the public, the solitary entrance onto the track, what I have always dreamed of, and above all the fabulous ovation from the stands."

Michel Laurent confirmed: "The best tactic was for Gilbert to get away with some good riders. They managed to keep a gap of two minutes for a long time. The only one who worried me was Van Poppel for he is very quick. After his attack I knew that he could go right to the very end."

As for Roger Legeay, his eyes misted up, he explained that he too had believed in this success since the Tour of the Basque Country where Gilbert had managed to follow the best of them, even on the climbs!

At the start of Compiègne, the main star was Jacky Durand. The man from Mayenne had a week earlier won the Tour of Flanders in an exemplary fashion, something which had escaped French riders since Jean Forestier's victory back in 1956!

So Durand was one of the favourites on the same level as the Belgian cohort led by Van Hooydonck, Capiot, Museeuw, Redant and several others. Kelly after his success at San Remo, was also returning to the Northern roads with legitimate ambitions.

Franco Ballerini was finally following in the footsteps of Francesco Moser who had never hesitated to take on the Flemish on their home ground: "It's a question of character" he said "the rider who is on form should not let himself be influenced by a little cold weather or some wind. In 1990 I won Paris-Brussels and the Grand Prix of Americas in appalling weather. Paris-Roubaix motivates me that much more for this event notably affected the careers of Coppi and Gimondi. I know too that the winner always goes down in history."

Gilbert Duclos-Lasalle was well aware of it. He said that very same evening that he would like to ride for another two or three years, would that not be to have another taste of Roubaix history? So a rendezvous was made for April 1993!

1992

LeMond satisfied with his work for his team mate.

1. Gilbert DUCLOS-LASSALLE (France) GS.Z
2. Olaf LUDWIG (Germany)
3. Johan CAPIOY (Belgium)
4. Peter PIETERS (Holland)
5. Jean-Claude COLOTTI (France)
6. Etienne DE WILDE (Belgium)
7. Johan MUSEEUW (Belgium)
8. Nico VERHOEVEN (Holland)
9. Greg LEMOND (USA)
10. Hendrik REDANT (Belgium)

M 0165 - 0419.0 - 6.00 F

L'EQUIPE

LUNDI 13 AVRIL 1992   LE QUOTIDIEN DU SPORT ET DE L'AUTOMOBILE   ★   47e ANNÉE — N° 14 287 — 6 F

DUCLOS LA CLASSE

A trente-sept ans et demi, Gilbert Duclos-Lassalle a réalisé un fantastique exploit en gagnant Paris-Roubaix pour sa quatorzième participation ! Le Béarnais s'est imposé en solitaire, après un énorme travail de toute l'équipe Z.   (Pages 2 à 6)

Magique

Jean-Jacques VIERNE

Duclos does it again - by a tyre's width !

"Never again will I come back to Roubaix!" exclaimed a devastated Franco Ballerini, with his head lowered. Dumbfounded, almost knocked out, the Italian just did not understand what had happened to him on the Roubaix track.

Crossing the grass, and before taking refuge in complete silence, several scarcely audible snatches came out of his mouth: "Never will I get on a bike again, what a con. Everything was perfect, I was so strong." A few moments earlier the Tuscan had been beaten by eight centimetres on the finishing line. Impressive all day long, alone in front with the inevitable Duclos-Lassalle at less than thirty kilometres from Roubaix, he could never have imagined such a terrible ending.

No doubt he had never been so sure of a victory and yet Duclos, the natural favourite of the public, close up against Ballerini's wheel since the entrance to the track had launched his sprint from a long way out in the back straight. The Italian managed to draw level with him and finally pass him, after the white line painted on the ground. Straight away in a magnificent gesture, he raised his arms to the sky.

The judge at the finish, perhaps impressed by the gesture, declared him winner before closely examining the enlarged frame of the photo-finish. There was no doubt, on the line, Duclos-Lassalle was first by the thickness of two tyres!

The announcement made the crowd erupt with excitement. Duclos-Lassalle, surrounded on all sides, was overjoyed, his children burst into tears.

He had achieved the double, he who had been waiting such a long time for a first success. His joy was total: "On the line I did not really know who had won," he said "I just simply threw my bike at the line like Ballerini. I was doing my job."

Duclos unleashed on the cobbles.

The same morning on the square at Compiègne the man from Bearn, as usual, appeared to be confident: "My rivals may not think that I am capable of doing it again. Personally, I still believe it." It was true that his unequalled experience, his exemplary form and his motivation, worthy of a junior on the morning of his first race, were major trumps for such a hard event.

However, "doubles" were rare in the history of the Queen of the Classics and the starting line-up excellent, as usual.

Certainly, the indomitable Indurain, plus Bugno, Chiappucci and Rominger remained totally indifferent to its outcome but the best classic hunters were there.

The GB-MG Squad, the new "dream team", so named because of its domination like the American basketball players at the Barcelona Olympics, was led by Johan Museeuw the superb winner of the Tour of Flanders, and Cipollini who was to be first at Wevelgem a few days later. However, for most people the strongest contender was Franco Ballerini. He seemed to be the best over the cobbles where his strength counted for so much.

Moreover, he was going well and dominating the situation as was to be seen by his second place in the Fleche Brabanconne and especially his sixth place in the Tour of Flanders although he had to play the role of team man.

Finally, the outsiders like Ludwig, who was always dreaming of winning, Capiot, Van Hooydonck, Sergeant, Wust, Tchmil and Kelly, never ready to lay down his arms.

Christian Chaubet, a one-time winner of the amateur Paris-Roubaix, launched the race. The man from Toulouse attacked in the middle of St Quentin. His lead reached a maximum of close to five minutes at Bohain but he was forced to capitulate after being away for sixty kilometres.

1993

Gilbert DUCLOS-LASSALLE
& PARIS-ROUBAIX

1978 : 28th
1979 : 25th
1980 : 2nd
1981 : 22nd
1982 : 20th
1983 : 2nd
1986 : 34th
1987 : 17th
1989 : 4th
1990 : 6th
1991 : 12th
1992 : 1st
1993 : 1st
1994 : 7th
1995 : 19th

One lap from the finish, Duclos laying in ambush on Ballerini's wheel ...

... victory snatched on the line.

For a moment Ballerini believes he is the winner.

On the podium...the family.

From the first cobbled sector at Troisvilles bad luck hit the Gan team. In just a few hundred metres Duclos-Lassalle punctured before crashing. Gouvenou, Lemarchand, LeMond and Colotti were also delayed.

The little group to whom Capelle and Casado latched on, embarked on a frenetic pursuit of twenty three kilometres in order to get back to the front.

The great manoeuvres started in the vicinity of Querenaing when thirteen riders went clear. Among them were notably Ludwig, Van der Poel, Marie and Sergeant, but above all four men of the GB-MG: Ballerini, Museeuw, Cipollini and Peeters!

In spite of the hard work of the latter two, seven men including Van Hooydonck, Tchmil and Duclos-Lassalle came up to them just after Arenberg!

At Orchies the group, now comprising of about twenty men, had a minute's lead. It was there that a lucid Duclos understood that Ballerini was the man to watch. He decided to stay on his wheel.

After several attempts, notably by Van Itterbeek, Van der Poel and Frison, Ballerini, followed by Duclos decided to accelerate.

In a just a few kilometres the issue was decided. Well protected by Museeuw who was in no doubt of the outcome at the velodrome, Ballerini was the man in the driver's seat.

It quickly became obvious that nobody could catch them, and as Duclos rode through the streets of Roubaix he knew he would never be happy with a second place in "his" race at "his" velodrome to the great despair of the fine Franco, ten years his junior, who for his part had all his future before him.

1993

1. Gilbert DUCLOS-LASSALLE (France)   GS.GAN
2. Franco BALLERINI (Italy)
3. Olaf LUDWIG (Germany)
4. Johan MUSEEUW (Belgium)
5. Adri VAN DER POEL (Holland)
6. Edwig VAN HOOYDONCK (Belgium)
7. Marc SERGEANT (Belgium)
8. Sean YATES (Great Britain)
9. Benjamin VAN ITTERBEECK (Belgium)
10. Wilfried NELISSEN (Belgium

Andreï Tchmil
goes down in history

Four days before the ninety second Paris-Roubaix, disputed on Sunday 10 April 1994, history was repeated for Franco Ballerini when at the finish of Ghent Wevelgem he was beaten by a few millimetres by his former team-mate Wilfried Peeters.

In fact, Ballerini so unfortunate, had moved to the Mapei team during the winter in the hope of forgetting all his torments.

The year 1993 had been a period of setbacks. Besides his Roubaix defeat, which had unquestionably left a mark on him, the Tuscan had first of all lost his father who had pushed him into sport, then less seriously he broke a bone in a mountain bike event. Quickly back in the saddle, the ride in Ghent Wevelgem had nevertheless proved that he was in good condition. His performance comforted him in the idea that he wanted to win at Roubaix, for he was to come back forgetting the promise he had made twelve months earlier at the finish, for he had no alternative than to arrive alone.

At the start of this 1994 season, the photo-finish equipment seemed a necessary adjunct for the finish of the Tour of Flanders was very close. The

The great style of Tchmil.

enigmatic Gianni Bugno snatched victory by several millimetres from a Museeuw who decided to get his revenge as quickly as possible.

There could not be a better place for him to do it as essentially he had always dreamed of only two events: The Tour of Flanders which he had won in 1993 and Paris-Roubaix.

Moreover, Museeuw, after the departure of Ballerini and Cipollini, had become the sole leader in the GB-MG team.

Opposing Ballerini and Museeuw were other pretenders such as Van Hooydonck, the powerful Olaf Ludwig, Johan Capiot, Andreï Tchmil winner of the Grand Prix E3 at Harelbeke and of course...Gilbert Duclos-Lassalle. Duclos faithful to the Tour of the Basque Country for his preparation, was not laying down his arms. He seemed confident and could envisage himself on the top step of the podium for a third time at Roubaix. "If I don't win" he said, "I will nevertheless have no regrets for I will have done all I could."

However, the man knew that triple wins at Roubaix were very rare indeed. In fact it had only ever been achieved twice: Octave Lapize who is today sometimes shamefully forgotten, and by Francesco Moser. On Sunday 10 April 1994 the weather conditions were bad. So it was in a snow storm that Lubos Lom escaped from the fortieth kilometre!

The Czech crossed St Quentin with a lead of four minutes over Steffen Wedesmann and nearly fourteen minutes on a dawdling bunch. He crossed over the first cobbled section

1994

L'OM laisse filer | Cantona sacré par les Anglais

L'ÉQUIPE

TCHMIL SABORDS !

with his lead intact but Lubos was in difficulty and, something very rare in modern cycling, stopped for a minute at the feeding station at Solesmes! Fifteen kilometres from there at Presau, after he had painfully restarted he was caught by the front of the peloton.

Between Valenciennes and Arenberg the peloton become feverish. Fifteen men went clear from the rest of them and the group included some of the favourites such as: Duclos-Lassalle but also Museeuw, Tchmil and Van der Poel.

At the cobbles of the Arenberg section the group had a lead of forty five seconds. However, some of them crashed and in the confusion some of the back markers joined the leading group so now the main bunch consisted of about forty men.

The Italian Boscardin tried his chance at Orchies before being caught, twenty kilometres further on, by Verhoeven, Museeuw, Van der Poel, Ballerini and Tchmil. Straight away Tchmil attacked. The sixty two kilometres to go to the Roubaix track did not seem to bother him too much. Rapidly he opened the gap, ten, twenty, thirty, forty seconds.

On the difficult sector of Ennevelin, Ballerini and Duclos-Lassalle locked up in the chasing group, both punctured just a few hundred metres apart. The motor bikes and cars with the spare wheels were far behind and the two rivals were obliged to ride on the rim for some time. Their Paris-Roubaix was over when finally they managed to get going again three minutes down. Museeuw managed to get clear behind Tchmil. The Belgian nibbled away at the seconds to the point where he could see him in front of him on the long straight sections.

However, Tchmil was still quite fresh and managed to hold off the menace. Museeuw was first of all joined by Willems and Bottaro, then by Duclos-Lassalle and several others at the crossroads of the Arbre, sixteen kilometres from Roubaix.

The way was open for Tchmil who arrived home (he lived in Roubaix in the winter) as the master of the situation.

At the velodrome the public considered him to be a Roubaisian and had an especially warm welcome for him. He had more than a minute on the astonishing Baldato then came the inevitable Ballerini, Ludwig, Yates, Capiot and Duclos-Lassalle.

A terribly disappointed Museeuw was only thirteenth.

For the first time, apart from the less prestigious win by Viatcheslav Ekimov in the Championship of Zurich 1992, an ex-USSR national had won a major classic.

It was hardly a surprise, for Tchmil was merely confirming the talent that most people knew he already had. Having turned professional in 1989 in the shadow of Konyshev, he seemed destined to follow the career of a modest team man. In fact his transfer to the Lotto team of Jean-Luc Vandenbroucke had opened new horizons for him.

Fabio Baldato for his part stole another second place from Ballerini. However, Franco was far less disappointed then he had been in 1993. In the showers he said that he liked Paris-Roubaix but (with one eye on Duclos) he had no desire to wait until he was forty before winning it.

On the other hand, Marc Madiot, nine years after his first success, left Paris-Roubaix for good after fracturing a bone on the cobbled section of Preseau.

The "Eastern Wave" was beginning to have its effect on the old continent, for a week later Evgueni Berzin was in his turn to reveal himself to the public by winning Liège-Bastogne-Liège.
Time marches on.

1994

Andreï TCHMIL
(Russia, 1963)

This resilient battler has entered the folklore of Paris-Roubaix as the first cyclist from Eastern Europe to win the classic.

1989 : 3rd Tour de Venetie
1991 : Russian Champion
       Grand Prix Cerami, Paris-Bourges
       Grand Prix Sanson
1992 : 2nd de la Coppa Sabatini
1993 : 2nd Tirreno-Adriatico
1994 : Paris-Roubaix, Grand Prix de Plouay,
       3rd Tour of Flanders,
       3rd Four Days of Dunkerque
1995 : Paris-Camembert, Tour du Limousin,
       2nd Paris-Roubaix,
       2nd Paris-Tours,
       2nd de l'Etoile des Besseges
       3rd Tour of Flanders

1. Andreï TCHMIL (Russia)
   GS.Lotto-Vetta-Caloi
2. Fabio BALDATO (Italy)
3. Franco BALLERINI (Italy)
4. Olaf LUDWIG (Germany)
5. Sean YATES (Great Britain)
6. Johan CAPIOT (Belgium)
7. Gilbert DUCLOS-LASSALLE
   (France)
8. Ludwig WILLEMS (Belgium)
9. Franky ANDREU (USA)
10. Nico VERHOEVEN (Holland)

Franco Ballerini at last

Many Italian champions have been fascinated by Paris-Roubaix. From Binda and Girardengo, who were hardly very successful, to Jules Rossi, the first of them to win on the cobbles and especially Coppi, Bevilacqua, Gimondi and Moser, there had been generations of riders who crossed the Alps in the hope of entering into legend.

Franco Ballerini was their worthy heir. Having turned professional in 1986 the Tuscan discovered his talent for the classics four years later after his victories in Paris-Brussels and above all the Grand Prix of Americas, a World Cup event.

Paris-Roubaix attracted him as much as it did Francesco Moser. There were no longer any secrets, he spoke highly of the merits and the consequences of a victory at the velodrome. Just like his predecessor, his style, his strength and above all his determination all added up to the fact that each year he was, without question, a potential winner. Unfortunately, bad luck had too often stopped his progress. Nothing had changed at the start of the 1995 season. Certainly, Ballerini had wiped out 246 days of famine by winning the Circuit of the Het Volk, but suddenly his hopes for Paris-Roubaix took a dive.

Four days before the event, a few kilometres before the finish of Ghent Wevelgem, Franco had crashed heavily in company with Museeuw and Bauer. His presence on the Northern cobbles seemed all the more compromised as his shoulder was quite badly injured.

According to his team manager, Patrick Lefévère: "There is only a thirty per cent chance that we'll see him at the start at Compiègne. However, it's much better to see half a Ballerini than no Ballerini at all." For his part, Franco, after a ride of one hundred and thirty kilometres in the region of Courtrai was not willing to give the

MAESTRO BALLERINI

L'ÉQUIPE

Battu à la photo-finish il y a deux ans, encore troisième l'année dernière, Franco Ballerini a enfin gagné Paris-Roubaix, et superbement, après s'être détaché seul à 32 km du but. Moncassin, premier Français, est 8ᵉ, Duclos-Lassalle seulement 19ᵉ. (Pages 2 à 6)

DEPUIS LE TEMPS QU'IL TRAVAILLAIT À SON PODIUM... ...CHAPEAU!

LUNDI 10 AVRIL 1995   *   50ᵉ ANNÉE — N° 15 219 — 6 F

M 0105 - 0410 - 6,00 F

Alesi bute sur Hill

Après une formidable course, Jean Alesi et sa Ferrari ont dominé Michael Schumacher, mais ont dû s'incliner devant la Williams-Renault de Damon Hill, qui, en Argentine, a remporté la dixième victoire de sa carrière. (Page

Andreï Tchmil in front of Museeuw,
Duclos-Lassalle, Moncassin
and the bunch

race up.

Johan Museeuw, who was suffering with his knee, was virtually in the same position. He was victorious a week before in the Tour of Flanders and he dreamed of joining De Vlaeminck in the record books for doing a double as Roger had in 1977.

Andreï Tchmil also returned to the theatre of his greatest triumph. This time the Russians seemed even stronger. For the rest there was: Ludwig, Van der Poel, a handful of Belgians and the irresistible Italian cohort led by Bortolami, Cipollini, Baldato and others. Gilbert Duclos-Lassalle, for whom the years did not seem to have taken their toll, came back from the Tour of the Basque Country with a stage victory. For him there was no secret, you had to keep going in spite of the difficulties: "Wet or dry, the cobbles always suit me. For years I have known that Paris-Roubaix is ridden at one thousand per cent!"

This time there would be no photo-finish for Ballerini at the velodrome. Thirty two kilometres from the end, at the exit to Templeuve, he escaped on a short cobbled sector. Well protected by his team mates Tafi and Bortolami he quickly opened a gap and reached Roubaix with two minutes lead. "Franco the cursed" at last entered Heaven! "It's the finest day of my life. Never up until today have I forgotten my cruel disappointment of 1993. I love Paris-Roubaix and this entrance into the velodrome was magic. It's a really unbelievable thing."

The race turned out rather lifeless. As they left Arenberg there was still one hundred men together. Then the selection naturally came into operation.

The German Dietz started the action before being caught by Tafi,

1995

Franco BALLERINI
(Italy, 1964)

After a second and third on the podium he finally achieved victory in 1995.
Like Moser, one of the Italian specialists of Paris-Roubaix, skilful and adroit over the cobbles.

1987 : Three Valleys of Varesines
1988 : Grand Prix Sanson,
       3rd Tour of Emile
1989 : Grand Prix of Camaiore
       2nd de la Coppa Placci
       2nd Tour of Campanie
1990 : Paris-Brussels,
       Grand Prix of Americas,
       Tour of Campanie, Tour of Piemont,
       3rd Ghent-Wevelgem
1991 : Tour of Romandy,
       3rd Tour of Lombardy,
       5th Paris-Roubaix
1992 : 2nd Tour of Campanie
1993 : 2nd Paris-Roubaix
1994 : 2nd Ghent-Wevelgem,
       2nd Paris-Brussels,
       3rd Paris-Roubaix
1995 : Paris-Roubaix, Het Volk

In one hundred years the means of communication have changed tremendously. Today the spectators at the velodrome can follow the race in detail, as it happens, on a giant screen ...

1. Franco BALLERINI (Italy)
   GS. Mapei-GB
2. Andreï TCHMIL (Russia)
3. Johan MUSEEUW (Belgium)
4. Viatcheslav EKIMOV (Russia)
5. Johan CAPIOT (Belgium)
6. Eric VANDERAERDEN (Belgium)
7. Fabio BALDATO (Italy)
8. Frédéric MONCASSIN (France)
9. Rolf ALDAG (Germany)
10. Gianluca BORTOLAMI (Italy)

Vanderaerden who had found his legs of yesteryear and Ekimov. The powerful Mapei team could hardly let the escape develop.

Capiot got away under their noses at Seclin but Bortolami and his team mate Ballerini rapidly came up to his wheel.

The Belgian crashed at Templemars and left the pair to make the junction a little later on.

At Templeuve the six men had a lead of forty five seconds, enough for the start of the "Ballerini festival".

Andreï Tchmil snatched second place to the detriment of Johan Museeuw. The French raised their hands with Frédéric Moncassin who was eighth, followed by Jean-Claude Colotti and Frank Jarno, who was excellent in his first Paris-Roubaix.

The latter had all of his future in front of him, in contrast to Gilbert Duclos-Lassalle who, unlucky once again, finished nineteenth. Disappointed with his performance he said at the finish: "Having failed so badly makes me want to come back next year!"

It was not to be, as on the eve of the Paris-Brussels the French champion announced his retirement from competition. A wise and difficult decision to take which, which it has to be said, left a lot of orphaned fans on the route of the centenary Paris-Roubaix on the 14 April 1996.

His career was intimately linked with this most famous Northern event. After Duclos-Lassalle, Paris-Roubaix found in the riders of Andreï Tchmil and Franco Ballerini its successors. Without question they are all of the same breed, they are Lords.

1995

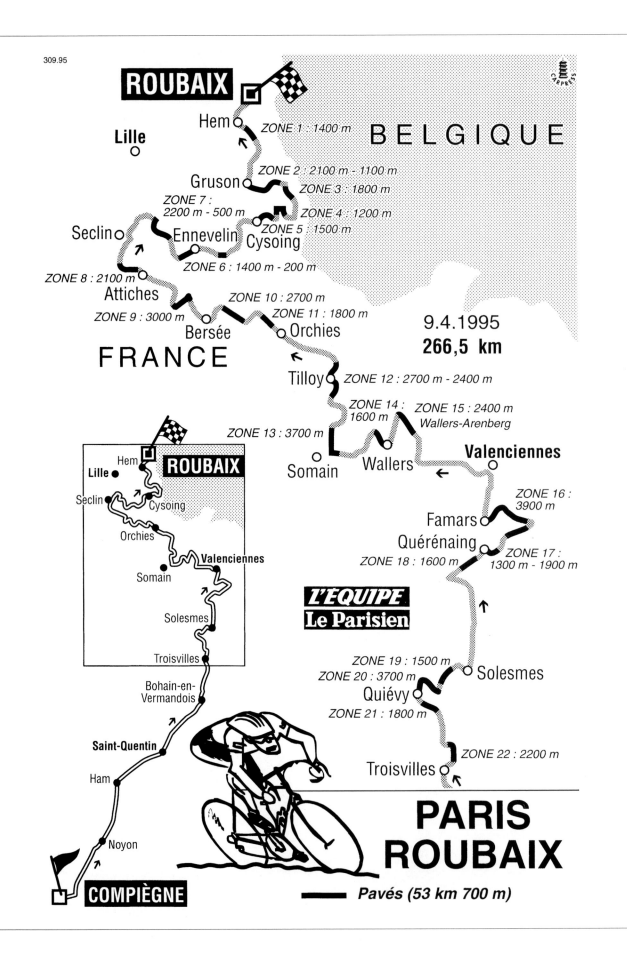

The legend of the century

Paris-Roubaix has embraced the century. The event has known how to resist and adapt itself to modern times in spite of several interruptions due to man's stupidity.

In February 1896, when Theodore Vienne and Maurice Perez had the idea of creating a "race arriving at their velodrome", never did they imagine the outcome. As a preparation event for Bordeaux-Paris, Paris-Roubaix quickly found its own place in the aristocracy of sport.

Thanks to them the undertaking was inexorably established. Paris-Roubaix was for the cyclists of course, but also for the heads of the cycle industry it was a wonderful publicity vehicle necessary for the expansion of several companies. From then on their cause was won.

Most of the great champions, with several recent exceptions, have won at Roubaix. Each winner has entered into legend for he has beaten other great riders and the traps of a route which has become more and more difficult.

The only fear today is that these last sections of cobbles might disappear. Already in the 1960's a first alarm signal was given by Jean Garnault and quickly confirmed by Albert Bouvet.

In spite of several crusades, mostly in the media, each year some more cobbles disappear forever.

In 1979 the writer Rene Fallet added: "Fortunate climbers, your mountains will never be eroded, cursed be those who destroy the cobbles and threaten redundancy. The De Vlaemincks of this world who are in peril of becoming as rare as the baby seals."

It seems imperative to not only preserve but also to restore certain existing sections so as to avoid falling into the trap of being discredited by a series of circus acts on farm tracks.

Today this is the main worry of the organising body, the Society of the Tour de France, but also of the Conseil General du Nord.

On this depends the future of the event which today has largely gone beyond the framework of sport to become a veritable institution and the showpiece of a region which is dynamic but often badly treated.

To be frank, would the month of April be the same without the Paris-Roubaix?

Photographic credits

The photos come from the archives of:

> The Society of the Tour de France
> Nord-Eclair
> Nord-Matin
> de Eecloonaar
> Het Laatste Nieuws
> Het Nieuwsblad
> Het Volk
> Gazet van Antwerpen

From Messrs

> Bruno Bade
> Roman Clauws
> Sebastian Jarry
> Bernard Libert
> Ivan Longueville
> Wim Verstraete
> Cor Vos

and from the personal collection of the author.

Special thanks to Mahdjoub Ben Bella, Dero, Serge Laget, Guy Sadet, "Le Sportsman" bookshop in Paris and to the cartoonist TEEL.

The author

Pascal Sergent, a former amateur cyclist, has remained passionately interested in the sport. Keen on history and born in Roubaix, he is naturally interested in Paris-Roubaix, the "Queen of Classics".

For many years he has been researching and discovering photos, articles and documents relating to this legendary event. Today he possesses an exceptional collection which permits him to organise exhibitions on a regular basis.

Born in 1958, Pascal Sergent is a press correspondent (Nord-Eclair, specialist magazines; Cycl'Hist, Vélo-Star, Infovélo) and also the author of several works on cycling and its history. Among these can be found "Chronicle of a Legend, Paris-Roubaix" in two volumes , "The Great Hours of the Roubaix Velodrome" and "Paris-Roubaix-Velo-City".

Recently he was the joint author of the history of the Cyclo-Cross World Championships. He is also the scriptwriter of the strip cartoon: "The Epic of Paris-Roubaix" published with his friend, the cartoonist TEEL.

Finally, Pascal Sergent was the historical advisor for "le Centenaire", the Official Film celebrating the Centenary of the Paris-Roubaix that is available in English, narrated by Phil Liggett.

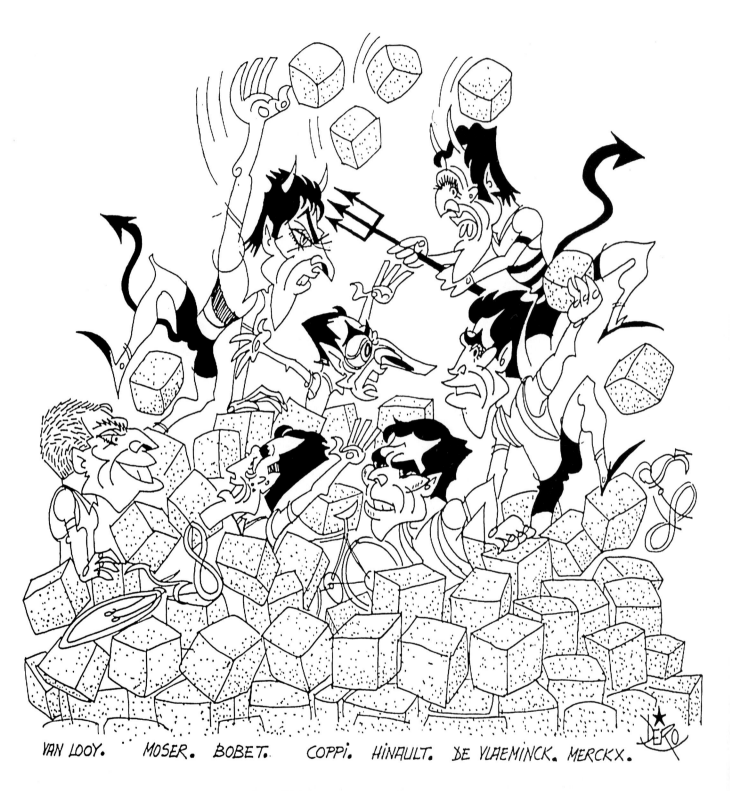

VAN LOOY.   MOSER. BOBET.   COPPI. HINAULT. DE VLAEMINCK. MERCKX.

"Fight in the Hel", Déro (1990)

the official book

PARIS ROUBAIX

1896-1996   le Centenaire

1896 : Josef FISCHER (D)
1897 : Maurice GARIN (F)
1898 : Maurice GARIN (F)
1899 : Albert CHAMPION (F)
1900 : Emile BOUHOURS (F)
1901 : Lucien LESNA (F)
1902 : Lucien LESNA (F)
1903 : Hippolyte AUCOUTURIER (F)
1904 : Hippolyte AUCOUTURIER (F)
1905 : Louis TROUSSELIER (F)
1906 : Henri CORNET (F)
1907 : Georges PASSERIEU (F)
1908 : Cyrille VAN HAUWAERT (B)
1909 : Octave LAPIZE (F)
1910 : Octave LAPIZE (F)
1911 : Octave LAPIZE (F)
1912 : Charles CRUPELANDT (F)
1913 : François FABER (F)
1914 : Charles CRUPELANDT (F)
1919 : Heiri PELISSIER (F)
1920 : Paul DEMAN (B)
1921 : Henri PELISSIER (F)
1922 : Albert DEJONGHE (B)
1923 : Henri SUTER (CH)
1924 : Jules VAN HEVEL (B)
1925 : Félix SELLIER (B)
1926 : Julien DELBECQUE (B)
1927 : Georges RONSSE (B)
1928 : André LEDUCQ (F)
1929 : Charles MEUNIER (B)
1930 : Julien VERVAECKE (B)
1931 : Gaston REBRY (B)
1932 : Romain GIJSSELS (B)
1933 : Sylveer MAES (B)
1934 : Gaston REBRY (B)
1935 : Gaston REBRY (B)
1936 : Georges SPEICHER (F)
1937 : Jules ROSSI (I)
1938 : Lucien STORME (B)
1939 : Emile MASSON (B)
1943 : Marcel KINT (B)
1944 : Maurice DESIMPELAERE (B)
1945 : Paul MAYE (F)

1946 : Georges CLAES (B)
1947 : Georges CLAES (B)
1948 : Rik VAN STEENBERGEN (B)
1949 : André MAHE (F) & Serse COPPI (I)
1950 : Fausto COPPI (I)
1951 : Antonio BEVILACQUA (I)
1952 : Rik VAN STEENBERGEN (B)
1953 : Germain DERIJCKE (B)
1954 : Raymond IMPANIS (B)
1955 : Jean FORESTIER (F)
1956 : Louison BOBET (F)
1957 : Alfred DE BRUYNE (B)
1958 : Léon VAN DAELE (B)
1959 : Noël FORE (B)
1960 : Pino CERAMI (B)
1961 : Rik VAN LOOY (B)
1962 : Rik VAN LOOY (B)
1963 : Emile DAEMS (B)
1964 : Peter POST (NL)
1965 : Rik VAN LOOY (B)
1966 : Felice GIMONDI (I)
1967 : Jan JANSSEN (NL)
1968 : Eddy MERCKX (B)
1969 : Walter GODEFROOT (B)
1970 : Eddy MERCKX (B)
1971 : Roger ROSIERS (B)
1972 : Roger DE VLAEMINCK (B)
1973 : Eddy MERCKX (B)
1974 : Roger DE VLAEMINCK (B)
1975 : Roger DE VLAEMINCK (B)
1976 : Marc DE MEYER (B)
1977 : Roger DE VLAEMINCK (B)
1978 : Francesco MOSER (I)
1979 : Francesco MOSER (I)
1980 : Francesco MOSER (I)
1981 : Bernard HINAULT (F)
1982 : Jan RAAS (NL)
1983 : Hennie KUIPER (NL)
1984 : Sean KELLY (IRL)
1985 : Marc MADIOT (F)
1986 : Sean KELLY (IRL)
1987 : Eric VANDERAERDEN (B)
1988 : Dirk DEMOL (B)
1989 : Jean-Marie WAMPERS (B)
1990 : Eddy PLANCKAERT (B)
1991 : Marc MADIOT (F)
1992 : Gilbert DUCLOS-LASSALLE (F)
1993 : Gilbert DUCLOS-LASSALLE (F)
1994 : Andreï TCHMIL (R)
1995 : Franco BALLERINI (I)

BROMLEY BOOKS

This English edition is published by Bromley Books,
the book division of Bromley Television International,
11 The Terrace, Barnes, London, SW13 ONP.
Tel : (44) 181 876 4671 Fax : (44) 181 878 3858

Translation : Richard Yates.

November 1997.

Printed and bound in "de Eecloonaar"
Industrielaan 44, 9900 Eeklo - Belgium.
Tel. 00 32 93 77 11 82 - Fax 00 32 93 78 12 34.

A catalogue record for this book is available from the British Library.

ISBN: 0-9531729-0-2

the official book
PARIS ROUBAIX
1896-1996   le Centenaire